THE EARLY SESSIONS

Book 3 of The Seth Material

SESSIONS 86-148

9/9/64–4/21/65

THE EARLY SESSIONS

The Early Sessions consist of the first 510 sessions dictated by Seth through Jane Roberts. There are 9 books in *The Early Sessions* series.

THE PERSONAL SESSIONS

The Personal Sessions, often referred to as "the deleted sessions," are Seth sessions that Jane Roberts and Rob Butts considered to be of a highly personal nature and were therefore kept in separate notebooks from the main body of the Seth material. *The Personal Sessions* are expected to be published in 6 to 9 volumes.

"The great value I see now in the many deleted or private sessions is that they have the potential to help others, just as they helped Jane and me over the years. I feel that it's very important to have these sessions added to Jane's fine creative body of work for all to see." –Rob Butts

THE SETH AUDIO COLLECTION

Rare recordings of Seth speaking through Jane Roberts are available on audiocassette and CD. (Further information is supplied at the back of this book.)

For complete information on Seth Books, Tapes, CD's and The Art of Robert Butts (Jane Robert's husband and co-author of the Seth Books) write to New Awareness Network at the following address and request the latest catalogue. Also, please visit us on the internet at www.sethcenter.com

New Awareness Network Inc.
P.O. BOX 192
Manhasset, N.Y. 11030

www.sethcenter.com

THE EARLY SESSIONS

Book 3 of The Seth Material

SESSIONS 86-148

9/9/64–4/21/65

Published by New Awareness Network Inc.

New Awareness Network Inc.
P.O. Box 192
Manhasset, New York 11030

Opinions and statements on health and medical matters expressed in this book are those of the author and are not necessarily those of or endorsed by the publisher. Those opinions and statements should not be taken as a substitute for consultation with a duly licensed physician.

Cover Design: Michael Goode
Photography: Cover photos by Rich Conz and Robert F. Butts, Sr.
Editorial: Rick Stack
Typography: Juan Schoch, Joan Thomas, Michael Goode

Library of Congress Cataloging-in-Publication Data

Seth (Spirit)
The early sessions: volume 3 of the seth material / [channeled] by Jane Roberts ; notes by Robert F. Butts.
p. cm.–(A Seth book)
ISBN 0-9652855-2-9
1. Spirit writings. 2. Self–Miscellanea
I. Roberts, Jane 1929–1984. II. Butts, Robert F. III. Title
IV. Series: Seth (Spirit), 1929–1984 Seth book.
Library of Congress Catalog Number: 96-69349

ISBN 0-9652855-2-9
Printed in U.S.A. on acid-free paper

I dedicate The Early Sessions
to my wife, Jane Roberts,
who lived her 55 years
with the greatest creativity
and the most valiant courage.
-Rob

SESSION 86
SEPTEMBER 9, 1964 9 PM WEDNESDAY AS SCHEDULED

(While trying psychological time on Wednesday, September 9, 8:15 PM, I had, after reaching a pleasant state, the rather strange sensation of having my legs pulled or stretched, as though some force was trying to elongate them. I felt rather strongly a sensation of gripping on the inside of each ankle, coupled with a downward pull, or stretching. It had some duration also; I had plenty of time to lightly explore the sensation.

(Bill Macdonnel arrived to witness the session. With him he brought some rolls of copper sheeting for our table, and incense and a burner. Both of these items, Jane had read recently, had been shown to be useful in psychic states by adding negative ions to the air. A negatively charged atmosphere has been shown to effectively increase one's psychic abilities.

(I thought the copper insufficient in quantity, but we unrolled it upon the table, and lit the incense. Its pleasant musty smell filled the room. I thought the trappings might bring forth some rather pungent comments from Seth, but kept my own counsel. Jane was not nervous before the session. She began dictating in a quiet and amused voice, quite slowly. Her pacing was also slow, her eyes dark as usual.)

Good evening.

("Good evening, Seth.")

I appreciate the many and varied preparations made this evening for my expected arrival.

Next you will undoubtedly suggest that I pose, contemplate what might pass for my navel, carve a likeness, and set it up in the middle of your table.

I do not seriously imagine that you would entertain such a ludicrous idea, but the situation certainly contains humorous overtones, and it would not be like me to let anything like this pass without comment.

My welcome to Mark, with his enthusiastic good intentions. Nor indeed is the idea behind all this ridiculous in any manner. Good intentions are highly important, and what you think will work, will work.

(It might be added that this evening it had rained, and now the night was very hot and humid. The windows were open; from a neighbor's house some distance

away, we could hear a phonograph playing, the sound carrying clearly on the heavy air. Traffic noise also seemed much louder than usual. Jane, dictating, seemed to carry her head at an unusual angle, as though listening. Her delivery was by now very slow.)

I would like to discuss some material that we have left unfinished, making certain that you understand that there are chemical and electrical reactions resulting from mental enzymes, that are also present in the process of constructing psychic energy into physical construction.

There are interactions here of utmost importance. For simplicity's sake you may say that ideas are electric, in that they spark enzymes within the mechanism, that then automatically begin the work of physical construction, in line with inner expectations as outlined earlier.

I have spoken of mental enclosures. Theoretically there is no such thing as a closed system. However for all practical purposes a closed mental system is one which allows the least amount of camouflage data to come through. It is not closed entirely but nevertheless it could be said to approximate in psychic terms the enclosure within which your so-called mediums work; that is, with a minimum of camouflage communication at hand.

(Seth began referring to mental enclosures, mental enzymes, etc., many many sessions ago, at the same time he began to give the information on the inner senses. By the time the 20th session was held these discussions of such material were in full swing.)

The system or the mental enclosure, again, is only closed comparatively speaking. An endeavor is made to close one opening from one plane, and keep the alternate or inner communication channel open. As an analogy here, the conscious ego could be said to exist within this copper tube, located at approximately its center.

(Jane had picked up a roll of copper tubing that we had not used on the table. Now she touched the left end of the tube as she held it before me.)

This end would then represent the <u>extension of the self</u> outward toward the physical universe. This extension, as I have mentioned, is theoretically endless. The world of inner reality would then be imagined as existing at the other end of this tube. And in the same manner that one end of the tube would represent the extension of the self into the world of physical reality, then so too would the other end of this tube represent the extension of the self into the inner world of reality.

(Again, as it has done quite often in recent sessions, Jane's voice turned abruptly deeper, and retained some of this heavier timbre for a while.)

Now using the analogy again, in our mental enclosure we attempt to close off this channel of communication with the outer universe. So. This end we leave open.

Now this is what you attempt when you experiment with psychological time, when your communication comes through the inner rather than the outer senses. And all living consciousnesses initially enter your plane of awareness by route of such a mental enclosure.

All psychic energy comes through such a mental enclosure. Now, we are leading up to a point. You remember, I am sure, that I spoke of extension and contraction, along with other discussions on the inner senses. Communication with the inner self, communication with entities on another level can be approached from one or the other of two methods. The approaches are different, and one is more often tried than the other.

I suggest your first break.

(Break at 9:26. Jane was dissociated, she said, but not to much of a degree. The neighbor's phonograph bothered her, she said, and so did the traffic noise. It was the first time she could remember that any outside influences had made themselves felt while she was dictating.

(Jane resumed in a voice a little deeper, but still with her very slow delivery, at 9:31.)

Now, it is only the initial approach which varies.

Extension of energy must have contraction as an after effect, and contraction will lead to extension. Therefore, if you begin in an attempt to contract your consciousness and energy, in the hopes of attaining communication with inner reality, then indeed will your consciousness, closed and contracted like a tight fist, open and expand. And if you seek to communicate by expansion of consciousness, then will this expansion come crushing and closing upon itself.

The end can be achieved in either manner. Concentration upon one minute, limited, contracted object will result in consciousness expansion, for have I not said that within even the molecule and atom there exists capsule comprehension?

A mental enclosure cannot be seen or touched, yet no man is ever within a mental enclosure but that he is alone. Here you seek not equalization of pressure, but a delicate, even precarious instability of pressures. No, no creativity arises from an evenness of pressure, but in constantly changing, new instabilities, ever seeking to achieve a balance.

This mental enclosure can be thought of as somewhat of a manufacturing plant, from which all material manifestations must come. The products that make up the form come through another entrance.

I am going to make this a short session.

There are some good reasons for this. The outside distractions from the street, for the first time it seems, are keeping Ruburt at a level of consciousness which is not quite adequate for my delivery of the discussion that I had in mind.

It may be significant that such distractions did not bother him until he read that they were supposed to. There is a reason also in that a deeper state of consciousness is sometimes needed when the upper level of his subconscious is concerned, as it still is since he gave notice at the gallery.

Usually we have little difficulty in achieving a deeper state in compensation. Tonight however a really satisfactory state was not reached, considering the rather difficult material I had planned to give you. A note here: Of course experimentation on your own will benefit.

I will now bring the session to a close regretfully, and despite the incense and copper so thoughtfully presented. Indeed, under most circumstances they could prove beneficial, although with all good respects for what you have in mind, you would have to literally line the walls with copper in this room.

The negative ions are of help, but you could not produce such conditions. But the attempt to produce advantageous conditions is in itself of help in any case.

A most fond and regretfully early good evening.

("Good evening, Seth."

(End at 9:55. Jane was dissociated to some degree. The music from across the way had stopped sometime during the last delivery, but Jane said the traffic noise continued to bother her. She had been reading that exterior stimuli should be excluded during such sessions as we conduct, and supposed Seth was right in stating that she may have allowed herself to be bothered. Jane said she would try to avoid this pitfall in the future.

(Seth's reference to experimentation on our part involved a discussion re holding another "seance" involving Jane, Bill and I. We had meant to set a date for such an effort but neglected to do so.)

(This material is included here because it is rather lengthy, and is not dealt with in the next session.

(Thursday evening, September 10, John Bradley visited us while on a selling trip to Elmira for his company, Searle Drug. It will be remembered that in the 63rd session, June 17,1964, Volume 2, page 159, Seth gave a date of September 2 for John, stating that on that day "plans may be born at that date which will affect his participation in his professional field." John was a witness to that session.

(Tonight John told us that on September 2 he was meeting at his home in Williamsport, PA, with his district manager, and that of course business was discussed.

John has in the past applied for a transfer to the West. The company to date has not granted his request. Seth has dealt with the upheavals going on beneath the surface of Searle Drug in various sessions, and in some detail; they are continuing, John informs us. It now develops that John's district manager is not too sure of his own job. Whether any actual plans affecting John were born at the meeting of September 2, time will tell.

(John also noted that he was keeping alert for any sort of trouble involving a woman neighbor who lives three doors down the street from him. Seth also mentioned this in the 63rd session. See John's map at the end of that session.

(In the 84th session, September 2, Volume 2, pages 329 and 331, Seth stated that Jane was blocking "a picture of Philip," Philip being Seth's name for John's entity. Without much thought Jane and I had taken the data given on this instance to refer also to John's September 2 date, since by coincidence the 84th session also fell due on September 2. This evening John said that he'd had no "disagreement in a kitchen, involving two women and a man, with a child close by," on September 2. So now we wonder whether the above incident is precognition, with the actual date being blocked by Jane, or whether Jane is just plain in error.)

SESSION 87
SEPTEMBER 14, 1964 9 PM MONDAY AS SCHEDULED

(On September 7 Jane had an odd dream. In it she was aware of an old woman, but not of her personal presence, of 83 or 85. The old woman had just died, yet her last day was filled with activity and work. She was a medium, and she passed from life to death with a smooth transition, continuing her work almost without interruption after death. Jane envied her greatly.

(Then, Jane in the same dream found herself in an old persons' home. She opened the door into a room containing one full-sized bed and another adult, though smaller, bed. Jane's friend Dee Masters, who had once been director at the gallery where Jane works, and who has been dealt with by Seth at various times, was doing something at an agitator-type washing machine. Jane also fussed with the machine, and a small quantity of water dropped from it onto the floor. Jane then had the feeling that somehow she, Jane, was the old woman who had died.

(On September 9 Jane dreamed that she spoke to two sick men, saying to them, "Don't worry. The material says I have cancer too." Meaning the Seth material, of course. Jane said the puzzling thing about this little dream was that in spite of its unpleasant content she felt no sense of alarm or danger or worry, that indeed she spoke to the two men quite cheerfully. She is concerned, though, wondering if the

dream might be precognitive.

(Jane was also concerned because of what she considers the poor session of September 9, when she was so affected by outside conditions. She was not nervous before tonight's session, however.

(Over the weekend Jane's father and his companion, Midge, stopped by in Elmira on their way to Florida for the winter. Jane wondered if the session tonight might deal with them, yet had no idea of its content to come. She began dictating in a voice somewhat stronger than usual, while pacing briskly. Her eyes were dark.

May I wish you a hearty good evening.

("Good evening, Seth.")

I have several items that I would like to cover this evening. And first of all, may I mention that I was ready to have a brief session last evening, because of the conditions, and because of the woman's need.

She would have been helped, and I could have shocked her into dispensing with her self-pity. The woman desperately needs help, and I could have handled her condition.

She would have benefited. I understood the reasons why neither of you wanted such a session. I was not calling one, but was willing to have one in answer to the woman's need.

I would also have greeted Ruburt's father, but indeed I was not invited to join the graceful family circle. I would not be one to upset such a quiet gathering. The woman, seriously, has found some comfort with Ruburt's father, but the personality is in sore trouble, and explosive. I will not devote any more time to this subject now.

Instead I would like to give you some more material dealing with mental enclosures. These are in some respects a different sort of camouflage, a self-formed, artificial and only partial enclosure, a beneficial psychic device within which the inner self momentarily and temporarily gathers and holds and collects as much psychic energy about it as it is capable of receiving, utilizing, and also withstanding. The mental enclosure in most cases is self-limiting then, since it represents a setting up of barriers on all sides but one. But it is limiting only for the ultimate purpose of intense concentration of energy, resulting in a burst or expansion of this energy that has been transformed and pressurized, so to speak, into new patterns.

The side which is open allows free flow of energy from the inner self, but momentarily the outlet for this energy is blocked up. This holding back, this gathering and collection without instant outlet, is one of the natural and constant processes involved not only in the construction of energy into matter, but in the construction of energy into any other form, and it is closely allied to the pause and pulsation that I have mentioned, as atoms and molecules appear and disappear imperceptibly, even while they seem to give continuity to any particular object.

You may consider a mental enclosure in its simplest terms to be somewhat like a cube. The dimensions may vary within, but the furthest side will be represented as open or transparent, the line itself being drawn only for convenience's sake.

Into the cube then pours psychic energy. The front or foremost line of the cube, like a gate, can open or close; and it points toward the outer world of physical matter. As energy pours into our cube it is momentarily held within it. Mental enzymes help transform the energy into incipient patterns, from which matter, physical matter, can result.

The front gates of our cube then open, freeing the transformed energy. But these front gates represent our subconscious and the signal to open, the permission for the construction of matter and its form, are dependent upon these subconscious gates. Even as incipient matter flows through, the final form is given by the way it brushes through these subconscious gates. It must be born and even shaped, finally, here.

The properties of matter have been given it, that is been given the energy, within the mental enclosure, as indeed the physical properties have been given. And a child is formed in the womb, but may be damaged in the act of passing out.

I suggest your first break.

(Break at 9:30. Jane was fairly well dissociated, and had no sense of being bothered by outside stimuli. However, since it was a cold evening our windows were closed, and the house itself was very quiet. She resumed in the same slightly heavier voice at 9:34.)

Now. Such enclosures are the innermost basis of any consciousness, regardless of the type of consciousness. They could be said to represent the inner psychic form even of the most minute cell.

They represent the necessary pause, though this pause understand on the physical plane is imperceivable. Nevertheless, the mental enclosures allow for a psychic duration in which energy, which is forever flooding, may be shaped to some extent and transformed, either into the properties of matter or into other forms.

We have to some extent touched upon the various ways by which this process is carried out. The process is carried out so quickly as to seem simultaneous on your plane, but the pause and resulting pulsation is always present. This mental enclosure is arbitrary, necessary again, a device used by the self. It would seem to limit the extension of consciousness, and yet it does not.

The dimensions of such mental enclosures are governed by the particular ability of the particular consciousness to receive, withstand and utilize energy. This ability is more or less elastic; that is, the ability can expand, and no rigid rules apply to it in a limiting manner.

Within it will be found the capsule comprehension of which we have spoken earlier. This is an attribute of energy itself in its pure form, and even when it is, so to speak, broken down or individualized, the capsule comprehension is in no way either lessened or simplified.

This point is extremely important. All consciousnesses, therefore, either of a complicated psychic gestalt such as a man or animal, or of simpler gestalts such as an individual cell or molecule, nevertheless operate in and form about themselves mental or psychic enclosures, within which is naturally contained the capsule comprehension which is an attribute of all energy.

And in this mental enclosure, also, the energy which is received is then momentarily held and transformed, either into matter or into other aspects. For the record, you realize that when I speak of consciousnesses I do not refer to that conscious ego, but rather to inner consciousness, that then helps form the material image.

I suggest your break.

(Break at 9:55. Jane was dissociated as usual. She resumed in the same slow manner; her voice was normal now, her pacing very slow. Resume at 10:01.)

This capsule comprehension I call capsule comprehension, since innate comprehension of itself and its workings is part of what you may think of as the fiber or makeup of <u>all</u> energy, regardless of any given particular form that it might take, or regardless of the camouflage it might form of itself.

The comprehension of itself and its workings, being an attribute and everywhere a part of energy, cannot be therefore pointed at, and is in no way distinguishable from energy itself, being a part and not an addition. It is distributed therefore throughout energy, or within it, in much the same way that creative ability is distributed throughout or within, say, a particular personality.

The results of it can be perceived in the actions carried out by a given personality, but as you cannot separate creative ability, or take it out of an individual for examination, so you cannot separate comprehension of itself from energy.

Now. This comprehension, latent in all energy, is not broken up and distributed piecemeal within individualized consciousnesses, but completely contained within as if it were condensed; and indeed it is condensed into a capsule form.

The comprehension is condensed, but the term capsule is merely one that I have chosen. All units of individual consciousness contain this capsule comprehension, and it represents the most minute unit of consciousness about which a mental enclosure, or self, can be constructed. There is no smaller unit, and cannot be, than this.

It is the ability of such a unit of consciousness to utilize or create other forms and dimensions of itself that regulates the dimensions of the mental enclosure and of the effective self. You understand that about this mental or psychic enclosure the other elements of self are constructed, the physical image and its extensions into physical environment. This process, in various fields, continually goes on.

The entity, each entity, was formed in this manner, it in turn sending out its creations in terms of other personalities, and these personalities sending forth their own psychic as well as physical constructions. When I spoke of energy being transformed within the mental enclosure, I mentioned that it was transformed into matter, but also into other constructions.

Certainly all energy does not go into the construction of physical matter, even on the physical level, as you should know; and I have mentioned in the past that dreams are not sterile, but also construct according to the nature of their own properties.

I will here mention Ruburt's dream, in which he spoke reassuringly to two men who were ill with cancer by telling them that this material said that he too had cancer.

This dream is a sequel to another, in which Ruburt was aware of the death of an old woman who was a medium, and I will need to explain the first dream, that is the earlier one, to make the other dream comprehensible.

In the first dream Ruburt remembered his earlier death. He was a woman medium in Boston, dying at 82 or 83 of cancer. He was not, then, afraid of death, knowing its true nature, and in the surrounding rooms there were other old people. Two in particular were men, dreadfully afraid of death, and both dying of cancer.

(See the details of Jane's dreams, detailed on page 5. For more data on the immediate past lives of Jane and mine in Boston, before the Civil War, see the 59th session, Volume 2, page 140. Our relationship with Dee Masters, mentioned by Seth in this session, is also dealt with briefly in the 59th session.)

In Ruburt's second dream he experienced no feeling of dread when he spoke of having cancer, because at the time he was not afraid. He reassured the two. One was a shipyard worker. One was a lawyer in his younger days but due to trouble he died poor.

The second dream was brought on by the memories subconsciously released in the first dream, and the whole memory block, oddly enough, was released by the fact that Ruburt had in the present some difficulty with his monthly periods. It had been on his mind, brought to his consciousness once the possibility of the difficulty as being a cancer symptom.

He threw this thought back to his personal subconscious, but by association it triggered memory of a previous death by cancer, which was then played back through the dream. But even then the reassuring dream came first. In the first dream, he was aware that the woman worked and was constructive until the last, and also that she passed the transition with little personal jolting.

It was only after this dream that the knowledge that the woman had died of cancer was allowed to emerge. The fact that Ruburt experienced in the dream, or following it, no sense of either fateful predestination or even fear, was a tip-off that the dream was not clairvoyant in terms of a future prediction.

He became worried about the dream only much later, because many other dreams have been clairvoyant in that fashion, and he wondered then what distinguished this dream from the others.

I—do you want a break?

("Yes.")

I will continue this after.

(Break at 10:40. Jane was fully dissociated—once again far-out, as she says. My writing hand felt little fatigue but I asked for the break because I thought Jane might want it. She said she felt fine. She resumed in the same normal voice at 10:47.)

The men, reassured by Ruburt in the dream, appeared without being old, although the original event of the past life involved men in their 70's. This was a distortion of the personal subconscious, to add to the seeming separateness of the two dreams.

On a conscious level, even though Ruburt remembered them, there seemed to be nothing to connect them. This is in keeping with the sometimes necessary inclination of the subconscious to block out such knowledge.

A point here: It is not understood at all that the uppermost or personal layer of the subconscious is concerned with maintaining the autocratic control and position of the conscious ego. Its inhibitions always are intended to protect the ego.

I will not extend this session for any length of time. You will find that an analysis of your dreams will further your inner development, and also make your way easier in the outer world. I suggest you keep track of your dreams, Joseph, when possible; and that copies of dreams for which you would like analysis be left on the table before sessions.

There is also a reason why Ruburt saw the former gallery administrator in the old woman dream, immediately after he perceived the old woman dead. I had mentioned that this woman was known to you in previous life. It is for this reason that Ruburt saw her. However, the elements of the dream were disintegrating, and he saw the woman in the form with which he is familiar with her in this life. The washing machine that he saw is an excellent example of subconscious knowledge distortion and fabrication.

He was bound up with you in the past life and what he did not know then, and he knew much, he has picked up telepathically from you, since the washing machine was a visual distortion of the idea of a ship, which he interpreted as a tub. And from tub he leaped to washing machine, filled with water.

This referred to a ship instead on the water, at a time when you crossed the Atlantic and came to Boston. In the dream the tub or washing machine leaked, but only briefly. This referred to a time when a leakage was discovered on the ship. This event, you notice, is even further back in time; and the cancer dream was also, though not so far back in time.

The dream sequence for that group of days involved perception, first, of Ruburt's actual previous death, and then leaped that same evening back further to much earlier events. The purpose of the whole sequence was reassuring, and in overall nature had to do with the personality's inner reaction to the season of an approaching winter and the ever symbolic death that it suggests.

On one level then Ruburt was psychically anticipating winter with its symbolism, and he involved you in his concern. The dream said that Ruburt died once and yet lived again, and that as you survived a leaky old ship at one occasion, so would the basic selves always survive.

At the same time the more nearly conscious worries present in everyone were felt by Ruburt in his cancer concern, and the dream said "You have already died of cancer, it will not happen again." So the dream had meanings on several levels.

There is no point in giving you a superficial analysis, since dreams usually impart knowledge that can be utilized by several levels of the personality; though consciously the information perceived and brought into meaningful context by the subconscious may not be at all comprehensible to the ego, it is nevertheless utilized by the whole personality.

I will here close the session, and wish you pleasant dreams.

("Good night, Seth."

(End at 11:15. Jane was once again far-out, losing track of the content of the material. We had barely begun to discuss the dream material when she abruptly

began dictating again while sitting across from me at the table. Resume at 11:18.)

I would add one remark. In the dream Ruburt said the material told him that he had cancer, because in a previous life he did have clairvoyant knowledge, through his psychic ability, of his future disease; and since his psychic ability has only lately come to light with this material, you can see the connection.

(End at 11:20.)

SESSION 88
SEPTEMBER 16, 1964 9 PM WEDNESDAY AS SCHEDULED

(At 8:50 this evening Jane had no idea of the material for the session tonight. She was very tired, in fact more so than I knew, and secretly she hoped for a short session. She did not tell me because she did not want to disappoint me.

(In line with the material of the last session, Jane had been studying her dream notebook with renewed respect, and I had resolved to begin one without yet doing anything about it. Jane began dictation on time; her delivery was slow at first, then speeded up; her pacing was slow also, her eyes dark as usual.)

I will now say good evening.

("Good evening, Seth.")

You should keep track of your dreams, Joseph. At times much information can be used from them, after analysis in conscious life.

All dreams are not clairvoyant. As there are levels of unconsciousness or subconsciousness, so do each of these levels have their own activities and translate, symbolize and often distort valid data, according to the different degree of subconsciousness through which the data were able to emerge.

What psychologists speak of as association is definitely an important psychological characteristic. What psychologists do not understand, however, is that in deep levels of subconscious activity associations may spring from the inner self's latent knowledge and experience of past lives.

There are of course peculiar sets of associations that have been collected in this existence only, but even among associations that seem to be from this existence there are those associations, usually key associations, from previous existences which merge with those of the present.

The topmost layer of the subconscious contains predominantly present associations, but in these are mixed and interwoven associations which have their origin elsewhere. These may be called self-unifying associations, since merely by their presence in the uppermost layers of the subconscious they provide a unifying sense of psychic continuity; of which however the ego is not aware.

For one thing, there are basic similarities between an individual's personality in various existences, so that quite naturally many associations of the same nature will arise.

When I speak of levels of the subconscious, I do so only for simplicity's sake, since there is after all no top or bottom to the mind, but only a present point of focus from which viewpoints may be taken, and new perspectives formed. It is theoretically possible, for example, to change the focus, to delve downward as it were two lives back, and look upward from that perspective to the present.

The ego cannot so change its focus, but the inner ego of which we have spoken is indeed the self that dreams, and is the "I" who experiences when the ego "I" sleeps.

When hypnosis is more clearly understood and used, and when certain other psychological devices are discovered, it will then be possible to change focus in such a manner, and through psychological testing discover the personality types, the individual types who dwell in various stages of the subconscious.

These various stages of the subconscious represent what was once the conscious ego of an individual, left now almost like living archeological heritage, from which the present individual may draw both knowledge, psychic continuity and balance.

What was once the subconscious of these individuals once more united with the inner ego, which always represents the true individual, and these then advanced according to their own abilities and desires.

I now suggest your break.

(Break at 9:25. Jane was dissociated as usual. Her delivery was now faster, her voice but a little heavier than at the start of the session. She resumed in the same manner at 9:30.)

Like the fossilized layers within the physical earth, so do the subconscious layers hold intact the traces of an individual's past lives. And as your physical eras of time may be deduced through studying the physical fossilized layers of rock, so can the time and place of past lives be deduced through studying the layers of the subconscious.

The personal present subconscious could be compared, using this analogy, with the topmost layer of soil dealing with the present seasons. Through it reach the roots of living emotions and desires. Directly beneath, still using our analogy, will be found the nutrients and seeds of those desires. The topmost layers of the subconscious hold then, first of all, almost conscious just-under-the-surface needs and desires; and under these those more deeply buried, reaching backward to birth, even as the loose dry autumn leaves still contain traces of earlier pigment.

The second layer, still of the personal subconscious, contains those elements most deeply feared for personal psychological reasons, those which somewhat frequently arise as in an earthquake, to shatter the seemingly solid surface of the ego.

Beneath this layer, in a third subconscious level, still dealing with the present personality, lie those possibilities of development which have lain barren and were not sufficiently strong to send up seeds to bloom in the sun of conscious ego.

It is from this layer that so-called secondary personalities may sometimes arise, usually due to one of the psychic earthquakes mentioned earlier. As earthquakes cause lava to boil up seemingly from the center of the earth, so do some secondary personalities in their explosive emersion bring with them debris from other levels of the subconscious, often personifying themselves in the guise of those buried and frightening fears that have, until then, found no vehicle for expression.

It is also possible that these secondary personalities, emerging, give access to buried abilities and benign constructive abilities which had been buried beneath heavier fears that weighed them down. In any case this level represents the last division of what we may call the present personal subconscious, and still only accounts for a small dimension of the inner self, being composed of only the most easily accessible portions.

There are methods, some of which you know, that make entry into these levels comparatively easy. Before I continue into a discussion of other layers, and hence into a following dissertation connecting various types of dreams according to their origin in these layers, I will make a present, pertinent statement.

The beneficial or detrimental effect of the emergence of secondary personalities must and may be judged by its effect for good or bad on the dominant personality, for in your existence the dominant personality is necessary and must be maintained in an authoritative position, to deal with the physical world.

(Now Jane smiled. With one foot up on a chair she leaned toward me and spoke in a most amused voice.)

I do not represent such a secondary personality. However I have included this material for your edification when you suppose that I am.

This phenomena is more common however than you would suppose, though unfortunately in many cases the secondary personality gives personification to buried fears and fantasies that are unhealthy to the dominant personality. Not only this, but because they are released by a psychic earthquake they emerge forcibly and sometimes with more vigor than the present personality can handle, so that they are in a position to dictate terms to the dominant personality.

The secondary personalities in such cases are, you see, of a whole, composed of powerful unified subconscious forces long denied outlet where the dominant personality, or the personality so far dominant, has long been holding the fort, and is set upon by those diverse divisions imposed upon it by society and environment.

I suggest your break.

(Break at 10:00. Jane was dissociated as usual. Although she had been very tired before the session began, she reported that she now felt fine. My writing hand felt no fatigue as yet, although it had been a rather fast session so far.

(Jane resumed in a normal voice at 10:04.)

Such personalities, that is such secondary personalities, do not represent past incarnations therefore, although some of the qualities may originate in a past life.

Such secondary personalities in many cases will often mask themselves by adopting for a while moral postures in keeping with those of the dominant personality; but these will be soon discarded as the secondary personality further insinuates itself.

<u>If</u> I were such a secondary personality for example, I would have long ago discarded any semblance of concern for Ruburt's own identity; and also the fear patterns of which I would have been composed would have long ago asserted themselves.

Nor would any intrinsically valuable information have come through, unless of course Ruburt had no strong, utilized creative outlets of his own. For oftentimes a benevolent secondary personality will indeed act as an outlet for creative abilities that the dominant ego has been unable to use.

Here for the moment we finish with the immediate personal subconscious.

Now, since we are thinking in terms of archeological layers, we would continue to express ourselves along those lines. So. Directly beneath personal subconscious you will find upon examination either through hypnosis or applied association, a layer dealing with the period before this life, and after the life before this one.

Since this period was to some degree at least free of camouflage, from it communication can be received dealing with the entity's knowledge of itself, and of uncamouflaged reality. From this undifferentiated gap of experience between camouflage existences, valuable information <u>may</u> be received dealing with the reality which exists behind, and independent of, matter.

From this focus position communication may be set up between personality essences no longer in the physical field, and those still in it, provided that those still in it are able to remove focus from the ego to this particular level. It is from this focus point then that communication between what is termed the living and the dead may take place.

The necessary focus point may be achieved through trance, hypnosis or self-hypnosis, or through certain other disciplines. It may happen spontaneously, as when a severe emotional reaction is set off; through external circumstances, and what Ruburt has read in the past along these lines is partially correct.

Emotional outbursts or reactions do cause chemical conditions, and certain chemical conditions can facilitate such communications. However, it is a fact that as a rule the communications cause the chemical reactions rather than the other way around.

On a particular level however this makes little difference, because such communications are carried on constantly at subconscious levels, seldom reaching ego awareness, so that individuals are subconsciously conditioned—and underline subconsciously conditioned—therefore expecting, all unknown to the ego, such communications when certain chemical changes come about; since these chemical changes also occur for other reasons when these conditions occur, on a practical level communications will then most easily happen. These chemical changes without the proper subconscious focus point, will result in clairvoyance or telepathy strong enough on some occasions to be conscious. When the proper focus point is reached however, these communications will result in rapport between the living and that portion of personality essences, or so-called dead, who are still at least psychically connected with life on your field.

I suggest your break.

(Break at 10:32. Jane was far-out, fully dissociated. She said that Seth was ready to continue. The pace had been so fast that my writing hand was beginning to feel it. Jane resumed in the same normal, if rather fast, manner at 10:40.)

Obviously people vary in their ability to change their point of focus. Many find difficulty in changing it at all. Some, because of excellent development, inner communication with the inner self, feel subconsciously secure enough to change focus spontaneously, as one might listen to one radio station and then another, still retaining knowledge of the basic "I" who listened.

This is entirely within Ruburt's natural ability. However controls adopted during this life made his abilities late in showing themselves, and now training and confidence must be given before he can spontaneously adapt himself.

His ego would have been in great danger of becoming a rigid prison for his intuitive self, because of the necessary defensive mechanisms it had to adopt against the most difficult and threatening aspects of his mother's personality.

As it is, he does not have sufficient inner confidence to give reign to his abilities, for changing his focus point. It was the outlet of creative writing, early adopted, that saved him from becoming a most rigid and frozen personality; and if he had adopted such a stonelike ego, then indeed he would now be in dangerous circumstances, since his strong creative nature would finally and disastrously have shattered the stone image.

Finding you Joseph, as a partner, and a complete psychic and sexual partnership, also helped deliver him from such an eventuality. He would have finally used his psychic abilities in any case, but they would have under those conditions been tools, or used as tools of the personal subconscious in diverse ways, shattering beyond repair the unity and integrity of the personality.

Beneath this undifferentiated subconscious layer we will find, and psychologists can find through testing and hypnosis, a layer composed of memories, dealing successively with each previous existence, and separated by a layer between lives that is, again, undifferentiated.

Historical knowledge and verifications of identity—identities—may be achieved through communication with those layers of the subconscious dealing with past lives. But no information may be gathered here that was unknown to the particular previous personality as a rule. <u>Some</u> particularly gifted <u>may</u> use one of these levels as a focus point, looking outward even to the present personality, but this is unusual.

Communications that give valid information concerning the reality beneath the camouflage world must be attained through one of the separating layers between lives.

At the bottom so to speak, will be found a layer of the subconscious dealing with racial heritage, concerning the dim first materialization of man; and beneath this a heritage dealing with a comprehension of reality as concerned in physical matter before the physical evolution of man, following backward to that first inner self within its mental enclosure, that was adept enough to translate and transform its psychic energy to form the first, most minute physical materialization, from which all other physical constructions then flowed.

These sessions come from, or are received through, what we may call, since we are using terms of succession, from the third undifferentiated level, beneath the limitations of Ruburt's personal subconsciousness.

Without his blocking therefore, he would have access to the previous three lives that he has lived, and in detail. And since his abilities are strong, he would also have access to your previous three lives, since he picks up much information from you telepathically.

I suggest a brief break, and then I will resume for only a short time. The dream material that I am leading up to will not be therefore given in this session.

(Break at 11:05. Jane was dissociated as usual. Her voice was a little hoarse at the close of the delivery, though she said she did not feel very tired. My writing hand was fatigued however. Jane resumed in the same manner at 11:10.)

These so-called layers of the subconscious, however, are not really layers at all, but part of the spacious present.

Actually, all of these previous lives, and the present life, happen simultaneously, but this idea cannot be comprehended on a conscious level.

The Frank Watts material represented communication on the first level of undifferentiated fields. Both Ruburt and Frank Watts were experimenting. According to an individual's abilities and development, he can change his focus so that it encompasses realities further and further from the concern of the ego, and in this Ruburt has come far. The phrase "give unto Caesar the things that are Caesar's" is a good one. You see I am better acquainted with biblical phrases than either of you.

(Jane delivered the above tidbit in high good humor.)

In other words, Ruburt's ego should be and is properly concerned with contact, development and progress in the physical field. His ego is a critical one. It is his inner ego which is intuitional and gives his critical ego the material from which his books are written; and I expect naturally that his ego, and yours, will critically appraise what we have done here, what we will do, and beyond doubt any suggestions to you that I might make. But also his abilities should be used to better advantage in our sessions, and this I know will only come about when his ego is assured, through examination of our material, of its validity.

This is as it should be. It is only because his abilities and his faith in you are so strong that we can put the material safely to the test, and he will become more freely accessible to the use of his own abilities as time goes by.

I am suggesting that psychological time experiments be again adopted for you both. Ruburt has great faith in such experiments when they are successful and when he knows I am not connected with them. The autumn will be an auspicious season in this respect. When our next session arrives I will discuss the furthermost level of the subconscious from the present ego, the particular advantage of the undifferentiated levels, and at least begin a discussion of dreams and the types of dreams that spring from the various levels.

I wish you now a fond good evening, with one remark still to come.

Dear Joseph, when I spoke of you both being in excellent overall condition,

I did not mean that I overlooked your yearly hay fever, into which we shall go in so far as causes and alleviation of symptoms are concerned, and shortly. I meant that both of your overall vital psychic reserves were being well utilized, and that your general health was, believe me, excellent. If you will remember your previous severe back trouble, and Ruburt's which has entirely vanished, you should be able to see what I meant.

I expect reasonable criticism, indeed enjoy it. But picayune comments find me most ungrateful. And now, old friends, you may call it an evening, or call it anything you like.

("Good night, Seth."

(End at 11:31. Jane was dissociated as usual. She ended the session on a note of heavy humor. She was now quite tired, and remarked that for the state she was in at the start of the session she had to be "out, all the way," to be able to give any session at all. My writing hand was also tired.)

SESSION 89
SEPTEMBER 19, 1964 10:10 PM SATURDAY UNSCHEDULED

(Saturday and Sunday, September 19 and 20, Jane and I spent visiting my brother William Richard and his wife Ida, in Rochester, NY. Bill has been acting as custodian of the second carbon of the Seth material. Jane and I have always made it a policy to have a carbon of any written material—prose, poetry, etc., in separate hands outside of our house, as a protection against loss by accident, fire, etc.

(We had not asked that Bill follow the material from session to session, feeling that it was for him to decide whether to pay any attention to it or not. Jane and I were therefore pleasantly surprised to learn that Bill and Ida had read some of the material; and while not hostile to it, they still expressed a healthy skepticism—an attitude Jane and I much prefer to any gullible, overenthusiastic belief blindly undertaken.

(Ida's brother, Louie, had also been following the material somewhat more thoroughly, and he visited the four of us at Bill's home Saturday night. Louie has had more experience than Jane or I with ESP activities; and when in the course of conversation the question of Jane giving a session arose, Jane and I were somewhat surprised, not anticipating this, and did nothing to push agreement to such an idea. However, when we finally became convinced that a session was quite welcome to Ida, Bill and Louie, if only out of curiosity, Jane and I agreed to try to hold one.

(We sat in the fully lighted living room. I held on my lap a sheaf of notepaper and had my pen handy. Jane sat quietly on the other side of the room while the rest

of us exchanged ideas on the subject. It was getting late, we had already put in an active day traveling and visiting, and I for one was not sure of how effective such a session might be. Jane had remarked that she had no idea whether she could give one, and no inkling of any possible subject matter.

(Jane then arose abruptly and began to dictate in a voice somewhat stronger than usual, without greeting. Bill called out the time to me. Jane spoke rather loudly but paced at an average rate. Her eyes, I noticed, were exceptionally dark.)

I will not here endeavor to deliver a full session.

Nevertheless I do here welcome all present, and hope that I am myself welcomed, into what we may call a pleasant family gathering.

It was not necessarily my intention to deliver a session this evening. Nevertheless, I did feel a legitimate welcome in advance; and since I feel already as if I know very well two of the present gathering, and since furthermore we have dealt with them in our material, I am more than willing to greet both of them personally.

(Here of course Seth refers to Bill and Ida, having given some information on their past lives in various sessions, many sessions ago.)

The other man was not involved with any of you in past lives, nor do I see him indeed at all in England in any era. Instead the Mediterranean area in the 1500's, and it is from this period that his present speech impediment indeed originated.

The impediment, beginning in this life, 1507, represented a time when he did not speak out, and he should have, for a man's life was at stake. He did not speak out because of fear, and now when he wishes most to speak out he cannot.

This can be remedied. A sense of guilt carried throughout one lifetime is somewhat understandable. A sense of guilt enduring psychologically since the 1500's is indeed carrying conscience just a bit too far. He has more than made up for the original offense, which was indeed understandable under the circumstances.

(Here Jane pointed at Louie.)

There was an army from another country, an invasion. A man in his company was thought to be disloyal. This man—

(Again Jane pointed to Louie.)

—was thought to be the disloyal member. He denied it; but when they decided that another innocent man was the culprit, a man whom he knew to be innocent, then to save his own life he let them think the innocent man was the betrayer.

He has paid time and time again for this. No one asked that you pay. He was then, even then, conscientious, and therefore fourfold bothered more than most by his own betrayal. In his immediately past life he plagued himself through a useless arm; right arm, you see, so he could not point out again. This time the self-adopted defect is less, a mere annoyance.

But such a mere annoyance becomes indeed a form of torture. There is no longer any need for this. In other ways, through constructive action, he has more than made his way.

(Now Jane pointed at me.)

You should know, and Ruburt should certainly know, that you form your own physical image in a most actual and practical manner, with all its defects, for your own reasons. And so has he.

The realization that he has more than made up for the initial betrayal should result, if he takes the information to heart, in a lessening of symptoms that should result, again, in their disappearance.

(Jane smiled.)

And, he knows the man whom he once so betrayed. In this life he knows him, and he—

(Again Jane pointed to Louie.)

—he has been kind to him, and he has given up much for this man whom he once, out of fear, betrayed.

Nor does karma say anything about an eye for an eye, nor is there in karma any suggestion of punishment. Karma is merely in the physical plane, the result of personal development, and represents the maturing realization that we are all psychically and physically part of All There Is, and that when we wound, it is not another that we wound but ourselves.

We do not have to bear such scars forever. There is a time when we must subconsciously forget where we have trespassed.

I suggest your break.

(Break at 10:32. Jane was fully dissociated. She had been worried about giving a session before three witnesses, she said, this being the first time for that many. During the conversation at break it developed that Louie in this life does not use his right hand for all things, but is somewhat ambidextrous. Ida associated this, which neither Jane or I realized, with the fact that in the previous life a right arm had not been used by Louie.

(Jane resumed in the same strong voice at 10:38.)

It is indeed a basic anxiety and fear. The personality can express himself very well. In the 1500's he was eloquent, and it is precisely because this eloquence, so persuasive, so smooth-tongued, caused his superiors at that time to believe the accusations against the innocent man, that he now fears to use an eloquence, because he once let it run away with him.

It is the present personality's desire to express himself, opposed by the subconscious memories of that past life, with its fear of the effects of eloquence used without discretion, that now cause his difficulty.

His present desire for expression will certainly not change. It is therefore the fear of expression that must be erased. Nor can this erasure occur without the realization by this personality that he can indeed trust himself. For both the fear and the anxiety is based simply upon a resulting distrust of his ability to handle eloquence or verbal expression.

Since I will not give a session simply to give a session, and because I will not let Ruburt parade me as part of his precious subconscious, I will indeed here speak for myself, but in terms that will help another and for the benefit of that other. And despite our anxious Ruburt's furious attempts to block me, I will indeed say that the person who was once betrayed by the personality involved was the present father of the personality, and he knows it—

("Who knows it?")

—subconsciously, and subconsciously the father knows. And why else would he demand from a son that which no father has a right to demand? He, the father, subconsciously knew and remembered this betrayal, and he would see to it that the present personality paid, and paid in full.

I am not implying that the father consciously intends either unkindness nor revenge, any more than I am implying that Ruburt intended unkindness or revenge on Walter Zeh; yet was this not the result, and is it not the result here?

(Jane pointed to Louie.)

He has taken at least as much as he gave, and there were sly and secret ways in which the father repaid him. Yet here we have further conflict, because indeed the present father loves the present son. It is not the son that he would wound. It is the man that son once was.

So, as the father pays back his old betrayer, he hurts the son without knowing why. He cannot understand his own cruelty toward him, or the acts which he is impelled to perform. Nor can the son, loving the father, understand either the father's cruelty or his own sense of gratification received from the cruelties. He, with his remorseless conscience, welcomes the cruelties, for they make him feel as if he is doing penance, and for what?

For an offense that has been paid for in full. And each cruelty committed by the father hurts the father more, for he is bewildered by the unkindness of his own actions toward the son, toward whom his conscious feelings are indeed fraternal. And again—

(Jane pointed to Louie.)

—he knows this, and he knows that by enduring the small acts of cruelty he gains two ends.

One, he attempts to convince himself of something that is indeed a fact. He has nothing else to do penance for. By enduring the literally endless small cruelties he does needless penance, but at the same time he strikes back by causing the father hours of remorse. In all relationships these intertwining effects exert, many times, most unpleasant effects.

The personality left, to return. He returned to reassure himself that he had indeed paid this subconscious debt, as indeed he had. But here again conditioning took over, and the old ways and the old responses.

(I believe this passage refers to the fact that Louie had returned to Rochester from California a few months ago. At the moment Louie is living with his parents, not being married, and is working in his father's place of business. Louie had also remarked that his speech impediment had not bothered him as much while he lived in California, as it does currently.)

I suggest your break. Nor do I here, despite Ruburt, apologize for what may be considered a slight invasion of family affairs. For if the information given is understood and applied, then the vicious circle of relationship can be broken, and a new constructive relationship can be at last attained.

(Break at 11:02. Jane was again fully dissociated, far-out. There followed a conversation mainly between Louie, Ida and Bill in which family matters were discussed. Not being versed in these, Jane and I could say little, and we had no way of knowing how valid the session's material might be, or prove to be.

(Jane resumed in the same forceful manner, with many gestures, at 11:20, pointing again at Louie.)

In order to rationalize, <u>this</u> personality and all personalities, to give to the present identity a more or less logical explanation for a symptom that is of past origin, the personality will bring forth an actual incident which can then be pointed at by the personal subconscious as a scapegoat.

Everything becomes plain. Such and such happened to me at the age of five or six, and ever after have I acted thus and so. So it is with Ruburt's eyes. The panic reaction, which is true, the fear of seeing reality as it was when he was a child; but this indeed is only a symptom of a symptom, and not an origin.

The incident, the handy incident which gave rise, or rather the incident which allowed the personality to project the symptom finally, in this instance occurred on a Saturday afternoon, and is not remembered consciously by the personality (*Louie*), and was not known to anyone else.

The incident, and I will mention it but consciously it will mean nothing, the incident represented the individual's final success after many failures to bring forth circumstances that would then allow, or seem to cause, the peculiar set of symptoms that he felt necessary in order to repay old debts.

Saturday afternoon he was five, not six, and for unforeseen reasons left alone for a mere ten minutes in a large house, circumstances being such that only for a brief time no one was present. He played with a large ball, and the actual incident was so simple and uncomplicated that under ordinary circumstances it would have resulted in no such results.

The time, 3 PM. He went out to the kitchen, where the ball after he played with it finally rolled. A portion of a stove had been left on; and though there was no danger of fire, the child was afraid of fire. But this was not the cause of his sudden terror.

It was indeed the sight of that portion of the stove glowing, however, that made him try to call out. There is somewhat more here, but our illustrious and pigheaded Ruburt has indeed implied that I should somewhat maintain silence.

The fact remains that the child did try to scream. At the same time a door close by slammed abruptly. Unused to being alone, the child reacted in the first place vehemently to the unaccustomed isolation. He ran to the stove, touched it, and as he burned but only slightly his right hand, the door slammed nearby very loudly.

This time when the child tried to scream he could not. The sound of the door was associated with the burn in his mind. When in a few moments his mother returned he tried to explain why he cried, for she had heard the first cries, and he stuttered.

He stuttered because the pain from the small burn through subconscious association became, for the first time in this existence, penance for the barely remembered past offense. Now. The stuttering did not, as is believed, begin continuously to show itself, but from then on it began to show itself more and more as the child experienced those necessary and trivial wounds that every child must indeed endure.

In many cases such symptoms show themselves immediately, even before a situation can be seized upon to justify them. In this case there was time, and the personality could have avoided them.

There is a subconscious domination of father over son, always an implied, always an insidious circle of reaction leading to reaction. It is not strictly necessary that the personality here involved change his environment drastically, if he can understand the circumstances that underlay the relationship between himself and the father.

If this is realized then the personality will not feel smothered. As it is, how can he dare express himself in the presence particularly of a man whom he feels he once betrayed? And when he speaks to him in syllables, he does not speak clearly. He does not owe the father any more than a normal filial devotion. He does not owe the father any more than that, and to seek the father's pleasure superficially, or to try to please the father in fields where he has no interest, will not lead either to personal development or success, and will not help the father in any way.

I will now end the session, in no way desiring to intrude myself any longer in your social gathering. I consider the session to have been a good one, and I wish each and all a fond and hearty good evening.

("Good night, Seth."

(End at 11:48. Jane was normally dissociated, gradually coming out of the state as the session neared its end. My writing hand was somewhat tired, since her dictation had been rather fast. Jane used the rather strong voice throughout the session, along with more gestures than usual also.

(The five of us were discussing the session when Jane spoke for Seth again, abruptly rising and dictating in the same strong voice. She spoke without wearing her glasses, but instead left them on the floor near where she had been sitting. Each time, pacing back and forth across the room, seldom looking down, it seemed she might step on the glasses, but she did not. Resume at 11:51.)

I will add here one note.

Communication is a field in which the personality will be extremely successful, for through electronics there is communication, and he can use his latent eloquence which now has no outlet, in this field. And may I here add that his interest in psychic phenomena is precisely caused by this need to communicate.

The whole personality, with its set limitation to vocal communication, will find satisfaction and success in a field or fields where the latent desire for communication can find outlet.

Indeed, it seems to me that I have given someone else, and a friend of yours, this same advice, quote: "Live alone." The personality, if he stays in this location, should find a dwelling place where he will be unsmothered.

His actual predicament is one where what he wishes, he feels will hurt others. And yet through living at home while helping the father, on the one hand, in the establishment, at the same time on unconscious levels by his very presence he says "I am not doing what I want to do, and you are to blame."

None of this, or very little, is conscious. The love that does exist between father and son can best be maintained and nurtured when the son stands alone, and lets the father know that he has the strength to do so. For the sacrifices unconsciously asked by the father, the father regrets, and the sacrifices made by the son, the son regrets.

The son is even now coming to an inner understanding. Indeed much of this I gain for Ruburt through subconscious telepathy from the personality involved. Were this not so it would be more difficult, but possible, for me to tell you what I do. And if I sound dour and heavy-handed it is only because I must sometimes deal with Ruburt with a heavy hand.

He does not believe that a houseguest should behave in any such manner, but then I am not a houseguest. And I will indeed close the session, with no more p.s.'s, and with my most sincere wishes for you all. I will not however give you a shorter session Monday, since I consider that I have done a favor, and I do not owe you another.

I may sound irascible, and if I do then indeed certainly I shall try to blame it on Ruburt, and say it is a distortion, though it is no distortion. I find it, however, a rather painful duty, self imposed, to delve into personal backgrounds, and consider myself rather dignified to adopt the pose of a Peeping Tom. But there are too few who can, either, look within themselves with candor, and if this material does anything, it must be oriented toward knowledge; and knowledge must be applied in your case in human terms.

(End at 12:07. Jane was dissociated as usual.)

SESSION 90
SEPTEMBER 21, 1964 9 PM MONDAY AS SCHEDULED

(Jane and I have not yet resumed the study of psychological time, although frequently as we are drifting off to sleep we will have brief experiences. I have had several vivid ones lately, including a fall tree in full color, and the head of a child with an open mouth.

(Company left this evening at 8:55 PM, and Jane had no idea of the material for the session. She had also been too busy to be nervous. She began dictation on time in a rather normal voice, and at an easy rate. Her pacing was average, her eyes dark as usual. And as she has done so often recently, she began without wearing her glasses, not appearing at all handicapped.)

I will here wish you a good evening—

("Good evening, Seth.")

—and open our quiet session.

Our last session proved to be a most beneficial one. It was good for Ruburt's confidence to hold a session away from home, and before people who though far from strangers, are nevertheless not closely associated in daily life.

It goes without saying that had Ruburt known beforehand the subject matter of the session, he would have blocked it. I certainly did not myself press for a session, though I was glad to be of help, as far as the personality about whose problems the session revolved.

It was however Ida's quite sincere curiosity, and her open-minded willingness to perceive, that subconsciously caused Ruburt to agree to the session. The rapport existing as a rule between twins, and that does indeed exist, between Loriza, L-o-r-i-z-a and her twin (*sister*), goes far to account for Loriza's latent intuitive, but partial, inner comprehension of the elements that work within, say, telepathy.

Twins use communication of the inner senses all unknowing, and what Loriza read of the material moved her subconscious to intuitive realization. The communication between twins is freer than it is with others. Twins are more used to using inner communication, and instances come more easily to mind.

(And here I must admit that although Seth gave the entity name for Bill's wife Ida, I did not think quickly enough to ask for the entity name of Ida's twin sister. Jane and I are curious to see if there is any similarity in entity names under such circumstances, and I will make it a point to ask Seth for the name.)

I knew that the material was being read. However I did not feel it wise to make a point of telling you because this knowledge in itself would have set up blocks, and on both of your parts.

It is reasonable, logical and even necessary at this time that you do not parade yourselves, giving sessions as one would put on a vaudeville act. Nevertheless when an honest request is made either to attend a session or to hold a session, and when you know that the person making such a request is sincere, and if other conditions are appropriate, then by all means it would behoove you to meet with the request.

I am not suggesting for example that five sessions, or four, be held in a week at this time; only that sincere requests should not be automatically denied because they do not fall within the scheduled time. And upon such occasions I will always make adjustments when you request them.

(At this point I began to sneeze. Hay fever season is not yet over, unfortunately. I sneezed many times, and Jane paused at intervals to let me catch up on the copy.)

Knowledge on your physical plane must be applied in human terms and human values, or the possibility of helping someone else either through the sort of a session we held last time, or through a more regular session, should not be ignored.

Would you like a break?

("No.")

The last session falls under a category of applied knowledge. I suggest your break.

(Break at 9:20. Jane was dissociated as usual. She said my sneezing did not bother her, that Seth was willing to wait; but also that Seth probably called the break early because of my continued sneezing.

(Jane resumed dictation in the same quiet manner, this time wearing her glasses, at 9:28.)

There must be abstract knowledge and concept before there can be any applied knowledge in real terms. The more philosophic material, or what could almost be called academic material, suits both of you greatly, and is indeed where my own interests mainly lie.

However the human element must not be ignored, and whatever personal help and inner understanding this material brings to others will incite their intellectual curiosity, and this is all to the good. Nor are the recipients of such help alone benefited, but so are you yourselves.

Your personal work, both yours and Ruburt's, will benefit whoever sees your paintings or reads Ruburt's poetry. It is performed however in solitary and divorced, as it must be, from an intimate contact with people. It is only natural that you carry this over into our sessions, preferring that <u>they</u> be held without such contact. This is not only understandable but in many instances profitable, in that it allows for a diversity of subject matter.

I abhor fanaticism of any type yet I do not feel, myself, that a sincere request under ordinary circumstances should be denied. It is true that conditions were far from ordinary on the evening when Ruburt's father and the poor personality of the woman were here, and under such circumstances generally, I would certainly not recommend a session.

It was the woman's deep need which would have let me make an exception, and yet I promise you that on no occasion will I try to coerce Ruburt into giving a session. By the same token I will not be coerced, ever, into giving a session.

(Jane delivered the above paragraph quite forcefully, facing me with one foot up on a chair. She now took a rather long pause, walking over to a window and looking out before resuming delivery. It might be added here that at the time of the visit of Jane's father, on the night in question Jane had, as she was explaining some of the Seth material to her father and Midge, felt definite emotional "nudges" from Seth to hold a session, whereas upon the occasion of our visit with Bill and Ida in Rochester, she had not. Yet in the latter instance she had finally acceded to the lively curiosity, and because both of us felt this welcome, held the session. Neither of us seriously considered holding a session for Jane's father and Midge, due to the turbulent circumstances.)

I hesitate because I am not certain whether or not to discuss the other woman, who is a sister to the twin before mentioned. I would strongly suggest however that Zibreth, Z-i-b-r-e-t-h (*Louie*), about whom the past session revolved, follow the suggestions given them, and also that he do the following.

He should take a half-hour's brisk walk. This will allow him to use constructively the aggressive energy which does not have outlet. I also suggest, merely as a matter of discipline, that he contemplate his part in the universe, so that he senses an enlargement of self in which personal worries and obsessions will not loom so large.

This next may sound Pollyannaish to an extreme, but he should make it a point to help another human being in any small way, without expecting thanks, three times a week. I do not suggest, you see, that he do this on purpose daily, lest it develop psychologically into a self-sacrificial ritual. And I also most strongly suggest that three times a week in a very quiet, disciplined but positive manner, he makes it a point to express himself when any matters arise where he holds a diverse opinion from the one being presented.

The personality is extremely sensitive, it does not take me to see that, and intuitional. It is also very strong, and the personality fears its own strength simply because normal aggressiveness has been denied outlet; and building up a practice of quietly but firmly expressing his own viewpoints will also help to release the inner pressure.

The personality should live alone for a while, and work separate from the family establishment. It, the personality, must avoid a rigidity of attitude, for this will not only hamper the native intuition but serve to divorce the personality from his environment.

A balance here is extremely important. There should always be this balance. The personality, being intuitively strong, should apply some of this intuition outward toward other human beings. If solitude is achieved through living alone, then the personality should so be able to relate itself outward.

A confident ego is indeed a prerequisite for psychic venturing, for it is only the confident ego which ultimately feels secure enough to give leeway to the inner self in the long run.

I suggest your break.

(Break at 10:00, Jane was dissociated as usual. She delivered the above material with many pauses, some of them of many seconds' duration. She resumed in the same manner at 10:03.)

For safety's sake a firm relationship between the ego and its environment should be considered a prerequisite for serious or extensive psychic investigation. The ego must have something to come back to. This is extremely important.

I do not mean to discourage the personality in his laudable interest in unseen reality. I do want to caution him that first steps must be taken first if his inner goals in this direction are ever to be achieved, without unnecessary difficulties for the ego.

With such a firm foundation he will indeed be most successful, and he can achieve such a foundation. Then he can apply inner knowledge to the ego's environment. The feet of the ego, of any ego, must not rest on quicksand, or when the venturing self returns there will be no sound foundation to receive him.

If this sounds difficult then indeed it is, because I will not deal in platitudes, and the exercise of the inner abilities demand, as a bulwark, the sometimes difficult achievement of an ego that can adapt itself in the outer environment, and so hold its own while the inner self is then freed to go its way.

Discipline then should not only be considered, as it is by some schools of thought, as a mere mental discipline over the muscles, or various portions of the body by the inner self, but indeed a discipline in terms of training of the ego by the inner self, so that the ego as a personality achieves a well-balanced relationship with the physical universe.

(Now, Jane's voice abruptly became deeper and louder, as if for emphasis. It maintained this tone and volume for a paragraph or two, then subsided somewhat, but did not quiet down to a normal pitch until the next break.)

And despite all comments to the contrary, this is by far the most difficult discipline; but without it the inner self is not secure in its journeys, and is like a boat with no harbor to receive it, and like the man without a country, with no place to return. The personality, to some (underline some) degree has been led astray by those who begin such a journey without first making certain of their return.

Legitimate, balanced psychic journeyings will result in a beneficial effect as far as the ego and its ability to handle its concerns are involved; and whenever such journeyings or investigations result in a lessening of egotistic control over circumstance then anyone so involved should instantly ask himself questions, and abruptly halt.

I do not speak here of acquaintances who do not understand the importance of psychic investigation. I speak now of the ego's ability to handle itself. And psychic investigation will, and should, increase that ability if it is properly begun, and if the ego is properly related to the physical environment.

The suggestions given herein, that the mentioned personality live alone, work apart from the family, walk briskly a half-hour a day, strike a balance between altruistically helping others and quietly opposing their ideas through expression when he does not agree, are very important.

A 15-minute daily meditation period would be excellent for three months. Then 3 weeks of no meditation; a month of half-hour meditation, followed by a week of no meditation; and for a year a daily schedule of no more than a half- hour meditation period, these periods to be regular however.

I suggest that they follow the lines of expansion rather than contraction, in that the personality projects itself outward toward All That Is, hence drawing upon the energy of the universe, and extending the reaches of the self.

This discipline however should be followed rigorously only with a program of ego orientation, in which the ego tries to discipline itself in the most difficult manner, for this particular personality, toward freedom. He should express himself when he feels a diverse opinion, when he feels wronged. It is only when aggressions are unexpressed that they are dangerous, and the repressed rage will hold back the desired psychic development. Even chemically such anger causes reactions that will make desired states of being difficult to achieve.

The personality also contains good intellectual capacities, and he should examine psychic experience in the light of his intelligence also. There are truths which the intellect cannot perceive, but the intellect knows the ego, and represents a firm and reliable pathway between the inner self and the ego; and psychic experience—I repeat, psychic experience—will not suffer from such scrutiny.

A steady program, such as I have outlined, because of its conditioning routine, will allow the personality a progressive and safe entry into psychic experience that is firm, and will also strengthen the ego in its relation to environment. This is not to suggest that the ego is weak in this case, for it is not. But its ability to relate to others on the physical plane needs strengthening, particularly since the personality is vitally concerned with psychic investigation.

I suggest your break.

(Break at 10:40. Jane was dissociated as usual. She said she thought Seth would end the session at about 11:00. My writing hand felt some fatigue. Jane resumed in a normal voice at 10:45.)

I will end the session shortly. This is material that I would have given if we had had the time in our last session, and for that reason I wanted to give it this evening.

We will return to other matters for our next session. I still find you both in excellent overall condition, regardless dear Joseph of the hay fever, and we shall take steps before next season to rid you of that.

Ruburt is coming along well in the gallery situation. You should have a good winter, both of you. If Ruburt can stand it, I would suggest a three-day period after he leaves the gallery, during which he does no writing. Perhaps playing about his apartment while instructing his subconscious to work for him in the interval, and completely divorcing his conscious mind from his writing for that period of time. Such a method will result in maximum use of his abilities, and more practical utilization of energy.

I will now, my two peachies, end the session. It has been most pithy. Soon, very soon however, after a few important sessions, we shall have to indulge in a bit of humor for variety. Even I am sometimes appalled at my dryness. Bon soir.

Good night, Seth.

(End at 10:52. Jane was dissociated as usual. My writing hand was tired.)

SESSION 91
SEPTEMBER 23, 1964 9 PM WEDNESDAY AS SCHEDULED

(This afternoon I had delivered to our landlord's supper club, here in Elmira, four large oil paintings which we mounted on the club walls. Our landlord had just finished redecorating his establishment, and wanted some original art for it. I plan to use his rather spacious walls as a hanging space for my work, rotating the exhibits periodically.

(Jane expressed a desire to see the work in place, so when I picked her up at the gallery we stopped off at the club to see it, where Jane made the impromptu remark that she wanted Seth to call off the session, so we could attend the opening of the club this evening.

(Jane had no idea of the material due, as session time approached. I described to her a vivid dream I had recently had involving my father, in the hopes that Seth would discuss it. I had not written it down, but plan to start my dream notebook before long.

(Jane began dictation in a rather fast way, in a voice a little deeper and heavier than usual. Her pacing was also faster, her eyes dark as usual.)

Good evening.

("Good evening, Seth.")

I am indeed going to hold a very brief session, out of the goodness of my heart, and for the sole purpose of letting you know that I do, if only occasionally, give you some time off. And also simply to break up your schedule for the sake of diversity.

(Jane now gave a quite satisfied smile as she paced about.)

I will not here take credit for Ruburt's novel outline. However you must admit the important inner guts, concerning space travel, did indeed come from our sessions. He will now, that is Ruburt will now, do very well.

(This we take as a reference to Jane's decision to leave the gallery and concentrate upon a writing career. This is the last week she is to spend at the gallery.)

Earlier he was not yet ready, for various reasons.

It is a particularly splendid autumn evening. You may go to your opening if you prefer, visit Mark's studio, or merely take a walk. In any case, I am through with you this evening.

(It will be remembered that Mark is the entity name for Bill Macdonnel, who has witnessed a number of sessions. Bill is in the process, incidentally, of moving out of his parents' home and into a studio and apartment in downtown Elmira, where he is going to live and at the same time maintain an art gallery. It will also be recalled that in several different sessions Bill was counseled by Seth to live alone, lest he suffer a recurrence of his lung trouble.)

To be less facetious, I am giving you a brief session also to let you know that since you did hold an unscheduled session, I will endeavor to equalize whenever situations occur of this sort.

I wanted to deal further during our last session with material originating in the unscheduled session, otherwise I would have cut the last session. I will not always of course necessarily miss a session because of an unscheduled one, since circumstances will always vary.

My hearty congratulations that your paintings are being seen now in your friend's establishment, and they will affect many people.

It always pains me to speak so briefly and run. However upon this instance I shall indeed do so, but our sessions this autumn shall be meaty ones, and I hope that you digest them.

My most fond good evening. I am amused because Ruburt is so surprised. Didn't you know, Ruburt, that I could be so magnanimous?

("Good night, Seth.")

(End at 9:07. Jane was dissociated as usual. She reported that while delivering the material she had a timeless feeling that belied the little actual clock time that had passed. She had thought it to be about 9:30 or so. Jane also said she felt somewhat put out, or "pulled up short" at the short session, although earlier this evening she had expressed the wish for either a short session, or none at all, so we could attend the opening of the supper club operated by our landlord.)

SESSION 92
SEPTEMBER 28, 1964 9 PM MONDAY AS SCHEDULED

(After supper this evening Jane told me she thought Seth might talk about

dreams and the subconscious at the session. In the event that Seth might do this, and also discuss our dreams, as he has mentioned doing by way of illustrating the material, I read to Jane just before the session began two very vivid dreams that I have had within the last two weeks, involving my father and other members of my family. The material I read to Jane was from my dream notebook, which I have finally begun.

(Jane was not nervous before the session. She is, also, taking Seth's advice and not writing for three days after leaving the gallery. This is her first day home, and she has begun to paint our apartment by way of diversion.

(As session time neared I lay my dream notebook on the table, as Seth had suggested we do. Jane began dictating on time, in a voice somewhat stronger than usual. Her delivery was average, her pacing slow, her eyes quite dark. And again, she began without wearing her glasses.)

Good evening.

("Good evening, Seth.")

I would like to continue our discussion concerning the layers of the so-called subconscious, in connection now with a study of dreams.

I had intended to cover this earlier but we were sidetracked. The preliminary discussion of the subconscious layers was necessary, since dreams originate in these various levels, and should therefore be interpreted according to the particular symbolisms inherent in the realm of reality to which they may belong.

Considerable confusion can result if a dream from one level of the subconscious is interpreted in the light of data which belongs to another level entirely. Many individuals feel easier with certain such subconscious aspects, with the result that they may be more aware of dreams that originate in particular subconscious areas, and be relatively unaware of dreams originating in other areas, which they may consider either fearful or at best unfamiliar.

We will find in many cases, first of all, dreams originating in that layer of personal subconscious, the most simple being those that have immediate reference to daily conscious life. While such a dream is less complex than others, it is nevertheless an amazing construction, and when we break down the obvious perceived objects or events of such a dream, we will find that the immediate objects and events that have application in daily life, that may be rehashed versions of the day, have nevertheless been carefully chosen.

(Here Jane smiled broadly as she paced about.)

And while it may seem that <u>all</u> dreams are random conglomerations of unrelated symbols or events, we will see that one of the most important attributes of <u>any</u> dream is indeed <u>discrimination</u>.

For out of a seemingly endless number of possibilities, our individual dreamer actually discriminates with great care, choosing only those dream objects or symbols that have meaning to him; and those dream objects that can best serve his purposes. And even a simple dream that would seem to be concerned with trivial daily events is in reality concerned with much more.

(Now Jane began to speak with much emphasis, and if anything her voice became a little stronger. She appeared to choose her words with great care. Her delivery did not speed up however.)

The dream objects are in fact chosen with such precise discrimination that in many instances, on deep examination they will be seen to embody not only data concerning the dreamer's daily conscious existence, but one and every dream object may be seen to apply on many levels at once.

The dream objects, then, are so cunningly, and if I may say so, almost slyly chosen, that the simplest of them may refer to instances in this existence, to personally subconsciously desired or feared objects or instances, to desired or feared objects or instances in past lives. They, such dream objects, may be the method or means with which the inner self warns the personality of future possible disappointments or disasters.

One dream object may represent simultaneously a simple daily and familiar portion of conscious life, a strong feared or desired portion of the immediately subconscious layer, an event or object from a past life, and a feared or desired future event or future possibility, as the case may be.

An equation exists here. One dream object has reality then in four or five different levels of reality simultaneously, the one object being more than itself, and equal to realities that have existed or will exist in your past or future; the past and future being therefore contained simultaneously within the dream object, by virtue of a quite real psychic contraction and expansion.

The expansion is the dream. The contraction is the return of the dream elements back into the original single object, that is dream object, from which the equation originated, as for example all numbers originate from the number one.

I suggest your break.

(Break at 9:30. Jane was fully dissociated. She said that for some reason she was aware that when the session began she would be "far-out" right away. She had not told me before the session began, but now admitted that she had been very tired by 9 PM, after painting all day. But now she felt fine.

(She resumed in the same forceful, if deliberate manner at 9:34.)

I will here digress for a moment.

Friends knowing of our sessions have asked at one time or another that I explain what appeared first in the universe, what started it all, and they ask with such ponderous voices. They want a first thing, or a first person. In this discussion on dreams we have indeed an excellent example of how creation is achieved.

At the risk of sounding childishly simple I will say, and I will not be understood, that each creation of idea or matter, physical matter, is a first creation.

It is only according to where you happen to come in this time, so to speak. Each dream, first of all, begins with psychic energy which the individual transforms not into physical matter but into a reality every bit as functional and as real. He forms the idea into a dream object or event with amazing discrimination, so that the dream object itself gains existence, and exists in numerous dimensions.

(Jane's voice remained at times quite loud, but her delivery became slower.)

It does not seem to exist in various dimensions. It does in actuality so exist. If a dream object or event does so straddle what you call not only time but space, and if as I say dream objects and creations maintain some independence from the dreamer, then you must see that although the dreamer creates his dreams for his own purposes, selecting only those symbols which have meaning to him, he nevertheless projects them outward in a value fulfillment and psychic expansion.

The expansion occurs, again, as the dream drama is acted out. For the dreamer a contraction occurs as he is finished with the events or drama for his own purposes, but energy cannot be taken back.

Energy projected into any kind of construction, psychic or physical, cannot be recalled, but must follow the laws of the particular form into which it has been for the moment molded. Therefore, when the dreamer contracts his multi-realistic objects backward, ending for himself the so-called dream that he constructed, he ends it for himself only. But the reality of the dream continues.

I do not care if this idea now appears impossible or farfetched, either to you and Ruburt or to others. The fact remains that it is so.

The fact also remains that on other levels but conscious ones, you know and every individual knows that the dream world that the conscious mind believes so foolish and irrational, is indeed constructed by the inner self with utmost care, with a precision known only by the intuitions. And each individual knows that such a splendid creation as this then exists beyond the self that was its origin.

Are your hands tired?

("No.")

(Jane looked at me. It was 9:58. My hand was in fact tiring, but I denied it because I thought Seth wanted to continue in order to make some particular point.)

It is therefore only in a world obsessed with objects, and to some extent necessarily obsessed, that the question of what comes first has any meaning.

Your conscious energies are focused upon the physical field, and the distortive cause and effect theory holds sway.

It is your focus, intensive, that of itself blots out other perceptions that would allow you to see that the question "What comes first?" is meaningless.

You create this universe individually and collectively, man and all other beings within it, in the same manner that you create your dreams. The only difference is that your conscious energies are focused upon only one rather minute aspect of creation, and all other larger fields of activity are closed off by the outer senses, simply so that the bulk of your attention be momentarily fixed upon one small area.

I will here suggest your break, since I do not want to stretch the area of your attention.

(Break at 10:05. Jane was again fully dissociated. She now put her glasses back on. She resumed in the same strong voice, and at a faster rate, at 10:12.)

We will indeed return to our dreams as connected with various levels of the subconscious, but this is in itself connective material so to speak, and I will continue.

I can hear anticipated objections. Even those who are familiar with our material, and know the various means by which individuals create a fairly cohesive body of physical data and call it the physical universe, even these persons will say that while they agree that the individual creates the physical universe with the cooperation of others, that universe has a unity and permanence and recognizable form that the dream world does not have.

They will then think that there is no real comparison to be made between the two, since each individual dream world would be a conglomeration of diverse individualistic symbols, even if they were projected into a type of universe of which the conscious mind was ignorant.

First of all, the physical universe is indeed a conglomeration of diverse individualistic symbols, none of which mean precisely the same thing to any two individuals, and in which even so-called basic qualities like color and placement in space, cannot be relied upon or agreed with.

You merely focus upon the similarities, and that is important.

(Jane laughed and knocked upon the table for emphasis.)

Telepathy could be called, indeed, the glue that holds the physical universe in precarious position, so that anyone can agree upon what a particular object is, or where it is at any given time.

So, when you consider the dream world, you have the same sort of a universe, only one constructed on or within a field which your outer senses cannot perceive. But it has more continuity than the world known by the outer senses so intimately, and there are similarities within it that are amazing to behold.

You know that many, but not all by any means, dream symbols approximately mean the same thing, but only approximately, and only for a particular group of human beings who experienced reality on the physical plane for a comparatively short period. The symbol of fire for example as a dream symbol, simply did not exist in the way that it does now to men born before mankind learned to use fire for warmth, or to cook his food.

The old symbol of fire still does exist, fire as mysterious grandeur or destruction. Only later did it become a symbol of hearth and warmth, so that to some extent dream symbols are cultural.

The basic symbols are beyond culture, and later I will give them to you.

I want to make a point however, that the dream universe is as real and cohesive as your own, and that the same glue of telepathy holds it together, and gives it not only as much reality but validity in actual terms.

For one thing, and I will go into this deeper shortly, those who now know existence on the physical level more or less because of certain cycles lived before on the physical level at about the same historical periods. They possess an inner familiarity, a cohesiveness that belonged to a more or less specific period, and to periods before, where they inhabited the same sort of physical universe.

Their dream worlds are not then so diverse in some ways as you might have supposed. Certain symbols are constructed into realities in the dream universe, then, in much the same manner that certain ideas are constructed into matter in the physical universe.

Do your precious fingers tire?

("No.")

(Jane spoke leaning close to me, quite amused. It was 10:36, and again I answered in the negative although my hand was tired, thinking she wanted to make a particular point.)

The same sort of psychic agreement holds the dream universe together as holds the physical universe together. If a man could actually focus his concentration upon those hidden, feared, mainly unknown, unrecognized elements in the physical universe upon which men simply cannot agree; if he could focus upon the dissimilarities rather than the similarities in the physical universe, he would wonder what gave anyone the idea that there was even one physical object upon which men could agree.

He would wonder what collective madness made or permitted man to select, from a virtual infinity of what would appear as chaos, to select a handful, a mere handful, of similarities and call it a universe.

So do you, viewing the seeming chaos of dream reality, wonder how I can say that similarity here occurs, and cohesiveness and actuality and comparative permanence. The dream means something to the individual who originates it, selects its elements most carefully, but in order for him to use it he must create it.

He projects it in a dimension unperceived by the conscious mind. But even though it has served his purposes and he contracts, the expansion and projection of energy has taken place and he cannot call it back. He can only withdraw from it.

As—you may take your break.

(Break at 10:46. Jane was dissociated as usual. She said she had indeed painted too long today; but although she was tired before the session began, she feels fine now. She said she could feel Seth close by now, but that he would end the session soon. She resumed in the same forceful manner at 10:49.)

The conscious mind does not even know, and cannot of itself command, the legs to walk across the floor. Is it any wonder, then, that the conscious mind does not know how it creates the dream universe?

But the legs do walk, and the dream universe does exist. As the entity expands and originates new personalities, and these personalities then become independent individuals, so do the individuals create dream or so-called dream realities and individuals of the dream universe, which are independent.

The term "dream" I use because you are familiar with it. It is not a good term necessarily. I will use the term, somewhat better, of hybrids, as the one to refer to personalities or individuals given existence by mankind in his dreams.

You may add to the word, dual-hybrid constructions. This is perhaps better.

At our next session I will continue with this, and continue into an interpretation of dreams as they affect the individual dreamer in the physical field, and connect them with the levels of the subconscious. However I wanted you to understand that the elements of the dream world, originating in energy, also continue in existence when the dreamer may have forgotten them; and that all energy or any energy, given or adopting <u>any</u> type of form, must then continue at least momentarily to adapt to the laws inherent therein.

All energy, once manifested in any manner, will follow the properties of its manifestation. It will ultimately be transformed but it cannot be annihilated. Its individual quality cannot be annihilated. Once manifested, the individuality of energy then comes under the law of value fulfillment.

Energy can be transformed from one state to another, but once it achieves a personalized gestalt the individuality which it has formed must follow certain laws of value fulfillment, and this involves distinctions which we have not yet covered in our sessions.

You have no idea of how little we have scratched the surface.

I will now close the session, with my most fond wishes to you both.

The ESP book and our material will indeed be published. Ruburt's abilities will expand, or his utilization of them will expand; and your own abilities in the expectation line have really begun to take a rather fantastic leap.

As always, I could continue. My affection for you both is very deep, and I hope the feeling is shared.

("Yes. Good night, Seth."

(End at 11:07. Jane was dissociated as usual. She had been all night, she said, otherwise she wouldn't have gotten by the first fifteen minutes of the session because of her weariness. My writing hand was very tired, in fact almost cramped.)

SESSION 93
SEPTEMBER 30, 1964 9 PM WEDNESDAY AS SCHEDULED

(While conducting these sessions, Jane and I have had remarkably few interruptions either during them or just before they were scheduled to begin. However, this evening we did have such an experience, although it was brief.

(At 8:50 a friend of ours, Howard Kimball, arrived. He is on the board of directors of the gallery, which Jane has just left. Howard wanted to look at some paintings, and of course some conversation ensued involving the new director at the gallery, who was discussed by Seth in the 74th session.

(Howard bought a small tempera of mine picturing two apples; and then to Jane's surprise he bought off the wall of our apartment a small abstract oil that Jane and I had produced jointly, in a humorous attempt at working together. The little painting had turned out well and attracted much notice. It was the first piece of art work Jane had ever sold, and she was pleased.

(Howard left at 9:11 PM. Jane said the visit had disturbed her somewhat, a fact that I had not appreciated from observing her. She stood beside my table, waiting. At 9:12 she began to dictate in a rather normal voice, although as the session progressed her voice gathered quite a bit of volume at times. Once again she did not wear her glasses. Her delivery was rather slow, as was her pacing. Her eyes were dark as usual.)

Good evening.

("Good evening, Seth.")

Due congratulations to Ruburt on the sale of his painting.

I hope that you will not find that he is now bigheaded, as well as pigheaded. He knows I speak only in jest. I did nevertheless tell you that he had been an artist at one time, did I not?

("Yes.")

(See the 2nd session, December 4,1963, Volume 1, pages 15 and 16.)

The interruption did bother him somewhat, as he was prepared for a session on time, per usual. I will however continue along the lines of our previous discussions.

Dreams, then, come from various levels of what you call the subconscious. But as a rule any particular dream, although it originates in a particular level, will nevertheless have meaning on all levels. The meaning however may well not be the same. That is, the particular dream may be a method of saying different things or bringing different messages, the one particular dream automatically being translated by the various levels of the subconscious in terms of the interpretation given by any particular subconscious level to the dream symbolism.

The dream could be said to be a message to the multitudinous levels of the self. For purposes of analogy only, imagine that each subconscious layer is personified into a personality, who is then subjected to rendition of a dream or more, who watches a screen upon which the dream images flicker.

Every subconscious personality then would see and hear the same dream, as many persons may watch the same movie; and as each person in a theater interprets the symbolism of the drama differently, so does each layer of the subconscious interpret differently the same elements of one dream.

Now. The "I" who dreams, who is aware of motion, action and participation in a dream, this "I" is of course the inner self, focused momentarily upon the particular subconscious layer at which the dream is originated.

I will here suggest that the term "subconscious layer" has served its purpose, and in its place we will refer to "subconscious areas."

In dreams the inner "I" changes its point of focus, and this is important. It is therefore able to view the self as a whole, with its past and present life. And because the focus brings it outside of camouflage time and space, it is also able to project itself into what you call the future.

In other words, a dream allows the inner self to view itself within the spacious present. Now, chemically the physical body does need to dream. That is, dreaming is a necessity if the physical body is to survive. This is the result of certain chemical reactions and chemical necessities, chemical excesses that build up during the days, inciting the mental dream mechanism.

Without dreams the outer camouflaged self would lose all touch with inner realities, or would be in danger of thus denying its own heritage; and therefore the physical body is so constructed that excess chemicals must be discharged and transformed into human action, or the physical mechanism would be clogged with poisons.

I suggest your first break.

(Break at 9:35. Jane was dissociated as usual. She now told me that she had been upset by the delay in starting the session. This time wearing her glasses, she resumed in a rather unhurried but emphatic manner, her voice a little stronger, at 9:40.)

When I spoke of the fine discrimination used in the construction of a dream, I had reference to the amazing work done by the inner self in the choice of its individualized symbols, which would have meaning to the many and various levels of the subconscious.

The dream objects are not randomly chosen, but only those are chosen which will be significant to the many layers of the self, according to the need or according to that part of the subconscious area which is to be instructed; that is, the portion which is directly a participant in the dream activities, and which plays out the dream drama while other parts of the self observe.

You must again realize that we speak of the self as being so divided only for simplicity's sake. While the self is whole, it is however compartmentalized for efficiency's sake, but beneath consciousness the doors are open. Again, the conscious self is most necessary. However it cannot be stressed too strongly that consciousness is merely a state of focus, and not a self.

Consciousness is the direction in which the self looks at any given time.

(Jane delivered the above sentence with much emphasis, her voice deepening considerably at times.)

That is perhaps the most important sentence of this session, and many others. For the direction or the focus of the self does indeed change, and even in your own daily lives you experience the fact that what is conscious today may not be tomorrow.

The self, in this manner, looks about. The direction in which the self looks is not the self. In dreams the self looks elsewhere, and the "I" is a conscious "I", and the working ability is tremendous. The inner self perceives realities that it observes in many directions, being free from the intense focus within limited directions of camouflage existence.

It then constructs its dreams in such a way that the symbols within will sift through all areas that are themselves less able to survey large vistas, but whose energies are focused along specific lines.

Without dreams the whole self would have no way of holding its various manifestations together, and the so-called conscious present personality would soon falter. Imagine if you will now a band of men, some in cars with the high beams of the headlights gleaming, so that some generalized conditions can be seen; and some with low beams showing only the road that the automobiles directly pass. The men can be compared to personified areas of the subconscious, with partial vision of existing conditions.

Another man in an airplane above sees the whole landscape, and through radio communicates to those below about those conditions which they cannot perceive. The man in the airplane, then, can be compared to the inner self, sending messages to other areas of the subconscious, whose energies and focus are necessarily used in limited fashion.

Only in this case the man in the airplane, instead of a radio message, would radio directly into the mind mechanism of the men below, a dream drama in the coded symbols which would be interpreted automatically by the men below.

Now. The conscious self responds without knowing it, often changing course and direction, to these dreams of which he is often not aware. The ego, the conscious ego, the so-called conscious self, is only the front man in the front lines, supported by multitudinous areas or portions of himself that he does not know, and whose messages come to him only through the correspondence of dreams.

I am, again, not minimizing the practical necessity for the conscious self as it appears to be. But man is much more than the conscious self, and what he calls the conscious self is merely the whole self as seen through the direction in which the whole self chooses to direct its energies and focus.

A man stands in the center of a room. When he looks to the right you say "This is my conscious self." When he looks to the left, we have something else again. You say "This is the dreaming self." The dreaming self, or if you will, the left-handed self, indeed is as important as the so-called conscious self. The whole self merely changes direction and viewpoint, and focuses its energies along a particular line.

It turns beams of attention off and on. It has many facets and many volumes and many dimensions. It acts out roles, but the whole self is entire, and every individual innately knows and is intimately familiar with the intents and purposes of the whole self. And in dreams and in intuitions and unspoken thoughts, the individual comes to terms with the whole self, <u>of which it is merely one portion</u>, and not necessarily the dominant portion.

(Now Jane perched on the table, sitting down upon it, and laughed and pointed at me.)

I will here give a brief personal example.

Our friend Ruburt prides himself that his conscious self, before the sessions began, started a book called *The Physical Universe as Idea Construction.* Ha ha, did he really now?

The idea that sparked the book came to him, though he may forget, in two ways. First as intuition; in other words from his inner self as he sat down to write poetry, and in a dream the following night.

Intellectually he followed the ideas, but his inner self gave him the all-important initial message. His poetry does not spring from the conscious self, yet he would not disinherit it for that reason. Intuition represents the directions of the inner self, breaking through conscious barriers.

Messages from the inner self if strong enough will pass through the conscious barriers, and the conscious ego is only too happy to receive them. But such intuitions have usually first appeared in dream form, appearing to the ego later; and many such messages appear in dreams ahead of time, to be released to the conscious mind when situations demand it.

I had forgotten your break. Take it by all means.

(Break at 10:22. Jane was fully dissociated; so much so, she said, that she hadn't followed the material at all, and had no idea whether it was any good or not.

(Jane well remembers the evening when she first consciously conceived Idea Construction, *and so do I. Checking her manuscripts yields the date of September 10,1963, as when she made her first notes. I remember walking out to the living room where she writes her poetry, having finished my own work in my studio in the back of the apartment at about 9 PM; Jane's first words were "Boy, have I got a great idea," or to that effect. She then told me about idea construction, which I didn't go for very much. Checking with her while writing this up, she said that she never did do any poetry that night; the idea came to her as she sat down to write poetry after supper, and she spent the evening on it.*

(It might be interesting to quote here the first paragraph of notes Jane made that evening: "Basic idea is that the senses are developed not to permit awareness of an already existing material world, but to create it. The inner image [idea] is projected by the senses outward to create the world of appearances. [Camera in reverse, for the eye, for example.]"

(As Seth states, Jane did have a dream about the idea the following night, September 11,1963. She recalls it quite easily. However she has no written record of the dream, since this was before she had cultivated the habit of keeping a dream notebook. As mentioned many, many sessions ago, however, her poem The Fence, *written in May 1963, clearly foreshadows the Seth material, dealing with [but not always by outright name] such subjects as reincarnation, dreams, unperceived worlds, etc. [See the poem on page 28, Session 5, in Volume 1 of* The Early Sessions.*]*

(Jane resumed in the same manner at 10:33.)

Now. The conscious mind perceives matter. Yet even then it does not perceive matter directly, but by a very indirect path, and only because the whole self directs a certain portion of its energies in that direction.

The conscious self does not perceive, or the so-called conscious self does not perceive, the equally valid dream constructions. You will discover that the whole self is composed of many so-called conscious selves. But neither of those conscious selves are aware of the existence of the others.

The dreaming self, dear friends, is not aware of the conscious self. The whole self, the entire inner self alone, holds knowledge of the direction in which it moves. The directions can be likened to conscious selves. Any individual on the physical level who has achieved great things has done so because his so-called conscious self was intuitively (and underline the word intuitively) aware of the selves of which he could not be consciously aware.

Men are not islands, even unto themselves. They merely perceive islands, or they perceive bits of realities. The dream correlates the various manifestations of the self with the whole portion. Dreams bring intuitive knowledge of the whole self to its own parts.

I will end the session shortly, after mentioning briefly an example of how various levels of the subconscious interpret a symbol. We will take Ruburt's dream that we have already interpreted on some levels, and one symbol only, that of a tub, t-u-b.

(See the 87th session, page 11, etc.)

The tub was the unifying symbol of the dream, interpreted by the various levels of the subconscious. On the most superficial level, dreaming Ruburt thought "One day I shall be an old tub," meaning an old worn-out vessel. This having to do with the disappearance of early youth, and having superficial meaning to the surface female personality.

The tub was next interpreted as a washing machine in a secondary level that was in itself a symbol leading to the next interpretation, belonging to a past life, that of an old tub that leaked. In his dream the washing machine leaked, leading him into a third level, where the tub was a symbol for the old ship that leaked when you, Joseph, were a passenger on your way to Boston in a past life.

The connection picked up again. The past administrator of the gallery was known to you in that life, and was a passenger on the same ship. Here Ruburt was led backward to the first level momentarily, being reassured, saying "I will not be the old tub, she was and is," therefore on a surface level overcoming jealousy because the former administrator spent so much money on clothes and appearance.

(See the 59th session for the data on the past lives of Jane, Dee Masters and myself in Boston, prior to the Civil War; and see again the 87th session.)

Ruburt knew he could look better if he spent half the time and effort, but was jealous anyway. So here the symbols coincided. He obtained subconscious information concerning your past life, the one symbol of the tub serving three purposes. It gave him information, it helped overcome his jealousy, and it was a transition from surface significance to deeper knowledge.

At the same time the word tub referred also to a friend of his, a woman whose maiden name was Tubbs, and informed him subconsciously that she was in difficulties, as when the tub or old washing machine leaked. Here the leaking of the tub referred to the leaking ship on one level, and to the difficulties that were being experienced by her old friend on another.

I am not sure here. The woman may have been in childbirth and the water bag broke.

(This bit of data really made me sit up and take notice. Jane has not heard from her schoolgirl friend Marie Tubbs for some months, and if Marie was pregnant we did not know it. They have exchanged a desultory correspondence for some years, and have not met since the early days of our own marriage, ten years ago. But because they were such good friends in school days, they have managed to keep in touch with each other over the years.

(Jane will now write to Marie to see if Seth is correct; if not, or the data is distorted, Jane will try to learn from Marie what association she could have been involved in with water. Marie's married name is: Marie Sterrett, of Boynton Beach, Florida.)

Now, in any dream you will find a unifying image that will seem as diverse as this to the conscious mind. But it will speak to various portions of the self. In that dream you found the word tub referring to many various meanings, but in many cases you will find various other images, all cunningly connected so that it seems most unfortunate to you that the conscious mind cannot interpret them.

However, I have said that the conscious mind is but a small portion of the whole self, and the information thus received through dreams is automatically acted upon or assimilated, regardless of conscious cognition.

This information itself may enable you to interpret your own dreams more effectively, and should enable others who read the material to interpret their own dreams with more sense.

It is not as important as you may think, since oftentimes you act with more wisdom automatically, and the conscious mind is extremely slow to assimilate knowledge that the intuitions know by heart.

I hope to get into your father's appearance in your dream. However the explanation will take nearly an hour, and is not what you think. I would suggest now that we end the session, although if you wish me to continue I will.

("I guess not.")

(Usually I would be willing to continue in such instances, but seldom do because it keeps Jane working longer.)

I will then wish you both a fond good evening, with the remark that Ruburt will make more this year through writing than he would have at the gallery. And if your poor Professor Von Jamesson appears at your door, do not be surprised. Be very kind and considerate, and say no to anything he may suggest.

My fondest good wishes to you both.

("Good night, Seth.")

(End at 11:02. Jane was dissociated as usual. She was wearing her glasses, but after the session she asked me how often she did have them on, since while delivering the material she doesn't see anything. I told her that lately she has had her glasses off perhaps a third of the time, something she did not used to do. Jane's delivery had been quite animated giving the last few pages of the session. My writing hand was also tired.

(I will include a copy of the very long, vivid and involved dream I had involving Jane, Bill Macdonnel, three friends of a family from Sayre, and my father, before whatever session Seth uses to discuss it. This dream also was followed by what I believe to be a sequel, a week or so later.

(The two dreams following are included here because they are dealt with extensively by Seth in the following, 94th session. They are taken from my dream notebook, which I have just recently begun to keep.

(September 18, 1964, Friday: This was a long, complicated and very vivid dream that seemed to consume hours. It was in full color. In the beginning Jane; Bill Macdonnel; Clark, Alice and Larry Potter; and myself were in an apartment I did not recognize but took to be occupied by Jane and me. [Clark and Alice Potter had been our landlords in Sayre, PA, for over four years. The four of us had liked each other from the start and had always gotten on well together. Larry is their teenage son, and they have another son, Norman, older by a year or two, who was not in the dream.]

(Kneeling beside an old-fashioned living room table with a shelf underneath it, I saw a foot-high pile of <u>Jane's</u> drawings and paintings. Pulling one out, I was surprised at the vivid colors in the drawing, and the marvelous three-dimensional form it contained. A pastel drawing of a green leafy tree especially charmed me, and I exclaimed to Bill and the others that Jane's drawings were much better than I had thought them to be, or had realized she could do.

(Then Bill and Jane were gone. I was in the living room of the apartment with

Alice and Clark, looking back toward a kitchen finished in brown wood paneling. In an intermediate room I saw Larry Potter. He was wearing a chamois-type fall jacket with knitted cuffs. He seemed to me to be taller and heavier than I had known him to be, which was about my own size. The amazing thing to me was that Larry was frantically busy at a wringer-type washing machine that was gushing forth a stream of water from its outlet, into a bucket that was almost full.

(Glaring at me, Larry shouted at me to get him a pie pan, that the washer was going to overflow the bucket any second. I yelled back that a pie pan wouldn't hold much. The machine was jumping around while Larry held it down. I don't recall any water on the floor. The next I knew, Larry was very angry with me; he stood right beside me and towered over me, yelling something about me being some kind of nut or dope, and that I needed a good punch.

(Then, Alice Potter and I were driving down Route 17 to Sayre. She was very sympathetic to me, and I may have forgotten the reasons. I believe she was wearing a nightgown but am not positive. Alice parked the car in front of my parents' home in Sayre, put her arm around my shoulder and said something. I then got out of the car and she drove away. I saw my parents' home clearly there on Wilbur Avenue, but I did not go into it. Instead I started walking up Mohawk Street, around the corner toward Keystone Avenue, a block away. I was going to a theatre, a big one, on the corner of Keystone and Mohawk, though actually none exists there. I was now in striped pajamas. [I have none like this.] I was well covered by the pajamas, which were loose and baggy, and not at all nude.

(Next I was walking up the center aisle of the darkened, crowded movie theatre, still in my pajamas but not at all embarrassed or concerned that others would or could see me. The place was dark of course but I could see well enough. I was looking for someone or something I could not find.

(Then the show was over and the crowds were leaving the theatre. It was night outside, and I was sitting on the green grass in front of the theatre, beside Mohawk St., again quite unconcerned as many well-dressed people passed me by. I still wore the pajamas and was quite in possession of myself.

(Then my brother Dick, looking perhaps a little younger than he is now [about 36], was approaching me, smiling down at me and saying something to me. He was fully dressed, wearing a jacket. Dick was accompanied by a thin, sharp-faced man in dark-rimmed glasses, neatly dressed in a dark suit and white shirt and colored tie, and a slim rather good-looking woman I did not know. This couple with Dick did not speak to me, as I recall.

(Next, Jane and I had been attending a party in a building on a busy downtown street corner, on the second floor. I did not actually see Jane but knew she was there at the party. Many people were about. I entered this part of the dream as I left

the stairway to move out on the corner for a breath of fresh air. I was now dressed, and it was daytime. As I stood on the corner with people passing me in all directions, I stretched my arms high above my head. Then to my surprise I saw my father ride past me, past the corner, on a bicycle. Father was wearing a familiar brown hat, and a long brown topcoat, incongruously enough, and he was his present age. His face was very smooth-looking and pink-cheeked, looking very healthy, and he seemed to pedal past me quite easily, as a youth would do.

(I was very surprised to see Father. As he passed me he turned his head to look back at me over his left shoulder, smiling serenely all the while. Caught by surprise with my arms up in the air, I quickly lowered my left arm somewhat, holding it stiff, and waved at Father with my hand revolving at the wrist. I did not bend my arm but waved at him awkwardly with it held stiff so that only my hand moved. Father did not speak a word to me, nor did I speak to him or call after him. He kept on pedaling, seemingly up a slight incline just beyond the intersection. This was the end of the dream, and it made quite an impression upon me.

(September 24, 1964, Thursday: Is this dream a sequel to the previous dream? Again in color. My two brothers, Loren and Dick, and I were in a room something like a courtroom, seated behind a long low polished dark-colored table. The three of us sat facing our mother, who was behind some kind of higher desk or bar. She was her present age.

(Some kind of steady noise pervaded the air. Mother spoke to us, or one of us asked her what the trouble was, I am not sure which. Mother answered, but though I saw her lips move plainly, I could not hear what she said. The three boys leaned toward her. I believe it was I who then asked her to repeat what she had said, over the noise which was something like a rushing wind. Leaning forward at the table, I then heard mother say very distinctly, "Father has a spot on one lung." This was the end of the dream, and it woke me up.

(These two dreams impressed me considerably, and I wondered whether they were clairvoyant in that they might presage an illness or farewell on Father's part. I might as well add here, as well as in the session, that the three boys do not get together very often—on the average less than once a year I would say—because we all live in different communities, Loren and Dick have families, and of course each person is always busy with his or her own life.

(However, the three of us did meet with our parents last Sunday, October 4, 1964, to handle some family business. None of us knew of any such meeting at the time of my above dream of September 24, simply because the meeting had not been scheduled yet, or indeed even thought of. And I must admit that such was the involvement in the problem at hand when the family did convene on October 4, that I completely forgot the dreams at the time, never realizing that I had dreamed of a

family get-together 10 days before it took place. This clairvoyant aspect of the second dream is discussed by Seth in the following session.)

SESSION 94
OCTOBER 5, 1964 9 PM MONDAY AS SCHEDULED

(Our landlord and his wife, James and Marian Spaziani, were scheduled to attend tonight's session, and to arrive by 8:30. The Spazianis have known about the Seth material from the beginning, and have read some of the earlier sessions; indeed, it was Jane's borrowing Jim's Ouija board in November 1963, that led to the flow of the Seth material.

(In spite of the fact that we are all good friends, Jane grew somewhat nervous as the day wore on, because the Spazianis had never witnessed a session, although both of them are interested in ESP, and Jim has read a great many books on the subject.

(By 8:40 the guests had not arrived, and Jane was up from her nap. Before laying down she had instructed her subconscious to inform her as to whether we would have witnesses, but upon arising she still had no answer. Jane then expressed a desire to obtain in the future as firm a commitment from witnesses as possible, well in advance of the session in question. Since we do not have a telephone last-minute verification is difficult, and we may have a phone installed.

(After supper Jane had read the two dreams quoted previously involving my father. My dream notebook lay open on the table. As session time approached Jane no longer felt nervous. I could tell however that she was somewhat tired, and when she began delivery I thought her voice had a peculiar, flat, expressionless quality that could be the result of fatigue. She spoke very deliberately, in measured phrases, in a voice somewhat lower than usual, but not loudly, and as though she were giving a lecture before a number of people. Again her glasses were off, her eyes very dark. Her pacing was also quite slow.)

Good evening.

("Good evening, Seth.")

I would like here to discuss a fact about which we have spoken briefly in the past; that is, that the inner world cannot be examined with the outer senses, that indeed the main purpose of the outer senses is the interpretation of the outer or camouflage existence.

The outer senses as you know are themselves camouflage constructions, specific tools formed for a specific reason to manipulate camouflage reality. They are not equipped to handle other realities, nor should they be expected to do so.

They were adapted to meet a specific situation in which the inner self found it must operate, and it therefore took unto itself the adoption of these specific constructions. Therefore since dreams are manifestations of inner reality, they cannot be interpreted or investigated with any success through the use of the outer senses.

They must be interpreted instead through the use of those inner senses of which I have spoken, for these are the basic tools of the inner self. I realize that it is frowned upon to speak in terms of a limited intellect, which cannot understand a whole reality because of a built-in deficiency; nevertheless while it is true that the intellect by itself cannot grasp or comprehend inner reality, this should not be thought of as a deficiency inherent in intellect.

A study or investigation of inner reality was not the purpose of the intellect. The intellect, again, was also and is a means by which the inner self relates itself to the camouflage physical universe which it has itself constructed.

Dreams therefore cannot adequately be understood or probed into on an intellectual level. The results of another kind of investigation may be given to the intellect, which may then be able to register the facts involved, but only with some difficulty since the intellect is bound and determined to study facts in the light of so-called cause and effect, which appears so logical to the intellect, since it deals so often with appearances registered by the outer senses, then trying to interpret them into some kind of order.

The investigation of dreams, then, must be accomplished in or on a subconscious level. In order to study dreams properly you must indeed immerse yourself in that medium in which dreams occur. The intense but limited focus of usual consciousness will itself distort the true nature of dreams, and the ego will hold any such conscious examination of dreams within rigid bonds.

Now. The tendency exists to suppose that any true evidence or proof of validity depends upon those effects that can be perceived through the outer senses. This tendency exists simply because you are unfamiliar with other types of validity, whose impact is every bit as real; so real in fact that once such proof has shown itself, even the intellect must be influenced and agree to a validity which it must admit it cannot understand.

Hypnosis is one method of examining dreams. Our method is perhaps the best one. The inner self constantly changes its focus. I have said that consciousness is merely the direction in which the inner self focuses at any particular time. In order to examine the reality of dreams it is necessary to change the focus of the inner self to those directions in which the inner self moves, when the ego does not limit its scope to camouflage reality only.

This in itself, this change of focus, is not difficult. What is difficult is the ability or facility to change focus from one area to another, always leaving the door open for a return to the usual necessary daily focus point, in order that effective balance be maintained and manipulation in the physical area remain fairly uninterrupted.

I suggest your first break.

(Break at 9:28. Jane was dissociated as usual. She had begun the session without her glasses but now put them on.

(I was somewhat concerned because once again she said that she was tired, and I felt her voice revealed her fatigue rather plainly. We discussed various alternatives, finally deciding that Jane would sleep for at least half an hour before a session whether witnesses were due or not, and whether they were present or not. We also talked of moving the beginning time ahead an hour to 8 PM, at least during the winter months when it gets dark early.

(I would like to remind the reader here that when Seth uses the term "area," he means what up until recently he has called a "level" of the subconscious. Actually, he states, the subconscious is not neatly divided into levels, but is marvelously intertwined, like a labyrinth. Seth has mentioned this at various times.

(Again in the same rather flat and deliberate voice, although it was a bit stronger now, Jane resumed at 9:34.)

The tools of investigation will therefore be different.

This does not mean that the investigation will not be as valid as those probes carried on with different tools.

Now during the dream drama the inner self may focus at various, or at <u>one</u> of various subconscious areas which it uses as a point of departure. This area, whichever one it may be, will be the one in which the main dream sequence originates and in which the dream activity occurs.

The dream objects and activities will then be interpreted at other subconscious areas, so that to understand a dream properly we should first discover at which subconscious area it originates. Individuals can be enabled to find this point of origin for themselves, after an attempt is made to recall any given dream or dreams.

A familiarity must be gained by an individual with the general nature of his own dreams first, as Ruburt now has some knowledge or intuition that enables him to distinguish between dreams that originate in areas having to do with past lives, and those which originate in other areas, though he is not yet able to further differentiate.

A state of dissociation is necessary, a letting down of egotistical barriers in order that inner symbolisms can be appreciated and distinguished. The change of focus alone will aid in intuitional enlightenment, and association can then rise more easily through the subconscious areas.

They will indeed burst through, or appear through, into the egotistical consciousness if given the opportunity; but the egotistical consciousness cannot go after them. The ego will always erect defenses, but intuitional understanding has always been able to pierce such defenses.

In the interpretation of your dreams then Joseph, as with Ruburt's, we must change our focus, for what appears as a logical interpretation through conscious examination is often distorted.

The basic and originating dream sequence occurred in that area of the subconscious having to do with past lives, and of course expanded into other areas. The dream was partially triggered, as is often the case between closely related individuals, by Ruburt's own dream in which the leaking vessel was featured.

(Again, see the 87th session for Jane's dream.)

It, the sequence, referred again to that ocean voyage, and gave you additional subconscious knowledge, informing you that the Larry Potter of your acquaintance was a seaman on the same vessel. He loomed above you in the dream because during that voyage he had rank, and <u>you</u> as a stowaway had none.

And when you were discovered it was he, a first mate, who had you pressed into duty, and who belittled your efforts until finally he struck you; a fact, incidentally, which you were not willing to face in the dream.

(True. See page 48. At this moment, there also popped to mind the fact that I have a collection of perhaps 30 books on old sailing ships, the sea, pirates, etc. I had not looked at them recently, indeed having begun the collection over ten years ago, before I was married, when I became interested in the subject while doing research for some artwork. But ever since I built up the collection, I've insisted on carting it about with us each time we changed location.)

Because of the present situation, where the man in your present life is a mere lad, the dream then changed levels. The vessel becomes a masculine symbol. The first symbol was built around Ruburt's dreams, which involved a female symbol; that is, the present Ruburt interpreted vessel as tub, hence washing machine, the leaking vessel becoming a leaking washing machine.

Your dream began with this, but you quickly changed into a masculined interpretation. A ship is thought of as a she. The symbol changed then to a woman: she who carries men within her. Because of the originating area of the dream, you chose the Potter lad's mother, and she was the connecting image from one area to another. Even in your dream, she carried you in a car from one location to another.

Even this, however, gave you additional information. The mate died during that journey. He struck you. You were then much younger than he. Two other sailors leaped to your defense, not out of great kindness of heart, mainly because they disliked him. He received a wound, not obviously critical, which developed blood poisoning.

You found out later and felt somewhat at fault. In the dream the lad's present mother is seen to comfort you, this being a way to relieve the past uneasiness that at a certain subconscious area still lingers. At the time the lad was in his very early thirties, but you were much younger.

("Do you know what year it was?")

No.

The ship had the word "maiden" in its name, however, and carried cargo from a Southampton to Boston.

You then found yourself, in the dream, wearing pajamas, first though deposited in front of your parent's home, but not entering. This being a symbolic connection again, a transference not yet into this life, that is not into your parents' home. But just immediately preceding birth you find yourself in the dream wearing pajamas, entering a theatre, looking for someone.

The pajamas merely represented symbolically your refusal to admit the fact of, first, nakedness; to hold off birth, to gaze about in the theatre of existence before permitting yourself to be born again on the physical plane, this deliberation always having been somewhat a portion of your makeup.

You were looking for the person who was to become your brother, and indeed you found him, or he found you. People in your dream did not notice your strange attire, incidentally, because in your dream you had not yet elected to be born.

A woman with your brother you did not recognize. The three of you communicated before your birth. The woman was your brother Loren as he appeared before. You then planned or decided to be born when the meeting was carried out. You also however intended to become intimately associated with the man who is now your father.

But though you met both the present Dick and Loren, neither of you knew what your relationship would be in this life. You intended a brother lifelong relationship with the man who is, instead, your father. Hence he passes you by, the bicycle being a symbol of youth. That is, because you imagined that he would be a contemporary in age, you saw him on a bicycle, a child's method of transportation, but because he was born earlier the vehicle carries him past.

You stretch, a symbol of the relatively sleepy, unrealized period of youth, early youth, in which you were caught, hence the stiffish arm that was not able therefore to keep the man who is your father with you in time. He smiles and nods, yet you do not speak because communication between you was always difficult.

His nod however was a blessing upon you. It was of course the knowledge that he would necessarily die before you will that gave rise to his passing by, but the dream did not involve an immediate clairvoyant knowledge of his death.

Now we come to a dream that originated on quite a different subconscious area, and that did include a certain clairvoyant knowledge. It gave you inner warning to prepare for last Sunday's very real occurrence, in which you did indeed to some extent sit in judgement. There was necessarily of course distortion, and rather tricky distortion at that.

Your mother sat in the dream before a higher bar, symbolizing your own inner conviction, based on early rather puritanical bases, that your mother and her actions should be judged, and a child's natural but unfortunate vindictiveness: "She who has hurt me, particularly if my mother and a female, shall meet justice." You have her in the dream before the bar of justice.

The other sons are present. On the childlike area of the subconscious you believe your mother mainly responsible for family difficulties. However her defense, which you recognize basically as insincere but superficially correct in this particular instance, was that your father hit her in the chest. You identified with your father, and could not permit, in this dream at any rate, an identification of this kind, since <u>at this childish level</u> you did not blame him and would have wished as a <u>child</u>, to have the power to do the same thing.

So, even in the dream you misinterpreted and distorted the violence. Instead of having your mother say "He hit me in the chest," and in order to punish yourself through your identification with your father, instead you translated the words to "He has a spot on his lungs," therefore punishing symbolically both your father and yourself for the violence.

However, the dream was basically clairvoyant, in that it foresaw the actual situation of Sunday, in which the mother ended up on trial before her sons; and it <u>did</u> prepare you so that you automatically adjusted yourself, coming through the actual situation rather intact, since you had already faced it on another level.

You were aware incidentally of your own misinterpretation, and the appearance of your father in both the dreams was opposed by the female vessel symbol, as the opposition between both parents has been an important element in your subconscious life.

A spot on the lungs also suggests bleeding or leaking, which returns you to the leaking vessel image once again, and also refers to the wound which leaked blood, that was inflicted upon the first mate.

You will find such sequences often, and this should be expected. The dream also allowed you to see ahead of time beyond the surface of the situation which did arrive on Sunday, and you were much easier on your father Sunday because the dream tipped you off as to the tactics that your mother would use on one level, and also allowed you to punish yourself and your father symbolically rather than actually, for a violent tendency which is now apparent in him toward her, but is not as readily apparent, but repressed, in yourself.

Had the dream not so prepared you, you may well have struck out verbally at your father most forcibly, in an actual attempt to make him suffer for his own rather restrained violence, because you would have feared and not been able to face its somewhat weaker but still definite latent manifestation in yourself.

Because I have kept you without your break, I will now close the session. I did not want to break the context or the continuity here, and it was much better that Ruburt remain in a constant state of deep dissociation for the most faithful interpretation of the dreams.

You will see from our previous discussion that such a state is by far the most beneficial if a faithful interpretation is to be received. I will continue the session for a few closing remarks after break, if you prefer.

("Okay.")

(Break at 10:50. Jane was fully dissociated, so far-out, she said, that she had no conception of the passage of time, whether five minutes or two hours passed. Actually we had missed two breaks. Toward the end Jane's voice had become quite dry and hoarse, and I had been on the point of asking for a break when Seth did take one.

(Actually, I had been well aware that Seth was skipping breaks, and had watched Jane rather closely to see if she became uncomfortable. This was her longest uninterrupted delivery by far since the sessions began last November 1963, and she appeared to go through it without any visible change in manner beyond the quite natural hoarseness toward the end. As for myself, I can state that by the time break arrived my right hand and arm ached all the way up to my shoulder.

(Since Seth had not actually discussed the very beginning of my first long dream, Jane and I spoke of this during break. It was a mistake, for no sooner did the subject come up than Jane began again with but one minute's rest. As it was, she remained seated at the table, sitting with her eyes closed and her glasses off. Her voice, surprisingly, was quite at ease.)

The dream of the drawings occurred on another level, and we will discuss in detail these various subconscious areas, though I speak of them as separated only for convenience.

The dream represented a correlation of past, present and future, a knowledge that Ruburt was indeed an artist in a distant life, that he has strong abilities in that direction now; and it represents your inner realization of the type of painting he can ultimately produce in this life if he utilizes the ability. Your surprise in the dream represents your feeling that he is not using the ability. Therefore the quality of the painting in the dream amazed you.

My fond and best wishes.

("Good night, Seth."

(End at 10:55. Jane was dissociated as usual. She said that while she was delivering the above material on one level, she also received the thought from Seth "on another level" that she should sleep for three-quarters of an hour after supper on session nights. She has reported this dual reception on a few occasions before, and as before she said she was able to give voice to but one level at a time.

(The pastel drawing of Jane's that I saw in my dream was so vivid that I still retain it clearly, and plan to do an oil painting of it soon. Both Jane and I of course have been aware of her artistic ability, and I have made various attempts to get her to use it more regularly. Although she understands perspective which I have tried to teach her, she has no feeling for it, and prefers to work without it; she calls her work primitive, and it has a childlike quality when she is left alone to paint her own way.

(Thinking the session now over, I then brought up the thought that I suspected a distortion in Seth's interpretation of the first dream, where he stated that before being born I saw my brother Loren as a woman. I thought I recalled Seth stating many sessions ago that Loren had been three times a man, but never a woman, and had a woman's life ahead of him.

(Jane, washing her face in the next room, agreed with me. Then to my surprise she came through again, striding out into the living room, speaking in a rather deep voice. Again she was without her glasses. Resume at 11:00.)

The man you know as Loren has never been born as a woman yet on the physical plane. The overall entity however is a <u>feminine</u> one.

This is why you saw <u>him as a woman</u>, and <u>why</u> you did not recognize him. The next life <u>will be</u> forcibly one of a woman. Or rather, the personality will manifest itself forcibly as a woman in most flamboyant terms, because it has thus far not used its abilities nor expressed the strong intuitive portion of its nature.

Because the entity has not expressed but withheld the basic femininity of its nature, it has fed back upon itself so that the overall identity of the entity appears as feminine simply because there is a backlog of those characteristics thought of as feminine.

An entity is composed of what <u>you</u> may call feminine and masculine characteristics, but when all energy is focused into masculine-oriented personalities then a backlog develops, so that the entity is left with only unused, unmanifested, so-far-denied feminine characteristics.

The same sort of situation develops if the male type of characteristic is repeatedly denied fulfillment or manifestation. I wanted to clear this up immediately, as the same sort of misunderstanding has occurred concerning Loren in the past.

And now good night.

("Good night, Seth."

(End at 11:06.)

SESSION 95
OCTOBER 7, 1964 9 PM WEDNESDAY AS SCHEDULED

(At 8:15 PM John Bradley arrived to be a witness. John has witnessed several sessions; with him he brought the first carbon of Volume 1 of the Seth material, which he has been reading. This consists of the first 38 sessions. John now had for us questions on beginnings and endings, inner reality, the inner senses, etc. John is also an indefatigable worker at finding people who are willing to devote free time to typing up extra copies of the material, and he had news for us on this score also. Needless to say Jane and I have been lax in this field, and we are most grateful to John for his efforts.

(It will be remembered that in the 63rd session, June 17, 1964, Seth stated that he could "also see a sort of trouble in September for a woman neighbor who lives three doors down the street from him" in Williamsport, PA, "the difficulty here somehow involving two children... A 'V' comes to mind..." See Volume 2, pages 159-60.

(John told us that although he had kept his eyes and ears open for news, he knew of nothing happening to any such neighbor, although as explained through John's map in the 63rd session, two such women neighbors with children live three doors from him. John had been on vacation for two weeks in September however, and said he may have missed out on something developing. The "V" given by Seth has no particular meaning for him, he said.

(At 8:35 Bill Macdonnel also arrived to be a witness. It will be recalled that John and Bill had been witnesses to various sessions, but not jointly before this. They had however met here before on other than session nights.

(The arrival of two unexpected witnesses made Jane a little nervous, but the mood passed rather quickly, she told me later. At 8:59 she was in the kitchen making coffee. She began delivery on time in a voice pitched little lower than usual, and

rather strong. Her pacing was slow. Once again her glasses were off, her eyes very dark.)

Good evening.

("Good evening, Seth.")

I will here welcome Mark and Philip to our session.

The material may be a mixed version of various topics this evening. At our last meeting we discussed dreams and the subconscious. Earlier I mentioned that your concept, distorted concept of cause and effect, led to the idea that all things must have a beginning and an end.

Also I mentioned that the spacious present knows no beginning or end, and that energy, of which everything is composed, can never be withdrawn. Nor can individualized energy ever lose its individuality, nor in a very actual sense can anything which has ever existed go out of existence, but merely change its form.

Since energy cannot be withdrawn but only change its form, then there can be no ending, but only a contraction such as that which I have earlier explained. And expansion must then follow, the expansion in your terms bringing a new beginning.

Ruburt, at the age of I believe seventeen, began a poem with the line, and if he will forgive me I will quote: "The end overshadows the beginning," end of quote. In your terms, you are obligated because of certain present self-imposed limitations, and necessary ones, to think in terms of beginning and end.

Ruburt in the child's perceptive poem could not let go this idea, and we must speak as he did then, in terms of beginning and end. But I disapprove of the terms, since in themselves they serve to perpetuate a most unfortunate distortive concept.

Energy is self-perpetuating. The universe and <u>all planes</u> and universes of existence, come indeed from what you may call energy, vitality, idea; or despite Ruburt's stubborn blocking, from a personality essence or psychic gestalt which you may refer to as God <u>if</u> you prefer. And this statement is an extremely simplified version of actuality.

(See the 81st session and the material on the God concept. By now, Jane's voice had strengthened, although it was not any lower. But she spoke with much expressive determination, using many gestures and smiling often.)

Before any universe as you know it, or as <u>I</u> know it, existed, there was first a <u>striving</u>. To make this as simple as possible is difficult, since it has been simplified for <u>me</u>. In ultimate terms, there is and <u>never was</u> a beginning, Philip. This strains the intellect, and so I will say that in your practical terms, of which we have somewhat spoken in the past, there was what <u>you</u> may all refer to as a beginning, when strife and striving and a wish to be formed itself and gathered itself sufficiently together to form a contracted whole in which all possibilities were latent.

You will ask me, then, the source of the wish to be. You will of course ask me the source of the source, and I will say again that only within the framework of your intense but limited camouflage universe does such a question have meaning or validity.

(Seth's next amused remark refers to Jane.)

Far be it from me to reinforce my little atheist's early catechism lessons. I must however substitute the word God for energy, but still say that energy always was and always will be.

It is not to minimize the importance of the intellect that I once again repeat: Inner reality will only be known directly through the inner self, and the inner senses. The intellect must deal and interpret the realities of camouflage existence, this being its purpose.

There is a constant, ever-enfolding and ever-expanding reality. The pyramids of psychic gestalts of which I have spoken represent in your terms all beginnings and all endings, which again expand into new beginnings and new forms.

Philip should read the sessions dealing particularly with the laws of the universe, that is with the inner laws of the universe, appreciating then the facts that this universe within all universes is spontaneous while having durability. It would be backtracking to repeat that long discussion, but as the inner universe has as its attributes spontaneity and durability, and as the spacious present is simultaneous while containing within it all pasts and all presents and all futures, and as Philip understands the meaning of expansion in terms not of time or of space but of value fulfillment, so will he intuitively then grasp that no contradiction occurs with actual reality when I say that there is no beginning and no end.

I will let you take your break before I continue.

(Break at 9:31. Jane was dissociated as usual. As soon as she sat down she put her glasses on. She resumed in the same strong and energetic manner at 9:36.)

As there is in actuality no beginning or end to a dream, so there is no beginning or end to any reality. A dream does not then begin and end, only your awareness of a dream begins and ends.

You come into awareness of a dream, and you leave awareness of a dream, but the dreams that you seem to dream tonight have been long in existence, in your terms of time. They seem to begin tonight because you are aware of them tonight, so you think that reality must begin and end.

You indeed create your own dreams, as you realize, Joseph. Nevertheless, you do not create your own dreams during a specific point in time. The beginnings, to use that distortive term again, the beginnings of dreams reach back into past lives of which you are not aware, and beyond even this the origins are part of a heritage before your planet even existed.

For every consciousness on your plane, or any other plane, existed simultaneously and in essence even before what you may call the beginning of your world. And what you are yet to be existed then and still exists now; and not as some still unfulfilled possibility, but exists in actuality.

What you will be, Joseph, what Mark and Philip and Ruburt will be, you all are now, not in some misty half-real form, but in the most real sense. You simply are not aware of these selves anymore on a conscious level than you are aware of what you refer to as past selves.

The material that I have given you concerning the nature of planes will be quite handy here. I have told you that a plane is not necessarily a planet, nor a place, but even a mere focus of awareness. A dream is an awareness of and existence in another plane, whereby the self changes focus to keep in touch with the various portions of itself so that inner communication can be maintained.

I do not believe that Philip has read the material dealing with the perspective universe, in which the dream is projected into a changing but durable and quite real existence, independent of the dreamer.

Now. I have said that any of you and all of you create a dream universe of validity, actuality, durability, and for Philip's benefit, self-determination, in the same manner that the entity projects the reality of its various personalities. As there is no contact between the entity and the ordinary conscious ego, so there is no contact on a conscious level between the self who dreams and the dream world which has its own independent existence.

And in the same way that the dream world has no beginning or end, neither does the universe with which you are familiar. No energy can be withdrawn, and this includes the energy used in the continuous subconscious construction of the dream world. You continually create it, have always created it. It is a product of your own existence, and you can neither consciously call it into existence nor destroy it.

We will now come to one main attribute then of all reality, and of that that is as ultimate as anything I know—that energy gestalt which may be called God.

For a compulsion is here that becomes an attribute, and this compulsion gives its opposite face a human character. For the one main and ultimate attribute or characteristic of this infinite energy is the compulsion to be. This is the driving force, the one main law from which value fulfillment then flows.

I will let you take your break, out of the goodness of my heart, and also so that I might have the benefit of your brilliant conversation between my material. I regret, and deeply, that we must still deal with concepts in terms of words strung out one before the other, for this method serves to reinforce your idea of continuity, cause and effect, past and present, and all such camouflages that I am completely determined to put into proper place.

(Break at 10:02. Jane was dissociated as usual. Again she put her glasses on at break, having delivered the above material without wearing them. My writing hand felt some fatigue.

(John and Bill, Jane and I engaged in a discussion of free will, and in an effort to make some points I was sure the material covered I again became aware of something that was becoming more obvious all the time: namely, that the material has now reached such a length, and has gone into so many subjects, some lightly and others deeply, that I for one can no longer keep all of it on prompt recall.

(Jane resumed in the same good voice, again without her glasses, at 10:17.)

My dear friends. There are no ends that must be accomplished by any given personality, no ends that must be gained by a personality for the entity.

There are only various planes of existence in which energy wishes, or may wish, to manifest itself. The entity then projects a personality within that plane of existence, equipping it with whatever camouflage senses, mechanisms, and protections that are necessary for survival on that plane.

The personality is on its own, with what you may call the power of self-determination and free will. If you had thoroughly remembered our material on value fulfillment, you would know that the only detriment to so-called free will is the built-in necessity for value fulfillment. The personality must gain experience, in other words, on a particular level of existence, on which or within which it operates, and it cannot choose otherwise. It must experience existence on the particular level on which it has been projected.

No child, no infant commits suicide. It is impossible. The adult who commits suicide has still gained experience to some degree within your plane. This law, the necessity for experience, operates only after complete materialization and orientation within your plane.

A child is not completely materialized upon your plane, nor is he oriented. A personality may refuse to gain such experience before actual birth upon your plane. This necessity for value fulfillment through experience upon a particular existence plane, is the only detriment, if you wish to think of it that way, to free will.

Now. No other commands are built-in, no other prohibitions given. But built-in of course into this necessity for experience, is the compulsion toward value fulfillment, and as you know this does not apply alone to growth, which is in itself a camouflage materialization of value fulfillment along one line only.

Personalities may indeed become entities. One personality may not be but one personality in your terms, as I have mentioned a man being one personality may be seen in terms of a father, a teacher, an artist, a community member and so forth.

The father does not negate the reality of, say, the artist. The father does not rob the artist of free will, nor does the entity rob the personality of free will. It is the personality who makes the choices. The entity may not either aid or prevent any choice that the personality may make. The entity may not like any particular choice made by the personality, but he, the entity, cannot change the course that the personality chooses to take.

If you say that the personality cannot take any choice of which the entity is not aware, then this is true; but it is also true that the entity is utterly incapable of changing that choice made by the personality, even though the entity knows about the choice ahead of time, so to speak.

With his superior knowledge the entity must leave hands off. His, the entity's, only hope is to allow the personality complete independence, for it is the personality who understands more clearly than he the conditions of the particular plane upon which his existence happens.

There is here no puppet, and there is no hand that moves the strings. If there were you see, you would indeed have a much more perfect world, but you would not have that one built-in prerequisite: complete as possible existence within all facets, and manipulation within all facets, of a given plane.

Now. What you call karma has meaning only in basic terms within your particular plane. I do not want to get too complicated. Nevertheless personalities on your plane work out individual problems within that plane through various existences. Here we have also free will, but a continuity so to speak of purposes. No purpose is forced upon any personality. He, the personality, adopts in various reincarnations upon your plane those purposes most in keeping with his own needs. And for Mark's sake may I say that levels of existence do not necessarily imply higher or lower levels, but concentric levels, even as the layers of the subconscious do not imply upper and lower levels, but are merely terms used for the sake of simplicity.

Mark should read the material dealing with capsule comprehension, as that portion will answer one of his questions.

I will let you take your break—all of you, those portions of yourselves that you know, for those other portions of yourselves as always continue along their own lines of focus.

(Break at 10:46. Jane was dissociated as usual, really out, she said, as she has been all night. Bill Macdonnel left for home because his cold had tired him out. Jane resumed in about the same energetic manner at 10:50.)

I will here begin to close the session, though like Philip's universe, the sessions never began at a specific point in time, and Ruburt knew of them long before he paced this floor, though he was not aware of them. And they will end, or they will end in <u>your</u> terms, with your change of planes. But they will not end, and as we have known each other in the past and in the future and in the present, so these sessions exist in the spacious present, where time as such has no meaning.

And incidentally, the events I mentioned in connection with Philip's neighborhood did occur indeed, as a check upon the newspapers might well show.

I will now close our session, though again <u>I</u> could go on for hours, and it is only <u>your</u> concept of time which slows down our flow of information.

("How about a clue as to those events in John's neighborhood, in Williamsport?")

My heartiest appreciation for Philip's attempts to have the material typed, and my rather impatient request that Ruburt begin his work of preparing the material for publication.

The woman involved, her initial a "V", the other information as given, and my fondest wishes to you all.

("Good night, Seth.")

(End at 10:58. Jane was dissociated as usual. See page 58 for a brief resume of the material involving John Bradley's neighborhood in Williamsport, PA. Again, John said the initial V meant nothing in particular to him, but when he returned home he planned to do what he could to ascertain just what did take place three doors from his own place, to a woman with at least two children, or who is connected somehow with children. I suggested that a visit to his local newspaper back-issue file might be the easiest way to check.

(Leaving, John took with him the first carbon of sessions 24-38, to test out his two female volunteers' determination in making copies of the Seth material. It is a massive amount of work—I can testify to that personally!)

SESSION 96
OCTOBER 12, 1964 9 PM MONDAY AS INSTRUCTED

(At 8:45 Jane had no idea of the material for the session tonight. She had tried to sleep at 7:30, without success. She said she still feels "a little odd when I don't have any idea of what he's going to talk about, or anything." Jane has also begun the study of psychological time on a regular basis, but has nothing of note to report yet, beyond a few glimmerings.

(I have yet to resume psychological time study. I now have my dream notebook in full swing, and since I had more dreams on the order of the two already discussed by Seth, I had my dream notebook open on the table as session time approached, in case these dreams were used in the material.

(Jane began dictating again with her glasses off, her eyes quite dark as usual. Her voice was normal, her pacing slow, and her rate of delivery rather slow and interspersed by pauses.)

Good evening.

("Good evening, Seth.")

A few remarks here, tying in with our previous session.

There is no <u>one</u> reality. There are many, in fact infinite, realities. There is no beginning and end. When beginnings and endings are spoken of, the implication is always there, that there must be but one reality, and that it must have a beginning in time and an ending in time.

I have tried to explain the distortions which make such questions seem intrinsically valid, but it is only from your own perspective that you think in terms of beginning and end, and only because of your self-adopted limitations that you continue along these lines.

Realities merge, one into the other. Personalities, or any type of individualized energy, may pass through various realities. The appearance of energy in one form could be said to end in that form were it not for the existence of the spacious present, in which all realities are simultaneous.

I could therefore with some justification let you continue to believe in beginnings and endings, and leave the more complicated explanations out, but this is not my way. And unless I am forced to do so, I do not like to water down information to make it more palatable.

It is true that the pyramid gestalts of which I have spoken can be said to merge into what you may refer to as a unitary and even sublime being, but this is grossly simplified.

We shall have a session dealing almost entirely with the nature of energy gestalts, and you will see that while these pyramid energy gestalts do, on the one hand, achieve a unitary character and sublime intelligence, on the other hand they form only an approximation of humanity's concept of a God. This unitary gestalt which we may call, and I prefer it to the word God, the primary energy gestalt.

This primary energy gestalt may be thought of as straddling all realities, or existing in the infinite realities of which we have spoken. Yet in this prime gestalt that is unitary, there is again an infinite diversity and literally numberless personalities. Nor are these personalities that compose the prime psychic gestalt dependent or submissive to any one dominating personality within the gestalt.

This material will take some studying. You will perhaps recognize a certain similarity between this concept and the Christian concept of a Trinity, except that the Trinity concept, while hinting at diversity within prime unity, was nevertheless distorted by man's own sense of his own adopted and unfortunate delusion of duality.

The Trinity concept in your terms was a masculine one, projecting to the one God concept the duality which all mankind feels, but because the theory originated with the male the duality is expressed in terms of the male viewpoint.

You have in the Trinity Father, Son and Holy Ghost. Here man attempts to externalize a division he feels within himself, individually. He is a son, and then a father, and always within him he feels that part or inner self which cannot be seen by another, which is neither father nor son, but which is within him while he is father, and while he is son.

This of course being the Holy Ghost, or rather that which he thought of in such terms. When he attempted to further formulate his God concept he then projected upon it those mysteries of self.

I suggest your break.

(Break at 9:28. Jane was dissociated as usual. She put her glasses on upon ending delivery, but took them off again upon resuming in the same quiet and deliberate manner at 9:34.)

As you know, inner data must be perceived through the inner senses. In formulating a theory concerning the primary energy gestalt, the data is distorted by the peculiar set of outer sensory equipment characteristic of any given plane of reality. This is known, that man forms his god in his own image.

The irony is that in part this image will be true. That is, it will represent one facet of the primary gestalt, but a facet so infinitesimal in the overall reality of the primary gestalt that it distorts beyond all recognition. Only by escaping momentarily from camouflage data can any larger concept be obtained.

A personality in the primary gestalt is indeed focused upon your present plane of reality, but to suppose that the whole primary gestalt is so focused represents mankind's ego playing with one of its most preposterous proposals.

The primary energy gestalt did not have a beginning in time, nor will it end in time. It is a result of an expansion, again, in terms of value fulfillment, an expansion that has nothing to do with either time or space as men conceive them.

The expansion resulted from a contraction of energy, but because of the unique attributes inherent in both value fulfillment and in the spacious present, there simply was not an initial or first contraction or expansion.

I will not say that there was, simply in order to make the material appear more logical, since only appearances can be made logical because they deal with, that is appearances deal with, data that you are physically equipped to handle.

You create appearances. You create outer senses to perceive the appearances, and so what you perceive through the outer senses seems logical indeed. But again, there are infinite realities, as vivid, and some indescribably more vivid than your own, but presently you are not focused upon them.

And since you are not, you do not have the peculiar sets of camouflage perceptors necessary to experience existence within them. Now. Within the same space and time that you at this moment occupy, there are numberless planes of reality. You simply do not have the camouflage equipment to perceive them.

They, or the inhabitants of such realities, do not perceive your plane of existence for the same reason. This does not mean that any one field or plane is more valid than another. The closest field or plane is that one that you create, that you call the dream world, and that you imagine to be unsubstantial, impermanent, fleeting, having no reality except during your own contact with it.

It may be thought of in an analogy, as a shadow, in that you create it or project it, but without conscious knowledge. It is a natural consequence of your own existence. But it does not vanish when the ego blots out the inner light from the whole self. Its existence is as permanent as your own.

I suggest your break.

(Break at 9:58. Jane was dissociated as usual, and again resumed wearing her glasses at break. During break I wondered aloud whether the inhabitants of another plane might be able to tune in on our dream world from the other side, you might say, and through the dream world thus locate our plane. Perhaps the flying saucer people had located our plane in that fashion.

(My writing hand felt some fatigue. Jane now did not feel particularly good, due to a sinus condition. She resumed in the same quiet manner, with frequent pauses, at 10:05.)

A note here. If Ruburt would resume his back exercises his sinuses will improve. The exercises should be done very slowly, however, and without strain.

At times he did them too quickly.

(Jane now took a rather long pause as she paced back and forth.)

There is more, but he is up to his tricks again, blocking me. I will get the material through for his own benefit in the near future. That will be all then for the subject now.

You know then from past discussions that the dream world as you know it is the result of your awareness of a plane of existence which you help create, and in which you manipulate. In other words, on an unconscious level you here manipulate in another plane of existence entirely, one in which your conscious camouflage ego may not enter.

It is not part of the particular camouflage necessities on that plane. Now. At other levels you exist and manipulate on other planes, which are consciously unknown to you, planes which are as valid as your own, and in which your existence is also a natural result of your own psychic makeup. I am referring here of course to all individuals.

This has nothing to do with reincarnation, but involves levels of experience, manipulations in other realities, that are a natural result of the psychophysical gestalt of a human individual.

The chemical and electrical construction of the human individual opens other pathways, and requires other activities in other fields than those with which the conscious ego is familiar. The mechanics are not important, but as dreaming is partially caused by chemical poisons that make dreaming a necessity for physical survival, so there are other mechanisms of this kind that are actually doorways, built within and natural to the physical mechanism, that at the same time necessitate experience upon other fields of reality.

Many purposes are thereby served. You have a focus in many more worlds than you know. One is a conceptual energy force reality which is much more than some theoretical world of ideas, but a reality in which individual energy is used in a constant manipulation of idea or concepts into constructions that, while not physical in your terms, is nevertheless a vivid and actual, concrete field of manipulated and applied force in which matter may be, but is not always, an end result.

This matter does not appear however in your universe, but is outside of it.

I am going to end the session somewhat earlier, as I am initiating you into new material.

An effort is involved here, as concepts of rather complicated nature must be broken into words between us for the first time, and this involves a discrimination most difficult, in order that the most evocative phrases be used while taking care that as many distortions as possible be avoided in word translation.

My best and fondest wishes to you both. As always I dislike leaving, but I am extremely pleased with tonight's material.

("Good night, Seth."

(End at 10:30. Jane was dissociated more fully, she said, than she had been earlier in the session. We were somewhat surprised at the rather abrupt end of the session, but not displeased either. My writing hand felt better.)

SESSION 97
OCTOBER 14, 1964 9 PM WEDNESDAY AS SCHEDULED

(At 8:55 this evening Jane had no idea of what Seth would talk about for the session. She did not feel good, however, and I was half-prepared for a short session or perhaps none at all.

(I thought she might be unhappy about a letter she received last Monday from the Macmillan Co. of NY, in which they stated that they liked her book of poetry, The Fence, *very much, but could not publish it due to their restricted list of poetry, having abandoned for the time being their projected series of paperback poetry books. The fact that Macmillan stated they thought another publisher would take on* The Fence, *had not, I thought, particularly cheered Jane, at least at the moment.*

(She began dictation on time, again without her glasses. Her voice was but a little stronger than normal, her pacing regular, her eyes dark as usual. Her delivery in the beginning was rather slow and interspersed with pauses, but after a page or so it began to pick up speed, until she had me writing at a pretty good rate. At the same time Jane's pacing also picked up speed.)

Good evening.

("Good evening, Seth.")

Ruburt's indisposition is the result of a rather uncalled-for sense of panic.

Were he not so honestly and unfortunately ill-disposed, the affair would be highly ludicrous. Last week he began and finished an excellent short story, and finished an outline, as well as holding our sessions, and beginning once more his psychological time experiments.

Monday he also worked, and the following day he did not immediately begin another story. And here we see his translation of this rather natural occurrence into tragic forebodings. No idea. And this further of course projected: no idea tomorrow, and a succession of days. But to hide from himself the dire imagined sequence he must have an excuse.

He is ill-disposed, and quite honestly so. Therefore he covers himself. If he does not get an idea tomorrow he has the excuse, anticipated, of being ill, and this also serves as a punishment. He will punish himself on any day that he does not put in his allotted hours in what he considers a constructive manner.

And incidentally, necessary business concerning the sending out of manuscripts, he does not subconsciously consider, should be considered part of his writing day.

Consciously he knows better. I will not put our session off this evening, though I may shorten it. He will learn shortly, and without any real difficulty, that while his new schedule will be, as it should be, followed with discipline, nevertheless he cannot expect a new idea every day.

It is ridiculous for him to so punish himself, and does not help matters, as his joyous spontaneity is so important in his working habits.

I would like to comment on a remark made earlier by yourself, Joseph. I find it most refreshing, rather drastic, however.

(Here Jane laughed, then took a long pause as she paced about the room. The remark of mine to be discussed was one I had made around supper time, and I was now rather surprised to see it crop up in the material.)

You spoke about this plane, mentioning I believe the possibility that the plane had some specified but unknown end, after which the cycle began anew, with of course new personalities participating.

You were indeed partially correct. However, even I pale at the idea of a specified—and that would be predetermined—end to your universe as you know it.

This would imply that despite the development of the inhabitants their world would end at a particular point, and this is not the case. However, your universe has had, and will continue to have, such cycles, but there is no predetermined end in those terms.

This is an extremely difficult subject. Certainly areas of the physical universe change form, are disassembled and reappear in other forms. This follows certain laws inherent in the field of nature as far as matter is concerned. Beyond this however, your idea would result in an end to your plane that was unavoidable. There are cycles, but they are brought about individually and en masse by the personalities active on your plane.

Probable universes are by their very nature existing universes. You mentioned that when and if you become an entity, and send forth personalities, that they would gain existence in the first periods of another such cycle; in another newer, say, fourth or fifth century.

You forget that in the spacious present you already are not only what you will be, but what you have been. Therefore, such personalities that you would project are already projected, and only the veil of unawareness divides you, as only the veil of unawareness ever separates one field or plane from another.

I suggest your break.

(Break at 9:29. Jane was dissociated as usual. Upon resting she put her glasses on. She reported that she felt all right while delivering the material, and also that she felt a little better now. She resumed in the same voice but at a little faster pace at 9:35.)

Concerning our friend Ruburt, another note. And that is that there is also a quite valid inner sense of guilt here, in that he has neglected his poetry.

At least an hour a day should be devoted to it. He was utterly and completely surprised upon learning that Macmillan had nearly accepted his book of poetry. He never <u>expected</u> any financial rewards from poetry, and it occurred to him that in his recent neglect of it he may have been cheating himself in more ways than one.

Because of his rather intense mental work, I would suggest walks and other physical activities. Small social relationships on an informal basis will be practical. They will prevent too much inner involvement, open new doors, bring psychic refreshment, and also provide our hungry friend with his diet of new ideas. As indeed his latest story was initiated by a remark made by a neighbor.

Rather frequent <u>informal</u> relationships are more practical than occasional formal ones, and Ruburt is already involving himself, again, in the satisfying for him diversified household chores, which are also a break from strict mental work. Even in winter time I will suggest he take walks, and these should be for pure enjoyment. Hammering at his subconscious as he does on his few walks negates their purpose. Too much of a good thing. After all, his subconscious would like some rest too. He is such a hammerhead in this respect.

We should have a balance here, and he must allow room for spontaneity. He remembers his early lack of discipline in working matters, but he is well disciplined now. On session nights particularly his working day is elongated, and regardless of my efforts there is some physical and mental strain involved, though these are greatly minimized.

His subconscious will provide all the spontaneous ideas that he needs for his own work, but he cannot sit it in a corner, lecture it, and demand very definite specific tasks. His subconscious knows better than he does consciously what particular means should be used to gain a desired end. It does not need minute by minute instructions.

I would not take up session time for this material except that my suggestions, if followed, will be most helpful. Also to him a note: even his adolescent, seemingly-undisciplined times were disciplined, giving notice of continuing ego strength, balanced and sometimes over-balanced by intuitional development, in that he never ceased writing from the day that he began.

He is face to face with himself, with his abilities, ambitions and limitations, now, with a whole day more or less to work toward his goal, and he feels great urgency. This is fine, a driving force, but his strength comes from among other things his very personal involvement with nature, and from his contemplation of it. Time devoted to what appears aimless thought and speculation will also bear its fruits.

I would have thought that any advice to Ruburt would have involved suggestions curtailing his robust and ever curious intuitional abilities, but he is holding them down with too heavy a hand. He so feared that he lacked discipline that he becomes too stern a keeper of his own inner fires.

I will close this part of our discussion, and suggest your break.

(Break at 10:00. Jane was dissociated as usual. She said she now feels quite a bit better. Her pace had speeded up and my writing hand was feeling it. She resumed in the same faster manner, although still with occasional pauses, at 10:07.)

We have not yet finished our consideration of the nature of dreams, which will be given more or less in bulk.

Dream interpretation will be an occasional but continuing proposition, and the general discussion of dreams will then serve as a guidepost.

The dream world is indeed a natural by-product of the relationship of the inner self and the physical being. Not a reflection, therefore, but a by-product involving not only a chemical reaction but the transformation of energy from one state to another.

In some respects <u>all</u> planes or fields of existence are indeed by-products of others. For example, without the peculiar spark set off through the interrelationship existing between the inner self and the physical being, the dream world would not exist. But conversely, the dream world is a necessity for the continued existence of the physical individual.

This point is extremely important. As you know, animals dream. What you do not know is that all consciousnesses dream. We have said that to some degree even atoms and molecules have consciousness, and this minute consciousness nevertheless forms its own dreams, even as on the other hand it forms its own physical image.

Now, as in the physical field atoms combine for their own benefit and individually into more complicated structure gestalts, so do they also combine to form such gestalts, though of a somewhat different nature, in the dream world.

I have said that the dream world has its own sort of form and permanence.

It is physically oriented, though not to the degree inherent in your ordinary universe. In the same manner that the physical image is built up of an individual, so is the dream image built up. You can refer to our previous discussion on matter if it will help you here, but the dream world is not a formless, haphazard, semi-construction.

It does not exist in bulk, but it does exist in form. This is not a contradiction nor a distortion. The true complexity and importance of the dream world as an independent field of existence has not yet been impressed upon you. Yet while your world and the dream world are basically independent, they still exert pressures and influences, one upon the other.

I will expand this discussion because an understanding of the dream world will bring you closer to understanding other fields of existence with which you are not so familiar.

I will shortly end this evening's session, so with your permission there will be no break.

(Jane looked at me for confirmation as she paced about the room, and I nodded. It was 10:28.)

It is important that you realize that the dream world is a by-product of your own existence. And because it is connected to you through chemical reactions this leaves open the entryway of interactions, in animals as well as men. Since dreams are a by-product of any consciousness involved with matter, this leads us to the correct conclusion—that trees have their dreams, that all physical matter, being formed about individualized units of consciousness of varying degrees, also participates in the involuntary construction of the dream universe.

I will here end our session, and am pleased to note that Ruburt feels much better. Had I put off the session he would have felt worse by far, feeling guilty. Now my two pigeons, good night from your crusty friend. We are all in the same pie together, save that I am the baker and the crust both. Some recipe.

("Good night, Seth."

(End at 10:38. Jane was dissociated as usual. She now felt much better; so much so that her last delivery was quite animated and cheerful.)

(These notes are taken verbatim from Jane's notebook, listing her recent experiments with psychological time:

(October 8, 1964, Thursday, 11 AM: Fleeting images; couldn't retain them.

(October 12, Monday, 3:30 PM: Elusive hallucinatory-type voices, unclear.

(October 13, Tuesday, 11:15 AM: Fleeting, forgotten images. As I first lay down, heard noise outside. Feeling struck me forcibly that it was caused by Marian Spaziani [our landlady]. Definite feeling, not a hunch, so strong I waited for her

knock, which didn't come. Thought I was mistaken. At noon someone in hall. It was Jimmy, Marian's husband. He had been working around the house for some time.

(October 14, Wednesday, 11:15 AM: No results.

(October 15, Thursday, 11:15 AM: Definite results. Eyes closed tightly but I saw a flood of light, same quality as daylight. In it, [as on a ceiling] a domed light fixture, unlike any here. So definite, vivid and unmistakable that I thought my eyes must be open—but they were not. Then it just vanished. I opened my eyes—definitely had not seen the light fixture in room, it was entirely different.

(October 16, Friday: Didn't try Psy-time, but lay down on bed for a nap, being tired. Exactly the same thing happened as yesterday, except that this time I saw a different light fixture, off to the left of my inner vision. Again, it was so clear I was almost sure eyes must be open, but they were closed. Again, fixture bore no resemblance to any in room.

(October 19, Monday, 11:15 AM: No results, except feeling of being light.

(October 19 also: Closed eyes, tired from reading. Saw clearly but briefly a red jewel, maybe pin, on a floor rather a distance off. Heard voices discussing the object. They may have wondered where it was. I snapped to, too, but don't remember what I said—sure that I wasn't speaking aloud. I heard my voice as I "heard" the others.

(October 20, Tuesday, 11:15 AM: No results.)

(For myself: I haven't begun regular experiments with Psy-time yet after the long layoff, but plan to soon. In the meantime I have had many fleeting experiences, usually soon after going to bed. The most recent came as I sat on the bed preparatory to lying down. It was dark of course, but I saw very clearly the figure of a blonde young woman in riding clothes, facing to my left. She was sitting down. Her clothes were brown. I saw this image as I was in the act of lying down.)

SESSION 98
OCTOBER 19, 1964 9 PM MONDAY AS SCHEDULED

(It will be remembered that in the 87th session of September 14, 1964, Seth began an interpretation of Jane's dream of September 7. The ramifications from this dream are still spreading. Seth again dealt with this dream in the 93rd session, of September 30. In it he said that although he was not sure, he thought Jane's schoolgirl friend, Marie Tubbs, now living in Florida, may have been in childbirth at the time of Jane's dream, with a possibility that the water bag had broken during birth. The unifying symbol of the dream had been a tub, and water.

(After this session Jane wrote to Marie in an effort to verify the above statement.

The two women have not seen each other for some years, but maintain a desultory correspondence. In her reply, dated October 11, Marie told Jane that she has not been involved in childbirth for two years. She did say that in July she had been on a cruise to Bermuda, in which she, her husband and friends had been on or near the water for about ten days. And at the time of Jane's dream, Marie said, hurricane Cleo had been descending upon them at Boynton Beach, and "we had plenty of water around then during the storm. It went right through here."

(So, since there was some kind of discrepancy here between what Seth at least considered a possibility, and the fact that Marie had not been giving birth, we naturally wondered what was correct, and hoped the session tonight would deal with it.

(Earlier today, feeling somewhat tense, Jane had visited a chiropractor for treatment. While talking with him she mentioned a hard lump that had appeared recently on the inside of her left wrist. It bothered her but little; the doctor stated that it could be an arthritic nodule; seeing that this upset her greatly, he reassured her by saying that it was more likely to be the result of an injury. Not remembering any injurious incidents, Jane came home quite upset.

(She was still upset as session time approached, and had been unable to take her nap before the session. She wrote out a list of half a dozen questions concerning the nodule, and left it lying on the table as session time came. She began on time, again without her glasses, and at a normal speed with some pauses. Her voice was normal, her pacing regular.)

Good evening.

("Good evening, Seth.")

I do not know precisely where to begin first.

Ruburt's mood is such that it is rather difficult for me. However this will be over shortly. I will therefore begin with the letter you received from Ruburt's friend.

The precise interpretation had to do with information in the dream pertaining to the cruise, the tub, here again, being interpreted in terms of a ship. This was incidental knowledge picked up telepathically when the woman in question described her journey, rather than from the trip itself.

The woman told the events of the trip to friends, then dreamed that night of the friends, and in this dream the woman retold these events. It was from this dream that Ruburt picked up the information connecting her friend with water.

In the friend's dream Ruburt played a small part, and this served as a connective.

("Were these two dreams simultaneous?"

(As usual in such interesting cases, I could have asked many questions, but settled by seeking to learn whether dreams could be simultaneous; offhand I did not

recall ever reading whether such a possibility had been dealt with by investigation. Let alone whether one dreamer could telepathically pick up the other dreamer's dream!)

In your time, yes. Water was of course all around.

A note here, pertaining to a different matter. Ruburt read that electrons spring from pure energy, and after our discussions on the nature of matter this should come as no surprise.

I have mentioned that atoms and molecules possess consciousness to a degree, as do electrons of course. The organizing principle of small particles into larger particles lies within the particles themselves, and is directed from within in all cases.

The organizing ability grows and potentials become more actual as such particles combine. However all potentialities are latent in each and every unit, regardless of size, and no combinations or coming-togethers are accidental, but are governed by inner principles of organization. All combinations of particles are voluntary, and based upon principles of value fulfillment, which operates within and causes those acts or motions which are conducive to the formation of more complicated gestalts.

Action and counteraction, operating through chemical enzymes, enable purposeful activity in which no motion is haphazard. The smallest imaginable particle gives evidence of that basic unity of energy adopting form, materializing the camouflage pattern necessary for efficient manipulation within your universe, that is composed of diverse but interwoven fields of apparent, semi-apparent, or unapparent activities and correlations. That is, many valid actions within your own universe do not, as you know, have solidity, and yet appear within and operate through the physical universe.

This should not seem strange. What appears rigid to your perception will not appear as rigid from other viewpoints outside of your system. What may appear to have no form within your system may well have form outside your system.

Effects which appear within your system, discernible by your instruments but without form in some, indeed many cases, represent speeds and velocities of activities or acts that actually have their origin from without your system; but because of their different speed and velocity they can travel through your system, and of course making their impression upon it.

Electromagnetic fields perceived and used within your system have their origin elsewhere. Nevertheless they affect your universe, even though you are not able to perceive them except in limited dimension.

I suggest your break.

(Break at 9:29. Jane was dissociated as usual, but more toward the middle and end of the delivery than in the beginning. Seth had not yet mentioned the nodule on her wrist, and we agreed that he was probably waiting until she attained a deeper state before he dealt with personal material of this sort.

(The last few paragraphs of the above material we thought to be an elaboration of Seth's rather cryptic statement in the 97th session, page 72, to the effect that in some respects all planes or fields of existence are indeed by-products of others.

(Jane resumed delivery in the same rather quiet voice, again with quite a few pauses, and again without her glasses, at 9:37.)

I will now endeavor to answer Ruburt's questions.

The formation on the wrist is not arthritic. You may repeat the statement for him to read. I have told him that he will not develop arthritis.

The hand was not injured, that is not knocked as by bunking, but was irritated due to a change of wrist motion occurring when he began to use a second typewriter, which he had not used for many years. The keys are spaced differently. The automatic wrist motion that he regularly uses in his touch typing was knocked askew, the pattern broken, and he used an erratic pressure that induced strain. This caused the irritation and the subsequent nodule.

The regular typewriter should be used. There is no use for me upon this occasion to do anything more than state the circumstances, except of course to suggest that Ruburt does not dwell upon the irritation.

I would state furthermore that indeed Ruburt did have occasion to be angry at the chiropractor, since with an emotional fear unthinking suggestions such as his, made with only the flimsiest of evidence, can be most harmful and destructive. And in an unwary, emotionally upset personality, particularly if under stress, such a suggestion could cause a harmless and protective nodule to be changed by the strong powers of adverse expectation, or rather expectation poorly used, into the form of what is feared; as a slight but harmless irregularity of heartbeat, with the unthinking suggestion of a doctor, can become through the patient's fears an actual functional disorder, so could suggestion turn a relatively harmless formation like Ruburt's into an arthritic condition.

Now obviously the unthinking suggestion alone is not responsible, or would not be responsible, for such circumstances. They would have to fall upon fertile ground; and given great enough emotional and subconscious fear an individual would need no outside suggestion. But those in position within healing professions have great authority, and any suggestions that they may make for good or ill are granted almost mystical validity by those individuals who visit them.

For one thing, individuals who finally visit such offices are oftentimes already emotionally upset. Oftentimes also those in attendance, the doctors or other healers are themselves tired, prone to the patient's emotional fears, and automatically in self-defense respond by giving voice to the patient's subconscious dread, picking it up telepathically but feeling it is directed at themselves, on a subconscious level of course.

And in many cases this is true. Again, subconsciously, the patient would wish to give his illness literally away, shove it from himself, so that often a healer responds subconsciously to what he considers a legitimate threat.

Nevertheless, because the patient is in a condition where he is most susceptible to suggestions, a great responsibility lies upon the shoulders of those who would treat illness. The chiropractor's suggestion that the irritation was an arthritic one was made positively; that is, without thinking he stated "Oh yes, that is not normal at all, it is an arthritic nodule." Later, realizing that the suggestion had been a poor one, and moreover one of which he was not certain, he amended the statement, adding that such a formation could also be the result of injury or simple irritation to the joint.

Despite Ruburt's understanding, his intellectual understanding of his fear of arthritis, he was thrown into an understandable and regrettable emotional state, with which he grappled with at least some success. But you see here what under other circumstances could have been the final straw, so to speak, the word of authority that would say "Your fears are justified." In such an instance and under certain conditions such an individual would have his deepest dreads, therefore, fastened upon him.

He would be convinced so of the diagnosis, that a disease that he might have escaped would be brought to physical manifestation. I am going into this clearly because the consequences that Ruburt escaped have often <u>not been</u> shaken off by others.

I will suggest your break.

(Break at 10:12. Jane was dissociated as usual, and also quite relieved at Seth's explanation. She had begun using her old typewriter for first drafts of her writings since leaving the gallery a few weeks ago, with the idea that since we do all the Seth material work on this machine, which is the best of the three we own, some wear and tear might be saved on it.

(Jane said she was "really out" while Seth gave the material on her wrist. She resumed in the same quiet manner at 10:21.)

I am pleased that Ruburt has begun his psychological time experiments again. His results are better than they would have been if he had not heeded my advice and had continued demanding results from the subconscious.

The consciousness of atoms and molecules can be likened to the subconscious as you now know it, in that it is generalized to a large degree, but energy-propelled. You should perhaps realize by now that the inner self, the mind and its components, is composed or forms a unitary force field of its own.

The subconscious is a radiation outward from the mental enclosure that can be considered as a nucleus. The conscious is the furthest reach, the outer radius of the primary field. Emanations from this field continue, traveling further, projecting energy that is transformed as you know into matter; and in a simplified version of your universe perceived in terms of such force fields, you would have seemingly endless atoms and molecules spinning about the nucleus, or an endless variety of such patterns that would appear on first appraisal random to an observer from another field.

This is precisely the appearance that your system gives. I am not speaking now necessarily in terms of size, although size as you know it is extremely relative, and it is only within the physical domain that size is granted importance, for outside of it intelligence does not need so massive a house.

We will go into this more thoroughly upon another occasion.

You do not have to wonder at the small physical symptoms which have bothered both of you lately. Before our sessions began your reactions were, as you might recall, much more vehement. The interaction between body and mind is always present. It is only when adverse symptoms arise that you pay it any attention.

Good health is as much a result of this interaction, you know, and more. Such symptoms as you have had have been mere annoyances, everything considered. I fear, however, that you are weary Joseph, this evening. If you prefer I will close the session.

("No."

(Seth-Jane had caught me yawning.)

Then I will continue.

I will return to the consideration of expectation and physical health, as from Ruburt's specific situation there is much general knowledge to be gained.

A disease of course is not brought about at any particular point in time, but is latent, and merely becomes perceivable enough to cause danger at what approximates a particular point in time. Psychologically there exists within a given individual the latent leaning toward a multitudinous variety of so-called diseases, these tendencies being picked up through early conditioning and environment.

This does not mean that the individual will necessarily fall ill to many of them, but it does mean that the physical structure has weak points that reflect, or are a result of, an inability along the lines of physical construction, that in turn result from an imperfection in manipulation.

Inner pockets of fear hold back needed energy, creating these weak points in the physical body. Efficiency may be developed through understanding, and through the efficient use of psychic energy. The deficiency is not in the matter itself, but is projected upon it.

Needed energy is held back in the fist of fear, and not used for fullest repair within the physical body. When the fear is activated it, the fear, drains more energy from the physical construction, contracting, the fear being like a short-circuit mechanism; and indeed definite electrical forces are here activated.

These can be measured. With this occurs a chemical overexertion, an attempt chemically to make up for loss of energy in a specific area. The body's defenses, with oftentimes insufficient energy at their command, attempt to hold the fort and make repairs, until the needed energy is again available.

A rather involved process here occurs. When it is understood that man creates not only matter but his own physical image as well, greater attention will be given so that early fear patterns of such extent will not develop.

I will also go into these matters more thoroughly, but Ruburt's situation gave us an excellent occasion. It is always wise to take heed, in your own speech, of remarks made pertaining to health or physical appearance, for the higher in esteem you are held by others, the more authority will be given to your suggestions.

I will now close the session, feeling that I have done well in setting Ruburt right at any rate. My fond regards to you both.

("Good night, Seth."

(End at 10:58. Jane was dissociated as usual. My writing hand was also tired. After the session was over, I realized that I had neglected to ask Seth to specifically clear up Jane's use of the phrase concerning her friend Marie as being involved in childbirth. I will make a point to inquire about this in the next session.)

SESSION 99
OCTOBER 21, 1964 9 PM WEDNESDAY AS SCHEDULED

(In an effort to further clear up Seth's rather involved interpretation of Jane's dream of September 7, I made it a point to ask Jane just before the session was due tonight about the statement Seth-Jane had made on page 46, involving Jane's friend, Marie Tubbs, in childbirth. Marie wrote Jane on October 11 that she has not given birth for two years, and Seth dealt with what looked like a discrepancy between the two sets of facts to a partial degree in the 98th session. See pages 74-75.

(Tubbs, of course, was Marie's maiden name. Her married name is Marie Sterrett, of Boynton Beach, Florida.

(John Bradley, of Williamsport, PA, who has witnessed several sessions, stopped by this afternoon on his regular rounds, but could not stay for the session this evening. Affairs involving John's work with Searle, the drug firm, are more or less quiet and uneventful, John reported. Seth has dealt with the machinations below the surface at Searle in various sessions. John now feels also that things are percolating below the surface, and he requested Jane and I find out what we could about the current state of affairs involving Searle, from Seth tonight.

(Jane had a rather unexpected opportunity, also, to verify Seth's diagnosis of the nodule on her left wrist yesterday afternoon. While on a walk to a neighborhood store she was given a ride by our family doctor. Sam Levine told her the nodule was harmless, the result of an injury, and called it a ganglion. He told her to leave it alone, saying it was protective and would probably disappear by itself. See Seth's diagnosis on page 77. Needless to say, Jane was pleased that Seth was verified.

(Also while on this walk, Jane had the thought that death approaches a personality when the personality becomes less and less able to focus his energies fully on this plane, when he can no longer control his physical image as well as in the past. She thought Seth might discuss this subject this evening.

(Jane began the session with a smile. Her voice was at a normal pitch, her pacing regular, her speed of dictation normal. Once again she began without her glasses, and her eyes were dark as usual.)

Good evening.

("Good evening, Seth.")

We will here embark upon our evening's journeys.

I find that the climate is more favorable this evening; and much to my amusement I discovered that Ruburt saw fit to collaborate my diagnosis of the condition existing on the left wrist, by speaking to a doctor, who did indeed collaborate my statement.

I understand the reasons that you seek such collaboration. I would, nevertheless, appreciate Ruburt taking me at my word sometimes. Later this evening, I may perhaps add a few remarks along these lines.

Ruburt did anticipate with some correctness part of this evening's subject matter, having to do with apparent deterioration of the quality of matter itself, that composes the physical body. Since you know now that all physical matter is constantly coming into formation, that it is formed by atoms and molecules so instantaneously, and that these atoms and molecules that give form to matter continually appear and disappear, so swiftly that the physical form that they compose appears permanent, then you must realize that there is no reason why physical forms should deteriorate as far as the atoms and molecules that compose them are concerned.

You are, however, left with the fact that physical matter, while appearing permanent for practicality's sake, nevertheless does exhibit disintegration in varying degrees. Since the cause lies not within that which composes matter in physical terms, then wherein does the cause originate?

Will it be possible, for example, to eliminate such causes to any astonishing degree, and therefore prolong mankind's individual existence within the physical field? This of course would lead to the further question: To what purpose would such elongation serve, in which direction would it tend? You are also aware that certain physical organisms seem to withstand this final dissolution, or hold it off for a greater period of your time. For this also there are reasons, which we will consider in due time.

We will begin by examining the cause behind the breaking up of necessary physical patterns so that survival within the world of matter is no longer possible. Now. Existence within the physical field depends upon a focus of psychic energy, in the subconscious construction of that physical organism without which material survival is not possible.

You may refer here to past sessions dealing with the mechanisms involved. Existence within <u>any</u> field of reality necessitates intensive focus within that field. It involves something like a sleight of hand trick, played by one part of the whole self upon another part. As an actor in a drama goes along with certain acts and gestures that make the play necessary, while at the same time he realizes that the play is a play, he must still focus his attention upon the lines spoken, and use the props available.

In much the same manner, existence within the physical universe involves the most intense self-hypnotic trance, where attention becomes riveted and focused along certain lines while other realities are of necessity closed out of one's perception and comprehension for a certain while.

No play can go on forever. Individual focus cannot be intensely maintained indefinitely. Neither can the vibrant, almost fanatical focus of the self within the limitations of one field continue indefinitely.

I will suggest your break.

(Break at 9:30. Jane was quite well dissociated, she said. Her delivery had become quite energetic. She said she felt as though she was listening to someone else speak, but could not retain what she heard, nor did she know what was coming next.

(She resumed in this newer more active way at 9:37.)

Energy cannot be imprisoned for long within one form. The individual whole self, by its very nature, will not restrain itself indefinitely to the particular set of necessities and perceptions necessary for survival within any one given field of reality.

It changes its focus, grows restive, adopts new forms in line with existence-necessities that exist within other fields. There is nothing inherent within the composition of matter as you conceive of matter to bring about a natural downfall, or natural inevitable disintegration.

Since matter does disintegrate, or seems to, you take it for granted that this dissolution is inherent within it, but this is not the case. The focus of energy that organizes the physical body weakens, strays; the trance state, strongest at what you call early adulthood, begins to lose its hold even as in childhood it has not yet attained its full depth.

The similarity here may not be easy for you to perceive, because of the diverse emotions with which you view childhood and old age. Nevertheless the child, to an unrealized degree, is free of the environmental necessities of his existence. Even while he molds and is molded by his environment, a part of his psyche is still uninvolved. His subconscious, on an uppermost personal level, is concerned with infantile fears of course.

Yet on a deeper level he still retains hold upon other existences, so much so that he even yearns subconsciously for those past realities, which mean safety, since their problems have already been solved. He is unbound emotionally and psychically by physical time, even while his physical body ticks with physical minutes.

By adulthood the trance, the intense focus, is most strongly upon him. It is after this period that the trance little by little weakens its hold. By the period you call old age the inner attention is already escaping. The strong focus of psychic energy needed to maintain the splendid physical image-organization is no longer given. The conscious ego with which you are familiar cries out its bewilderment, for has it not always sensed immortality?

But the outer ego as you know is that portion of the whole self that is given over to the maintenance of physical manipulations, and it perceives only through those physical equipments, those outer senses. It sees its dominion in jeopardy and rises up in arms. It, the ego, is that small portion of the whole self which the whole self has allowed to be completely, or almost completely, bewitched by the self-hypnotic trance. It is that portion which believes implicitly in the given specifications of the hypnotist, and as such it will be last to leave the trance.

I suggest your break.

(Break at 10:02. Jane was dissociated as usual. Again she put her glasses on during break, only to remove them as soon as break was over. She resumed in the

same manner at 10:12.)

During that period you refer to as old age, once again emotionally and psychologically the individual is less bound by physical time. He no longer, that is the whole self no longer, makes available sufficient psychic energy however for the maintenance of the physical organism.

This accounts for the disintegration. There is much more that must be said along these lines, and in time we will go into further discussion. However, the main focus of the whole self has already begun to stray, and the energies used in necessary pattern organization for the physical plane are already being returned, taken from their attention to physical matters, and becoming more attuned to the whole self from which they were originally delegated.

Now. A more complicated, involved, intricate physical organization, such as man, necessitates on the part of the whole self a tremendous outlay of energy for maintenance of the psychic- (hyphen) physical structural relationship.

There is not only a physical survival at stake, but also a highly delicate balance to be maintained. Since man is aware subconsciously of a heritage for which he ever seeks, and yet which for many reasons he cannot grasp while in the physical state, he must know and not know, and there is a strain here that no fish or bird or worm experiences. This subject also will be fully elaborated upon.

I also intend, and had intended this evening, to go into the causes behind the difference with which various physical individuals and species manage to make their physical forms endure, as far as continuity in your time is concerned. But this will have to wait.

As far as Philip is concerned, they are also waiting in Chicago. Only one man is for doing anything, and this man is not the man whom Philip suspects. He is not, this man is not, in as strong a position as the man whom Philip suspects.

("Can you give us a name?"

(It will be remembered that Philip, incidentally, is the entity name of John Bradley.)

He has brownish hair and glasses, and a slight mole on one of his cheeks. He is not even aware of his own feelings in the matter, but considers himself something of a father image as far as Philip is concerned, and feels somewhat betrayed.

Two other men up rather high in the organization make no difference. Philip will not achieve certain stated goals unless he takes strong measures, but certain unstated goals on his part will be met.

There was no distortion but some confusion as far as the childbirth and water bag episode was concerned. As is sometimes the case, there is a misinterpretation, which I will attempt to clear.

Ruburt's dream itself dealt with vessels. The correct interpretation was that of a vessel, the ship, in which the Tubbs woman toured; the breaking bag, winds unexpected during a day of travel during the cruise.

For his own reasons Ruburt did automatically receive the correct interpretation for himself. However, I have said that we must deal with words, breaking down symbols first of all.

Part of Ruburt's dream, you see, did have to do with a ship; and here with a second vessel and the water, you find that information was given on a subconscious level to Ruburt concerning his friend's journey. If you will reread that session dealing with the main dream you will see the connection. However, there was a deep sense of bewilderment upon Ruburt's part with his friend, who is a mother, since neither of them as adolescents considered motherhood as a part of their personal futures.

(True. Jane and Marie went through high school together. Both girls were interested in writing more than motherhood. Through the years I have heard Jane wonder aloud, many times, about the fact that Marie decided to have children, rather than place her emphasis on writing, as Jane chose to.

(For the data given by Seth on Jane's dreams, see the 87th, 93rd, 98th sessions, as well as this one.)

This sounds extremely involved. But while Ruburt did get the correct message, another topmost layer of his subconscious took childish revenge by changing the symbolism of vessel as ship, into vessel as womb, container of life. On this level, which also achieved its purpose, the water image was translated into a bag, or the bag of water that burst.

The Tubbs woman was to be given still another child, when no more were desired, by Ruburt in childish retaliation. Both literal interpretations were true, you see, but Ruburt took the opportunity (unconsciously of course) to use valid information, that of the trip, as a method of getting back for the imagined and unreasonable treachery of her friend.

You must understand that such occurrences are in no way unusual. If our dream interpretations appear complicated, it is because dreams are complicated, and we are viewing them from the entire group of levels in which they have meaning. To interpret them upon one level alone would be indeed simplicity in itself. But such interpretations lack any full validity, since they lack knowledge of that rich tapestry, the subconscious folds of which dreams are composed and in which they have their validity.

Nor have we yet discussed those dream elements which have sufficient energy propulsion to maintain existence in the plane upon which they were created. Such material, I am afraid, must wait, as you do not have the necessary background in fundamentals to give it comprehension.

Thoughts and dreams do indeed possess a validity and reality of which the subconscious has always been aware, and there is in some sense a responsibility here involved.

It is impossible to discuss fully in one session the particular topics which may arise, but they will be taken care of in time. An added little personal note, if I may be permitted.

("Yes.")

And at the danger of being considered a nag, despite Ruburt's insistence that the bedroom looks better the way it is, your bed should be moved so that the head is upon the wall that I specified months ago.

You should know by now that my homey little suggestions have worked out, rather amazingly to your view, for your benefit.

(Still quite amused, Jane pointed to a kind of barrier arrangement of bookcases that we had set up, to shield the table at which Jane writes from the rest of the room. She had said it gave her a sheltered feeling that she appeared to need.)

This arrangement, while rather a conglomeration, does help to serve a purpose that I mentioned last spring. Some sort of a <u>permanent</u> fixture might set you at rest Joseph, since you would be harassed no longer.

Now briefly before I close, and again on a personal note: the condition of Ruburt's wrist will take care of itself and vanish. He should faithfully continue the back exercises, which he usually resumes and then forgets. The turning around of the bed will alleviate a soreness of his ribs on the left side.

I will not go deeply into this, but there is an interruption of vibrations there, and a crosscurrent. It is too late to discuss this fully. Psychological time for <u>both</u> of you should be maintained, for psychic education and for the physical benefits achieved through momentary release from physical time. For Ruburt, salt is beneficial during some periods of the month, and not beneficial at other times.

("When are the good times?")

Most of all, the hand will clear up. It should not be babied in any way. The back exercises will help it also. The period after menstruation is good for salt. I will here close our session. I will be more than glad to hold a question and answer session, whenever you prefer.

(Again Jane laughed, and indicated the bookcase barrier.)

The permanent setup, whenever and if ever arranged, will here be most beneficial, and in ways that I will not now, because of the time, discuss. There is a connection with mental enclosures though it is a subconscious and psychological one.

Now, my most fond best wishes, and my congratulations to Ruburt, the old firekeeper, in connection with the furnace. He stokes his own flames fairly well also.

("Good night, Seth."

(End at 11:11. Jane was dissociated as usual. Many months ago Seth had suggested putting the head of our bed to the north, without going into much detail as to reasons. He referred above to a question and answer session because I had mentioned the idea to Jane earlier in the day. We plan to work up a list of questions. The furnace reference concerns Jane's manual operation today of the usually automatic gas heating plant in the house, after the thermostat developed some as yet undiagnosed trouble. In connection with the bed data, Jane has been mentioning for some time now that she has a vague soreness of the ribs on her left side.)

(The following psychological time notes and related material are taken from Jane's notebook:

(October 21, Wednesday: No results. Interruption.

(October 21, Wednesday: A small incident. In the morning I thought strongly of Venetian blinds, that I would like some on the kitchen windows. I visualized them, although we have none to fit and cannot afford to buy them now. This was a spontaneous, vivid wish on my part.

(Going down cellar at noon to check on the furnace, which had been acting up, I found three Venetian blinds, set out in plain sight where none had been the day before. I am sure of this because I was in the cellar yesterday also, because of the furnace trouble. Our landlord was with me, and told me that I could use the blinds, since someone in the house had obviously decided they no longer wanted to use these. So I took them.

(October 22, Thursday: Feeling of lightness, but no real results.

(October 23, Friday: Brief but clearly—saw brass door lock with chain.

(October 26, Monday: I saw a large scrapbook filled with pasted-in newspaper articles, then an envelope in the book. Half in and out of the envelope was an old snapshot of Rob and me.

(Also: I also had a very brief impression of standing up and off to the right of myself, only I was in the body of an older woman that I didn't recognize. It was not my body surely, but must larger, with a bony frame, dark hair, a more square face, and glasses.

(October 27, Tuesday: No results. Interrupted.)

(I would like to add here something that might be of interest.

(On October 21, last Wednesday during the session, a remark I made led Jane to recall that on the night before she had had a dream involving a washing machine that leaked and flooded; she told me that she was not sure whether it was the automatic washer in the cellar of the apartment house or not. I wrote it down as a matter of routine.

(Last night, the washing machine in the cellar sprang a leak, a pipe rupturing, and flooded the cellar. Our water was cold this morning. Inspecting the cellar after breakfast, Jane discovered a foot of water there, and of course immediately called the landlord.)

SESSION 100
OCTOBER 26, 1964 9 PM MONDAY AS SCHEDULED

(Our first session took place on December 2,1963, after a few preliminary and quite brief gropings during November 1963.

(This evening Jane and I had supper with Marian and Jimmy Spaziani. Jimmy is our landlord. We were back home from their place in Pine City, five miles distant, by 8:40. Jane had a "slight" feeling that someone would attend the session, yet she was not sure the feeling was legitimate. She could not say why she felt that way, being unable to determine at least yet when such feelings are legitimate. As it developed, we had no witnesses.

(The Spazianis know about the Seth material, of course. This evening Jimmy asked if Seth could help him locate the missing cover for the thermostat, which is located in the downstairs hall of the apartment house. Since the furnace has been misbehaving to some degree lately, he is quite anxious to find the cover, which he believes he misplaced some months ago, in order to keep people from tampering with the delicate thermostat mechanism. We promised to ask Seth's help.

(The Spazianis also related a mutual experience they underwent recently, involving Jimmy's deceased father. They asked for Seth's interpretation of this quite vivid happening. Since it is rather involved, I will insert an account of it in the session where Seth takes note of it. This page of the session will also be used for future reference.

(I have yet to resume a planned study of psychological time, but as noted previously I continue to have small experiences almost daily. Usually they take place just after we retire, when I am in a relaxed and drowsy state.

(Jane was not nervous before the session, and had no idea of the material to be dealt with. Once again she began without her glasses. Her eyes were dark, her voice

normal, her pacing regular. Her rate of delivery was somewhat slow, with pauses.)

Good evening.

("Good evening, Seth.")

This will be a fairly informal session, and I am indeed aware that it is our hundredth session.

(Now Jane smiled broadly as she paced about.)

As I told you many sessions ago, I tell you once again: Our sessions are but barely beginning. I did want to mention the fact that Ruburt is doing very well with the initial chapter that will introduce our material.

I also hope that you both realize how your abilities have begun to ripen, and how our sessions have led you into an increased awareness in all avenues of focus and activity. We are as I have told you going slowly, and yet the progression will be a steady one that rests upon disciplined sensitivities, without those possible dangers that can result when there is an overly intensive or fanatical attention to one line of focus, and a lack of disciplined understanding.

We are not attempting to enlighten the intuitions at the expense of the intellect. We are attempting to work in such a manner that added knowledge from the intuitional inner self is also made known to the intellect.

Ruburt, in writing his Introduction this afternoon, used a term which is an excellent one.

He spoke of the undiscovered man in terms of the whole self, whose abilities are so little known, and this is precisely what we are here attempting to bring to light: the vast areas within the self which have been left undiscovered and unknown.

We are attempting in these sessions to develop both of your abilities in many areas, while we still maintain a most necessary balance of development so that one part of you does not get top-heavy, and topple over. I say this partially in jest, nevertheless there is a definite reason for such a steady, balanced progression. From the beginning of our sessions you have been learning the method with which we will explore the whole self, but we have not plunged headlong into any foolhardy expeditions.

We are equipping ourselves with the necessary background and knowledge. This does not mean that a stiff restraint should be used on either of your parts. Ruburt now can allow himself some additional freedom. The ego however is a necessary protector, and its barriers should not be lowered by force or pressure. It must first feel secure and become flexible while still retaining the integrity of its nature.

(In line with the above material, it might be noted that Seth had cautioned Jane to go easy with her "ecstasy" experiments in the 54th session, May 18, 1964.

She had achieved this ecstatic state, as she described it, several times by that date. She had also been concerned as to how far to go along with this experience while she was alone in the house. Seth stated that he did not realize Jane would achieve this focusing of inner energy so early in her studies with psychological time, and furthermore said that it could have unpleasant effects if it was unwittingly directed toward someone else. Nor was this possibility "shades of witchcraft. Any energy can be used for almost any purpose."

(After that session Jane stopped trying to reach this state, and has not experienced it to this date.)

It is actually a most dependable measure, as far as its attitude and condition is concerned, in that if it becomes overly concerned the concern is caused by a fear for its own survival. And its survival is obviously a necessity for existences within the physical field, if it is to deal effectively with camouflage reality.

The ego however is not an afterthought disconnected from the whole self, and when the intellect becomes aware of data given to it by the intuitions or the inner self, it is then capable of informing the ego, which then changes its attitude accordingly. This way we are assured of the cooperation of the whole self, and avoid any possibility of splitting one self, one part of the self, against another.

This is one of the main reasons why I advised Ruburt at one time to discontinue certain particular experiments, which I believe he can now handle.

In the past few sessions we have begun discussing some material that will be the basis for many other sessions, and well may be considered as a general outline for another year's work.

There are many specifics to be filled in on past material, simply because at the time you did not have the background for fullest comprehension. This is why, for example, I did not go into the molecular structure of the dream world. It differs from the material world with which you are familiar in many instances, and yet the material dealing with the nature of matter was a necessary prerequisite.

I suggest your break.

(Break at 9:28. Jane was dissociated as usual. After a slow beginning she delivered the bulk of the above material at a steady, comfortable rate. She resumed in the same manner at 9:33.)

You will make many gains during the following year. You must realize that your own attitudes have changed for the better, and this is finding its reflection in your daily life.

I am tempted to give you some new material this evening, although I had decided to hold a brief session, merely because of certain rhythms and crests of activity, that ebb and flow. I had intended this to be an <u>in</u>formal, generalized discussion, and definitely mean to mention again that the general setup of this room is now excellent, regardless of what additions or so forth you might choose to make.

The division here in the room into spheres of more or less separated activities is of great benefit. The bed is again in the position that I suggested, I notice. An additional small detail that I make (it is a fact, but I also mention it to tug at Ruburt's leg a bit) you are both better off, actually, without the radiator being covered, because of the collection of dust particles.

I am myself rather dusty this evening, since I am very relaxed, and indeed come with a certain smug satisfaction in having survived one hundred sessions; and you may feel a smug satisfaction also.

It is no small feat. The maintenance of overall equilibrium has been excellently maintained, with nevertheless optimum results as far as the development of your psychic abilities. The early stages of our sessions were the crucial ones in that respect. Yet there is always the necessity of maintaining an overall balance of spontaneous inner freedom with disciplined attention. Both are required.

I am fully aware that your landlord and friend has asked me to locate his old thermostat cover.

(Jane now began to take some rather lengthy pauses as she delivered this more personal material. I did not feel that she was worrying about its accuracy particularly, merely that such information is evidently more carefully presented by Seth lest it arouse such outer ego fears; hence it "comes out" at a slower rate. *See page 88 for information on the thermostat cover.)*

He intended to place it on a shelf in the cellar, but instead shoved it with other metal objects, where it ended up on the floor of his Jeep, with or underneath some rubbish.

It was dumped either someplace on his own property or in a public dumping area, whichever area is by a hill, and it is still there. Not destroyed, but partially damaged. I trust this will satisfy him.

("Can you tell us when this happened?")

There were two occasions. One when he took the thermostat, threw it by mistake into the Jeep, where it lay forgotten and hidden; and another occasion three weeks later when it was dumped. I believe both occasions last spring, early in spring.

He had removed it and let it sit off, then in a hurry later he noticed it and intended to put it in the cellar so it would not be lost. He did not want to bother putting it back on then. That is all.

Upon another occasion however, we will discuss your relationship with him and his wife, and the rather bizarre circumstances that surround the man and his youngest son.

(Jimmy's youngest son, J.J., is six years old. The first time Jane and I saw the two of them, over four years ago, we were struck by the unmistakable similarity between them, not only in physical appearance but in manner. If anything this likeness between father and son has grown with the passing years, until now it is a standard topic of conversation when the Spazianis and the Buttses get together. As Jimmy's wife Marian said to us this evening at supper: "Well, there must be a few drops of my blood in J.J. somewhere..." Jimmy of course is Italian. Marian is Irish and French.

(Jimmy is obviously proud of this similarity between J.J. and himself. This evening he showed Jane and I a family photograph taken when he was about J.J.'s age, and of course the physical similarity was even then unmistakable. This old family photograph, incidentally, included Jimmy's father, whom Jane and I had not met, and who is referred to in the following session material.)

I am of the opinion that your psychological time experiences will shortly become more vivid, Joseph; and also Ruburt's. The inner spontaneity is coming back to Ruburt, after he tried too hard during the last of the summer.

The informal social engagements that you have been enjoying are most beneficial, and within reason should be continued. The change in the direction of the bed will also aid in psychological time experiments, when tried there.

(I might also add here that in the short time since the bed was changed in position, so that its head points north, Jane has lost the persistent soreness of the ribs on her left side. See the note on page 87.)

Most of all in this session, I merely intend to congratulate you both for your perseverance, and I hope you will congratulate me for mine. The experience on my part has been most enjoyable.

("Is this the first such experience for you?"

(Jane now smiled.)

I will never cease to enjoy the tricky note of your voice when you are trying to catch me off guard. And I have already upon one occasion answered your question. Also if you recall, I early told you that I considered myself an educator, and gave you some hint of my educational philosophy.

You may if you prefer ask me questions, or since I left this evening's session relatively open, you may take the occasion to rest and close early.

("Let's take a short break. I'll ask you one question and then we can close.")

As you prefer.

(Break at 10:05. Jane was dissociated as usual. I did remember Seth's previ-

ous answer concerning the top question above, and it was to the effect that his experience with Jane and I is his first, at least on this plane. I was hoping he would elaborate on the experience. I regret that I am unable to give the reader a page number for the previous answer. I am making my own version of an index for the material, and have not yet covered that particular session.

(Talking it over at break, we thought that at first we could ask Seth to comment briefly on a very vivid dream I had on Friday evening, October 10, 1964. Then I thought it better to ask for a comment on the vivid experience Marian and Jimmy Spaziani had, concerning Jimmy's deceased father, recently. We made that the official question. Marian had described the experience to Jane a few days previously, but at supper this evening the Spazianis went over it again for our benefit. And since it is still fresh in mind I will note an account of it below, although Seth does not discuss it in any detail in this session. This account can be used for future reference.

(The experience: Jimmy operates a supper club in Elmira, which Jane and I visit frequently. Some of my paintings hang there. Jimmy usually closes after 1 AM; by NY law he cannot serve drinks after 1 AM. On this particular evening during the first week in October 1964, he had some extra work to do. Shortly after 1 AM he took a waitress to her home in his Jeep. With him he also had some fresh tomatoes, and with these he stopped at his mother's home while on his way back to the club.

(His mother's home was dark, of course, and not wanting to disturb her merely to leave the tomatoes, Jimmy left them on the back porch. His father had died a few months ago, and while he stood in the backyard, a place he knew and had loved since childhood, Jimmy thought to himself: "Now, if I could see my father's apparition, then I could tell Ma, and she'd feel a lot better," or words to that effect. Jimmy waited beside the dark and quiet house, staring out into the backyard, but he saw and heard nothing unusual. He is well acquainted with the literature on psychic phenomena.

(He estimates that this little episode took place at about 1:20 AM. Getting back into his Jeep, he drove back to the club, a few blocks away. He arrived there at about 1:30. Just as he entered the kitchen the telephone rang. It was his wife Marian, in a state of high agitation. Marian then described to Jimmy a most vivid and startling experience she had just undergone.

(Being tired, she had gone to bed a little after midnight, instead of waiting up for Jimmy as she usually did. She fell asleep immediately. Unaware of the passage of time, she then was awakened out of a sound sleep, not dreaming either, by a thunderously loud voice which shouted to her or at her: "Good night!" Marian told us this was so real to her, so loud and unmistakable, filling the entire room as with thunder, that she sat bolt upright in bed, fully awake and quite frightened. She had not

been having a nightmare, or even dreaming. It so upset her that she immediately went to the telephone to call her husband. That is, she took a short while to collect herself, then put in the call. The voice was that of Jimmy's dead father; Marian said she recognized it unmistakably.

(Jimmy of course related to Marian his thoughts about seeing his father's apparition. Doing a little figuring concerning the time, he arrived at the conclusion that Marian had had her experience at approximately the same time he had been standing in back of his mother's house, thinking about his father. Jimmy speculated that perhaps Marian had received a message from his father, in answer to his wish, even though he, Jimmy, had seen or heard nothing.

(Jane now resumed in a somewhat faster and louder manner, at 10:14.)

I should have known better than to have expected a simple yes or no question.

Now. The experience involving your landlord, his wife and his deceased father, was a legitimate one; but one that I should like to use as an example for a rather long discussion of questions directly resulting from some recent sessions. That is, the question as to the survival of the physical image after the point of so-called death, and the lingering about the physical plane of <u>portions</u> of the personality.

I do not want to begin an involved discussion this evening. I will say that the mentioned experience did involve a communication of the father and his son, taking place through the cooperation of the wife. I will not continue with this this evening, though I will begin the discussion at our next session if you prefer.

("Okay.")

(Jane and I now wonder if it is coincidence that we were discussing this same matter a few days ago, and wondering when Seth would begin to cover the subject.)

The woman involved could gain immeasurably through the development of her own abilities. However she is fearful of them, fearing mostly a quite actual lack of discipline. The ego, her ego, is presently too concerned with other problems to allow her any such inner freedom. At the same time the difficulty experienced by her ego cries out for the sort of fulfillment that could be achieved through the development of these abilities.

Such a development would result in the strengthening of her ego, in added self-confidence. And her abilities are strong enough so that they <u>do</u> operate with some efficiency when her ego does let down its guard.

The man represents, now, an example of a personality highly endowed with intuition, and inner senses that are highly developed. There are some rather unusual circumstances here, in family and past family situations.

The boy, the youngest son, is also well endowed, with already efficient inner senses. The father did communicate. The living however can within certain limits make it difficult for those personalities who are finished with the physical field, because of a lack of understanding of circumstances. We shall discuss this later.

(This reference to J.J., Jimmy's youngest son, reminds Jane and me that Jimmy has often mentioned to us that as soon as he began to talk, J.J. started to tell his father about the "playmates" who kept him company through the day. At the time Jimmy was quite intrigued because the only playmates J.J. had were his older brothers and sisters, and these were not the people he was describing. Jimmy states that J.J. related such stories to him up until he was about four years old. J.J. is now six.)

We shall discuss this later. A personality, or personalized energy, is never destroyed; but transformation of form remains a <u>necessity</u> for continuation of <u>each</u> personality, and in some cases an emotional denial on the part of the living, of this fact, can lead to resistance in so far as the personality of those no longer connected with the physical field. This resistance must then be coped with, and results in difficulties that could be lessened through understanding on the part of those so-called living.

You must understand that to me now, mankind's insistence upon recognizing as alive only those personalities with which he deals in the physical field, is a most limiting concept.

I will go into this more deeply. I will also discuss your dream at another session. Since I attempt to use such incidences as examples to expand your comprehension along many lines, it is almost impossible to bring up a great variety of such incidences as they occur.

I will say however that the dream involved experience along many lines, and that the coat represents something far different than you imagine. And for this evening I will close, with again my most warm good wishes.

("Good night, Seth."

(End at 10:42. Jane was dissociated as usual. She was now quite tired, as she had been at the end of the last session.

(Almost as soon as she began delivering this last material, I regretted having asked her to do so, since I could see her visibly tire. Jane remarked upon the fact that after some sessions she feels less fatigued than before they began, while after others she is tired; at the same time she said that fatigue has no meaning for her while she is delivering the material.)

(The following material is taken from Jane's psychological time notebook:

(October 28, Wednesday: Feeling of lightness, etc. No real results.

(October 29, Thursday, 11:15-11:45 AM: Two fleeting effects. I had an

impression of Rob striding forward, saying something like, "I'll tell you what I think we [or you] should do with the wedding license."

(I then saw something, an item that I now forget. I heard someone say, "That's Lizzie's. She was the one who used to buy them." The voice was a mental one.

(Now, at 1:20 PM, Rob tells me: This morning a newly married couple visited him at the office. They were there from about 11:25 until noon. There was talk and kidding about marriage, etc. But he does not recall any specific mention of a marriage license as such.)

(I have resumed the study of psychological time on a regular basis, and the following material is from my notebook:

(October 27, Tuesday, 11:45: Upon retiring, I had a definite and durable feeling of stretching in my legs, as though a force was pulling at my feet, as though with hands. At the same time, my familiar old thrilling sensation flooded over me quite strongly.

(It may be coincidence, but upon checking my back records I find that the last psychological time experiment I had listed, for September 9, was <u>identical</u> to the one above. See my notes on this on page 1, the 86th session.

(October 28, Wednesday, 5:30 PM: Today I had been working on a painting of apples. Trying psy-time, I saw apples twice. The first time they were in shades of gray and violet, and I saw small sections of them from a close-up position, as a stem detail, etc. The second time, I again saw the apples in sections, but this time in full color. I could discern easily the grain of the board, the brush strokes in the paint, etc.

(In between these two sightings I saw a middle-aged man in rolled-up white shirt sleeves, sitting at a kitchen-type table and staring to my right. His profile was to me. He had a definite cauliflower ear. His complexion was ruddy, his hair had a reddish tinge. He did not move. He reminded me somewhat of Bill Macdonnel's father, but it was not him. I also recall a small pencil drawing Bill has done of his father in a similar position, but from a full-face angle.)

SESSION 101
OCTOBER 28, 1964 9 PM WEDNESDAY AS SCHEDULED

(Jane slept from 8 to 8:30 this evening, and upon arising felt quite uneasy. She does not like to get up when it's dark out, she said. Actually she slept but the last few minutes of the allotted time. She decided that after this she'll nap sometime during daylight hours on session days.

(She had no idea of the material for the session as the time for it approached.

She began dictation in a normal voice, with some pauses, and again without her glasses. Her eyes were dark as usual, her pacing average.

Good evening.

("Good evening, Seth.")

We will be concerned with many various subjects this evening.

I will indeed use an explanation of a particular instance to add to your general knowledge. I have told you that the communication between your landlord's father and himself was a valid one, and I believe that other communications have taken place. In at least some of these, as in this instance, the man's wife acted as a relay station.

(See the account of the experience on pages 93-94.)

The father is mainly finished with the physical field. He is on what you may call a midplane of existence. Personalities in such transition are thereby allowed to acclimate themselves in a period of neutrality and relative passivity.

They exist in actuality, but not in a form with which ordinarily you would be familiar. The neutrality is protective, a duration within the spacious present, where nevertheless there is a certain acceleration in terms of value fulfillment.

(See the 41st session for Seth's first long dissertation on the spacious present. This was delivered April 6. The 44th session includes much on the basic laws of the inner universe also, as do the other sessions received during this period. As this material continues to expand it becomes more difficult to pinpoint references on a subject to a given few pages.)

The relative, neutral passivity is attained as various portions of the whole self once more collect together. The acceleration, which is mental, begins as those divergent portions of the whole self interact. This is an electromagnetic sequence or action that will eventually help provide the impetus for projection of the whole self into another field of actuality, as the rate of acceleration increases and becomes more unified.

At this point of course the self moves beyond or through the particular midplane involved. The term itself merely applies to a reference point duration that has meaning only in so far as it is related to a specific personality that is in a transitional frame between dimensional actualities.

The personality itself therefore, as a mental action, is responsible for the point or midplane, for without the personality or mental act, this particular reference point or midplane would have no meaning.

You will need perhaps to reread your material on the spacious present, since our explanation here will be necessarily in terms of sequence of events, when as you know in the spacious present events are actually simultaneous. When the personality withdraws itself from the physical image therefore, in a sort of slow motion of actual simultaneous happenings, this is what occurs.

The physical image does not immediately disappear, for a number of reasons. The personality, through the inner self, has indeed created or constructed the physical form, but the very material from which it was constructed also contains its peculiar consciousness, as you know.

This consciousness of organs, atoms and molecules, cells and other components, is left undiminished with whatever degree of consciousness and vitality they originally possessed, not enough of course to hold form or organization to any degree. However, the image is also maintained partially by those others who view it. An explanation for this you will find in our discussion of the nature of matter.

There is much involved here that a reading of past sessions on matter will make plain. You realize of course that the atoms and molecules within the physical image continually change during existence on the physical field. Openings, so to speak, for the influx of new material into the physical form, are made possible by the inner self. When it abdicates it closes up the possibility of this repairing type of molecular action.

I suggest your break.

(Break at 9:30. Jane was dissociated as usual. She felt much better now that the session was under way. Again with her glasses off, she resumed in the same deliberate manner at 9:37.)

Remembering again your material of the spacious present, a portion of personality retention however still surrounds those physical reference points with which the personality was familiar.

In actuality this retention is mental, a mental attraction to other mental actions or personalities; but this attraction, while mental, still projects in certain fashions into the physical field. The attractions weaken, but during their duration, when certain conditions are met, communication can take place.

There is usually strain involved here, since points of reference must be changed. The personality is already immersed in a dimensional transformation; when the emotional need of those within the physical plane call out for communication, they add to the pull or force of the attraction still present, binding portions of the personality to the physical field, and <u>can</u> add to the resistance encountered by personalities in transformation.

This may cause bewilderment and disorientation to such a transforming personality. Later, so to speak, when entrance into another and higher is achieved, then such a higher-dimensioned personality may without difficulties of this sort communicate with your field.

By this time he can change his reference points, although his experience is so much more vivid, and so much fuller proportioned, that to him the experience could be likened to going down into a small cramped tunnel.

This is one of the difficulties with our sessions, in that you cannot take in concepts directly. That is, you cannot experience them directly, and I must cut them down, dimensionally speaking, in order that you can perceive them in your more limited dimension.

Ruburt, incidentally, is to be congratulated, as he is just beginning to read books on physics, in order to intellectually keep up with the material as I give it. Never having read such books before, he was astounded to discover that I knew what he did not. He should be used to this by now.

(Jane delivered the above paragraph with a smile. It is true that she, and I to a lesser extent, have begun to read up on our physics. Both of us have largely neglected the subject since school days, although of course we came across references to it in other reading, since the subject plays such an important part in everyday life now. Jane has been quite surprised to find many references in these books that tally with what Seth has said. Many other points in the books have served as jumping-off points for Seth's material, also.)

In his reading he came across a statement to the effect that imaginary two-dimensional people could not comprehend a three-dimensional system. You are obviously in the physical system, and according to your terms fourth dimensional. Your dream world, of which I have spoken, could be compared to a third-dimensional universe. However, the dimensions of which physics speaks are, again, the result of your own point of reference, and of the system in which you are enclosed.

A fifth-dimensional universe does not have to possess all the attributes of the previous four, for example. Once you progress beyond a fourth-dimensional universe, then freedoms are attained which will make the attributes of previous dimensions unnecessary.

This will be the direction toward which physics must travel in the future.

Before I mention briefly the fifth dimension of which we have already spoken, many sessions ago, I suggest your break.

(Break at 10:02. Jane was dissociated as usual. See the 12th and 16th sessions, among others, for material on the fifth dimension.

(Again with her glasses off, Jane resumed in a faster and more animated manner at 10:10.)

Beyond a certain point freedoms are attained. There are many, literally numberless, other dimensions which physicists cannot imagine because of the limitations of your system.

Width, height, length have no meaning in dimensions that do not have existence in space as you know it. Time as a reference point has no meaning in a dimension that has its existence wholly within the spacious present.

Such a reference point does not exist there. I have told you many times that planes or fields, or dimensions of activity, whatever you prefer to call them, move through each other often, and do not collide. If their reference points were the same, they would collide.

I have told you also, long ago, that what appears as weight or mass on one plane may appear as something else entirely upon another. And this long before Ruburt picked up his book on physics.

I have told you that a plane was not necessarily a location in space, but a field of mental vitality. The material that I have given you on the fifth dimension will here prove invaluable. I have told you that it is space, since this was the beginning of our discussions. During our earliest session I used the term space for simplicity's part for your sakes, while still explaining most carefully that this fifth-dimensional space was far different than what you consider space to be.

(I presume here that by "earliest session" Seth refers to his first material on the fifth dimension, given in the 12th session. Space as a fifth dimension was however also referred to in the first session. See Volume 1, page 8. This first session material was given to us through Frank Watts, however. Frank Watts is a fragment of Seth's entity. Seth stated recently that the Seth material begins when he announced his presence to us by name, and this would be in the 4th session. See the 85th session, Volume 2, page 336, for Seth's statement concerning the Frank Watts material.)

The imaginary framework that I set up for you is an excellent one, a particularly good model for the actuality. And even such a model as I carefully described could not be constructed physically within your particular system, since it contains degrees of mobility that your system has no room for.

(Jane smiled.)

I would suggest Joseph, that when you find the time, or if you can coerce Ruburt into doing it for you, insert here for any reader's convenience a copy of the early material, in which I set up the imagined structure of mazes.

You can see that in that fifth-dimensional existence there can be no constants as far as reference points are concerned, since by the very nature of the dimension, camouflages are adopted to fit numberless other dimensions as the structure itself continually changes.

A rereading of the material will make this plain, but there are still other dimensions based upon entirely different systems. And between these there can be no communication. They are strange to me.

When I say there can be no communication, I speak of course from my own points of reference. There are even other physical dimensions which do not appear physical to you, your antimatter being one. But there are many others. Some dimensions, or planes or fields, contain others, and some are sufficient unto themselves, with others dependent upon it, as for example <u>your</u> fifth dimension as I have explained it.

But there are dimensions that can never be understood by any algebra, whose basis rests upon emotional equations that can never be solved, or even approached from your system. These emotional equations however form effects that oftentimes react within your system. And your own emotional explosions <u>appear transformed into mass</u> within one such system.

I will continue for a short few moments and then end the session, or if your hands are tired you may take a break.

("Okay, I'll take the break."

(Break at 10:35. Jane was fully dissociated—far-out as she puts it. "Somebody found a way to get a lot more out of me than I knew I had in me," she laughed. She had been going at a good pace and my writing hand was nearly cramped.

(She resumed in the same brisk manner, again without her glasses, at 10:40.)

I will not keep you much longer.

We will indeed before too long delve into the means by which these sessions are made possible, and the reasons also for Ruburt's fatigue at the end of <u>some</u> of the sessions, and his exuberance at the end of others.

There are chemical as well as psychic reasons for these effects, and at some times of course he operates more efficiently than others. During sessions there is a constant translation of energy from one dimension-plane to another, and on his part a change of reference points, allowing for such translations to occur.

The psychic organism is much better equipped to handle such transformations and translations than is the physical organism, and there are also influences, quite natural, from surrounding psychic environments within your system that can act as resistances.

These resistances of course require added energy on Ruburt's part. They do not affect me. We will go specifically into these matters at a later date.

I will say merely that when during these sessions Ruburt is open, so to speak, to other reference points both within and without your system, there is a vulnerability to other influences. He has spontaneously set up automatic resistances that block such influences, or open channels through which their effects may enter your system.

This takes energy, and on those occasions when there is much activity of this sort, he will be seen to become fatigued. The resistance is obviously necessary, however. It is this same sort of resistance, on a much simpler level, that he uses to block me whenever his ego becomes overly concerned.

Now I will indeed close our session. It has been a most fruitful one, and I feel quite close to both of you this evening.

(End at 10:53. Jane was fully dissociated again, and ended the session with a smile. She was tired, but not so much as at the end of the last session.

(From Jane's psychological time notebook:

(October 30, 11:30-12 noon, Friday: Immediately upon lying down I felt strongly that I would hear by mail this weekend, today or tomorrow, about a sale of the ESP book to Fell, I believe, with a contract. It could have referred to a sale of a short story I suppose, but did think it meant the book. I had emotional high spirits at the time of the experience, as if I'd already heard.

(The whole half- hour was a study in psychological sensation. My left foot, first, began to feel airborne, ready to disappear. I wiggled my toes to check its presence. The feeling went partially up my left side. Slight but definite feeling of cavity where chest is. Breathed through nostrils deeply, handkerchief over closed eyes. Suddenly intensity of all sensations deepened. I felt as though I could rise up. Area behind eyelids became whitish, seemed to expand. Tingling sensation.)

(From my psychological time notebook:

(October 29, Thursday, 5:30 PM: I saw a close-up of a child's baby face, from the 3/4 front facing to my right. Pink cheeks, parted lips. This was followed by traces of my thrilling sensation. [Also, while painting this afternoon I had felt the same sensation in stronger form.]

(Then my feet [in shoes as I lay on the bed] lying about six inches apart, felt as though they were connected to each other by a bridge or rope of flesh. This was a definite pull, with several minutes' duration. The sensation was quite strong. At the same time my heels ached and stung.

(At one time all of my limbs felt as though they wanted to lift up out of themselves. The left arm especially felt as though it was stiff, and hinged at the shoulder so that it would lift up stiffly like a lever.

(October 30, Friday, 8:10 PM: A variety of effects. Many instances of my sensation. Once this was very strong when my hands felt crossed upon my waist, although actually they lay by my sides. My feet felt jammed together at the heels quite forcibly, and at one time my hands felt enlarged. Several voices. Once a middle-aged man with graying hair said to a young woman: "You're my oldest daughter. I have great faith in you." I forgot other instances before arising.

(October 31, Saturday, 8 PM: Again a variety of effects. Shortly after I lay down my sensation came over me from the feet to the head. Minutes later it came from the head down to the feet. At one time my hands felt very large, and several feet

[3] apart, though in actuality they lay at my sides. Once my hands and feet felt as though they would rise up. I had snatches of voices and vague pictures. This was rather a steady progression of experiences.)

SESSION 102
NOVEMBER 1, 1964 11:05 PM SUNDAY UNSCHEDULED

(Perhaps the affairs of this evening were set in motion several days ago, when Jane and I voiced the thought that we might try an ESP experiment of some kind on Sunday night. This, of course, provided we were alone.

(Through last week, also, Jane had enjoyed a burst of painting activity after a rather long time away from it. She enjoyed herself doing these pictures very much, and we discussed them at length. She sensed a conflict between what she wanted to portray, and her limited technical abilities in getting the actual images on canvas. I thought her work was better than ever, surprisingly so, and that her ideas were good and her extremely personal handling of them in paint very fresh. Jane persisted in thinking of her paintings as childish.

(We had company after supper. Before this couple left, Bill Macdonnel dropped in. Jane, Bill and I were eventually left alone, and since Bill is also an artist, the three of us joined a rather animated discussion of Jane's latest work. It lasted for perhaps an hour.

(Here, I would like to call attention to my dream of September 18, 1964. See page 47. Seth has discussed this dream in considerable detail, without saying much about the opening sequence of the dream. In this opening sequence, Jane, Bill, the members of the Potter family, and myself, were gathered in a living room. I was pulling out some of Jane's drawings and paintings and showing them to Bill, and Jane, Bill and I were animatedly discussed them. Particularly did we express surprise over their high quality. It then struck me this evening that the discussion between Jane, Bill and I, over Jane's new work, bore some rather remarkable parallels to that opening dream sequence, and I wondered whether that portion of the dream could have been clairvoyant. Seth may comment on this in the next scheduled session. The main difference between the dream and "reality", of course, is that the Potter family was not present this evening.

(Since it was getting late, any ESP experimentation this evening seemed improbable. We did discuss the feasibility of trying a "seance" of some kind, without doing anything about it. We were by now rather tired. We discussed the apparition Bill had seen in the bath doorway, described in the 68th session. This in turn led to Bill's telling of some very vivid and upsetting dreams he had been having in recent

days; in these dreams his bedroom had seemed to be peopled by apparitions or strangers, he said, entirely unfamiliar to him. From the recent material we had received on the dream world, I said it sounded as though Bill was in contact with other parts of his inner or whole self.

(It will be recalled that at various times Seth has said that Bill Macdonnel has much natural psychic ability, and that it is largely untrained. Seth stated that Bill was gifted in many lines of psychic ability, among them the perception of apparitions. Seth also stated that Jane and I did not see as much as we might because we were both too "fussy" about what we would allow ourselves to see.

(Now as the discussion progressed the three of us sat in the living room around our coffee table, staring into the open bath door and exchanging half-joking remarks about apparitions. Bill then announced that he sensed the "feeling of a form" within the doorway, in the same manner detailed in the 68th session, except not to that degree. Jane and I could see nothing, as before.

(I would like to say here that recently Jane had remarked, several times, that she would feel better if she herself could see some physical evidence of psychic phenomena. She had not seen the apparition, nor of course had I, and she had not been able to see the change in her features, again described in the 68th session. Even though I reminded her that she was the prime mover in the sessions, she still expressed the wish to "see something" that would "prove" to her that the material was legitimate. We both remembered of course that long ago Seth had said in no uncertain terms that he was not in favor of demonstrations for demonstrations' sake, and that he would not perform on call.

(Since the subject had been under discussion for some time by now, so that a certain mood or feeling might be said to have been engendered, Jane remarked that she could feel Seth "buzzing around." This announcement did not mean much to us, and we paid little attention. Instead we tried to discern the form Bill said he could see in the doorway. We did not succeed.

(I then became aware, at 11:00 PM, that Jane had fallen silent. She sat on the divan, her legs drawn up beneath her, across the coffee table from me. Her expression was smiling but fixed. She stared at me. I saw that her eyes had grown very dark beneath the lower lids, a rather peculiar manifestation that cleared up shortly after she began dictation. Jane held a cigarette but seemed to be unaware of it. She had taken her glasses off.

(I had an impulse to try to get back to my studio to get some paper and a pen; this was followed by another impulse—to forget about notes for a change, even though Jane was obviously about ready to give a session. I followed the latter course, since she seemed unconcerned about whether notes would be taken. Bill and I waited. Jane began dictation in a rather strong voice that was pitched somewhat lower

than normal, and maintained it for the whole of the session. She remained seated throughout. As soon as she began to speak she closed her eyes, and to my continuing surprise she kept her eyes closed throughout the session, except for one brief instant that shall be mentioned later. There followed a rather strange procedure, for when Jane addressed either Bill or myself she kept her eyes closed but faced the pertinent one, and gestured in the correct direction also. After a while one tended to forget that her eyes were closed, since there was no evidence of confusion on her part. In addition, the closed eyes played a part in an interesting little development that will also be mentioned later.

(As soon as the session was over I began notes on it, and covered the range of material given. Since what follows is reconstructed from memory it is to some extent out of chronological order. I found that I could write out rather easily an abridged version of the material Seth covered, and did not miss any of the major points. Undoubtedly I missed some minor asides, and changed phrasing and punctuation. Yet I feel that what follows is a good account.)

For once Joseph will not have to take notes.

I have been with you this evening for some time, as you no doubt knew. Notes are not particularly necessary to what I have to say; and Joseph, you should enjoy the rest.

I am not, as you know, particularly in favor of physical effects, but since Ruburt is such a well-known doubter I will go along. We will have to have our physical effects, effects that even <u>he</u> will not be able to deny.

What will be necessary is that, at least in the beginning, the <u>three</u> of you will be necessary for this to be possible. I hereby suggest that the three of you attend a session at least once every two weeks. In the beginning three will be necessary. Later two may be sufficient. And with the three of you we will need dedication and discipline.

Joseph is committed to these sessions. He believes. Ruburt is a doubter, from way back. He is intellectually intrigued but he is not yet emotionally committed. You, Joseph, make these sessions possible. Without you Ruburt would not let me come through. Without you Ruburt would never have held a single session.

Ruburt has been in search of discipline. He was always in search of the discipline he lacked. His intuitions were always very strong. Well, now he has his discipline, but it has been overdone. It has come to hamper the very strong intuitions, and it must be lessened. Spontaneity, inner spontaneity must be restored. He is now doing better with his psychological time experiments, and he must let this spontaneity expand into other aspects of his life. Ruburt must be <u>fully committed</u> to these sessions for them to accelerate in scope.

If he wants physical effects he shall <u>have</u> his physical effects. But I repeat, three at this time are necessary.

You, Joseph, had the discipline always. You were afraid to trust your intuitions, and the circumstances of your early life encouraged this fear. But you have now learned to trust yourself and have expanded accordingly. You are now free, and you will continue to expand your abilities, in your painting and other aspects of your life.

Mark, you need discipline, but it is discipline that you will acquire in living. And here let me say that Ruburt's strong feelings are correct. Ruburt knows what he knows. You should move into your gallery as soon as possible. You will be asked to give shows of your paintings by two people whom you should refuse; you will be asked to give shows by other people, whose invitations you should accept. It will be up to you to use your inner knowledge, your intuitions, in determining which persons to refuse and which to accept.

(It will be remembered that Mark is Bill Macdonnel's entity name. Bill is now in the process of transforming a downtown store into a combination art gallery and living quarters.

(As Jane delivered the above material in quite an animated fashion, Bill picked up a piece of paper lying on the coffee table, and Jane's pen. He made a quick sketch on the back of the already used paper and passed it to me. I saw that he had roughed out Jane's features, stressing her closed eyes. I also saw that he had drawn, upon the closed upper eyelid, an iris, thus superimposing upon Jane's closed eye an open one. I nodded to Bill to show that I understood that he was seeing an eye or eyes upon Jane's closed lids.)

Also, Mark, you should not be afraid of your dreams. They do not mean what you think they mean. They are, briefly, part of your whole self. You have been in contact with other parts of yourself for a long time. You have learned more in the last year than you learned in the last fifteen. If you want to learn more about your dreams and what they really mean, I will discuss them in a regular session. But above all you should move into your own place.

(Telling us about his recent dream and apparition experiences, Bill had mentioned that at times when his eyes were closed he was aware of the feeling of a white light, or glow, that varied in intensity at different times. Jane was interested in this description because it tallied with an effect she attains quite often in psychological time experiments—this feeling of a light within, even though the eyelids are squeezed tightly shut. At times Jane has seen images after the appearance of this inner light, but Bill has seen only the light. I have experienced this type of inner glow on a few isolated occasions, but have seen few images in this manner.)

If it is physical effects you want then I will go along. After all, I must please Ruburt to some extent, since without him I could not speak. The reason that his paintings upset him is that they reflect his inner knowledge, of which he is well aware. It is true that his poetry does also, and over the years he has come to take this for granted. But the paintings, especially the late ones which are so much improved over his earlier efforts, are new to him. And since he is still a doubter of the material, he sees this inner knowledge in a new light, and is upset.

(Jane smiled broadly, gesturing as she sat upon the divan.)

We have all known each other in the past. We have been more closely connected than you can imagine, and have had more experience in different realms than you can now know. I cannot at this time make it all clear to you. But there will be reunions and reminiscences, mark my words.

And there will be physical effects if the three of you want them, but you must meet faithfully, and in a committed way. There will then be effects that even the greatest doubter cannot deny.

Nor is it any accident that those certain people come to the sessions, the ones who did come, just as it is no accident that Philip's mother is also a bedridden arthritic, just as Ruburt's mother is.

I have been with you while you stared into the doorway. Indeed I am with you more than you know, and I am never really far from you.

Ruburt's psychological time experience recently was correct, in that he will soon hear about a sale. I cannot tell you more about this now.

(See Jane's psychological time experience of October 30, page 102.)

As for a party, I don't see why not. Joseph does not have his house, but I think that I am perfectly capable of producing as good effects here as I promised you at the housewarming.

The physical side of these sessions is accepted by Joseph. He knows what he sees, but perhaps we can aid in our Ruburt's commitment. He demands proof of the validity of this material, his psychological time experiences notwithstanding. He demands physical effects and then freezes up. He questions everything that happens in the sessions, and sometimes I think he believes none of it.

But I will do my best, and it will be considerable. I will not parade any so-called effects for you tonight, however. I demand discipline and respect at my sessions, no matter what I said about Ruburt and discipline earlier. But we will have our effects, never fear.

And now, my best wishes and good night.

(I did not think to note the time the session ended, but certainly it was within half an hour. Jane said Seth knocked her out quickly, and that it was her deepest trance except for the self-induced one of January 10, 1964. See Volume 1, page 83.

Yet as usual she could hear herself speaking, although she could not follow the sense of what she was saying, nor did she try to.

(Jane spoke with her eyes closed throughout except for one instance. Her cigarette had burned very short; stabbing her hand toward an ash tray on the coffee table, she struck it a glancing blow on the rim and knocked it aside. Her eyes popped open for an instant.

(Bill Macdonnel explained that the superimposed eyes he saw upon Jane's closed lids had no pupils, but resembled instead eyes clouded by cataracts. He also said that whenever Jane spoke to me and gestured in my direction, the eye effect followed, yet I noticed nothing unusual in Jane's features. For Bill this effect began when Seth first mentioned him in the session.

(Philip, of course, is the entity name for John Bradley, of Williamsport, PA, who has witnessed several sessions.

(Seth mentioned the physical effects often throughout the session, hence my repetition of this. He did not say anything, however, about what <u>*kind*</u> *of effects he would produce. Jane spoke at a somewhat faster rate than usual, although had I been taking notes I believe I could have kept up for the most part.)*

(Bill's first sketch of the effect he saw on Jane's closed eyes during the session.)

(Bill's second sketch. "Exterior eye," he wrote. "Her eyes are closed. White iris.")

(After the session Bill finished for Jane and me the "press-release" kind of account about his gallery that he'd worked on while we talked before the session. This can be used for radio and newspaper publicity. He signs his paintings by his middle name, Cameron. Bill wrote:

(Elmira artist opens gallery to promote abstract and expressionistic art in the Elmira-Corning-Binghamton, New York area.

(Cameron Macdonnel will hold a grand opening of the Cameron Studio Gallery at 344 East Water Street on Sunday, November 8.

(The purpose of the gallery is to provide an outlet for painters, sculptors, and ceramacists to bring their work before the community. These artists will be welcome to arrange for one-and-two-man showings.Group shows will also be featured in the future. Interested area artists can contact Mr. Macdonnel between 1:00 and 3:00PM on Saturdays and Sundays at the gallery.

(The Grand Opening exhibition will consist of a two-man show of sculpture by Harold Spaulding and Walter Buhr, two well-known Binghamton-area artists. Along with this Mr. Macdonnel will have on display some of his oils, watercolors, and graphics. Walter Buhr has had his work shown in numerous galleries in New York State as well as in Pennsylvania. He is starting a sculpture class as well as working at his own sculpturing. The media he works in range from terra cotta to bronze to wood. Harold Spaulding has exhibited at the Roberson Gallery in Binghamton, and has participated in a two-man show at Two Rivers Gallery in that city. He has had a one-man show at I.B.M. in Owego, New York. His art has also been exhibited at Arnot Art Gallery in Elmira in group shows, and in Scranton, Pennsylvania.

(Cameron Macdonnel is a graduate of the State University College of Education at Buffalo, New York, where he received his Bachelor of Arts degree. He has had his work exhibited in many galleries in Buffalo, including A.M.A.'s Gallery, J.N.'s Gallery, Encores Gallery, and Carl Briedmier's Gallery. His work received favorable reviews in both the Buffalo Evening News by Trevor Thomas [well-known English art critic], and in the Buffalo Sun Bulletin by Larry Griffis.

(Mr. Macdonnel teaches art in grades 1-9 at Painted Post Junior High School.)

(From Jane's psychological time notebook:

(November 2, Monday, 11:30 AM: Feeling of vibration, body and bed, maybe three minutes duration. Uneven in sensation, never violent. Also sensation of circular motion inside closed eyelids. Light feeling.

(Later, resting on bed after work with eyes closed, saw a quick but rather violent vision of a round, very bright daylight-type light. But this light seemed to be clearer than daylight, and to be almost like a mirror that was reflecting another

mirror. At the same time it spun around, or else the dark area around it spun around, with a sudden violence that actually made me dizzy. Yet the whole thing was incredibly brief.)

(From my psychological time notebook:

(November 1, Sunday, 12:30 AM: Upon retiring after the unscheduled session, I saw a whole host of football players in activities connected with the game. [Had watched football on TV that afternoon.] This lasted for several minutes. I also saw full-face heads, usually in sections, as half a face, etc., coming closer to me, usually with the lips moving soundlessly. As I saw the first head my sensation swept over me quite strongly, and continued for some little while.

(November 2, Monday, 5 PM: Varied sensations upon lying down for a nap. My legs felt as though the bed was bent downward beneath them. Then chest felt quite strongly as though it was scooped out on the left side. This was very definite. My hands grew thick and fat upon the backs, as though they would lift out of themselves. I saw many varied female heads, rather vague, mostly facing to my right. I had my sensation and heard vague voices.)

SESSION 103
NOVEMBER 2, 1964 9 PM MONDAY AS SCHEDULED

(By 8:55 PM Jane had no idea of the material for the session tonight, nor was she nervous.

(She began dictation on time in a voice somewhat stronger than usual; it became almost loud at times. She spoke at a rather slow rate however, with some pauses. Again she spoke without her glasses. Her eyes were dark, her pacing regular.)

Good evening.

("Good evening, Seth.")

Our session may be somewhat briefer this evening, to make up for the unscheduled one.

It is of course true that within our rather rigid schedule we miss some excellent occasions for sessions, as far as Ruburt is concerned. That is, we miss instances when his abilities are at high peak. Yet overall we balance out fairly well. And particularly in the beginning such regularity is important.

When a particular situation arises, or when his abilities are unusually attuned, we have in the past held unscheduled sessions, and I have always attempted to compensate by cutting the next one short, or cutting it out entirely.

(Offhand, I do not recall any instance where Seth has eliminated a session

entirely. But I can think of many instances where a succeeding session has been cut short in compensation.)

For reasons of convenience on your part, completely unscheduled sessions would not be practical. With your permission, we may attempt to take better advantage of such peaks of activity in the future, but if and when we do we will still maintain a general practice of not holding more than two sessions a week.

At some still rather far date, the present rigidity of our schedule may give way to a more spontaneous framework. Such a future framework, and a method whereby we take fuller advantage of high peaks would also tend to cut down distortions. This would obviously be most valuable.

This kind of procedure, while appearing less disciplined, would in actuality require added discipline, since this would be necessary to avoid the imbalance of either too many or too few sessions.

If the procedure were attempted prematurely it would also tend to place an added strain upon you both, particularly upon Ruburt, who would have to make the decision in the last analysis.

Also here a word concerning wine, in connection with sessions.

It is a fact that alcohol is a depressant, that conscious inhibitions become lessened with indulgence of varying degrees. Ruburt has not indulged to any degree. Since, however, he has noticed that occasionally, without touching a drop of wine during a given session, he nevertheless feels as if he had been indulging, so I would like to make a brief explanation.

(Jane smiled as she paced about the room. I had heard her mention often that after a session she would feel as though she had drank a little too much. She is rather in the habit of sipping at something during sessions, since she uses her voice constantly. If she uses wine it is seldom more than a glass or two. Most often she favors milk or iced coffee.)

It is quite simple. At certain stages a state of dissociation is achieved with the indulgence of alcohol. This stage is reached by Ruburt without such indulgence, and it is this state that he recognizes.

Now. Conceivably at times during a social evening several glasses of wine, under certain conditions bringing him quite naturally to the same sort of state that he goes through and passes beyond in these sessions, could lead him to misinterpret his data, or get his signals crossed.

There is little real danger of this, but a state of dissociation is a state of dissociation, and this must be kept in mind. There is however a distinction here which he is already beginning to recognize. It is simply that he becomes vulnerable, or more sensitive, to inner data in a dissociated state, regardless of what causes the state to come about.

This was true long before the Seth sessions ever began, and it is generally true. In such a state, regardless of its cause, any individual is more sensitive to inner data. I am making this plain, naturally, for your own benefit.

There is little danger here except under the most unusual circumstances, merely an inconvenience or a feeling of disagreeability on your parts. Actually there is only a certain rather well-defined period within which the dissociation is conducive to our sessions. That is, while Ruburt drinks socially to some quite limited extent really, the fine balance of dissociation that allows our sessions to begin would not be possible, if for example our Ruburt drank more some evening than good sense would ordinarily permit.

He has wondered about this. However, he does not have to worry ordinarily about beginning a session on the spur of the moment under the influence of too much drink. If he had truly <u>that</u> much, he simply would not be capable of a session, even if I were idiotic enough to agree to one. And I assure you that I would not be.

I must tell you however, that a session begun through mistake, so to speak, after a few drinks, would not suffer as far as the <u>material</u> itself were concerned. I mention the affair in general merely so that you can be alert to the possibilities, and to aid Ruburt in the development of his inner distinctions.

In any state of dissociation <u>any</u> individual is more sensitive to inner data. This sensitivity varies in accordance to the ability of the individual in general in this line, which is why I make the point. In an intimate gathering of close friends, if a few glasses of wine are drunk, and if Ruburt happens to then be increasingly aware of inner data, there is not anything out of the way in holding a session, if this happens only occasionally. Indeed a <u>judicious</u> (underline judicious) use of wine is somewhat beneficial, but never to be overdone, and this is very important.

Under circumstances of which I do not approve, I will not permit a session. My distinctions are not always the same sort as your own, however. There are certain social, peculiar niceties that are held in changing, shifting, sometimes meaningless patterns, to which I would not respond. That is, I simply would not be attuned myself to social situations or social transgressions, or what might seem social transgressions to you.

So in these purely superficial patterns of behavior you and Ruburt must judge. I mention here as example—do you want your break?

(Jane interrupted to look at me. It was now 9:35. I shook my head, since she seemed to want to go on, and was not talking so fast that I had difficulty keeping up.)

I mention here as example the evening when Ruburt's father and his woman visited. You and Ruburt had been drinking, but to no great extent more than usual. The woman, unfortunately, was not as restrained in her drinking habits.

Now. Ruburt was in a splendid state of dissociation. He was also emotionally and intuitively attuned because of his father's visit, and in an inner state of irritability, meaning excitability, which often accompanies dissociation. There is an outer aloofness, but an inner sensitivity to different stimuli.

Ruburt was more than ordinarily affected by the woman's inner plea for help with problems that she finds she is less and less able to cope. Ruburt received that message, and in a conducive state was also in communication with me.

I was perfectly willing to hold such a session. I knew your reluctance, but you see I did not truly appreciate considerations that were strong with you, and as you recall I did not come through. But this was in deference to you and Ruburt personally. To me the social entanglements and—ah—possible social disagreeabilities did not exist.

(Notice Jane's hesitation above. She delivered this material with some groping for the right words, evidently, and used many facial expressions and hand gestures as she did so. "Disagreeabilities" certainly is not common usage.)

I would always catch any real possibility of danger. I would catch any occurrence that would be strongly disagreeable if it were actually going to occur. I would know beforehand, but I am not necessarily aware of what you might consider possibilities in that line, unless I use particular effort, so these possibilities are not considered by me. In the particular instance that we are discussing, if such a session would have led, if held, to a strongly unfortunate situation, then I would know in advance, and not hold such a session.

I will let you take your break.

(Break at 9:59. Jane was dissociated as usual, in fact very much so, she said. She had talked steadily for almost an hour, pacing the while, with few pauses on either count. Her voice had quieted if her pace had picked up, and she resumed in this manner at 10:06.)

In such cases therefore you must make your own decisions, and you should not have a session if for any reason you do not feel comfortable about it. This applies to both of you.

There must be an agreement on both of your parts or the session will suffer. Dissociation opens or makes available lines and possibilities of communication, but there is no necessity that they be used at any given time or instance.

Your feelings on the mentioned evening were legitimate as far as you and Ruburt were concerned, even though those feelings, for many reasons, were not mine. This information should be used as guideposts in the future.

Now if, and this has occurred, Ruburt finds his abilities unusually attuned, and circumstances are advantageous, it is perfectly legitimate to hold a session, though it is not a scheduled one. I will automatically make adjustments. This refers to sessions with or without witnesses.

Naturally, conditions being beneficial, such sessions may allow us to take advantage of high peaks of activity and increase our spontaneity. And with increased spontaneity we will decrease any distortive effects. These effects very rarely occur, except in personal material, or in cases where Ruburt feels under pressure because of doubts. During high peaks of psychic activity the doubts are minimized.

I am aware of your resumed psychological time experiments.

This will not be a long session. The effect seen last evening was legitimate, and I will discuss it at a later date.

(Jane now took a rather long pause as she paced about. The effect Seth referred to, Jane told me later, was the one seen by Bill Macdonnel during Sunday's unscheduled session—the opaque white eyes superimposed upon Jane's closed eyelids.)

There will indeed be a welcome sale on Ruburt's part. He unfortunately blocks me at this moment as to details.

The increased appearance of his ability creatively, as seen in his own writing, should be apparent to you Joseph, and is objectively apparent in the letters he has received. The increased focus of his abilities I predicted <u>during</u> an unscheduled session, if you recall. His short stories dating approximately from that time display a much increased facility and knowledge.

(See the unscheduled 82nd session. In this one Seth for the first time mentioned that Jane should work full time at her writing. This was August 27. By the end of September she had left the gallery where she had worked part time four years. This move was not dictated wholly by the Seth material, but certainly this played its part. Since leaving the gallery and buckling down to work, Jane had received many very favorable letters from publishers. Invariably they comment on the much improved quality of her work. This improvement has seemed to blossom like magic, and we feel that the time when Jane begins to sell her work regularly will soon arrive.)

The poetry is also steadily improving, and this inner increased spontaneity, that are the results directly of intuitional powers, are flowing over even into his paintings, allowing him to use knowledge that had not been previously available to him.

Such results are also now showing in your own work. The understanding and inner freedom is enabling you to use more and more facets of your own ability, and to develop these further.

(This, I can testify, is certainly true. In recent weeks alone, my work has improved remarkably; I am objective enough about it to be able to see this. In several recent paintings I have solved problems, almost effortlessly it seems, that I have been contending with for years. It may be coincidence that the studies are finally paying off, but it is also interesting that it should happen at this particular time. At times while working recently, I have had an almost magical ability to achieve whatever it was I wanted to do.)

In quite practical terms also you have been selling paintings, because now you do not hold back, and you will continue to improve; and this improvement will cause others to be drawn to your work.

I told you a while ago that what seemed impractical was practical, and that value fulfillment is the only true practicality.

I will here close the session. We are doing well. Nevertheless I want to make sure that our precious balance, in terms of energy involved and so forth, is maintained, though I am in fine form and per usual could carry on for hours.

I would suggest when it is convenient that your recorder be repaired, and that it be kept in a handy place in this room, set up for recording for any occasions when I could speak less formally, that is also quicker, conversationally, without the need of your taking notes.

This would not happen very frequently, since in the long run it involves just as much work on your part, in then transcribing from the machine.

My best regards to you both. I am in the mood for capering, but I will stick to my word like a gob of glue. Good evening to you both.

("Good night, Seth."

(End at 10:35. Jane was quite well dissociated. Seth, she said, "came through real clear and strong from the beginning."

(Jane said that the fingers of her right hand had been slightly "fat" late in the session, particularly her index finger.

(This was the first manifestation either of us had had of such a sign for many sessions. The 59th session furnishes an example of hand enlargement, which Seth labels as the attempt of the physical body to expand in rhythm with psychic, or inner, expansion. See the detailed measurement data in the 55th session also. As in the past, Jane's sensation began to diminish as soon as the session ended; by the time I looked at her hand I could not see anything out of the ordinary.

(Jane said that Seth gives breaks just for our own benefit. When she talks for an hour, for example, she ends up in a deeper state of dissociation usually than in the half-hour periods.

(Seth's remarks about the recorder point up the reason we do not use it to routinely record the sessions for later transcription. Not only would I sit through the

session with Jane even though we were recording, but in doing the transcription I would have to expend an equal amount of time listening to the session again, plus the time necessary for typing, and starting and stopping many times.)

(The following is from Jane's psychological time notebook. Her extraordinary experience of Wednesday is listed separately.

(November 3, Tuesday, 11:30 AM: Not much of anything. I saw a mechanical gadget of some sort, quickly but not clearly enough to describe. I don't know what it was.)

(The following are from my psy-time notebook:

(November 3, Tuesday 7 AM: Getting dressed for work this morning, I abruptly had the rather clear thought that I should walk back to my studio and look out the back windows, because I would be able to see that a car was parked in front of the garage, blocking the exit of my car from the garage. Looking out the windows, I received a jolt when I did see a car so parked, blocking off the exit of my own car.

(I wonder: The car blocking mine belonged to a young man who lives in a downstairs apartment. By agreement we park so as not to block each other's automobile comings and goings, and the system works well. I do not know why on this particular occasion his car was parked as it was; perhaps because another car had temporarily taken his regular place, then left later. Since my friend of downstairs knew his car must be blocking mine, perhaps I received a telepathic communication from him upon arising this morning. Going downstairs after breakfast, I saw the car was gone, which meant my neighbor had moved it considerably earlier than is usually his habit, since he leaves for work sometime after I do.

(November 4, Wednesday, 8 PM: After lying down for a few moments I experienced my familiar sensation on two occasions, not too strongly however. I then had many instances of hearing voices—sentences, or bits of conversations, some quite involved. I saw many faces, male and female, and some had some duration, as a fat man with glasses and wearing a white restaurant worker's uniform, etc.

(It is of considerable interest to me that since I have resumed the regular study of psychological time from October 27, practically all of my visions have involved people. Jane on the other hand had received visual data on many inanimate objects, particularly lights, light fixtures, door fixtures, etc.)

(Jane's Account of Psychological Time Experience November 4, 1964. [Wednesday]

(A rather crazy experience today—I will separate it into parts as it was divided, part in the morning and part in the afternoon. I am writing this while I am still

not myself as I do not want to fall off to sleep as I am tempted to do, don't think it wise, and would like to describe both experiences while they are still fresh.

(I put in my usual morning writing hours 8:30 to 11:30 and then tried psychological time according to schedule, from then until noon. I set the alarm clock, lay down in the bedroom, closed my eyes and relaxed without giving myself any suggestions except that for complete relaxation. Was in good relaxed state but nothing was happening or anything. I said to myself, "Am I really going to make a good sale soon?" [meaning a book or story] and the words, "Evelyn's grandmother," sprang to mind. I figured that was meaningless and ignored it.

(Then, suddenly, the whole thing began. I was laying straight in bed, arms at my sides. Without warning I felt as if the bed was disappearing beneath my hands, as sand will shift away, leaving pockets of nothingness there, that kept enlarging. My thumbs definitely felt as if they were grasping the edge of these holes of nothingness; the holes enlarged further, spreading out beneath. A few minutes later, this is most difficult to describe, I felt a quick definite and physical whoosh outward as if I was suddenly shooting or rushing out through my head, longwise—strong frightening sense of motion and being completely carried away. Instantly panicked and stopped... whatever it was, at least I think I did.

(Then I was angry because I had been frightened but was still cautious and didn't want to get in over my head. Told myself then that I could travel anyplace safely and return safely but that I would go slowly; that I was safe and confident and would welcome such a valid experience. Feeling resumed of bed disappearing beneath my hands. Strong red color behind closed eyelids. Feeling of heat in head, shoulders, back of neck, and then cold in same places. Sense of expanded radius inside closed eyelids. Then felt as if legs, arms, belly...dissolved, I guess is the best description. Feeling of suspension but not of motion. Then the alarm rang, yet still I lay there, had some slight difficulty in opening eyes but did so. Even with eyes open feeling of being suspended continued. Felt some resistance [on chest?] against rising, but decided it was not wise to experiment beyond normal time limit, and got up.

(Was left with light feeling [not a weakness or anything], feeling as if I could rise up bodily, and quite definite sensation of having an empty space above my wrists. Took our cat out though, sat on steps waiting for Rob to come home from work; feeling diminished. Got lunch, told Rob what happened, left house for walk to post office to mail manuscript, and to grocery store. During lunch very slight but noticeable lightness in wrists and hands. Mentioned it, but didn't think it at all important. Intended to do my errands, come home and write from 1:30 till 4:30.

(Second Part

(It's a terrific autumn day, sunny. Walked perhaps half a block or so. Remember thinking suddenly that Seth might say the following in tonight's session:

Material world of physical matter doesn't actually exist as such at all, in a real sense. Atoms and molecules etc. are our names for the stuff of which we compose our images or transpose them into apparent validity. Then the next thing I remember is a marvelous feeling of lightness, I felt not so much buoyant as free of resistance; physical resistance. Free of physical bulk, of physical pressures, as say, sometimes we imagine we might have felt sometime in early childhood. This didn't register at first though; just felt unusually good, enjoying my walk, conscious of the lightness of my step, aware of a satisfying unity with creation.

(Remember going to post office. Regular store was closed due to death in family, sign on door said this, and a woman going by so informed me. Decided to go to another store though this would make a longer trip than I had planned. Stood on corner to cross street. Telephone company men working on wires; two men high on pole. One man on road. Somehow the wire dropped, came down, falling maybe two feet from where I stood. I never noticed; it didn't seem important. Ordinarily I would have jumped.

(Headed across playground to strange street, not on my ordinary route. From there in, the sensation of lightness spread throughout my body except for chest region. Seemed no effort at all to walk, completely effortless, as if there was no resistance at all to overcome; no sense of muscular motion for example. Fabulous sense of well-being; of floating along the street. Walked this way about four blocks; went to store, feeling the same; talked to woman who works there in ordinary manner.

(Left; started way home. By now, however, felt as if lightness rose through body, and this changed so that suddenly I felt as if lower part of body had dissolved completely, up to chest. No muscular knowledge of carrying bag with three quarts of milk, and book and cigarettes that I'd purchased at all. Suddenly worried; realized for the first time that I wasn't in state of something like just plain extraordinary good humor or good health or ordinary but unusual exuberance. First, I was aware that I <u>felt</u> as if body had dissolved below chest; but then thought that it really might have. Went up curb on Church St.; beyond doubt it took no effort at all; the usual effort you feel in lifting feet for steps. Shoes bothered me though; they seemed heavy, holding me down. I know this is silly, but felt scared that if lower part of body was dissolved; and all that was left was chest and shoulder and head region, then I would just fall down; a chest, shoulders, and head on street. Didn't think I was going to do this; but the image popped into my head. By this time, worried to some degree but still enjoying the delightful...suspension...looked from Walnut Street through yards, to my own windows that showed through trees. Noticed that it seemed that I was floating by...rather than walking. Afraid I might...leave body or something...unprotected in street. Got home. Told Rob. He made me drink coffee, had me sniff ammonia.

(Got home about 1:50 PM Feelings continued, though beginning to lessen. At

3 PM though, just after I began writing this all down, went to downstairs front door to see if mailman had come, still felt same sensations though to lesser degree. Rob and I in living room area; I told him about the mailman and all of a sudden I had the odd and striking feeling as I walked around my table that I passed through a "hole of nothingness"—and passed out of it again immediately. It is now 4:15. I feel more like myself now, though tired. In fact, I'm OK now, or close to it.

(Guess I went too far again, without realizing it. Strange to me that the second experience began after eating lunch and while walking.

(During the experience I viewed my environment from some sort of different perspective or something; everything looked terrific, extraordinarily brilliant. I felt very happy.

(Forgot to mention: during the morning experience, before the whole thing started, felt that "ecstasy" sensation, don't know what else to call it; a physical flow of pleasurable waves over body.)

(My notes and comments re the above experience:

(As soon as Jane returned home from doing her errands and mentioned that she still "felt funny", I suspected that we would see something like a repetition of her adventure of January 10, 1964, Volume 1, page 83. On page 89, in the 100th session, Seth had stated that Jane could allow herself more freedom now, and since she had mentioned the feeling of what she calls ecstasy to me this noon, I thought she was indeed doing more than usual. I also wondered whether she had done too much.

(Again, see my notes on pages 89-90, concerning Jane's ecstasy. From some of her recent psy-time experiments I had thought she was close to achieving that state again. She had been giving herself suggestion lately, that she would be able to travel psychically, during her experiments. From the following session it will be seen that Jane was correct in thinking that the rushing-out sensation she felt, through the top of her head, was definitely an attempt at traveling.

(Jane was also correct in suspecting that her suggestion to go slowly, after her first ego-alarm, was literally interpreted by her subconscious; hence the later manifestation of symptoms quite a while after her experiment had "ended." This was much more her idea than mine.

(When she returned home her eyes were very clear, her skin color good, her pulse normal. Her hands also felt normal. Her manner was quite smiling and relaxed and at the same time surprised. I was not concerned particularly, except on the general score that in these experiments I prefer to make haste slowly. She had no trouble talking, although as she walked about at times I noticed a lilt to her step; at other times her knees would bend a little more than usual, as though her legs were rubbery; but to no great degree.

(I made her coffee, which she did not seem to want very much. The ammonia capsule we tried as an experiment; we did not think she needed it, but we wanted to see what effect the pungent odor, being a kind of shock, would have. It had none that we could detect, except that Jane coughed briefly. I talked of a cold shower but we did not try it.

(The effects took some time to wear off. She first began to type up her copy on the experiment at about 2:30 PM, but appeared too relaxed to want to exert much effort in this direction. She had no trouble with coordination, [could type easily enough, etc.] as she had in the January episode, when she could not even use a pen effectively for a time. I felt that even at its height she understood the state she was in, and was not alarmed. She agreed with me that she had overdone it, however, and we spent some time discussing ways in which either of us could appreciate the first warning signals, and halt any experiment that involved too much, too fast.

(Ever since she traveled to her home town, Saratoga, NY, psychically, Jane has wanted to travel again. (See Volume 2, page 65, April 30, 1964.) She believes that her experience today was an effort at travel, and wondered why it was apparently so much more difficult to accomplish now than it was last April. Seth deals with the problem somewhat in the following, 104th, session.)

SESSION 104
NOVEMBER 4, 1964 9 PM WEDNESDAY AS SCHEDULED

(Naturally, after Jane's experience with psychological time earlier in the day, we wondered whether there would be a session at all tonight. As the day wore on however Jane appeared to feel all right. We made plans to hold the session as usual, provided Seth himself did not eliminate it or Jane had a change of heart. Jane had no idea of what material the session might cover, as far as foreknowledge went.

(Jane and I have talked to our landlord, Jimmy Spaziani, concerning the data given by Seth in the 100th session, concerning the missing cover to the thermostat in our apartment house. Seth stated that Jimmy inadvertently disposed of the cover "either someplace on his own property or in a public dumping area, whichever area is by a hill, and it is still there." Jimmy states that with Seth's reminder, he does recall cleaning out some rubbish from the house last spring; the description, according to Jimmy, matches that of Elmira's city dump, which Jane and I have not visited. Jimmy states that the area is all small hills, and covers many acres. I asked Jimmy if by any chance he could recall where in the dump he disposed of that load of rubbish, but he could not. Jimmy states that attendants there direct him to a different spot each time; the size of the dump precludes any detailed search, so we conclude that the cover will

probably never be found.

(Concerning Seth's statements that Jane will soon make a writing sale, she has nothing to report yet. See pages 102, 107 and 114 in this volume. She continues however to receive very complimentary letters concerning her work.

(Jane began dictation on time in a normal voice, and in a rather slow manner, then gradually speeded up. Again her glasses were off, her eyes dark.)

Good evening.

("Good evening, Seth.")

Our Ruburt has already put in quite a day.

If you recall, I told you that the psychological time experiments would prove more fruitful now, but Ruburt really came up with a peach.

(See page 92 in Session 100.)

Again, we are involved with the necessity for a delicate balance between spontaneity and discipline. Considering the circumstances and all in all, Ruburt handled himself very well.

The experience did involve several experiments that he was making without, of course, conscious knowledge. Several lessons may also be learned from this. The inner self is well aware of its innate capabilities in certain directions, and directs its efforts along these lines.

Ego in its own way senses these particular potentialities also; merely senses them as say a dog might sniff danger, and it directs its efforts to block them. A frightened dog takes very careful handling, or you may lose a hand and gain very little.

Ruburt's strategy was brilliant from one standpoint. The rushing-out feeling through the head represented the initial flow of the inner self from the physical image.

(While delivering the above sentence, Jane took several long pauses as she paced about. She had not been speaking very rapidly, but her rate of delivery now slowed somewhat, broken by frequent pauses.)

It happened so quickly that Ruburt's old dog of an ego was taken by surprise almost completely, and the whole affair might have been successful, as far as its purpose being achieved, had not a quick preliminary sensation caused the ego to rouse from its pleasant doze.

The sensation occurred mere seconds before the outward rush, but provided just enough of a dim warning to the ego. The ego could not prevent the outward rush. It did not react in time. The warning was not therefore sufficient from the ego's standpoint. It yelped and pulled the escaping inner self back by its imaginary coattails.

Quietly but firmly, without antagonizing the ego further, Ruburt quieted it down by the suggestion of safety and slow motion; as you suspected the slow motion suggestion and/or coupled with the cautionary warning, was interpreted rather expertly, that is slyly, by the subconscious, which then waited a good interval of several hours before trying again.

(I would say a little less than two hours, actually.)

In the meantime, that is for the remaining half-hour, it experimented with preliminary acclimating and familiarizing sensations, with which the ego, somewhat conditioned and convinced of the benefit of these experiments, could find nothing really objectionable.

As a rule Ruburt's ego will jealously guard its interests. When he feels it shout at him it is good to lessen the pace during the rest of the session, as he attempted to do. The wording of any suggestions is very important, however. The phrase, "I will progress safely", is an excellent one to use, since it allows for continuation and progress balanced by safety.

The word slow, or slowly, is not good in this connotation, since of itself it does not necessarily suggest safety, but a mere neutral and temporary putting off. So far Ruburt is doing well, and will learn as he progresses how to operate inner acceleration and flow, or rush of energy, so that he is comfortable. And the ego, through experience, will learn that the inner self will always return safely. And it would be most unjust, and needlessly cruel, not to give the ego this necessary reassurance; and also the inner self should manage to communicate to the ego its gratitude for the ego's protective concern.

This involves a simple communication both ways. Familiarity with such experiences, again, will quickly teach Ruburt to use the right touch, to learn how to control this acceleration and rush of the self, going either inward or outward; that is, leaving the physical image and returning to it; as with your airplanes, I believe, landing is important, without a crash.

We anticipate no airline disasters, so to speak. Perhaps, inevitably, a few bumpings along the ground. These controls in the long run must be learned individually, directly through experience, but I can be of some aid.

I suggest your break.

(Break at 9:34. Jane was dissociated as usual. She was speaking somewhat faster by the end of her delivery. She said that the above material, dealing with the outward movement of the inner self through the head, reminded her that in her earlier psychological time experiments she had sometimes experienced a "bump on top of the head" sensation, momentarily, that had been rather unpleasant. This would be several months ago.

(When Jane began dictating again her voice had changed from a rather normal voice to one that was quite a bit more formal and harsh in tone, and somewhat

louder. At times it had a hard-to-describe singsong quality, emphasizing certain syllables and elongating them. Her diction became very elaborate. She maintained this voice, moreover, until the end of the session. Resume at 9:39.)

There are always new things to be learned as new levels are reached, new controls to be mastered, new balances to be maintained, new disciplines that must be adopted; and initially this does involve a natural, added exertion of energy and increased activity, before the whole self learns to deal with the new level, and is comfortable in its manipulations.

For the present Ruburt's ego will exert balancing resistance, like an anchor perhaps, or a weight. However the inner self has also tasted new freedom, so there will be a brief jolting while the relationships and forces work themselves out to achieve a new, integrated balance.

I expect no real difficulties. If any should develop, not really develop, for we will pull back before then, but if any give evidence of causing any unwarranted or really uncomfortable turns, then we will do either or both of two things for an interval.

We will either cut our friend down as to allotted time per day for a while, or we will not have him experiment alone in the apartment. Any difficulties would be caused by a temporary impasse of ego and inner self, which should clear itself up. I do not foresee difficulty.

It is a matter of Ruburt's own forces, that must always work in balance. Some rather harmless diversities of purpose, and temporary imbalance, may most probably be expected at various times while the whole self becomes acquainted with a new level of achievement.

This is to be expected as minor adjustments are made. Without them there would be dangers. Too much smooth sailing could then lead to overconfidence, before the whole self had mastered the controls and disciplines really necessary.

We find here a difference between this experience and the one in which Ruburt journeyed psychically, but actually, through space and time to a Saratoga of quite some years ago. That journey was powered by emotional impetus, personal emotional impetus.

(Jane had this experience on April 30, 1964, at 11:30 AM. See Volume 2, page 65. This was a few days before the 50th session. Checking over my account of Jane's experience on that date, I notice that I did state that this experience began with a feeling of "a blow on the head." It is included in Jane's dated version. On April 28, 1964, Jane also underwent this rather unpleasant sensation; perhaps in preparation for the Saratoga Springs journey two days later. And the sensation of rushing out through the head that she experienced this morning was, Jane said, very similar to

those earlier "bumpings.")

The personal emotions and memories loosened, freed him; but the journey was necessarily destined by the particular emotions that powered it, and the destination was one, incidentally, familiar to the ego, and to some extent at least one to which both ego and subconscious were nostalgically connected.

It was therefore along the lines of a preliminary test flight, and one to which the ego would not therefore object. This incident today was vastly more complicated, though it did not completely come off.

The ego is now somewhat in the confidence of the whole self, therefore we have more to contend with. We are no longer tricking the ego, which it would ultimately and sometimes almost disastrously resent, but taking it into the confidence of the whole self, so that it will allow departure from the physical image, as a mother can finally be convinced that it is safe for a son or daughter to go out alone.

This analogy is not a very good one however, since the child <u>does</u> eventually leave the parent, but it is a true one because the inner self does indeed leave the physical image with which the ego is so concerned, when it passes beyond the physical field.

During ordinary plateaus between levels, there is little such difficulty. Such relatively harmless difficulties however are more than compensated for by increased confidence and achievements that emerge as the difficulties are met, and controls learned.

Also this ability to handle energy is carried over into other life areas, that is other areas in this life. It is no coincidence that Ruburt's writing, and even his painting, is also showing advancement to a higher level of its own, as your work also shares in your increased abilities to use and handle inner energy.

You have each your own characteristic ways of advancement. You will discover, Joseph, that your ability to receive so-called telepathic data is showing itself in psychological time experiments and dreams, as well as in spontaneous flashes during regular consciousness.

(See my notes on my experience of November 3, involving the car blocking our garage. This may fall within the telepathic category. I have not asked Seth about it simply because of the time problem. Jane and I cannot cover all the subjects we would like to. Many times when we would like something at least mentioned by Seth, we mention it before a session in the hope it will be dealt with. This particular instance is on page 116.

(Also notice that on page 116, I mentioned that I have received many human images during psychological time experiments, and that often the people I perceive appear to be talking to me, but soundlessly.)

You are allowing more of this through than previously. The images will come more clearly within the near future. More data could be received by you, and will be as you allow further data to emerge from the images; that is, feelings that emanate, say, from the images of the people. You are somewhat closed down to these, which add extra and necessary dimension that would round out and focus the information.

If your hands are tired you may take your break.

("Okay."

(I meant that I felt okay, although my hand was tired. But since it was 10:15, I thought the session would end soon.)

This is your present line of development, and you have utilized it in the past through your portraits, faces of those that have appeared to you in telepathic images of which you were unaware. Closer attention should be paid to your dreams, the suggestion given by you that you will recall them.

I am going to end the session, even though our friend is doing extremely well, since he has dealt with quite enough this week already. I shall make it a point to look out for him in a protective manner during his experiments for a while, and we shall keep a check upon his excellent progress, which should continue. And also assure ourselves that proper controls are being maintained.

My most sincere wishes to you both. One note further: The sale has developed at this time, and future sales have been set into motion through stories. That is all.

("Good night, Seth."

(End at 10:21. Jane was dissociated as usual. She had maintained her unusual sing-song voice until the end. It had been a strong voice also, and she now said that her voice had felt different to her; as though she was not using her own vocal chords, but served as a vehicle or channel through which this strange voice emerged. Jane did not particularly care for the idea of serving as a channel. To me there was no doubt that the voice was recognizably hers.

(Seth's statements about my receiving telepathic images interested me greatly, since I have been aware for some years now that I would much rather do a portrait without a model. That is, I greatly enjoy setting to work to "make up" a character, then paint it. I have found that for me working from a model is rather boring and somehow limiting. My best drawings, particularly in ink and oil, have been produced in this fashion, and I used to think it rather strange that I liked to work this way. In fact, Jane has often mentioned the fact that I have seldom used even her as a model. I have done so a few times. The situation is about to be remedied however, since as my work continues to expand I now discover that I want to use models also, and have several paintings planned in which she will appear.

(Concerning Jane making sale of her writing soon, the last statement of the session above now makes four times that this bit of information has come to us, either through sessions or Jane's psychological time. See pages 102, 107, 114, and 125. In writing out the last line of the session from Jane's dictation, I took it for granted the information referred to one sale. Jane then told me, as soon as the session ended, that it referred to two sales; one now accomplished, and other future sales. While we were discussing this point, Jane suddenly resumed her feet and began dictating again. Her manner and voice were more subdued now, and grew progressively quieter and slower as she talked. I will indicate pauses where they took place. Resume at 10:26.)

A sale has already developed *(Pause)* period.

Future sales having to do with stories will result in the near future. These have not yet actually developed, but the framework that will ensure them has already been laid.

Communications, not physical, have been established through elements of energy both within the stories and between certain individuals and Ruburt, although Ruburt is not physically acquainted with these persons.

(Jane's voice now became even quieter as she paced about.)

A collegiate-type man, graying hair, large feet, and mustache of—of reddish faded color, two children, that is, he has two children; and another tall, thin, gawky-type man whose eyes are <u>some</u>what protuberant. A woman might have something to do with one sale, through influence. An office with a modern red leather chair, small room, stories high, not at all elegant. Office used at various times by three men.

A manuscript now from Ruburt lays on a desk. Some excitement over it. Ten o'clock, PM. New York City. (*Pause*) One man, enveloped in a large overcoat, enters. He has three children. I cannot get more through. Pushing Ruburt will cause distortions, this time, that would result from tiredness rather than unwillingness.

I give you what I can. This sort of thing Ruburt is not yet acclimated to, and distractions from other places nearby may cause him to confuse images. That is all.

(End at 10:40. Jane was again dissociated. She ended upon this very quiet note, speaking quite slowly. As soon as she sat down, Jane told me several things. One was that as she spoke for Seth about the red leather chair, she had a mental image of this chair. It had short round wooden legs with a light brown finish, a cushioned seat and back [the back leaning back, of course] and was without arms. Jane could not describe the floor upon which it rested, or any other furnishings in the room, or a door, a window, etc.

(She did say that as she mentioned "stories high" she had a definite impression

of looking out over many other lower buildings. While talking about the chair she also had an impression that "some source, something" was trying to tell her about a rug that either usually was on the floor, was sent out for cleaning, or else was never there. The only thing she is sure of in this instance is that she was trying to receive something about a rug. She had no vision of it.

(Jane has quite a bit of material out to various publishers. From past experience we have learned to be careful in trying to interpret this kind of material, and so will not try very hard with this information, preferring to see what develops and then include it in the record.

(It might be noted here that Seth/Jane also gave a brief physical description of a person on page 84, in the 99th session. This was in connection with material on John Bradley's superiors in, presumably, Chicago. We have no verification on this yet, not having seen John recently. Since John goes to Chicago rather infrequently we may have to wait a while for it.

(I was tempted to ask Seth whether he referred to distractions around Jane and me here in Elmira, or possible ones in say New York City. But it was obvious that Jane was tired and ready to end the session.)

(The following material is from Jane's psychological time notebook:

(November 5, Thursday, 11:30 AM: Very few fleeting images.

(November 6, Friday, 11:30 AM: A very definite prolonged feeling of body dissolving below chest. First, feeling of imbalance, as if head was tilting to one side, the left, causing my eyes to feel as though they shifted to lower left. Then sense of whole body vibrating gently to and fro. Then both hands terribly cold. Then they moved of own accord sideways, followed by sensation that they rose, but do not think they actually did. Persistent feeling that they were going to, sort of gentle pressure beneath them. Feeling from feet up of body dissolved, but the coldness at the same time. It reached my upper left arm, which ached with cold. [I was actually partially dressed, and beneath spread which was doubled.] I had the feeling my body might rise without it, since it felt dissolved below the chest. The alarm rang. My limbs very cold to the touch. As I write this at once my hands and feet are still abnormally cold. Was shaking with cold when alarm rang.

*(Now in the very beginning, I felt a sudden need for Rob. * Quite emotional, as if he was dead and I wanted him. Spoke his name in ejaculation in my mind. Quick intense sorrow. Had just thought consciously how much he meant to me. Feeling vanished. I forgot it until now. Rather unsettling. I asked mentally if Rob was in any trouble, got no answer. [As I wrote this down, in the second sentence with the * I found myself substituting Rob's name, no, Walt's name for Rob's. Maybe something happened to Walt? Notice the correction in last sentence—there wasn't any*

sense of danger; sorrow after an event? Nor did it seem particularly an immediate event, or even necessarily one in near future.]

(November 9, Monday, 11:30 AM: Lightness etc., good state. Had upsetting dream last night. Asked about it mentally during session. Can't remember whether the following vision happened before or after request, but think after. Saw two nurses, or a doctor and nurse, in white. Heard conversation. Forget some, but got the words, "Well, she's coming out of shock." They were looking down at bed or table, which also seemed to be my own observation point of them. Very quick duration. No feeling of danger on my part during experience. Since last night's dream involved, I think, a <u>*warning*</u> *of a woman's death, then the affair seems to tie in. But am cautious in attempting to interpret such data.*

(Also November 9, Monday, 7 PM: In doze, asked silently if I was being warned about a death. If so whose? If not, what was the message? Few seconds later I saw a brown hand mirror held out. I saw it edge on. I got scared, wouldn't look, I guess afraid I'd see my own face. As it vanished it occurred to me that the face wouldn't have to be mine. Upset. Checked with the pendulum. It said warning was of my mother's death, in December. And that the psychological time experiences, today and Friday, were connected with the warning from Helen McIlwain. Linda was not involved. Don't know how trustworthy the pendulum is.)

(The following account is from Jane's dream notebook. It is included here so as to present all the pertinent material together. The material is dealt with extensively in the following, 105th, session.

(Jane's dream, Sunday night, November 8, 1964:

(A boy handed me a long, legal-sized black envelope. Helen McIlwain's name was the return address, written in black ink on the envelope. [She was a friend of my mother's, now dead.] I took the envelope to contain notification of my mother's death. I guess I opened it and read inside, though now I don't recall doing so. Then with relief saw that the death was not to be that close. Not my mother, but a young girl. Got the name Linda, and the last name, which I think I've forgotten—don't think it was Butts. But there was a connection with Linda.

(I was relieved that it wasn't my mother, but my reasoning was cold-blooded. First I thought: "Well, I've always feared my mother's death," and I was almost relieved that it was over. Then relief when it wasn't her death, but someone else's.

(If it is a death, and in Rob's family, say of Linda, which I doubt, then why the return name of my mother's friend? [With whom I was not close?] Maybe one of my nieces, instead of Rob's? Joan? In dream I think the death must have already happened. My death? No feeling that it was, though I could have substituted names. But the person [to die?] was younger than I am, I think. And who was the boy? He wait-

ed while I read the message inside. But can't remember reading it, just interpreting it. Somewhat unsettling dream.)

(From my psychological time notebook:

(November 5, Thursday, 8:15 PM: Mild sensation upon lying down. Few vague people and voices. Used Seth's suggested phrase from the 104th session, "I will progress safely," as a safety measure.)

SESSION 105
NOVEMBER 9, 1964 9 PM MONDAY AS SCHEDULED

(Last Friday, November 6, John Bradley, from Williamsport, PA, visited us briefly. John could offer us no confirmation on Seth's data concerning John's home office in Chicago. This information was given in the 99th session, page 84. John recalls no one fitting the rather general description given by Seth.

(Seth also stated at that time that John will have to take strong measures if he wants to achieve certain goals. John reported that he has been visited by his district manager this week, and that indeed the two men have been covering John's route together. The visit has given John a chance to state his case for transfer and more money, and John has been vigorously doing just this.

(Jane has been quite concerned because of her dream of November 8, which she feels to be clairvoyant, and her recent psychological time experiences, which she feels are related to the dream. She has come to think that these experiences, taken together, may forecast her mother's death. She is uncertain as to how much credence to give the pendulum experience.

(She had no actual idea of the subject matter for the session as the time for it approached. She began dictation in a rather normal voice, that occasionally struck a deeper undertone. Her glasses were off, her eyes dark. Her pacing was slow, and she spoke rather slowly, with frequent pauses.)

Good evening.

("Good evening, Seth.")

I can see that you have both had quite a time.

Ruburt's abilities have indeed jumped up another level, and that is why he is jumpy, if you will excuse the pun.

I realize that Ruburt in particular is in no mood for levity, and I would for his sake tell him that the information contained in his psychological time experiments, and in his dreams of late, is merely the fabrications of his subconscious, of which in the past he was not aware.

However, I cannot tell him this, since he has indeed received a communication from someone he knew as his mother's friend. And he received further information or collaborative information, in his own psychological time experiences.

(It might be of interest to note that Helen McIlwain, the communicant in Jane's dream of November 8, has been dead for perhaps two years. Jane's mother so informed her in a letter. Jane had not met Helen McIlwain for at least fifteen years, she estimates, and remembers her best from her, Jane's, grade school years.

(Thus, Seth seems to be saying in the above paragraph that Jane received a communication through a personality that has been dead for two years. When Jane described her dream to me I had mistakenly taken it for granted that Helen McIlwain was still alive.)

First of all, when he cried out silently for you during a recent psychological time experience, it was because he sensed, through inner communications, a situation concerning a death in which he would need your support. The poor Rob cry was his regret at having to depend upon your support, taking, he feared, energy from your work; and a regret, based on fear, that he always feels whenever he is forced to rely upon someone's strength.

(See Jane's psy-time experience of November 6, page 127.)

He fears that he will be loved when he gives support, but not loved when he must rely, or ask it, from another person. Sensing a death, immediately fearing that it was yours, Joseph, since he heard himself call for you, he hastily attempted to sacrifice his previous husband in your place. Therefore the mix-up of names when he wrote down his experience.

He then attempted to forget it. Last night's dream—

(Jane now paused beside my table, her eyes closed. She lifted a hand.)

Ruburt is trying not to block me, but there is some difficulty, which we will attempt to overcome.

Last night's dream was a communication from the Helen who was the friend of Ruburt's mother. The message was directed to Ruburt. He did not pick it up from his mother. The envelope, the black envelope, was obviously a symbol, but it did enable Ruburt to see the name of the woman who was sending the message. And the import of the dream was clear to him merely in the perception of that simple data, the black envelope, with the return name in the left hand corner, and though he does not recall it, his name on the envelope as the person to whom the communication was sent.

Even in his dream he was stunned, afraid that the death was his own. This is why he could not remember that the envelope was addressed to him. In his dream, therefore, which he knew he would remember because of his training, he then added shielding fabrications, interwoven with the valid information.

His mother's name—let this pass. We are doing well, but for now we find this sentence cannot be completed.

(Jane had again paused and gestured, hands up, eyes closed. Her voice was now quiet, and she paused often. I had become rather concerned, considering the content of the material, and watched her closely. I was prepared to end the session at once if I thought intuitively that it was necessary. Jane's face was drawn, her eyes very dark beneath. She paced about with her eyes lowered mostly.)

He then attempted to substitute the name of Linda, your niece, and pretended not to know whose death was being perceived. Nor could he recall reading the message, or the name that was inside. That is why he cannot remember actually opening the envelope. In any case, opening the envelope was superfluous.

The relief he felt after deciding that he had safely tricked himself, he thought in the morning, was due to the fact that the future death was not his mother's or his own, but one involving a relative at least somewhat distant. The relief of course was the result of his partial success in distorting the information, but despite distortions the sender came through, and the sex of the person whose death was unfortunately perceived.

(It might be added here that last September 2, Jane's dream notebook reveals, Jane had a dream involving Helen McIlwain's brother. The brother has been dead for at least five years, and quite possibly much longer, Jane states. Jane remembers the brother rather better than she remembers Helen, actually. The dream involving the brother was a rather ordinary one, Jane believes, and at least on the surface does not involve clairvoyance. Nor, superficially, does it appear to signal a communication from the brother.)

That is, in your state of affairs, a future death certainly seems unfortunate to the ninth degree, but the perception of it is beneficial, insofar as it will serve to prepare those in any way involved.

We are going about this explanation in our own way; Ruburt and I have a pact, now, of which he is not consciously aware, and if I observe certain niceties or conventions, which I am perfectly willing to accept, then he lets me through. As a rule he will. It involves my not shocking him right away with painful data, but working around it rather craftily, and yet still in my own way getting the material across.

Are your hands tired?

(Jane paused to look at me. I nodded no, thinking it probably better that she continue. She did not look well, I thought, yet appeared to be holding her own. Since the trance state appeared to be acting as a shield or buffer, allowing her to digest the

material at a slower rate, I did not insist that she take a break.

(Jane had also begun rubbing her hands together in a way, I remembered, that meant they again felt "fat" or enlarged to her. Many sessions ago, notably in the 50's, this phenomena had been common to both of us. The last recent instance of it occurred in the 103rd session on a rather mild scale. It was now 9:30.)

I would prefer then to continue without a break, but I will end the session early if it appears advisable to do so.

It is <u>more</u> difficult for Ruburt if he has a break under such conditions as those that exist this evening.

The boy who delivered the message in Ruburt's dream was partially a dream construction, representing a George Pilotte Junior, with whom Ruburt felt an affinity in early life; a relative, a cousin who is also psychically connected with Ruburt's mother, and who is subconsciously connected in Ruburt's mind with the death of his grandfather, since the boy, who is now a man, was kind to Ruburt at that time.

The psychological experience today was a reinforced message, tied in with the others, which again Ruburt tried to forget and could not quite manage, because he has now trained himself to recall such data.

Such communications, though not necessarily tragic ones, are being received by every inner self. In this case, even while distortions come through, there is a validity of basic undistorted material.

I here suggest that Ruburt break after all. Give him a glass of milk and a bit of solid food, and then if he is up to it, and I think that he shall be, we will continue.

(Break at 9:40. Jane was dissociated as usual. She was also physically sick to her stomach. She said she could not have continued without a break. The thought of milk seemed most unpalatable to her while she felt this way, but upon taking some she began to feel better. She was surprised, and ate a few cookies.

(Jane said that she felt the material was a burden at this point. She was not trustful of it at the moment. She hadn't really thought Seth would say that her dream and psychological time data were correct; she didn't think, moreover, that Seth would ever come out with such material, no matter whose death was involved.

(Again, I was prepared to end the session at any time Jane seemed unable to carry on. The food and drink seemed to be most helpful, however, and she resumed dictation in a quiet voice. She paused often and paced quite slowly. Resume at 9:54.)

The distortions referred to, represent those occurring in the dream and in the psychological time experiences, particularly in today's experience in which Ruburt saw the white-gowned hospital personnel.

This made him more worried that the future death foreseen was his own, since he was looking up at a nurse and doctor while they looked down at him. He heard the words spoken by a nurse, "She is still in shock," but he distorted the words so that he remembered them as being, "She is coming out of shock."

The incident or hospital scene was valid, in that the death will occur in such surroundings. It reinforced the sex of the person involved, and it added the environment. Ruburt however constructed the images subconsciously, and then perceived them.

The particular event as he saw it was not valid, but the information contained therein was valid. The words, "She is still in shock", however referred not to the person whose death was being perceived, but the words referred to Ruburt (as Jane) still being in a state of shock because of the clairvoyant information.

Thinking that the words referred to the physical condition of the person whose death was foreseen, Ruburt changed them as mentioned in an effort to better the situation. You will see here that indirectly but clearly we have given you the identity of the person whose death is foreseen, particularly when I add to the positive statement, though it may appear negative, that your mother, Joseph, is in no way involved.

(Jane's voice was much quieter by now.)

Ruburt is calmer now, and I may add not only that his death was not involved in any manner, but also that his death will not occur for many years. He is extremely touchy, for all his training, upon this subject in general.

We can progress now to the subject of the car incident.

You thought you hit something in the road, a stone perhaps, and Ruburt was insistent that he had seen a cat, and that the car had struck it. He wondered what had happened to the cat, and you went back together to see.

There was no cat. The above mentioned matters were on his mind. His eyes under good circumstances are inefficient. He saw a gray brown bag of cloth used to collect leaves, and usually connected to lawn mowers. It lay on or by the curb with leaves in it and it, uh, it had, ah, metal eyelets and another projection.

(Jane had paused here, groping for the right words. Standing with her eyes closed, she attempted to describe to me by gestures what she meant by eyelets and "another projection." I didn't get it.

(The incident Seth is describing took place this afternoon. Long after it was over it was on our minds, for we did not like to think of an injured animal that had, perhaps, crawled away to die.)

It had been disconnected from a mower. The man left it momentarily. He was called inside. You hit this and threw it, but it did not fly up, and the color mixed well with the pile of leaves there. It was gone when you returned.

Now that this is finished, we can return again to the subject at hand, and the mirror instance. The mirror, again, would have offered valid data had Ruburt looked into it, but again he grew frightened. And the mirror was, once more, a means by which information could be made intelligible to him, and specific, though the mirror in larger terms did not exist.

This does not make the experience any less valid. Merely it was the use of a mental implement, through which valid information could be received. He did not use the implement, that is he would not look into it.

Now. We can say that Ruburt has received valid information concerning his mother's death, which has not yet occurred; but the conditions which will cause it have begun.

(Jane took long pauses before and after the following sentence.)

I will not give you a date at this time.

The physical conditions are irreversible, because of conditions that are not physical within the personality.

I will here close the session, giving you a fairly brief one because of circumstances, and I suggest for the rest of this week that Ruburt limit his psychological time experiments to fifteen minutes a day, rather than a half-hour, simply because he is under some strain.

You will be given all support from me, and from others, in the situation which will develop, and Ruburt will find that he will come through with a minimum of difficulty, considering the normal discomfiture involved in any circumstance of such nature. That is, there will be no added strain, due to the unusual relationship that has existed between him and his mother.

The situation for his mother would be much worse if she lingered, and she will find an exuberance, well-being, understanding and sense of peace, that she simply has not known in this particular existence.

I close now with sympathy and best wishes as always, and with some regret that I find myself in a position of corroborating this type of material. Needless to say, your increased abilities will make you aware of much added joy, and bring much pleasure, as well as sometimes bringing you tidings of this kind. And again, even now they serve to give you time for inner preparations.

("Good night, Seth.")

(End at 10:31. Jane was dissociated as usual. She was not sick now, if also not hilarious, and also looked much better. Actually she said, she felt much better for having the information out in the open so that she did not have to constantly wonder whether it was valid, distorted, etc.

(A reminder might be added here that Jane obtained the December date for her mother's death through the pendulum only. See page 128. Seth seems to be saying

that the event will occur soon, but we must wait. Jane has not seen her mother for some years now; the two women do correspond regularly, however.

(One development of possible interest concerning her mother took place last month, in October. Jane received a hand-knitted sweater from her mother as a Christmas present. In her accompanying letter Jane's mother wrote to the effect that she was sending the sweater ahead of time because she did not "expect to be around" by Christmas. I remember that Jane and I were struck by the tone of the letter, but in all honesty neither did we take it overly seriously. Jane may still have the letter. If it is found it will be filed with other data pertinent to the Seth material.

(At the close of the session Jane's right hand felt "fat" or enlarged.)

(Since Seth's suggestion Monday that Jane confine her psychological time experiments to 15 minutes, she has nothing to report for Tuesday and Wednesday, November 10-11, except for a rather mild feeling of general lightness.)

(The following material is from my psy-time notebook:

(November 10, Tuesday, 8:30 PM: Strong sensation several times, flooding over whole body very pleasantly. Followed by an alternating vibration in my feet, as though they felt or sensed an unheard vibration, a mechanical rhythm as of machinery. This had good duration. This was followed by several glimpses of a father and son, in old-fashioned clothes, pedaling about city streets on an old-fashioned bicycle, the kind with a large front wheel.

(Also Tuesday: While falling asleep near midnight, I saw my brother Loren very clearly if briefly. He was with a group of young men and women I did not know. It appeared to be summer. Loren wore a colorful short-sleeved sport shirt and a light brown straw hat with a narrow brim. I believe he carried a pipe in his left hand. He stood on the left side of my field of vision. Smiling at me, he held out his right hand toward me. I did not hear him say anything.

(Thursday, November 12, 7 AM: This morning, again while dressing for work, I had an experience very similar to the one of Tuesday, November 3. This time I did not have a clear-cut thought that I should look out my studio windows. Instead I found myself walking back to them, and looking out I saw that, again, a car was blocking the exit of my car from its garage. It was also the same car as before, belonging to a tenant living downstairs. This is, I repeat, not the usual system for parking here.

(However I did not think much of this, and since Jane was already getting breakfast at the other end of the apartment, I forgot to mention it to her by the time I sat down to eat. And as before, by the time I left the apartment, the other car had been moved.

(What I did not know was that right after I left the apartment Jane had a sudden strong urge to walk back to the studio and look out. She found herself doing this almost without thinking, for she felt that my garage was blocked by another car. She did not see the car that had been blocking my way, for it had been moved by then. She saw me back out of the garage as usual. I did not look up to see her for I did not expect to. Jane says this is the first time she can remember that she has checked up to see if the garage was blocked. Nor does she watch me leave for work. She too forgot the incident until I happened to mention my experience at lunch.)

SESSION 106
NOVEMBER 11, 1964 9 PM WEDNESDAY AS SCHEDULED

(Today marks a week since Seth's statements concerning a writing sale on Jane's part. See the 104th session, pages 125-6. Jane has yet to receive word of a sale of any kind.

(She does continue to receive encouraging letters from publishers. The latest arrived yesterday from Playboy Magazine. It was a long letter, and the editor asked to see more of Jane's work. She met this editor some years ago. She has not met two other executives there who have taken some cognizance of her work, and we now speculate that the situation described by Seth on page 126 might apply to Playboy. It will be interesting to check future events.

(It is also interesting to note that the nodule or ganglion on Jane's left wrist is almost gone. Seth dealt with this in the 98th session. See page 77. Seth stated that the nodule would disappear. Jane had in fact forgotten about it. She was reminded of it because of a slight ache, incurred when she held her arm over her head for an extended period of time.

(Jane had no idea of the material for the session. She was not nervous. She appeared to have fully recovered from the impact of Monday's session. Her manner was normal in all respects.

(Again, she began dictation with her glasses off. Her eyes were dark as usual, her voice normal, her pacing rather slow although it speeded up a bit later. Her delivery was not fast, and also broken by pauses.)

Good evening.

("Good evening, Seth.")

I have been promising you a short session so long that tonight I may finally give you one. Unless of course I get carried away.

I am most pleased with the chapter that Ruburt has written to open our book, [*How To Develop Your ESP Power*], and as you shall soon discover, events will work out as I predicted they would in the late summer.

Of course we have more material yet to cover on the nature of matter as it appears to you. Much of this material will be discussed along with data concerning the construction of the dream dimension. There will be completely new subjects also to concern us.

I am holding a rather brief and quiet session this evening because of the effort involved for Ruburt in our last session. It quite made up for two regular sessions, and I will not go into that subject matter at all this evening.

Nor will we discuss clairvoyance, except to mention that such incidences may appear frequently within the sessions as Ruburt gains confidence. Indeed, that details have appeared is evidence of increased confidence on his part.

I do not consider these small helpful hints of future events to be the sort of demonstration which in certain circumstances could annoy me. And any annoyance that I do feel is merely with the impatience that requests for demonstrations may hide.

You are both moving into a most profitable season, and a most fulfilling one in many respects, and this is the result of discipline and focused energies on both of your parts.

One small note here that I meant to mention earlier. It is true in one respect, in a very large respect, that your physical universe as such does not exist, in the manner in which you suppose that it does. In another sense it does legitimately exist, but in a way in which your ordinary senses would never perceive it.

(Note that this relates to the ideas Jane had during her trance experiment of November 4. *See page 116.)*

As you know, it is the focus of your perception upon certain reference points, to the exclusion of others, that helps to tie your universe together. If you distinguished other quite legitimate reference points also, then your physical universe would be indistinguishable to your perceptions; that is, physical perceptions, lost in a maze of seemingly chaotic data. Such data, such other reference points, come into your perceptions however as you are ready for them, and they change the horizons and whole conception of your universe as they do so.

As for example Freud added a dimension to your world with his discovery of the true subconscious, as far as he was able to perceive it.

Before this your psychological world was a flat one, and discoveries can now be made, and new reference points be recognized, that would have been impossible before.

These points are highly significant, and the world of the inner man will be found to gain depth, shape, motion, in and through space and time.

Discoveries in this realm will be fully as magnificent as those like discoveries in the world of physical matter; and again, because ideas and psychic energy form the basis of the physical universe, an expansion and thrust in the realm of idea will serve to actually expand and change the nature, scope and dimension of your physical universe, and in a way that could be achieved in no other manner.

I suggest your break.

(Break at 9:27. Jane was dissociated as usual. She said she felt fine, and did not know whether she needed the rest or not. We soon decided however not to press for a longer session. Jane resumed, again without her glasses, in the same manner at 9:30.)

Ruburt's attempt at predictions is an excellent idea and should be continued. He may find that his scope of perception may enlarge.

It is difficult, rather, for me to leave you so early, since I enjoy our sessions. Nevertheless I will follow my own resolution. Ruburt has sufficiently worked already this week, and his energy should be directed elsewhere while he recuperates. There is no serious energy loss here. My purpose is to keep you both in a state of disciplined exuberance however, and I keep a most cautious eye on any, even minute, psychic fatigue. He is not suffering from psychic fatigue. This is a mere and perhaps unnecessary precautionary gesture on my part.

His own work will go well this week, and his energies be refreshed through his usual activities, and also through painting if he finds time. The fifteen-minute limit for psychological time experiments should be kept until our next session, at which time I will give other directions according to the situation.

My heartiest good wishes to you both. With your permission I will look in on you from time to time before our next scheduled session, simply because I enjoy your company.

("Good night, Seth.")

(End at 9:39. Jane was dissociated as usual. She felt somewhat let down and disappointed that the session was so short: "It seems real odd. I feel like a person who expects company for a nice long chat, only to have them just say hello.")

(The following are from Jane's psychological time notebook:

(November 12, Thursday: 15 minutes; merely a light feeling.

(November 13, Friday, 11:30-45 AM: Definite feeling of lightness, or weightlessness. Odd sensation of inner, not physical, motion, and of pulsation.

(Falling off to sleep, I saw very clearly a dark brown doorknob that was on a white door. So plainly I thought my eyes were open.

(November 16, Monday, 11:45 AM: Good state achieved.)

(The following account is from Jane's dream notebook, and is included here because Seth mentions it in the 107th session. This dream is also directly related to Jane's dream of November 8. See pages 128-129.

(Jane's dream, Monday, November 16, 5 PM [as Jane took a nap]:

(I was with Doctor Kiley and another man who was also a doctor. Doctor Kiley is also dead, has been for some years, at least seven, and was a brother of Helen McIlwain; she was in my dream of November 8, relating to my mother and Seth's subsequent statements concerning her death. Now, Doctor Kiley and this other doctor were joking and clowning around, laughing about another doctor in connection with my mother.

(Somehow, Doc Kiley grabbed me, spun me around in the air and hugged me. My clothes were in disarray, I told him laughing. Was the joke on my mother? Or on the other doctor they spoke of, or both?

(I remember Doc Kiley best from my grade school days, just as I do his sister Helen. I didn't see as much of them by the time I was in high school, then college. I remember his last years were tragic ones; he killed a woman while driving, and became an alcoholic. When I was small he gave me presents. In particular I remember a toy merry-go-round. He was a big heavyset man with a square jaw.)

(Then I was in Saratoga Springs, I think. I pointed to a spot in the air beside a telephone pole, and spoke about the two men—Kiley and the other doctor—who had "crashed through" a <u>barrier</u> of some kind. And that's how or why I was in Saratoga. Not clear here.

(I then spoke to Nan Zeizing, a girl I had gone to high school with. I am not sure, but think I said to Nan that those two men had come to get my mother.

(Nan also said Playboy was a good magazine; I agreed, saying that if one was to read uncritically, as most do, then Playboy would hurt you least of all. They had good stories, and were considering my work, I told her. Nan sat on a railing or in a doorway.)

(The following are from my psychological time notebook:

(November 12, Thursday, 8:55 PM: Strong thrilling sensation briefly. Good feeling of enlargement in tops of feet and hands, with duration. Arms especially felt as though they would lift up out of themselves. Also some vague glimpses of figures.

(November 13, Friday, 8:30 PM: Moderate sensation a few times. Hands and feet enlarged on the tops again to some degree. Once, very quickly, the bed beneath me "rippled." For a moment I thought I might be attempting to travel or lift up.

(Also saw a boy's head with dark curly hair on an unrolled scroll of some kind. I didn't know him. Could have been a drawing. Another glimpse of a boy

also, profile, though this was not clear at all.

(November 15, Sunday, 8:30 PM: Moderate sensation; some enlargement in hands and feet. Good state achieved. My hands then felt as though they were crossed upon my waist, though actually they lay at my sides.)

SESSION 107
NOVEMBER 16, 1964 9 PM MONDAY AS SCHEDULED

(While taking a nap late this afternoon, Jane had the dream detailed page 139.

(Reading some of the recent sessions on dreams earlier today, Jane got the idea that Seth would talk about dreams this evening.

(Jane did some work on one of her paintings last night. She later told me that while working on it she felt quite uneasy. The feeling lasted for some time. No definite thoughts came to her about the sense of unease, and she had difficulty putting it into words.

(She began dictation on time and in a normal tone of voice. Again her glasses were off, her eyes dark, her pacing rather slow. She spoke with some pauses, and continued to use them. However as the session progressed her tone and manner became rather more determined, and even a trifle grim.)

Good evening.

("Good evening, Seth.")

I am somewhat taken back to discover that Ruburt, upon learning to use his abilities, would also attempt to censure the direction of their use.

It is as if, with his ordinary eyesight, he tried to so censure himself that he saw only sunlight. Oftentimes information such as he has been receiving, is received but not correctly interpreted or understood, with the result that the physical and psychic organism is bound in nervous knots of apprehension, for which there seems to be no cause.

(And this certainly seems to fit the mood Jane was in last night.)

You cannot deny the normal coming of night by refusing to face it, and closing the outer eyes would only result in those very characteristics of night which the self tried to avoid. Nor would the pleasant characteristics of night be ever known, but night would forever mean terror and chaos, since it would never be given the recognition due it, and never explored.

So. The information that Ruburt has been receiving, by the very fact of its source, and by the very fact of the method of communication used, the information itself is proof that death is much more than an ending.

(Jane's voice now became much louder, briefly.)

If this information comes from a personality no longer in physical form upon your earth, then surely this is an indication that death is but entrance into another dimension.

The information brings, because of its nature, much more than you might think in its implications. In wishing to close himself to such information, Ruburt would wish to close himself off from beneficial knowledge, and from the kind of exploration which in itself expands, and opens barriers that are not really barriers but doorways.

This sort of experience does, for you, indeed have its unpleasant side, and the ego most naturally combats. Nor is this to be unexpected for any physical death, or knowledge of any such physical death, is considered automatically as a threat by the ego. Hence Ruburt fears that he, and not his mother, is here involved.

I wanted to explain this clearly.

Now. Connected with the above material, but rather opaquely, I will continue along other but parallel lines. I would return again to those questions asked: What was the first act of creation? How did it all begin?

It is basically as meaningless in essence, to ask this kind of question as it would be to pause in the middle of a dream, and wonder when first the dream location was created: To stand facing a dream landscape and wonder at what point in time the rocks had their origin. For there is a great similarity between the so-called world of dreams and the so-called world of matter, as you should know.

The material of the physical universe is created spontaneously and constantly, even as the dream locations in the dream world are so created; and as it is impossible in terms of time as <u>you</u> know it to set a point of beginning in the dream world, so it is impossible to attempt to do the same as far as the physical universe is concerned.

There has always been development, but not along any single line. You are only aware of development along certain lines because you focus upon some, and do not focus upon others. There is a give and take between the dream world and the physical world, and each makes or causes effects in the other.

In time as you know it, there simply is no point of first origin, since in the spacious present the past does not exist, as the future does not exist in those terms. The dream world is more closely connected with uncamouflaged experience in the spacious present, but it still is in a camouflage perspective, dealing with recognizable projections of material reality.

Because of its relative freedom, however, the self, returning from the dream world, can impart to the individual knowledge of much the physical self could not ordinarily be aware. Much of this knowledge, then, resides in the subconscious while the ego goes on its way.

I will suggest your break.

(Break at 9:30. Jane was dissociated, she said, but not to her usual degree. When she began dictating again she maintained her deliberate and rather determined manner; at the same time she spoke a little faster. Resume at 9:35.)

This connection between the dream world and the world of material is not unusual.

While the two dimensions seem entirely separate, and while it is most difficult, nearly impossible, to dwell within both simultaneously, there are effects which occur in both. The two perspectives or dimensions do exist simultaneously, even though you cannot inhabit them simultaneously.

The barrier, if it may be so called, is not so much in the nature of the two dimensions themselves, but in your own limitations, since presently you are focused mainly in <u>one</u> of these. Until a certain area of psychic development is attained, awareness, or rather <u>direct</u> awareness, is only possible in one dimension at a time, though experience in other dimensions in varying degrees may be received separately.

As awareness develops, so do the abilities develop that enable the whole self to handle ever-varying data, and therefore to manipulate it and function within the perspective of its meaning. There are—

(Here, I abruptly had a coughing spell as I attempted to swallow a sip of milk. It was rather severe and I had to stop my taking of notes. Jane waited quietly, watching me while I tried to breathe. Perhaps a minute passed.)

I suggest a brief break.

(Break at 9:43. Jane was this time more fully dissociated, she said. She felt "funny" when I started to cough, since even though she stopped dictation she still felt suspended between the trance state and the regular state of being. She said she couldn't pull out of the trance easily until she said we should take a break. She wasn't able, for instance, to quickly run over to try to help me. As far as I can recall this is the first time an interruption of this kind has occurred during her dictation.

(Again without her glasses, Jane resumed at 9:48.)

There are other dimensions, some of which you are almost ignorant, in which however you exist, or have some valid effect; where you are projected and where in one way or another you form a reference point.

You are not known for what you are in these dimensions. You are not recognized in your human form. You are known only by effects. In some of these dimensions you are chemically and even electrically a reality, in others electro-magnetically.

In some, only the constant telepathic psychic communications are picked up. These, in this particular other dimension, appear as something that could be compared to the winds that sweep across your own earth.

These projections, from this dimension into others in this manner, again, are not unusual. Projections in terms of reference points appear also in your dimension, and you have as little knowledge or understanding of their true nature, as inhabitants of other dimensions have of your own.

In all these cases the available projections are interpreted according to the set conceptions of those in whose dimension they appear, and the data can only be interpreted according to the particular camouflage patterns which are inherent for existence within a given dimension.

Yet these projections or effects from your dimension into others, and from other dimensions into your own, do cause definite reactions within the plane in which they occur; and various attempts will be made, and are made to interpret them, but always within the framework of accepted, known phenomena. Therefore such attempts in this manner are doomed to failure.

As you know, camouflage elements are formed from the vital energy, which itself forms of itself all dimensions and all realities. It exists within all camouflage, since the camouflage itself is merely the form that is adopted. The inhabitants of any dimension, or whatever makeup, are still whole-self constructions.

The whole self as you know has its existence in uncamouflaged energy, and is therefore capable of the assimilation of knowledge in so far as it can, if it chooses, be basically unaffiliated to any one camouflage dimension or perspective. In actual practice this takes a supreme development, but even for general purposes the inner self retains a freedom from camouflage perspectives, and is aware in varying degrees of other perspectives, and of its existence outside of them.

Through the inner senses, therefore, some enlightenment can be received as to both the actual existence of dimensions that the physical self cannot perceive; and also through the inner senses, a sense of confidence and continuity can be achieved through the inner self's knowledge of its freedom.

The subconscious has great and rather astounding effect in dimensions other than your own, and it sends vivid projections into these other perspectives, that appear there and are in their turn perceived in distorting manner by the outward camouflage senses of those inhabitants. And yet their inner senses give them hints of your reality.

You exist and have effects in more realities than you know, and you perceive bits and pieces of other perspectives that appear in your own dimension. This is why I have told you, long ago, that your cause and effect theory was ludicrous. It only applies to your own dimension, and will never make headway in explaining those numberless projections that appear within your universe from a dimension separated from it.

I will not say outside of it since in many instances, if you speak in terms of space as you know it, then in space many perspectives occur together. It is not space that separates, it is the focus and the form of energy.

You may take a brief break.

(Break at 10:15. Jane was fully dissociated this time. My writing hand was also tiring, since her rate of dictation had continued to be fast.

(Jane had been delivering the material while pacing barefoot around the room. At one point she inadvertently knocked her foot against a metal coffee table leg. The blow made a good noise and I expected her to break off dictation, or at least wince. However she continued on as though nothing had happened. She now told me she felt her foot strike the leg of the table, but that ordinarily it would have bothered her a lot more than it did.

(Jane resumed in a slightly slower fashion, with more pauses. She laughed as she began, and this accompanied her remarks concerning her practice of psychological time. Resume at 10:19.)

I am indeed going to end the session shortly, giving Ruburt some relatively brief ones.

He has been doing so well at his homework.

I still do suggest the fifteen minute limit that he has adopted for psychological time, until the end of the week. And then we shall see.

You will find that we have gone somewhat ahead this evening in our material. I wanted to mention the fact that the subconscious has definite effects, and casts definite projections into other dimensions or perspectives, as a basis for a more thorough discussion on the levels of the subconscious.

So far we have covered the areas of the subconscious from almost a one-dimensional view, using depths to be sure, but only in the most shallow of terms, and we will progress as we should.

There are here in what you call the subconscious, abilities and realities of which you know little, and as you see how the subconscious projects itself into other dimensions, so will you see more clearly how energy is projected outward to form your own world of matter. There is much here to be explained.

My most dear friends, I will now close our session, and may I say to Ruburt, if he will let me: Be of good cheer, for there are lights where you think there is darkness. And may I again assure him that his existence is in no way involved with any of the information he has received, at all.

Your help, Joseph, has been most beneficial to him, and it is difficult naturally for him to manage this sort of data; but if he could not manage it he would not have received it, since we are developing an integration here. And I have protected him from a vulnerability to experiences that would be, or that would present, a danger to the overall balance of the personality.

I am developing, or helping him develop, his abilities with all caution. Your abilities are indeed developing and even now growing, in a different manner, beneath the surface, but they will show themselves, and much to your benefit.

Now, my most fond good wishes to you both.

("Good night, Seth."

(End at 10:32. Jane was dissociated as usual.)

SESSION 108
NOVEMBER 18, 1964 9 PM WEDNESDAY AS SCHEDULED

(Trying psychological time for fifteen minutes on Tuesday, November 17, and Wednesday, November 18, Jane achieved an excellent state on each day.

(I have little to report concerning my recent psy-time experiences, achieving little beyond a moderate sensation. This appears to be a low point for me.

(Yesterday a friend from our Sayre days visited us. We had not seen Sonja for several years. She is a nurse, has married a doctor from Turkey, and is spending a few months in this country before joining him in Turkey. Sonja has always been attached to a portrait I had painted before Jane and I were married, and at various times had urged me to sell it to her. Yesterday she asked me again to sell her the painting, and I did even though it had sentimental value for Jane and I.

(The portrait is one of my "people" that I had painted without a model, which is my favorite way of doing people. Seth has said that I paint these portraits of unknowns because I have received telepathic data on them. At one time I had decided never to sell the portrait, but gradually changed my view on this in the light of my own feelings, along with Seth's statements concerning my using my work to influence others. Yesterday I thought I had more understanding why Sonja wanted the painting, and so decided to sell it. I felt it might possibly remind her of a past life, or a past-life location. The painting was rather abstract, but hinted at a Middle East background, and the head was in a turban of sorts.

(I did not know it at the time, but Jane would have preferred that I keep the painting. Truth to tell, we both missed it after Sonja left. However I have pho-

tographs of it and will now do another one similar to it. The results should be better since I am a better artist now.

(Jane had no idea of the material for the session. She began dictation in a voice a bit deeper and stronger than usual, and again without her glasses. Her eyes were dark, her pacing slow, and she spoke with her usual pauses.)

Good evening.

("Good evening, Seth.")

I also miss the painting that hung there upon the wall; and while I will not take up much of this session with this material, I will nevertheless make here a few comments concerning the person to whom the painting was sold.

No doubt here of jumbled relationships as far as the personality is concerned. We find here a personality once a warrior in the very early period of the Ottoman empire, and no coincidence that the personality is now involved with that country.

No coincidence here either, the difficulty of establishing definite sexual role. The painting always struck the personality deeply, reminding him, because of the face portrait and the background, of the bare and ancient land from which he had once come, and to which he returned.

I would like to speak this evening further along the lines of camouflage. Matter is as you know camouflage, the <u>out</u>wardness of energy. The outwardness is formed through the <u>in</u>wardness, not the other way around.

There is always an excess of this inwardness, struggling to express itself in an outward form. For this reason a study of the outwardness will never result in true comprehension of the inwardness. There will always be that inside which is still unexpressed.

The inwardness is individualized. This is the rule. There is no unindividualized energy. There is no energy that is not to some extent aware of itself; having sought and achieved expression through physical form in one way or another, it is not satisfied but forever seeks more complicated gestalts.

The inwardness therefore flows through and forms matter, and the inwardness remains when it has finished expression in any given form. As you know in the case of man, memory, experience and value fulfillment is not lost as the inwardness disregards one form. This would deny value fulfillment itself.

I have told you that energy always regenerates itself, but the implications here psychically are astounding, as the inward energy forms gestalt after gestalt; and each gestalt itself then continues to go on, itself regenerating, forming new personalities which are never destroyed.

The entities, like master memory cells, store knowledge of its, or their, gestalt personalities; and even these entities are often split in many pieces, and each segment retains the complete data that belonged to the original entity.

Here you see, psychically and electromagnetically, something close in concept to your birth process, but without the eventual death of the parents. For this psychic creation is spontaneous. This inwardness of course is the basis for all existences, and pushes its way into everything that is, since it is the inwardness of all.

There are possibilities in all inwardness, that seek to establish conditions that will make it possible for them to come into existence. They, the possibilities inherent in inwardness, collect magnetically, so to speak, about other like possibilities, setting up coherent fields of like attractions. In your universe they began with the psychic possibility of a world of physical matter, born in consciousness.

They formed atoms and molecules, after first spreading out a positive field. There was also therefore from the beginning here a negative field, and as they weaved matter in and out of this psychic beginning meshwork, they formed both the world of matter and of negative matter.

The inwardness, as you know, is conscious of itself; but forming this new universe it could express its consciousness only through matter as it formed it, beginning with the innate, rather generalized consciousness of atoms. When sufficient atoms were formed from inward energy, then more various combinations became possible, and with them an accelerated consciousness could be made apparent.

I suggest your break.

(Break at 9:30. Jane was well dissociated for a first delivery. Her diction had again become quite positive and elaborate, almost forceful and loud. She resumed in this manner at 9:39.)

This inwardness is so adaptive and self-generating, seeking all outlets and possibilities, that it not only in your case formed a physical universe, but found new ways, operating through the new physical universe, to construct an additional field or plane within and completely through, or on the other side of while yet within the physical universe; this being your dream world, which is made possible because of the physical mechanisms and involvements themselves.

And then within this same physical universe, the inwardness was not content to find expression through but one form only, but in multitudinous forms and degrees. What you call reincarnation is only one aspect of a particular interest in the whole regenerative psychic process within your physical universe.

Remember now that the abilities of the inwardness determines the outward form, species and so forth. In the beginnings within your universe psychic characteristics grouped into units of attraction, so that mental enclosures were formed that could be compared to the smallest physical particle.

Initially these mental enclosures formed as much matter about themselves as they could manage, capturing other such enclosures through attraction when possible, in which case the two groups thusly joined both benefited by the additional matter that they could form. For there is this excess of inner energy, and when two such enclosures joined they could between them form more matter through interrelationships, than either could alone.

The unified units, then stronger, began again the process of joining with other such units through attraction. Some such units closed their boundaries and therefore captured, so to speak, no other psychic inwardness, but were content at this stage; and they became self-contained, relatively changeless physical units.

These units however, while not adding any more matter to themselves and being self-contained, could and did become units that were used as building blocks by other units which continued, not yet completed. And here the self-completed building block units, while not expanding within themselves, still became part of more complicated gestalts.

It will be found in some important respects that the dream universe, which began even then, has somewhat the same relationships to the physical universe, but on a psychic level, that the physical universe has to the universe of negative matter. They represent skins, layers of skin, all belonging to the same fruit. Someone holding the fruit might be able to peel away the layers, but as for the fruit itself, the layers while making up the fruit are to all intents and purposes separate.

I suggest your break.

(Break at 9:59. Jane was again well dissociated. Again with her glasses off, she resumed in the same energetic and definite manner at 10:02.)

A note here.

In your paintings, Joseph, you attempt to show the inwardness behind the completed physical construction, to hint at the endless nature of the inwardness which is imprisoned briefly in the outwardness.

When Ruburt attempts his paintings he tries to catch the inwardness before its moment of construction, with the form not yet fully in appearance, but between. It is for this reason that he has so much difficulty with his perspective.

He is concerned with inwardness just before it materializes within your perspective. You, Joseph, look through the outward in its physical completion and perfection, through to the inwardness which fills your paintings of physical objects, as it fills physical objects themselves.

Through the outwardness, beautifully constructed, you hint at the significance within, and you bring it out, actually through, the form. Ruburt shows the inwardness, trying to express itself in form, the coming together at the point just before the physical event.

He hints at the object, looking from the inside out. You do not see here a sort of partnership that applies to your relationship in general, the reason also for his technical inability in painting, and his technical ability in writing.

Allegorically speaking, from the inside he reaches outward, his hands full of inwardness, but it is you who form the inwardness. In the past you have been afraid of what you considered, but no longer consider, the chaos of inwardness. And he was afraid of what he considered the frozen nature of the inwardness, once formed.

He is now more able to deal with this, and you are much better equipped now to grapple with the inwardness, so that you have both helped each other immensely in this way.

This has been somewhat, though not too far, off the subject. I had intended, and still will, involve us in a discussion of the parallel development of the physical universe, the world of negative matter, and the dream world. For each one depends upon the existence of the other.

There are so many interconnections, and with the construction of the physical universe inward energy was so inventive, that even further possibilities began early to show themselves. Anything constructed, in any field, attains reality.

Reality means consciousness, and through the very physical apparatus developed by inwardness, which was aware from the beginning, further embellishments became possible for consciousness itself. The inwardness not only formed physical matter then, but formed new dimensions of inwardness itself, new dynamics from which consciousness could originate.

As within your universe, as a personality reincarnates into different form, you have the retention of the original personality, intact, with its memories in the subconscious; and you have the additional formation of a completely new personality time after time.

There is a splitting away from the original psychic branch, but with memory of previous individual existence.

(See the 54th session, May 18, 1964, Volume 2, page 91, etc. Seth deals with this fact to some extent as far as his relationship to Jane is concerned. Jane is not Seth now, he states, not his subconscious mind; nevertheless Jane's entity Ruburt is, now, an extension and materialization of the Seth that he was at one time, centuries ago.

See also the 63rd session for a brief mention of the same theme.)

The individuals continue to exist, and express themselves according to their development in other fields not connected with yours, when they are finished on your plane. No particular identity is ever lost. If so the whole process would be meaningless. And in other ways to lesser degrees, through abstract thought, through art of any kind, the physical human being, having been formed by consciousness, in his own way then working through and with matter, constructs other fields or planes of attraction, which according to their abilities expand.

This is not difficult to understand when you consider the relative difficulty in understanding even the simplest of physical phenomena alone.

You may take a break and I will continue briefly, or if you prefer we can end the session.

("I'll take a short break, then.")

(Break at 10:29. Jane was again well dissociated. My writing hand was tiring, otherwise I would not have taken the break. Jane's pace had been fairly rapid. She resumed in the same active manner at 10:34.)

It is impossible to go into many matters which you are waiting for until more tie-ins are made.

The communications occurring from your landlord's father, for example; none of this is forgotten on my part. It is merely that the questions you may think simple often require a complicated background in an answer.

Nor have I forgotten any of the psychological time incidences. These will all be covered in a particular sequence of particular material devoted to them in a chunk, so to speak. Nor could I have even begun this explanation of the relationship and growth of the physical universe, the universe of negative matter, and the dream universe at a much earlier date. The preparations had to be laid.

There is a communication possible between your universe and the universe of negative matter, but it does not involve the physical self. You are, in your present, confined to our imaginary fruit, yet to some extent you can know it much more thoroughly than you do, and its three layers can be understood to a much greater degree.

When you attempt space travel for example, you are attempting to travel around the complete fruit, but only within or upon one layer of skin. The circle is indeed important; and traveling in one dimension only about it, on the physical plane even, would require more, much much more, abilities than you have available.

There will be much more said here, but it cannot be said now. It would not make sense to you.

I am afraid that I will have Ruburt continue with the shorter psychological time period again until our next session. This will keep things in proper balance, and whether he realizes it or not, he is becoming accustomed to controlling energy acceleration, and automatically adapting himself.

(Jane now gave a broad smile as she paced about the room.)

This session has been extremely fruitful, all layers considered.

It amuses me, as a last thought, that your word "pit", in sound, is like a core, and suggesting depth for considering inwardness as the pit. You see how the matter is built around it.

I will have more to say also about your paintings, Joseph.

I will now close, although I am in fine form and coming through very clearly, and could indeed carry on splendidly for quite a while. However, I will here consider your convenience, and so I say a most fond good evening to you both.

("Good night, Seth."

(End at 10:50. Jane was dissociated as usual. Seth, she said, "came through like a bell." My writing hand was tired.

(As this material continues to expand, Jane and I realize more and more that indeed nothing is simple in explanation. For this reason we have curtailed our questions concerning a quick explanation on any subject that might interest us at the moment. Most of the time now we do not even ask.

(Both of us have kept strict records of our psychological time studies, for example, with the hope that Seth will eventually discuss them. The records have now piled up to such an extent, however, that we do not really understand how Seth can ever cover them, as he has promised to at various times, in very much detail. Even if he began a discussion of them they would still accumulate. The same problem arises with dreams, with material on the inner senses, etc. So we settle for what we can obtain each session. Actually the time set aside for gathering material is quite limited, yet it keeps us busy.

(I am not sure that Seth's statement on page 150 constitutes a distortion, when he mentions that a communication between our universe and the universe of negative matter is possible. In the 63rd session, again, he deals with the two companion universes to ours, calling them a beforeimage and an afterimage, and lumping them under the general terms of negative or antimatter. In the 63rd session Seth states that our universe and the two universes comprising the universe of negative matter can never meet. Perhaps the point here is what kind of a "meeting" he was referring to in the 63rd session. He is referring to a psychic communication in the present session.)

(The following material is from Jane's psy-time notebook:

(November 19, Thursday, 11:30 AM: Excellent state achieved.

(November 20, Friday, 11:30 AM: Same.

(November 23, Monday, 11:45 AM: Saw a funny tall cylinder structure covered with red wood. It was not wood inside. I heard the name "Toby" mentally. Thought it might be a person's.

(It will be recalled that Jane is still limited by Seth to fifteen minutes of psychological time practice a day. See the 105th session.)

(The following material is from my psy-time notebook:

(November 19, Thursday, 8:30 PM: Mild thrilling sensation upon lying down. Hands enlarged somewhat on tops. The unusual thing achieved this time was that my left heel came to feel that there was nothing beneath it, as though it hung off the edge of the bed. The sensation had good duration and was unmistakable. I verified that my foot actually was on the bed by exerting pressure. This sensation is like some Jane has experienced recently. She achieved a much greater degree, however, as when she attempted to travel psychically and ended up in her trance of November 4, 1964. See page 116.

(November 23, Monday, 8:15 PM: This was my most active experience since resuming psychological time study. I experienced sensation, sight and sound. Most of the sightings and sounds are now hard to recall, frustratingly enough, but they were very vivid at the time, and I did achieve partial duration in memory.

(Among other things I saw a skull, rather humorous, popping up on a wobbly stem above a box of some kind like a jack-in-the-box toy. There was no fright or concern involved on my part. It flashed very briefly, in the middle distance. Also I saw a bright yellow light flash behind the seated figure of a man at a desk. I did not know the man.

(When I first lay down I had the feeling that a door had opened out of my vision to the left, letting light creep slowly in. I had to squeeze my left eye shut to make sure it was closed. The right eye was not so affected. My sensation swept over me several times. One time I saw a group of men and women walking out of a deserted house into a field of knee-high brown weeds, and heard them talking plainly.

(Monday night, November 23, 12 PM: Upon retiring I experienced with good duration many sightings of painted trees, brush, etc. in fall colors. Had been working on such a landscape today.

(November 24, Tuesday, 12:00 PM: Again a very vivid experience. First upon retiring I had a recurrence of seeing the painted trees, for some little time. I then switched to receiving other vague scenes which I quickly lost track of.

(Then, evidently in a good state between waking and sleeping I had a most vivid sighting. From high up in the air I found myself looking down upon a white

snow-covered landscape with white mountains and flat white expanses, and a vivid blue sky. It was rather brief but very clear. I saw a round hole, evidently cut into ice; at the hole were two men wearing white fur suits, and moving about the hole as though perhaps fishing through the ice.

(The scene flickered at full strength for a second then was gone. I was so surprised I spoke aloud; Jane answered and I then described it to her so I wouldn't forget it by chance until I could write it down in the morning. After speaking to her, I again saw the two figures less clearly, walking or climbing in the rough white terrain.

(Seth's recent statement that my psy-time experiences would shortly become more vivid seems to be working out. See the 100th session.)

SESSION 109
NOVEMBER 23, 1964 9 PM MONDAY AS SCHEDULED

(Jane feels she could have had a session at about 3:30 PM, Saturday, after a rejection from Playboy arrived in the mail. The rejection slip was not accompanied by a letter and this made her angry. She thought of Seth's statements in the 104th session, concerning a sale that "has developed," and wondered just what the statement meant. She doubted its veracity. She then received from Seth, mentally, a firm statement repeating that a sale <u>has</u> developed. I was talking to her at the time but she did not mention the incident to me.

(Around suppertime Saturday when we were again discussing the matter of interpretation of prediction data, Jane again felt Seth nearby. This time she mentioned it to me but I left it up to her, as to whether she wanted a session. She did not take me up on the situation and so none was held.

(As session time approached Jane had no idea of the material for the session. She told me she "still feels funny" even after all this time, when she hasn't any idea about the material to come.

(Jane began dictation in a normal voice, at an average rate. Again her glasses were off, her eyes dark, her pacing regular.)

Good evening.

("Good evening, Seth.")

We have a variety of topics for this evening.

A small note here, mentioning a fact of which Ruburt is surely now aware. The momentary difficulty in the short story that he did not finish was simply caused by a very temporary relapse because of pressure: He did not wait for his subconscious to deliver an idea, as he has been long accustomed to doing.

When he grabs upon a definite whole piece of autobiography, it is usually caused by impatience. He is past that momentary lapse.

I would like to speak concerning the parallel development of the universe of matter as you know it, the universe of negative matter, and what is truly the universe of dreams.

We have spoken concerning the relative impossibility of first origins as you consider them, occurring at a particular point in your time. Inward, individualized, aware energy existed before the conception of your time, your time obviously being an interpretation of the spacious present, from which all creation not only originally began but continues in terms of value fulfillment. Without such a development before the conception of your time, indeed, your universe would never have come into existence.

There are points, quite imaginary, that can be used as references. However, those who ask concerning the time of the origin of consciousness within your universe, are those who do not understand that the most minute physical particle, the most microscopic, is a materialization of inner, aware energy.

To those who ask concerning the origin of that inward energy you may say that the inwardness came from itself. In the spacious present there simply is no past. There can be no point of origin in time as you conceive it. It is only within your camouflage perspective that this remark appears illogical, but this does not mean that you still cannot grasp some of its meaning, using your own inner experience.

Every man dreams. I have told you that as the dream is only connected by the smallest thread to your time, so also, although it is difficult, you could manage to pinpoint the apparent beginning of a dream in clock time. This time, you know intuitively, has no psychological inner relationship to the dream experience.

It is true that physical stimuli may signal a dream, but the stimuli, the physical stimuli, does not actually signal the beginning of the dream; but it calls your attention to the dream, which has been in progress, as if you walked into a darkened theatre and began to see portions of a production which had been going on.

You would know better than to think that your awareness of the movie signified that the movie began only when you appeared. You construct dreams automatically, so to speak, with one level of your being in the main, whether you wake or sleep, and whether you are aware of the dreams or not. This is an inner symbol manipulation that is carried out as automatically as you breathe or walk, a by-product of your own physical and psychic structure, of your chemical and electromagnetic constitution.

As the dream does not begin then at any particular moment, neither did your physical universe begin at any given moment, and neither did the inwardness become born in terms of cause and effect.

These are not mysteries. You have simply not tried to understand them. Actually your physics will soon glimpse the truths behind these statements, but they will merely glimpse possibilities.

(Now Jane smiled. She was quite amused as she paced about.)

I will truly confuse you. I will here add however not only that the universe you know had no particular origin in your time; and I will add that its roots, if we may so speak, continually go in all directions. Within your terms then they may be said even now to be traveling as far backward as they are forward, simultaneously.

I will suggest your break.

(Break at 9:29. Jane was dissociated as usual. She put her glasses on as soon as break arrived. She said that while delivering the above material she felt a strong sense of certainty that the sessions did not come from her subconscious; she felt an energy she knew she did not have available ordinarily.

(Jane's delivery had gradually become more emphatic as the session progressed, and she resumed in this more energetic manner, although still with pauses, at 9:35.)

The first origin, my dear friends, is constantly reoccurring, but never in the same or exact manner, never in terms of a rehappening or of a record played over and over.

(Seth has touched upon this subject before. See the 97th session, page 70.)

Again, it is your comparatively one-lined perspective that makes you think in terms of one particular beginning. This will undoubtedly be difficult to consider, nevertheless there are countless beginnings, even of your own universe, occurring at different reference points in various perspectives; and it is impossible to trace backward your own thin line, since it is interwoven and actually a part of so many others.

You, any man, participates in more varied perspectives than he knows consciously, and appears in one way or another in more dimensions than he knows. You may again recall our fifth dimensional imaginary structure. Since all parts were ultimately interconnected, it is impossible to give any one part an origin in terms that could be comprehended by anyone who inhabited a particular unit within.

(See the 12th session [in Volume 1] for most of the material on the fifth dimension. Note that this is an early session; it was held on January 2, 1964.)

I am again, not here praising the intuitions above the intellect. They are both intended for different purposes. They tune in on different realities, and all realities are actual. Nevertheless our last session, with its simplified explanation of development in terms that you can understand, should lead you to realize that because of the parallel development of the dream universe with the physical universe, the study of the dream universe will help you comprehend the basic inwardness behind the physical world that you inhabit.

Both the dream universe and the universe of negative matter then, are by-products of the physical universe, in that they were formed as inward energy attempted to form itself in a physical way.

The physical materialization was so constructed that it resulted in further regeneration of inward energy itself. I would like to repeat that dreams occur constantly, whether you wake or sleep; and this has always been the case. The dream universe has also affected your own physical universe, as the physical universe has strongly affected it.

Concepts, ideas, realized in dreams, have then been constructed physically. Physical constructions and inventions, purely in terms of a new intellectual comprehension of physical matter, have also transformed the nature of the dream universe, and enriched it, adding to the symbolistic freedoms possible there.

Earlier I mentioned fire, which was intellectually grasped by man and therefore materialized in the world of matter. Previously the dream world symbolically used fire only in terms of its power to transform matter. Man was not able to see fire earlier in terms of beneficial warmth or comfort. He could not for example in his dream universe then manipulate fire, except in terms of what he considered destruction.

With his intellectual appreciation of the benefits of fire that followed his physical mastery of it, then his dream universe became enriched with a new freedom. This is but one simple example. While development of the two universes overall is parallel, no exact evenness in all respects is achieved. That is, a concept may be brilliantly alive in the dream universe but unexpressed physically, or for one reason or another an intellectual comprehension in the physical universe may not find expression in the dream universe. But overall there is parallel development.

I will let you break.

(Break at 10:00. Jane was dissociated as usual. As soon as she stopped dictating she put her glasses on again. Without speaking any faster, she resumed in a somewhat louder voice at 10:07.)

The relationship between these two universes is truly astounding, and such interchanges have great transforming effects.

There are breakthroughs in the dream universe from the physical universe, as well as from the dream universe into your own. The dream universe, for the purposes of our explanation, is a specific one. For you I must speak in terms of directions, since there is difficulty due to your insistence on placements in space.

So for simplicity's sake I will have you imagine that the dream universe occupies a position on the other side of the physical universe, with the entity separated from the dream universe by the physical. Do you see?

(Jane had delivered the above material with many pauses, some of which were quite long. Now she looked at me and attempted by gestures to show what she meant. I nodded.)

Imagine the analogy psychologically again, using the physical universe as the ego, with the dream universe in one direction and the entity on the other.

It goes without saying, or should, that the inner self sends its projections of inner senses through both the physical universe and the dream universe; yet all this talk of space and placement is a mere convenience. Yet, in terms of physical construction this is what you would find, and this, if it were understood, is what is seen in the actual construction of the most minute physical particle under observation in your laboratories.

But the significance is not seen. No energy is not used. Entropy does not exist. It is the appearance only of an effect within the physical perspectives; that seemingly unusable energy helps form your dream universe. That energy from which you seem to get no work physically, that energy which seems to diminish in value, is plowed backward into inwardness, regenerated and used to form universes without which <u>you could not exist</u> even as physical beings.

For without the dream universe you could not exist physically. I am going to quickly embark into the universe of negative matter, but briefly, only to show you the interwoven quality of existence; and how we will follow it in discussion.

For energy regenerates itself. And as I have told you consciousness, conscious energy, continually manifests itself in various forms. Now. Remember last session's explanation of mental enclosures, composed of inward, individualized, aware energy, materializing itself in physical form, and at a particular point closing off and becoming more or less a closed system.

Do you recall?

("Yes."

(See the 78th session, August 10, 1964, [in Volume 2], for Seth's rather long discussion on the fallacy of the entropy concept in physics.)

A closed system could become captured, so to speak, and be used as a building block, still retaining its individuality, by other systems still expanding. In this manner your physical universe, dream universe, and universe of negative matter have come together, while retaining their boundaries as a more or less closed system.

You will have to understand that I speak for simplicity's sake, since no system is completely closed. Now. We have not said nearly enough about the dream universe, to really launch a discussion concerning its by-product. Nevertheless I shall tell you that its by-product is the world of negative matter.

I wanted to make this point for your edification. You will know where this material is going. But there is much to be explained before you can grasp the interconnections.

Now—you may take a break, or I will continue briefly; or you may at your pleasure end the session. I am that good-natured.

("All right, I guess we'll take a break.")

(Break at 10:29. Jane ended the delivery with a smile. She was well dissociated, she said, and had indeed been in a good state all evening. My writing hand was tiring, otherwise I would not have taken the break.

(Jane resumed at a somewhat faster rate at 10:37, again without her glasses.)

For practical reasons for our discussion, we will speak of these universes forming a closed system.

Energy seemingly lost or dissipated or unusable in the physical universe does indeed leave it; but it transfers itself, seeps into the dream universe, and there it helps to insure the existence of the physical universe itself, since the existence of each of these fields or universes is dependent upon the existence of the others, in most actual ways.

The energy is then transformed in the dream universe, and again regenerated and used in the formation of the universe of negative matter, into which it seeps from the dream universe. Our discussions will have to thoroughly discuss the nature of the dream universe before we can hope to consider the universe of negative matter, but it will not hurt if you keep the above mentioned facts in mind.

All the universes, while seemingly closed, have their origins one within the other. I mentioned sessions ago the connection between negative matter and positive matter, concerning the pulsations of energy into atoms in your universe. I also told you that you existed as long out of the physical universe as you existed in it, but I did not say that you existed identically.

(See the 61st session, June 10, 1964, [in Volume 2], for Seth's discussion on pulsations, and negative and positive matter.)

In some manners you do exist identically in the world of negative matter, but in most manners you do not. Psychologically, dear friends, you do not. I will at one time discuss a fascinating facet, though important not shattering, concerning identical twins, in which slip-ups have occurred in this line.

Psychologically there is no identity, although some aspects are shared. I am speaking here of identity between your selves and the existence of a parallel self in the world of negative matter. That parallel self would not be recognized by you, as psychologically identical, and is indeed quite independent, and a by-product. But since all beings can be said to be by-products in one respect, this does not imply any lack of equality.

We have gone quite far enough this evening, and I will shortly close. One note: Ruburt should remain for a short period only, still on the short schedule for psychological time. And in no case has there been a distortion in our predictions concerning Ruburt's sales. Not distortions as such. There has been somewhat a lack of correlation; and as you supposed, Joseph, sometimes in interpretation.

(This last statement would refer to the 104th session, November 4, 1964. See pages 125-6. Here Seth made rather strong statements concerning sales by Jane of her writings. Since none have developed yet as far as Jane being notified is concerned, we wonder how we should interpret such material.)

Ruburt's own experiments with predictions will accelerate his ability to let longer segments, concerning any one particular prediction, in our sessions to come through. You have received some quite legitimate bits and pieces, but the data have not been correctly correlated in your terms, so that you do not know how to put them together. But with practice there will be better, and if you will excuse the pun, more predictable results.

I will now close, though again I myself am in a frisky, companionable mood; and if you ever get your recorder serviced we can use it now and then, only on such instances; when the regular session is concluded and your hands are tired, we can chat.

My heartiest congratulations with your own progress, Joseph. And now good night, most fond chums.

("Good night, Seth."

(End at 10:55. Jane was fully dissociated. My writing hand was also quite weary.

(Seth has mentioned using the recorder before. I have wondered however just how much we will use it, when it is fixed. Usually by the end of a session Jane is tired, ready to quit. I would not be in favor of extending her labors in such cases. She would have to continue in the same manner as when dictating to me; my having a respite would do her no good.

(I presume Seth's congratulations to me refer to the accelerated rate of my painting sales, since I began to put some of his advice to use. Sales have been growing, much to my surprise. Indeed, I now have two advance orders for work not yet finished; this is the first time I have been in such a pleasant position, as far as sell-

ing paintings goes.)

(The following data are from Jane's psy-time notebook:

(November 24, Tuesday, 11:30 AM: Good state achieved.

(November 24, Tuesday, 12:00 PM: Before falling asleep, I saw a page of a Time magazine and was reading it. I don't recall what it said. I asked to see the headlines or cover. I then saw what I think was the cover. It was in big red block type, but blurred.

(November 25, Wednesday, 11:45 AM: Good state achieved.)

(The following data are from my psy-time notebook:

(November 24, Tuesday, 12 PM: By mistake I included this day's data on page 152; that is, before Monday's session instead of before Wednesday's session.

(November 25, Wednesday, 7:30 PM: I saw my painted trees again, and again with good duration. I also had some other sightings, and heard voices which I could not retain. However, I had an excellent experience which was reminiscent of mine on November 19, in which my left heel felt as though the bed had disappeared beneath it. Today the same sensation came, but this time I felt that the bed was gone from beneath both legs from the calves down. Both feet thus felt suspended in air. I could verify the fact of the bed beneath them in actuality, by exerting a downward pressure.

(The sensation lasted for many minutes and was quite pleasant. At one time I again had the feeling, also, of a "bridge" or connective of flesh, this time from my left heel to the inside of my right big toe. At the same time I experienced the sensation of having my wrists connected in the same way to my sides, as I lay upon my back. All three of these sensations were very definite. I also experienced my standard thrilling sensation a few times, to a mild degree.)

SESSION 110
NOVEMBER 25, 1964 9 PM WEDNESDAY AS SCHEDULED

(On Tuesday, November 24, we had as dinner guests Dee and Joe Masters. They no longer live in Elmira. It will be remembered that Seth has discussed both of them at various times in past sessions. Until about a year ago Dee was Jane's supervisor at the art gallery. Some predictions concerning them will be found in the 63rd session for June 17, 1964.

(Jane and I tried some ESP experiments with Dee and Joe, and obtained good results. In one of them Dee achieved a light trance state. I have notes on the

proceedings, and will include them in the record should Seth ever discuss them at some point in the future. Seth was not involved in Tuesday evening's activities in any way.

(On Wednesday, November 12, Jane sent a copy of the 44th session to A.J. Budrys, science fiction editor of Playboy Magazine. Jane and A.J. have met once, at a science fiction conference some eight years ago in Milford, PA.

(At this conference Jane, A.J. and three other science fiction writers formed a group they called "The Five." Letters were exchanged for some little time. In her letter of November 12 Jane asked A.J. a few questions about The Five. A.J. replied on November 22, stating that before he could answer Jane's questions he would like Seth's answers to three questions: "When was the last time you grew up?", "What do you love?", and "When is the self born?"

(A.J.'s letter arrived this afternoon, Wednesday, November 25. Since a session was due tonight, Jane studied the letter in the event Seth would choose to deal with it this evening. Just before the session was due she read the three questions aloud. Jane did not feel up to par and was not particularly in the mood for a session.

(The session turned out to be one of the slowest I can recall. Jane began dictation on time and in a normal voice. She spoke very slowly and with many pauses. Again her glasses were off, her eyes dark as usual. Her pacing was also quite slow. A.J.'s letter lay on my writing table.)

Good evening.

("Good evening, Seth.")

We will indeed at least begin with the questions which are being asked, though I will answer them in my own way.

(Jane smiled and picked up the letter.)

And I answer them, also, out of politeness, and also because parts of the answers will add to some of our own discussions.

I will also, though not necessarily at this session, but in this session or the next session, have some remarks concerning the man who asks for the answers.

(Now Jane lay the letter on the table and bent over it, studying it.)

I will answer now. The first question I presume refers to growth in the terms in which growth is usually considered, a coming toward maturity in terms of physical and mental approach to a hoped-for fulfillment.

In these terms, and giving the simplest explanation since your friend is not well acquainted with our previous discussions, my last growing-up period occurred in Denmark, in the same approximate period as the one given previously for a previous life of your own, Joseph, and of Ruburt's.

That was the last time that I grew up, in what was a town called Triev.

("Do you want to give me the years on that?"

(In the 4th session, December 8,1963, Seth stated he lived in Denmark three centuries ago, and that Jane and I did also. According to Seth Triev no longer exists. It was situated near Eastern Roads. The use of the word Roads in this connotation may have a maritime meaning. See Volume 1 of The Early Sessions.

(Note also that Seth did not answer my question right away. This is often the case.)

I will continue. In terms of maturity I did not fulfill myself at that time. I am still growing as far as value fulfillment is concerned. Growing up, to your way of thinking, implies a growth or expansion also of physical stuff. The value fulfillment of which I speak carries no such connotation.

As to what I love, I find that question itself has many complications. I love the inquiring consciousness in whatever form it may appear. This is the simplest, most direct and spontaneous answer that I could possibly give.

(Jane smiled as she paced about the room.)

Another thought here is the love of continuing creation, which is continually formed by, through, and because of inquiring consciousness. It, inquiring consciousness, is as you know always individualized, and it is because of this amazing diversity that so many forms are possible.

Everything that is, is a materialization of aware, individualized, inquiring consciousness; and to love this is a personal, almost all-encompassing discipline and devotion. I say discipline because whenever, individualized inquiring consciousness expresses itself in form, it not only expresses its spontaneity; and this is not contradictory: But even while expressing its spontaneity, it disciplines it.

Form always implies a discipline. The love of individualized inquiring consciousness has always been my strength, and the source of my energy.

As to the third question, I suggest your break and I will answer it. I am, incidentally, giving fairly brief and spontaneous answers, as requested.

(Break at 9:28. Jane was dissociated as usual. She said she felt all right while delivering the material, but not as good during break. Her rate of delivery was so comparatively slow that perhaps half as much material as usual came through.

(She resumed in the same manner at 9:33.)

Indeed, as for my not defining terms, it is impossible not to define terms.

I experience concepts directly, as you know. These must of necessity be broken down into words that follow one after another, for our communications to take place. As such, I must end up trying to use your language rather than my own.

(Again Jane bent over A.J.'s letter as it lay on the desk.)

Words are quite ineffectual methods of communication. The question, "When is the self born?", would take many sessions to answer. As simply as possible the self, the inner self with which the ego is only vaguely familiar, that self which is the inner strength, continuity and identity, that gives the ego its vital meaning, that <u>inner</u> self, dear friend, is constantly being born.

There is no point in time as you know it, when the self is born. It is constantly in a state of becoming. It expands and develops in terms of value fulfillment, in a way that has nothing to do with space and time.

It develops, again, as <u>you</u> know, Joseph and Ruburt, it expands as an idea expands, taking up no space. The self may project itself into the dimensions of space and time, but the projection is a small part of its actuality. Even the uppermost or surface elements of the self with which you are familiar, the ego and the uppermost layers of the subconscious, even these cannot be said to be born at any given time, in time as you conceive it.

The self, Mr. A.J., is more than you know. It is capable of intelligence that you do not use. It is capable of making distinctions finer than you now imagine. The self, as other sections of this material explains, has methods not only of perception, but of criticism and judgment, that man in general does not take advantage of nearly as much as he could.

The self is limited only by its own idea of limitation.

Man has always feared what he could not objectify. He has always attempted to objectify, to separate whatever realities he could from himself, to hold them in his hands, so to speak, so that he could observe and study them.

Those things, those realities which were most intimately connected with himself, those realities which he could not objectify and hold in his hands, he feared. He attempted to deny the existence of such realities, yet he cannot. You cannot hold a psychological experience in your hand as you can a rock, though its weight may be indeed heavier than a rock. You cannot put it on a scale. Though its color, to continue our analogy, may be as gray, you cannot see a psychological experience as you can see a gray rock.

A psychological experience may take up no space as a rock takes up space, but when a psychological experience happens it may fill you up. Yet you do not deny the existence of a psychological experience, though you cannot rip it apart from yourself and examine it with the physical senses. Still it has its effect, and its validity is well known to every man. So also are there other realities that cannot be examined through the use of the physical senses, realities so close to the self that they cannot be separated from it and objectified.

This does not mean that they do not exist, nor does it mean that vivid, valid and definite evidence for their existence cannot be received; and evidence which will be accepted by the intellect. The method of investigation is simply different.

I suggest your break.

(Break at 10:02. Jane was dissociated as usual. She now said that she felt much better than she had before the session began. She still stuck to her very slow delivery however.

(During break we quickly looked through the early sessions to see if we could establish the year of Seth's birth. It had not been given. We did find that he died in 1655, in a fire in Sweden. Much of the reincarnational data is incomplete. Jane and I asked many questions about this kind of material in the beginning sessions, but as the material began to unfold such questions were pushed aside. Seth has said at various times during the year that we can bring such information up to date, but it seems that we do not get around to it. Thus it becomes one more category about which we have many unasked questions.

(Jane resumed in the same quiet and slow manner, again without her glasses, at 10:12.)

There must always be a balance maintained between spontaneity and discipline.

A combination of intuition and discipline can be used with most valid and definite results, as a tool for investigating those parts of the self which are so interwoven that they cannot be separated from the self.

In a very actual respect chemically, electromagnetically, extensions of any given self permeate your universe. For practical considerations, and to reduce the amount of data that need concern the self, rather arbitrary divisions are set up, where the self at one point is said to exist and at another is considered nonself.

Outward extensions of the self can be more clearly objectified, the concentration at the outward extensions being less, and identity correlations being kept in more concentrated areas within the boundaries of the physical self. The eye sees but it cannot see itself. In like manner the self is, but is not consciously able to examine that which it is. Therefore man must take his abilities and travel inward, since going outward will not allow him to perceive the inner portions of himself.

He has not done so to any great extent. Until most recently he would not admit the existence of anything unless he could objectify it. Now, even in his scientific studies he discovers that his senses have often misled him, his precious solid objects for example found to be solid only <u>to</u> his senses, an appearance given by the limitations of his sensual perceptions.

It is not that the senses are not to be trusted, merely that they are trustworthy only within the framework of certain definite limitations.

I am going to end our session. For your information Joseph, I was born in that existence in the year approximately 1486, and lived most of that life in the town called Triev, in the eastern part of the country, as a merchant dealing in spices.

I was indeed rather spicy myself. My kindest regards to Ruburt and yourself, and my regards to the man who asked that the questions be given to me. He lived two other lives, one in Spain approximately 1341, and one in England in the 1800's; this one as a banker in London. He as a personality has often been in the position of being distrustful of strong elements of compassion within himself in this life—

("Can you give us his entity name?")

—and alternates between an over-reliance on discipline on the one hand and intuition on the other, not yet able to weld the two so that they become two edges of one reliable tool. Strong abilities in both directions, however. Entity name Salden, S-a-l-d-e-n. I will now end the session. I cannot obviously in one evening cover all the matters that have been suggested here.

("Good night, Seth."

(End at 10:50. Jane was dissociated as usual. She felt much better than when the session began. Note that the date of Seth's birth, given as 1486, is probably wrong. Jane and I think it should be 1586. I did not catch this during the session and so did not ask about it. From material given in various sessions we think the date of Seth's death, given as 1655, is more likely to be correct. If Seth had been born in 1586 he would have been 69 at his death in 1655. I will ask about the discrepancy in the next session.)

(During our first test on Saturday, November 28,1964 at 8:10 PM, I told Jane that I would think of a series of random numbers. Each time I told her I had a number in mind, she tried to match it with her spoken answer.

Rob	*Jane*	*Rob*	*Jane*
6	*791*	*43*	*25*
23	*806*	*36*	*3141*
1	*73*	*54*	*2*
81	*203*	*89*	*94*
5	*1001*	*1*	*5620*
7256	*77*		

(In the second test, each time I spoke a word Jane answered it as quickly as she could, without thinking. She felt blocked at times.

Rob	*Jane*
news	*media*
good	*bad*
friend	*foe*
distant	*relative*
book	*(blocked)*
story	*(blocked)*
NYC	*(blocked)*
cat	*dog*
ice	*cold*
food	*fill*
rain	*snow*
night	*dark*
story	*sale*
playboy	*magazine*
house	*street*
tree	*cat*
dog	*cat*
car	*key*
shop	*worn*
book	*buy (slow)*
manuscript	*(blocked)*
sale	*boat*
Seth	*material*
Little Daddy	*grampa*
Dee	*Masters*
food	*bill*

Rob	*Jane*
clothing	*dresses*
cover	*all*
hardcover	*book*
script	*writer*
radio	*(blocked)*
anticipate	*state*
Malba	*(blocked)*
king	*features*
couch	*pillow*
apartment	*store*
Marian	*Spaziani*
type	*writer*
storyteller	*writer*
tale	*graph*
news	*media*
walk	*good*
fire	*machine*
automobile	*car*
editor	*A. J.*
NYC	*publishers*
announcement	*marriage*
Linda	*Butts*
Willy	*cat*
studio	*apartment*
painting	*Robby*

(Resume of the events of Saturday evening, November 28, 1964.

(Jane and I usually go dancing Saturday evenings, leaving the house at about 9 PM. Shortly before 7 PM Jane told me that she felt herself to be in an excellent mood of pleasant anticipation; she thought she might be trying to receive information, but did not know how to go about it.

(I was working at the time but we decided to take advantage of her mood. It was now dark outside. The night was windy and wet. We turned off the lights and sat at our table by the bay windows in the living room. Shadows were active; the room was rather well lighted by lights from passing traffic.

(First we concentrated on trying to move a small brass ring lying on the table between us, without success. At times the moving shadows gave us the illusion that

the ring did move. Next we sat in our living area, away from the windows, and concentrated on our Kennedy rocker. It did not move. Jane asked for help in attempting this from anyone who might be present. She still felt quite strongly her mood of anticipation. Again, the changing shadows gave us the illusion that the rocker did move slightly at times.

(Next, in an effort to "break through" Jane's mood, we tried a matching numbers test that failed. Then I tried a word association test. I could see well enough to write without turning on lights; the test revealed that Jane was concerned with some associations connected with books, publishers, stories and New York City, but did nothing as far as enabling her to "accomplish" something this evening, at least quickly.

(Now we turned on a closet light and left the door ajar so that the living room was softly lighted. Jane said her mood had leveled off somewhat. It seemed we would accomplish little. We began to exchange random thoughts. Jane did not want to call on Seth and had not since the beginning; she was more interested in obtaining some kind of effects that she could see herself, instead of being the one observed by others.

(By attaining a certain mood, and then talking quietly, Jane had in the past produced the Sarah Wellington and the Malba material. See Volume 1, pages 64, 103 and 127. She had shown rather subtle voice changes each time. For Sarah she had spoken in a rather more childish manner; for Malba she had sounded rather petulant, grown, not too bright and poorly educated. In each case there was no doubt that the voice was Jane's.

(Nor was there this evening. Sarah and Malba were of course female. I believe the voice and the personality Jane used or displayed this evening was largely male. We sat on opposite sides of our coffee table. Jane's back was to the light source and I could not see her features clearly. Her voice never became loud. Instead it acquired a very dry and light and hesitant quality. She used many ahs and ums and other such bridges, but I felt that these reflected the personality's manner rather than Jane's groping for the next word or phrase.

(Jane began speaking in this manner as we exchanged idle conversation. I was not aware of any sharp point of transition. As soon as I did become aware that a change in her state had taken place I began to ask more pointed questions. What follows is my reconstruction of our conversation. I did not attempt to make notes. We merely exchanged words in a normal manner and at a normal rate.

(Jane began by telling me that "Several of us are much older than you are. We watch and we try to help you develop your abilities. I am not at this time able to give you my identity, or that of the others."

(I never did obtain any hints of identity. I tried three times specifically; and each time in a most dry and amused, even pleased way, the personality said firmly

that Jane and I could not be told why at this time. I learned that three were involved in the watching. The group had not been with us very often in the past. They knew Seth. They said he was an educator, and that they were also. One of the more interesting points the spokesman made was that much instruction was passed on to our plane of existence through dreams; this when the ego was more relaxed.

(Jane had recently had some more levitation dreams. The nameless personality said the group had assisted in these dreams, and that Jane had done better psychically, with them, than she had so far done physically. It also developed that Jane had begun to develop her psychic abilities as a child, as a means of protection and escape from a very unhappy family situation. I named some people, now dead, with whom Jane had been closely involved in her maturing years. The spokesman said these personalities were on "other" planes, and that he could not contact them.

(In a most amused way the personality said he and the others did not think much of our fumblings around with various tests this evening. The group was not with us when we tried moving the ring; it <u>*was*</u> *with us when we concentrated upon the rocker. "A corridor had been open" then. I did not ask for predictions and none were volunteered. Future contact was a possibility. The group was "interested" in watching our progress with Seth. They thought Seth was "all right" as a teacher. We could not be told now why they must remain anonymous. Although some instruction was given to personalities on this plane through dreams, it was difficult because of the ever-guarding ego. They were able to accomplish more in the way of education after personalities had left this plane.*

(The foregoing sums up the bulk of our conversation. The nameless personality announced that he and his fellows would leave us, and a moment later Jane had left the state. It did not last more than fifteen minutes, and was finished by 9:15 PM.

(Jane remembered parts of what had been said. Her mood was now normal. As far as I recall, the personality I spoke with had nothing to say about any reasons for her excellent mood earlier in the evening. Nothing about this being Jane's way of trying to establish contact with the group, for instance. Jane did not speak at all like Seth, either in manner or inflection. At times her voice sounded so dry it had a rasp.

(The closest I came to getting any kind of personal information were a few remarks about our Denmark existence, three centuries ago. But here I was politely told I would not even be informed as to whether the connection was family.)

(The following data are from Jane's psy-time notebook:

(November 27, Friday, 11:45: Feeling that some part of me was leaving the body, very slowly and gently through the head, rising and curling up outside my body. Not alarming.

(Upon retiring for the night I saw clearly a bed lamp and a yellow china vase

or bowl, with dark gold trim.

(November 28, Saturday: During the late afternoon and evening I felt strangely excited, almost exultant. This evening, trying some experiments with Rob, I got the "group" contact. See pages 167-68.

(November 30, Monday, 11:45 AM: Good state achieved. Hand moved of own accord.

(It will be remembered that Seth still limits Jane to fifteen minutes of psychological time experimentation daily. See the 105th session.)

(The following data are from my psy-time notebook:

(November 26, Thursday, 8:30 PM: No results.

(November 27, Friday, 9:45 PM: Good sensation of enlargement and of rising up in hands and forearms, and lower legs and feet. A hint of voices.

(November 29, Sunday, 2:00 AM: While dropping off to sleep, I saw many calligraphic-type symbols of squares within squares, triangles, circles, etc., in white line on a dark ground. They appeared to be moving about. Similar to white chalk diagrams on a blackboard.

(November 30, Monday, 8:15 PM: Quite a few glimpses of male and female faces and figures. One was very good: the figure of a heavy-faced man, smooth-shaven, well dressed in a tan topcoat, in the act of bending to his left, as though to pull out a chair. Several different women.

(Also, quite definite and with some duration, I had the feeling that my hands were once again crossed upon my waist, when in actuality they lay at my sides as usual. At one point here the definite feeling was that my thumbs especially were extending themselves through the tips, toward each other in an effort to meet across my body.

(More calligraphic symbols upon dropping off to sleep.)

SESSION 111
NOVEMBER 30, 1964 9 PM MONDAY AS SCHEDULED

(Jane was somewhat tired before the session began, and had no idea of the material that might be covered.

(Shortly before the session was due I mentioned that I hoped Seth would clear up the discrepancy concerning the date of his birth. It was given as 1486 in the last session. We think it should be 1586, to tally with material given in various previous sessions.

(I also mentioned that I hoped Seth would say something about our experience

of last Saturday evening, when Jane contacted the nameless spokesman for the "group." See pages 167-68. In particular we were interested to learn why we were given so little actual information.

(Jane began dictation on time, in a voice that was pitched just a little lower than usual. Her delivery was faster than last session's especially slow manner. Her pacing was regular, her eyes dark, and again she was without her glasses.)

Good evening.

("Good evening, Seth.")

We may have a brief session.

First of all, I will mention that the 1500, not the 1400, date for my Denmark existence is correct.

Our prospects for the immediate future will involve discussions of our threefold universal fields, their development, interrelationship, correlations and reference points.

Data from one such universe can and does serve as a reference point in another. In such a circumstance, the data is of course interpreted according to the universe in which it appears. An action may occur therefore in the world of matter, and be perceived in both the universe of negative matter and the dream world, but in such a case each universe interprets the action according to, and within, its own framework of reference.

There will be seen to be correlations that will appear in each of these universes. They would seem to be distortions. They represent however almost reflections of the same action, and are viewed from different dimensional points.

A study of the correlations with their distortive effect would seem to yield entirely different data. Only an observer from without the three-field system of universes could judge that one action, and not three, had occurred. It will be simplest to discuss at first such correlations occurring within the dream universe, and the universe of matter, since the dream universe is closest to you in both psychic and electromagnetic terms.

As we progress and pick up the study of our dream universe once more, we will be involved also with the study of mental events as they occur within both systems. And because I am presently uninvolved within your system, it is possible for me to give instances as they occur of such mental actions, as they are perceived in both the universe of matter and the dream universe.

These acts are not only interpreted differently, they also of course have effects which are caused not only by the initial action but <u>also</u> by the distortive <u>appearance</u> of the action in a given system. The reaction to such a mental act is made not only to the act itself; but the reaction is made to the <u>appearance</u> of an initial act, as it is projected into the second system.

Its very appearance or projection into a second system, therefore, causes an apparent change in the act itself. To all effects and purposes such an action becomes a different one, while in actuality it is the same.

If you will again recall our material on the fifth dimension, you will see how this must be the case. It will be far more simple to see such a distortive effect of one mental action as it occurs in the dream and matter universes. In all such cases the mental action occurs simultaneously in all systems in which it will have a reality; in which it can be used as a reference point in other words.

All mental actions are not used as reference points in all systems. I will not go into the reasons for this now.

(See the 12th session [in Volume 1] for material on the fifth dimension.)

There may be the appearance of a time lapse of one kind or another between mental actions and their appearance or projection into other systems, but this is a distortive effect. Such distortive effects, such distortions, are often correlated within a given system, and accepted as a foundation for the nature of reality. And all further data is then accepted according to the easiness with which it can be accepted within this framework, the distortions being mistaken for the actuality behind them.

We will have many sessions yet dealing with the dream universe. Beside the interpretation of dreams specifically, in which I realize you are most interested, beside the explanation of dreams as they apply to your manipulation in the world of matter, we will discuss dream symbols as they apply not to the world of matter but to the dream universe itself.

We shall look in from the other side, for there is a looking-in also from the other side. I have mentioned before that beneath camouflage the fifth dimension is truly transparent. I have said that dream universe data has its effect upon your universe, as <u>your</u> universe has its effect upon the dream universe. It is also true that the <u>dream universe is at least as familiar with your own universe</u> as you are familiar with it; and as <u>you</u> tune in on <u>it</u>, so to speak, and while you are necessary for its survival, creating it, so does the dream universe tune in on you. So is your survival dependent upon its survival, and so does it create you as a by-product, <u>if</u> you are looking at your universe from the other side.

I suggest your break.

(Break at 9:32. Jane was dissociated as usual. She said she could feel Seth building up throughout the delivery to the last paragraph of material.

(Her delivery had been rather fast, but it slowed down when she resumed at 9:38)

The last statement should not surprise you.

All systems, and this is a general statement, all systems are to some extent interinvolved. This applies to the smallest and the largest systems.

I have said and I will repeat: In fact, there are no closed systems. They may appear closed to those within, but they are not closed, and there are openings in what appear closed places. We will deal directly in our future dream material with specific mental actions, and with the different appearance of the actions in the dream and matter universes.

This will involve as much work as we have already done on the nature of matter, and will involve us further in that discussion. I must always pick up multitudinous threads as we go on, in order to make even one point clear. The habit, when it becomes vigorous, of trying to view your system from the outside will serve you greatly.

We touched briefly on this when I spoke of objectifying. The study of the dream universe will require a journey inward, through the subconscious and beyond. It will also require a certain objectivity, in that you must try to see your own universe then from the other side. This involves definitely a change of focus, and willingness to momentarily detach the abilities of both the intellect and the intuitions from familiar camouflage reference points.

Keep in mind here, though a discussion will wait for quite a while, that a like relationship occurs between the dream universe and the world of negative matter. There is surrounding this threefold system an envelope, so to speak, of uncamouflaged psychic phenomena. In other words, psychic energy gestalts, of which we will speak much later. They are important however; and from what you now know you realize that these energy forms represent mental enclosure units, operating in the same manner as our earlier ones of which we spoke when discussing the early development of energy within the physical field.

These therefore for all intents and purposes close ranks, encompassing the three systems and accepting no further additions at this given time. As they evolve they may attract other energy forms, and build extensions to the system.

The inwardness, or inward energy which forms all these systems, is the inventive stabilizer; and yet in its search it ever creates new outlets that result in creative chaos, a lack of temporary balance which is then balanced. It is from the inwardness then, operating through its forms, that all innovations come, and from which the most seemingly unexpected developments can be expected.

I suggest your break.

(Break at 10:00. Jane was dissociated as usual. During break she mentioned that she wanted to know if she could resume practicing psychological time for half an hour a day, instead of fifteen minutes. And I said I hoped Seth would say something about the "group" Jane contacted Saturday night. See pages 167-68.

(Jane resumed in the same rather slow and deliberate manner at 10:07.)

Now. Your experience the other evening was indeed quite legitimate.

My friend's manner was meant as a gentle reprimand to me, and as a joke between us, since I had told him that I did not want him to confuse you, or to discuss matters being covered in our material.

I did not want him coming in as a substitute teacher, and with all good intentions in the world causing any misunderstandings in my class. So he, as a joke on me, would tell you nothing at all, and answer hardly any of your questions.

We are well acquainted. Our educational methods vary. That is all. Perhaps for your amazement or amusement we may come together some evening, although not during a regular session. And this is not anything but a probability.

I have told you that this will be a fairly brief session, and so it shall. Ruburt may try a half-hour psychological time experiment tomorrow and Wednesday, if he chooses, and then we will see. This has been an excellent session. My most fond good wishes to you both; and if you do not want to carry on conversations with my friends you do not have to.

I told them you were both very particular about what you saw, and to whom you would deign to speak. Particularly that hardheaded Ruburt. And now after my weak joke I will say good evening.

("Good night, Seth."

(End at 10:17. Jane was dissociated as usual. As she sat down she said, "He may have said good night, but he isn't gone yet. 'Night, Seth." We sat quietly for a minute or two in case Jane resumed dictation. Then she announced that Seth was gone.

(Jane ended the session with a smile. Evidently she picked up my thought about conversing with Seth's friends. As I took her dictation I was wondering just how we would go about speaking with more than one entity at a session. She then answered my thoughts in closing out the session.

(The following data are from Jane's psy-time notebook:

(December 1, Tuesday, 11:30 AM: Excellent state. Toward the end of the period I had the definite feeling that I could rise. It was equal over all the body.

(December 2, Wednesday, 11:30 AM: Again a good state achieved. I "saw" a white-covered table, with an item on it. I wanted to see what it was. I then had the feeling that I glided over to the table, in some fashion, since I did approach the table. I saw that the item was a hamburger; then it faded. The sandwich wasn't very thick looking. [I also had, slightly, that feeling of being hit on the top of the head.]

(Note: Jane tried psychological time for half an hour in both the above

instances. Seth had agreed to this in the last session.)

(For December 1 and 2 I tried psychological time also, but have nothing to report beyond a few minor sensations in the hands.)

SESSION 112
DECEMBER 2, 1964 9 PM WEDNESDAY AS SCHEDULED

(By coincidence this session fell due on the anniversary of our first session. We made contact with Frank Watts in that session. Seth did not announce his presence until the 4th session. See Volume 1, page 23.

(Jane had no idea of the material for the session tonight. Again she was quite tired. She has increased her writing day an hour recently, and is still not used to the change.

(She began dictation on time in a normal voice, and at a much faster rate than she has been using lately. Her pacing was also faster. Again her glasses were off, her eyes dark.)

Good evening.

("Good evening, Seth.")

Our bright-eyes Ruburt has been less than bright-eyed lately.

This is merely due to the additional time that he has added to his schedule, and he will quickly acclimate himself to the new conditions.

For a daily schedule however, six hours of writing should be sufficient. And yes, a daily walk should certainly be prescribed.

Mental activity does demand more energy of one kind than does physical activity, and the reason here is a rather strange one, in that in many respects creative work demands the extra energy used in a sort of repression. The ideas, for example, are not directly carried out or fully constructed in a material way.

They are expressed yet they are repressed from, or they are kept from, active complete physical construction by the very act of artistic creation. There is a division of self involved.

The idea is bared, not permitted expression in complete physical form. The energy then that would be used in complete physical construction of the idea into material form is, rather, transfixed; held, suspended more or less alive, yet incompleted, and therefore in many respects immortal.

The extra energy needed is that energy that is used to hold back the idea from finding completion in concrete terms, and forcing it to flow into a different channel. The impulse for such creativity within your field is mainly two-fold, although other elements may enter into it; there is the exuberant desire to express, the same desire exhibited by all energy. There is also however a deep dissatisfaction with the universe as it is interpreted, and a disinclination to add to it in its own terms. Hence the search for a condition of existence which will be both within and without the ordinarily conventionalized framework.

As with a landscape there is often an attempt, my dear Joseph, to *steal*, so to speak, those elements of life with which the artist is pleased, and transpose them or transfix them, in such a manner that they will attain an *in*vulnerability to other elements with which the artist is *dis*satisfied.

Such processes are extremely complicated. The human psyche adds its own distortive effects, and it is of these that we have been speaking. Nevertheless there are important correlations existing between man's creativity and the inherent impetus of all energy toward creation and innovation; for energy itself forever seeks to perfect itself in precisely this fashion.

Ruburt has added more time to his writing day, and is now also doing more painting. The same kind of energy is being used. It will take a very short period however for him to catch up, and soon he will have *more* energy by far, than he expected.

I will close this discussion.

Now that you know something about the nature of matter, you will see that all matter is objectified mental action, and that basically such action happens simultaneously in the spacious present, formed by individualized energy through the formation of mental enclosures.

These simultaneous actions, happening at once, appear in multitudinous fields of activity. And it would seem from within those fields that time as you know it is involved. You know however that time is not involved. The appearance of this time is caused by the apparent changes or transformations of the action as it enters any given camouflage field.

The action is only apparent or visible in a particular field when it adopts the camouflage coloration of the field in question. Basically the action has not changed. The camouflage distortion is like the effect that water reflections have upon the image that falls across the water.

A tree reflected in the water is still the same tree, and unchanged as the mental act is unchanged. As the reflection of the tree, however, gives a waving and distorted appearance, so as the idea is projected into another field it also is seen in a distorted fashion.

The distorted reflection of the tree in no way changes the actual tree. The distortions that occur as a mental act appears in another field in no way changes the mental act.

You may take your break.

(Break at 9:33. Jane was dissociated as usual. She felt all right while dictating, but tired as soon as break came. She had produced quite a bit of material than average however. She resumed in the same brisk manner at 9:37.)

Now. I used the above analogy to make the point that I made. However, there is also an important difference here that will be rather delicate in the telling.

In your field, when the tree is reflected in the water, the tree itself is stationary. In our basic universe the tree, while remaining stationary, would nevertheless fall crashing into the water.

(Jane smiled as she paced about the room.)

This would happen as follows. The action, the mental action, constantly attempts to recreate itself. It recreates itself in the moment of its birth, with multitudinous slight variations and differentiations; and in so doing automatically plunges into, or projects itself into, those fields which attract the particular range of those differentials.

Yet these projections or reflections do not alter the fact, or change the basic nature of the so-called original mental act, and it remains as untouched by its own reflections as does the stationary tree remain independent from its reflections in the water.

We are merely adding dimensions of actuality here that your tree does not have, and we are also adding a differential mobility which your tree does not possess.

This discussion may require more understanding than you or Ruburt possess, but I do not believe so. In all of this, when I use the word original or initial, I speak only to make certain ideas clear, because you think within a reference of continuity.

I wanted to give you this material because it is basic for any comprehension of mental acts as they occur in the dream universe and the universe of matter. There will also be additional information concerning the concept of time, as the experience of time is strongly connected with the motion of mental acts, as they are projected outward from their center into the fields of various camouflage systems.

It is the effect of the camouflage which is responsible for the experience of time as you think of it.

I suggest your break.

(Break at 9:53. Jane was dissociated as usual. Note the unusual, early break time. She still felt tired. She said that Seth would have ended the session by 10 o'clock, but that she decided to continue.

(Again without her glasses, she resumed at a slower pace at 9:59.)

Time is merely the effect caused within a given system by the system itself, operating upon a mental action as the action enters within its framework.

There is something else here also, concerning the appearance of time, that I could not have undertaken with you earlier, since you would not have understood it. It is an important point, and it will be the last main point that we will cover this evening.

If you recall, when we spoke of the development of conscious individualized energy within your field, we spoke of units collecting material about themselves, and at various points becoming more or less closed systems, accumulating within themselves a more or less stable reserve.

(Among others, see the 86th and 109th sessions.)

Now. In much the same manner as these atoms behaved, so also do other units behave, including large ones such as various field universes. Remember, no systems are really closed, but only appear so. There is however a resistance about or around such units, large or small; and it is this resistance through which a mental action must appear, and within which the characteristics or camouflages of the units operate.

For all systems, so-called time is measured with the entrance or projection of any given mental action through this resistance barrier. The mental action projected must continue to project. When it passes completely through a system, then within the system it appears that the mental action has ceased to be, and again time is marked.

The apparent lapse between the entry and departure points of this motion appears then as a convenient measurement within the system, that is referred to within your system as time.

Because both of you seem weary this evening, and since the material has come through that I wanted to deliver, we will have a short session. The regularity of the sessions is the important factor, and as you know their length will vary according to many circumstances. However, the sessions are coming along extremely well. I realize that your Frank Watts introduction is a year off, and hope that you both understand how much you have learned and how much you have progressed. What you have already learned can never be taken away, and will serve you well.

As for me, I have been around now, here, for quite a while myself, and have found the experience most enjoyable. It is because I hope for many years of such sessions that I am not overly concerned with the length of any particular group of sessions.

I hope you do not tire of me. I will now wish you a fond good evening.

And Joseph, you could give me at least a comradely smile. You have been more serious this evening than I usually am, and that is saying a lot.

("Good night, Seth.")

(End at 10:18. Jane was dissociated as usual. Both of us had been rather glum throughout the session.)

(The following data are from Jane's psy-time notebook:

(December 3, Thursday, 11:35 AM: Good state of lightness achieved.

(December 4, Friday, 11:30 AM: Impression that someone "drifted up" and kissed me on the check. I saw dimly a glass, and a lit pinup lamp with a shade. Also, quickly, I saw clearly the birds on our rooftop, through the living room window.

(While lying down for half an hour this evening, I saw the street outside our house clearly. I thought for a moment my eyes were open, but they were not.

(December 7, Monday, 11:30 AM: No results.

(Jane is now trying psychological time for half an hour daily.)

(From my psy-time notebook:

(Thursday, December 3: Missed.

(December 4, Friday, 9 PM: A general expectant feeling of being about to rise. I seemed to weigh less. The sensation had some little duration. My hands and arms seemed to rest upon a somewhat higher level than the rest of the body.

(December 5, 6, 7: Missed.)

SESSION 113
DECEMBER 7, 1964 9 PM MONDAY AS SCHEDULED

(Jane had no idea of the material to be covered in the session as the time for it approached. She began dictation in a voice somewhat stronger and faster than usual. Her pacing was also faster. Once again her glasses were off, her eyes dark as usual. She smiled.)

Good evening.

("Good evening, Seth.")

I wanted to give you the following, I suppose welcome news, that you will have some time off. I had not meant particularly to hold so many sessions without giving you some sort of vacation.

I get quite carried away for one thing, and our material has been coming over so well that I quite forgot that a rest period has been due. It will not be of much duration. However, it will suffice to give you both a breather.

Even though such a period is due, I find myself jealous of missing any sessions, as you might guess, knowing me by now.

I will despite my own feeling end the session very shortly. There will be no Wednesday session, and that will be your rest period. It is not long. I had planned to give you tonight completely free, but I want to make a few points first.

It is necessary, even regardless of your physical health which is in good condition, and your mental health which is fine, it is still necessary that I give you a period of relaxation from time to time. It will probably be so for quite a while yet, but in a more distant future this will not necessarily apply.

I prefer this period to fall now rather than later in the winter for several reasons, having to do with situations relatively unimportant, and effects which I will explain later merely for your convenience.

The point that I wanted to make is that in all instances energy, individualized energy, materializes itself on any, or within any, field through mental enclosures; which are of themselves not formed of any camouflage, but represent entry points formed of pure energy for its entrance and eventual manipulation within a given field.

Again, such entries or projections of individualized energy are initially simple, with however all potentialities for possibilities of complexity inherent in them.

This must be understood, for it will be the basis for further discussions of our three close universal fields. If it were not that I know better, I would jealously not give you a rest period until you requested it. Nevertheless I am aware of my responsibilities in this matter. I will expect truly excellent sessions to follow. There may be the possibility, <u>if</u> you request it, of one session off during the Christmas holidays, but only at your request.

(By now Jane was in high good humor. Her voice was still stronger than usual. She smiled often as she paced about the room at a fast rate.)

I have told you myself that I would close now, yet still find it difficult. I am such a windbag. <u>I</u> may say this, you may not. I may look in on you now and then. It would be quite difficult for me to let you go completely for one whole week. We shall come back even stronger. <u>Two</u> weeks would really not be detrimental, but you do not really need that much, and so I see no reason for taking it.

My heartiest wishes to you both. What are you going to give me for Christmas?

("I don't know. What do you want?")

I should certainly get a present of some sort, or perhaps I should give you one. We shall see. I will not come loaded with lights like a Christmas tree, but you can never tell. I may come decked out in some other manner. If so, you will know.

And now, until next Monday, good evening; and enjoy yourselves while you have the opportunity. It may be another six or seven months before you have another opportunity.

("Good night, Seth."

(End at 9:23. Jane was well dissociated for a first delivery, she said. She was as surprised as I was at the short session and the extra time off. We have been feeling fine; if we needed a rest from the sessions we were not aware of it. It hadn't occurred to us to ask for any time off.)

(The following data are from Jane's psychological time notebook:

(December 8, Tuesday, 11:30 AM: A very good state achieved.

(December 9, Wednesday: Missed.

(December 10, Thursday, 11:30 AM: An excellent state achieved.

(December 11, Friday: Missed.

(December 14, Monday, 11:30 AM: I saw a brass doorknob again. I also heard voices but didn't retain what they said. Felt I could see through my closed eyelids.)

(From my psychological time notebook:

(December 8, Tuesday, 8:30 PM: Quick full figure glimpse of Lois Williams, as she stood facing me and making a comical gesture. I then saw a gaunt blonde woman sitting in a chair, profile, facing my right, with her head tilted away from me at an angle. She was smiling. I then saw a short, dark-haired man wearing black horn-rimmed glasses. He seemed to be an Oriental. He appeared to stand right over my left eye, so that I had to "look up" to see him. He carried some kind of notepad and said something like, "Now, if I may be permitted to do it like this...."

(I had good duration with feeling of enlargement in the backs of both hands. My legs from the knees down felt considerably lighter. Along with this sensation they also felt curiously stunted, with the right leg bent and drawn partly up at an odd angle. In actuality they lay straight on the bed.

(Also at times my body felt lighter, as though it was engaging in exploratory movement.

(December 9, Wednesday, 8:30 PM: This was a very interesting session. After achieving a good state I began to feel or sense various small "ripples" or movements while lying prone. Then abruptly I felt my whole body swing headfirst to the left, then to the right, as though horizontally pivoted at the belly. The sensation was quick

but quite definite. It was followed by more, lesser feelings of movement. During this experience I had my thrilling sensation twice, to a fair degree.

(Then the central part of my body felt depressed down to bed level; I had the odd thought that I was more aware of the bed beneath my middle body than I was of the body itself. It was almost as though that part of the body wasn't there. At the same time, my arms and hands, remaining where they were, then felt elevated. This feeling was also definite, with duration.

(When the alarm rang to end the session, my eyes opened as usual. The room was quite dark, very nearly pitch black. Yet before me I saw, like an afterimage, a symbol that Seth had described in the 84th session. It was a half arc with one crossed line diagonally, almost like an inverted cent sign. Seth stated that this small symbol, with some initials, was on a rowboat at Provincetown, MA, and that Bill Macdonnel should have seen it while he spent some weeks there. Bill has no memory of it, however.

(The symbol as I saw it appeared to be suspended in the air several feet away from me, and although the room was dark I can only say I seemed to see it in black line. Naturally, what I did see is my personal reconstruction from the data furnished by Seth.

(December 10, Thursday, 8:30 PM: Good state achieved.

(December 12, Saturday, 2:00 AM: Jane and I had been dancing, and upon retiring I saw many visions of male and female dancers. I also experienced a whole string of glimpses of people, some of them very striking close-ups of features, as eyes, etc.

(December 13, Sunday, 8 PM: Few little hand sensations, etc.

(December 14, Monday: Missed.)

SESSION 114
DECEMBER 14, 1964 9 PM MONDAY AS SCHEDULED

(This is our first session since last Monday, December 7. It will be remembered that Seth gave us a brief rest, eliminating last Wednesday's session.

(Jane had no idea of the material for the session as the time for it approached. She began dictation in a voice a little stronger than usual, at a rather slow rate with quite a few pauses. Her eyes were dark as usual, and she took her glasses off as the session began. Her pacing was quite slow.)

Good evening.

("Good evening, Seth.")

I hope that you enjoyed your brief vacation.

I would like this evening to speak more concerning the interrelationship of various units; for when I speak of the interrelationship of universes, remember that these universes are also units, or if you prefer, systems.

They are merely of a more complex gestalt, yet they share in the properties inherent in all units or systems, regardless of apparent size or complexity. Once again, there are no closed systems or units, although some may appear closed to those inhabitants within.

There is an interrelationship between all systems or units that are. This interrelationship is independent of time, as you conceive time to be. The interrelationship between units or systems is, therefore, between not only those that now appear actual to you, but between all systems or units that you assume to be future or past, with those that appear to be present.

This interrelationship is not in terms of cause and effect, as this law is a distortive misinterpretation of actuality. The interrelationship between all units or systems has nothing to do with continuity in your terms. The systems or units are basically simultaneous actions. As participants within one system of action, you are to a large extent limited by the very participation that gives you reality within the action system.

Man is himself a particular system or unit of action within other systems of action, and he is himself composed of other units of action. This unity and interdependence is in itself responsible for that interplay of mental and psychic action which results in the individual consciousness, that is, with the ego.

I have told you that for various reasons all inner energy cannot be objectified within any given action. That part of the entity which does not find expression within a given system seeks it elsewhere. There is, nevertheless, a portion of individual psychic energy that resides, you may say within or behind, every physical manifestation; and this constantly seeks inventiveness in whatever direction is open to it.

So do portions of each entity find simultaneous expression within various systems or units of action, and they must then progress within these systems according to the specific properties of the systems. Units or systems then are open, interdependent and simultaneous in actuality.

They are formed as I told you earlier. Individualized, aware energy is the basis for their camouflage frameworks. I have said that they are not continuous, meaning that they are not strung out in your time, one before or after the other. Because they are units or systems, they do possess at their outer limits a resistance which serves to give them unitary identity, a resistance which tends to attract like and repel unlike elements.

Yet also at this point of resistance will be found, in the case of your system, particles that are part of your system and also part of another system. In other words, where two systems merge the outer resistant edges of each are the same.

I suggest your break.

(Break at 9:28. Jane was dissociated as usual. At break time she then realized that she hadn't smoked at all during the first delivery. As a rule Jane smokes steadily during sessions; even I hadn't noticed she was going without cigarettes.

(By now I was also aware of a mild feeling of enlargement in the fingers of my right hand. The third finger was the most involved. Neither Jane or I have had many experiences of this kind in recent sessions. See the 47th and 55th sessions [in Volume 2] for more pronounced effects of this kind, including measurements.

(Jane resumed in the same quite slow manner at 9:36.)

These particles attract and repel, both.

If we may speak in an analogy, then these particles have two faces. If you consider them as soldiers guarding the barriers or the boundaries, then you would have to imagine a strange creature, our particle, as a soldier on a boundary facing toward and away from the country in question.

He would be composed of the stock of each country, so that neither country could decipher any alienness within him. This is a rather important point, for it concerns all units or systems. The inner alignment and electromagnetic structure of such particles is the main issue that allows them to be, or to operate within, two different units or systems. And while these particles act as resistant boundary forces, they are also uniting forces, forming so to speak the connective tissue that both separates and unites.

These identifying particles, as we will call them, that both close about a system yet still unite it to other systems, these particles are also inherent properties of any unit or system. Availability of energy and energy transformation into the particular camouflage necessities of the system are other properties.

No system is able to utilize all of its energy however, and a residue of energy is another characteristic of a system or unit. Camouflage initiative is another such characteristic. Within the limitations set by itself, a system may nevertheless, from the opportunities available to it, vary its camouflage patterns.

A system may say that within its limitations there is room for still further transformation of energy into still more various camouflage forms. It may be generally said, but only generally, that the most advantageous system is that system which has great diversity of camouflage patterns, in that energy, always individualized, is then given expression within the system in different materializations, which then allow for further individualization to the benefit of the whole system.

The system exists basically, again, not in space, nor does it expand in space as you conceive it. It exists and expands in terms of depths that take up no space, in terms of value fulfillment.

We have discussed this before but it should not be forgotten in any of the discussions. The urge and drive toward value fulfillment provides the spark for the initiation of any system or unit. Increased consciousness and awareness of itself, through the manipulation and materialization of its own energy into more complicated camouflage patterns, is another characteristic of a system or unit.

None of this goes on in any one level. There is great interplay, and as I mentioned in an earlier session, inward energy is itself transformed and affected and enriched by the camouflage forms or units that it produces.

I suggest your break.

(Break at 10:03. Jane was quite well dissociated. Again, she had not smoked since last break. I still maintained the feeling of enlargement in the fingers of my right hand.

(An interesting little experience now came to light. Jane's delivery had become very slow; as slow as the 110th session, which was as slow as any I recall. When I mentioned this Jane was quite surprised. It developed that while dictating she felt she was speaking rapidly. In actuality, her delivery had been so slow that at times she paced from one end of our living room to the other before giving voice to the next word. Thus it is seen that we had much different appreciations of the same amount of camouflage time. It might be added that during the 110th session, Jane was aware that she was speaking at a slow rate.

(She resumed in a somewhat faster manner at 10:10.)

The particles of which we spoke may be regarded as not only boundaries but as gateways, both separating and dividing systems.

To you they would be seen as mysterious connectors or links. Energy passes <u>through</u> these particles from one system to another, more or less constantly; yet they themselves, taking energy from system A, transform it into an adaptation that can be received by system B.

These particles are, then, transformers of a kind; receiving energy from system B, they transform it before passing it through. These particles contain both positive and negative ions within their own unitary system, for they are of course also units in themselves.

This transformation of energy should be quite comprehensible since you know that you subconsciously transform energy into physical, mental, creative or psychological states, manipulating it to your advantage. I have used the word "particle" to explain those units which are gateways and yet boundaries. While many are particles, this is only because they can be said to fall within the framework of your definition.

They are smaller than small, to be sure, but soon your scientific instruments will detect them; though I do not believe their significance will be understood. But many such units cannot by any stretch of the imagination be considered as particles in these terms; and while certain of their effects are detectable both chemically and electrically within your system, they cannot be examined directly with instruments.

Dreams are such connectives, for you see that this preliminary material is very much to the point as far as our dream universe is concerned, and is itself a connective to that discussion. This will be the basis for our next session, for you will see how dreams also serve as the other face, so that man himself stands at a threshold that is also a barrier, or stands at a barrier that is also a threshold.

The dream universe and your own are both actualities, and both separate systems that are interconnected.

(Jane's voice had by now become a little deeper and quite a bit more forceful. She rapped upon my writing table for emphasis.)

This interconnection means that the reality and actuality of each system is made possible by the existence of the other. Yet both are separate. This brings us to several points that I will leave for our next session.

It goes without saying however that the characteristics of any system or unit that I have given here must apply to the dream universe, and to your own universe. These characteristics vary only in terms of intensity from system to system.

This has been a most rewarding session, and I have enjoyed it. I would suggest here that our hardheaded friend, Ruburt, refresh himself tomorrow by loosening his schedule somewhat, and gaining new reservoirs of creative energy, through perhaps an aimless walk, or quiet contemplation.

And now I will close our session, hoping that you will apply tonight's material to others, that is other sessions, as it adds to the total picture that I began to paint for you when I spoke of the so-called initial appearance of matter within your system.

And now, fond friends, good night.

("Good night, Seth."

(End at 10:35. Jane was again well dissociated. And again, she did not smoke at all during the delivery. She still felt that she had been speaking rapidly. The tempo of her delivery had picked up since last break, but to no great degree.

(I was still aware of the feeling of enlargement in my right hand. I was careful not to confuse this with any cramping effect from holding a pen for so long. However, the feeling now became more pronounced, so that when I made a fist my fingers felt thicker, against a thicker palm, giving a feeling of restricted movement. Usually such

effects begin to wane as soon as a session ends, but in this instance the sensation was stronger than ever five minutes later. It lasted for some fifteen minutes or so, during which time it gradually declined.

(For the record, I note here that I also experienced the same sensation, in the same hand, for a few minutes on last Sunday afternoon, December 13, while working in my studio. Seth has said that in such instances the sensation implies my sensing his presence, if only subconsciously.)

(The following are from Jane's psychological time notebook:

(December 15, Tuesday, 11:30 AM: I experienced, internally, a lateral rocking sensation, and one also from head to foot.

(December 16, Wednesday, 11:30 AM: A good state achieved. I saw a very wide closed opaque curtain, and an interior wooden wall.)

(From my psychological time notebook:

(December 15, Tuesday: Missed.

(December 16, Wednesday, 8:15 PM: Another quite interesting experience. After achieving the desired state, I saw a few vague faces, male and female. I then began to tell myself I would visit Ed Robbins, in his house in New Paltz, NY. After a few minutes of this I abruptly became aware that my lower legs felt as though they were off the edge of the bed, suspended in space. The feeling was startling and quite definite. I was aware of it in the left leg from the knee down, and the right ankle and foot. I could not feel the pressure of the limbs upon the bed.

(While this sensation attained some duration, I began to experience my feeling of existing upon two levels again. I haven't had this one lately, however. This was also definite and prolonged. First, my middle body felt depressed [or nonexistent] upon the bed. I then became aware that my left arm and hand felt itself to be some inches higher than my right arm and hand. Yet beneath both limbs I felt the presence of the bed. It appeared that the point of transition between the two levels existed somewhere within, or beneath, my body, but I was not aware of it consciously. While I knew the bed lay beneath either arm, note that I was not aware of the bed beneath my lower legs. Good duration for both effects.)

SESSION 115
DECEMBER 16, 1964 9 PM WEDNESDAY AS SCHEDULED

(Jane had no idea of the material for the session as the time for it approached. She said that a day or two after any given session the memory of it seems like a

dream; she has to read it to verify that it actually exists.

(She began dictation in a much stronger voice than normal, and maintained it throughout the session. At times it was quite loud, without growing much deeper. She also spoke somewhat faster than last session. Again her glasses were off, her eyes dark as usual. Her pacing was regular.)

Good evening.

("Good evening, Seth.")

I would like to speak a few words concerning the nature of realities.

This will serve as a further connective to our discussion of the dream universe, and its interaction with the world of physical matter. It goes without saying that your definition of reality is extremely limited, and excludes more than it includes.

Even within the experience of men there are realities that are entirely different from the realities of physical objects. Psychological experience is one such indisputable reality. Ideas are another, and dreams are still another. Secondary effects of such realities may appear in material form, but the original reality of such experiences cannot be captured within physical matter.

If such experiences appear less real than more obviously material realities, they also have at times a peculiar vividness that cannot be overlooked. Their nature is simply different from the nature of physical realities. If they seem occasionally insubstantial, it is because their substance is of a different quality.

They appear to lack the apparent physical durability of, say, a table or a chair, the table and chair being examples of physical realities. And yet their effect is much more durable, and they impress and to some extent manipulate physical realities, in their strong and sometimes explosive emergence into your universe. Such realities do not bow to the artificial time measurements which so often limit <u>you</u> in daily life.

They move through psychological time. Their existence continues after your awareness of them has vanished. Just because <u>you</u> focus—

(At 9:15 there was a knock on the door. Jane stopped dictation in the middle of a sentence. She looked at me wordlessly as I walked toward the door, but before I reached it I heard her say, "I'm all right now."

(It was the paperboy. I paid him, and both of us joked with him for a minute or two before he left. Jane's manner was her regular one. After the boy had gone Jane said his knock stopped her delivery abruptly, but that she did not come out of the light trance quickly enough to go immediately to the door. She could have, however, within thirty seconds, she said.

(She resumed in the same strong, almost loud voice, at 9:20. In contrast to the last session, she was smoking during this one.)

Just because your attention is no longer focused upon such realities, this does not mean that they do not continue to exist.

You do indeed give them energy, as they also give you energy. Dreams, or the dream universe, exists even while you wake, and you only become aware of certain portions of it even while you sleep. You do create it, but it is also to some degree independent of you. As your ego experiences changes in its relationship with the physical world, so do you change aspects of the dream world accordingly, and enrich it.

The dream universe also enriches your own existence. There is great interplay here, and a continual interchange of energies, and of energies that are transformed and recharged, so to speak, through their constant passage between fields. Dreams, perhaps more clearly than anything else, can help you understand the concept of value fulfillment, and of the expansion that does not take up space.

(Jane now smiled broadly as she paced about the room. If anything, her voice was a bit stronger. It was close to 9:30.)

Dream locations do not exist like physical objects in your head. How could your small skull hold a replica of a cement building, for example, even though the skull might be a rockhead? You need not take that remark personally, Joseph. I couldn't resist making it, however.

These dream locations are realities. They do exist, even though they do not exist in space as you know it, and certainly they do not take up space in the skull. There would be no room for anything else. As a brief byline here, I mentioned once the Crucifixion, saying that it was an actuality and a reality, although it did not take place in your time. It took place where time is not as you know it. It took place in the same sort of time in which a dream takes place, and its reality was felt undeniably by generations, and was reacted to. Not being a physical reality, it influenced the world of physical matter in a way that no purely physical reality ever could.

(See the 81st session for Seth's statements on the Crucifixion. This session and the 96th, among others, dealt much with the God concept, psychic gestalts, myths, etc.)

The Crucifixion was one of the gigantic realities that transformed and enriched both the universe of dreams and the universe of matter, and it originated in the universe of dreams. It was a main contribution of that field to your own, and could be compared physically to an emergence of a new planet within the physical universe.

The reality, the physical reality, of fire was such a contribution made by the physical universe to the universe of dreams. Physical man, observing fire, dreamed of it, thereby immeasurably enriching the universe of dreams. His discovery in the physical universe of domesticating fire was another such contribution to the dream universe.

The ascension of Christ did not occur in time as you know it. It is a contribution of the universe of dreams to your own universe, representing knowledge within the dream universe that man was independent of physical matter ultimately.

I suggest your break.

(Break at 9:42. Jane was dissociated as usual. After some thought she said she was aware that she was speaking in a strong voice, during dictation. But she had no sense of quickly passing time like that she had experienced in the last session.

(Again without her glasses, she resumed in the same strong, not overly fast, manner at 9:51.)

You necessarily limit your own knowledge, or the knowledge possible to you, when you limit your definition of reality, or possibilities of reality.

Many concepts, huge advancements and practical inventions, simply wait in abeyance in the world of dreams until some man accepts them as possibilities within his frame of reality. Why man so often mistrusts the dream reality would escape me, if I did not know the nature of the ego.

It feels insecure at best in a world with which it is fairly familiar, and it vigorously fights any new adoptions within that world, for it must then change accordingly.

Now, and this can hardly be called a controversial statement, the imagination is waking man's connection with the universe of dreams. Imagination often restates dream data, and applies it to particular circumstances or problems within the physical universe. Imagination is never basically destructive. In some cases the ego construction may be weak, or incapable of holding its own, in which case the imagination is often said to be too excitable, and to be at fault.

I cannot impress upon you too strongly that imagination is another such basically nonphysical reality, with a basis however, and interrelationship, in both dream and matter. Again, its effects may appear within matter but it is of itself not composed of matter.

These realities, because of their continuing effects within your system, and their actual transformation of it, should be studied thoroughly, for much can be gained in this way. Like transformations are made by events in your universe upon the dream universe. Often, again, the dream universe possesses concepts which will, some day, completely transform the history of your field; but a denial of such concepts as actualities or possibilities within reality, hold these back, and put off breakthroughs that are sorely needed.

Such developments would mean the releasing and availability of added energy into your field, that would have endless possibilities in all directions. Ideas and concepts are nonphysical actualities that attract unaligned energy, direct and concentrate it. The dream world exists more closely in that spacious present of which the inner self is so aware. It is not as involved with camouflage constructions as your own universe, and its actions are somewhat limited within its own framework.

It might be said then, that in many ways the dream universe depends upon you to give it expression, in the same manner that you also depend upon it to find expression, although in this case you have other outlets, and it has few. The impact of any given dream has physical, chemical, electromagnetic, psychological and psychic repercussions. These are also actual and continuing, and they not only represent a part of your environment in all of these cases, but they affect most deeply the ordinary channels of everyday life.

The type of dream, or the types of dreams experienced by any individual, is determined by many factors. I am speaking now of the dream experience as it occurs, and not of the remnant of it that his ego allows him to consciously recall. As an individual creates his physical image and environment according to his abilities and defects, and in line with his expectations and subconscious and inner needs, so does he create his dreams; and these interact with the outer environment which he has created.

However, with the ego at rest the individual may allow communications and dream constructions through, past the ego barrier, in such a manner that he becomes in some ways free. If for example his present expectations are faulty, when the ego rests he may recreate a time when expectations were high. The resulting dream will then partially break the circle of poor expectations, with their shoddy physical constructions, and start such an individual along a more beneficial path. In other words, such a dream may begin to transform the physical environment through lifting inner expectation.

I will continue at our next session. My fond wishes to you both.

("Good night, Seth."

(End at 10:29. Jane was dissociated as usual. She maintained her strong voice until the end of the session, without apparent strain.)

(The following data are from Jane's psychological time notebook:

(December 17, Thursday, 11:30 AM: I concentrated on traveling psychically to Marian Spaziani's kitchen, and kept repeating her name over and over. For a second I glimpsed a small kitchen, that reminded me of Marie Colucci's. Was Marian perhaps there? I had a feeling of extreme lightness, and a slight feeling of rising. Also

another hard-to-describe feeling, one of an overall inner motion.

(December 18, Friday, 11:30 AM: Again a feeling of extreme lightness. Feeling of no bed under ankles or feet, after first feeling as though my lower arms and hands rose. My thumbs then seemed to hold on to a pocket of "no space."

(In my upper left field of vision I then saw a note that was handwritten in possibly dark pencil. It was torn along the edges and wrinkled, as though it had been smoothed out. It was rectangular in shape. This was a visual image, yet I couldn't read it.

(Now came a second image, partly visual, partly impression. I felt the action was continuing and was still there, as though I could "tune in." Saw several men who seemed to wear some kind of uniforms of dark green, with helmets or helmet-shaped hats on. A work crew perhaps, busy at an activity, something like an evacuation or disembarkation. I then saw one digging in something other than snow. I saw this in several successive tries to see it clearly.

(During the whole half-hour of the experiment I shivered constantly, and felt very cold even though I was covered by a blanket. The shivering was in some kind of rhythm of varying intensity.

(December 21, Monday, 11:30 AM: Heard mentally, separately, the names: Foster, Lancaster. I was speaking them mentally. I also saw two people dimly. I had the impression of a doctor and a nurse, ushering someone into a side room and then closing another door that blocked my "vision." I don't know any Foster or Lancaster.)

(The following data are from my psy-time notebook:

(I would like to note here that one night during the second week in December, possibly around the 11th or 12th, I awoke out of a sound sleep to become aware that both arms and hands were involved in my rather familiar sensation of enlargement and of elevation. The feeling of enlargement centers mainly on the tops of the limbs, as though they were swelling, and is not to be confused with the overall thrilling or tingling sensation I often refer to. I have now experienced both sensations many times. As far as I can consciously recall, this instances is the first I have experienced upon coming out of a sleep. I was lying upon my back at the time, and this is the position I use while trying psychological time.

(December 17, 18, 19: Missed.

(December 20, Sunday, 8 PM: Another interesting experience. Upon lying down I experienced my familiar thrilling sensation three separate times, the last time strongly. I saw briefly various male and female figures, some of them apparently monster types.

(My enlarging sensation began on backs of hands and in feet quite soon. I believe I then either dozed briefly, or attained a very good state. I had been telling

myself I would visit Ed Robbins. I became aware that my whole body felt as though it were gathering itself together, charging itself with some kind of energy, in preparation for travel. The sensation was very strong and expectant. My stomach felt empty or gone, my arms and hands elevated. Arms and legs felt enlarged. This was the peak of the experience as I waited to see what developed. Briefly, and I could be mistaken, I thought I had a sensation of being suspended perhaps a foot or so above my body.

(After this I saw, as though in the distance, a group of small gleaming knives, carefully arranged in two parallel rows. They were identical in design and had wooden handles.

(December 21, Monday, 8:15 PM: Interrupted by baby crying downstairs, but prior to this a good state achieved. I saw a few figures, male and female.

(I had one interesting experience, before the interruption, and felt that I could have had more. I was on the sidewalk of the main street of a small town. I looked up the rather empty and depressing street a few doors to an evidently empty storefront with big gray-colored plate glass windows. There was an indistinct male personage or figure on the sidewalk before me, passing the empty storefront. I then heard <u>my own voice</u> coming out of the store, saying something to this effect: "Now, you've known me before." At this the personage began to scramble <u>backward</u> up the street toward the store, falling backward as though losing its balance at the same time.)

SESSION 116
DECEMBER 21, 1964 9 PM MONDAY AS SCHEDULED

(Jane received her first intimation that something new might develop in the sessions when she was reading over last Wednesday's session after supper tonight. She came up with the idea that she might give part of tonight's session while lying down. Her first thought was one of acquiescence. Her second thought was one of panic, in that she wouldn't know the passage of time as usual, etc.

(It might be interesting to note that at the time Jane received this idea, I was working on an index for the 35th session, of March 16, 1964. In this session Seth talked of having us try various experiments involving the use of the inner senses; tonight's session was of course in the nature of an experiment. Jane did not know what session I was working on, and we were also separated by two rooms at the time.

(Then, lying down at 8:15 this evening, Jane felt that she went into a deeper trance state, one that was experimental and yet controlled. She was not particularly trying psychological time, yet she felt that she was familiarizing herself for a new development. She did not "see" or "hear" anything. She did not feel Seth around. She was, however, worried somewhat about what control she would have over the

material if, in the prone position, she was in a deeper trance.

(Jane had no idea of the material for the session as the time for it approached, although she said her arms felt a "little light" from the state she had achieved at 8:15 and later. Nor had she been thinking recently along the lines outlined above.

(The session did begin in a new way. At 9 PM Jane was sitting opposite me at our living room table, where I take my notes. She took off her glasses as usual, but instead of rising to begin pacing about the room she remained seated. Her eyes were closed, and remained closed whenever she delivered material throughout the evening. Her voice was normal, her delivery rather rapid but with pauses. For the most part she sat with one leg drawn up, an arm resting upon the knee, her hand to her head as though propping it up. She held a lighted cigarette in the other hand.

Good evening.

("Good evening, Seth.")

We may possibly this evening try something, not drastic, in the way of a small experiment.

I will speak concerning the ego's censorship, and even to some extent concerning the censorship of the personal subconscious.

Communications such as this must sift through many channels and make many interconnections. We shall achieve important progress this year, I hope, in getting more material through the censorships. I will in no way press for Ruburt to go further than is beneficial for him.

He is also however somewhat anxious to develop his abilities, and if he is to do so we must progress. For future reference, Joseph, and I repeat future, you should not probably need this for awhile, the words "All right Jane, you're back now," will always suffice to return Ruburt to his more usual condition.

We are merely now experimenting. If at any time Joseph, you do not agree with any particular procedure or condition or situation, you may immediately speak the words that I have given you, and the situation or condition will become the normal one.

This procedure, and your consent, will give Ruburt a feeling of trust without which I do not believe he would otherwise proceed. In other words, the situations and conditions will not be out of your hands at any time. Nor shall we necessarily keep to any one procedure. I believe that certain experiments will allow us to get more complete data through censorship.

(Jane still sat opposite me, her eyes closed. Her delivery was easily heard, yet more halting in manner than usual. Her eyes were still closed. Her cigarette had now burned down, and to put it out she groped about for the ashtray on the table, as she talked.)

Nor would I have attempted such a procedure until I knew that Ruburt was ready for it, or at least ready to begin it, for this is but a beginning. He is doing well. This is of course a training period, and he may become momentarily uneasy, but never frightened. It is simply a matter of new orientation, and doing without certain props that are basically unimportant, but practically extremely convenient; such props as the divisions of sensation, fenced in from each other by pickets of minutes.

Clock time is one prop that even in our usual sessions Ruburt is accustomed to rely upon, though not of course to the extent that he relies upon it in the periods of more ordinary consciousness.

The pacing back and forth has always been a symbol and a manifestation of his insistence that he stay on his feet, this of course relating to his invalid mother; also a manifestation of control on his part as far as the sessions are concerned. Nor is he now relinquishing control. He is merely shifting focus from one level to another, and allowing me to speak in this manner, because he now realizes that I am no threat to any portion of his individuality as a self.

There may be a slowness or unevenness as we attempt such an experiment, and this is to be expected. I ask you now if you give <u>your</u> consent, Joseph.

("Yes."

(I gave this answer almost as a matter of routine. It is now quite a few days later as I type this material, and Jane and I have had time to think it over. She has not shown outright opposition to experimenting, but from various remarks of hers I know she is still not enthusiastic about giving up any of the props she has become accustomed to—the pacing, the open eyes, etc. This is quite understandable. Jane's hesitancy here reminds me of her hesitancy in the beginning sessions, when it early became apparent that she was receiving the answers to questions mentally, even though we were using the Ouija board. She did not want to dispense with the board for some time.

(As for myself, I have qualified the approval I gave, making it dependent upon Jane's own approval. Our approach is cautious, as usual. I do not want to unwittingly push her into anything she does not really want to try. For the moment, then, we have decided to see what comes. If either of us does not like the developments, we plan to return to the method we have been using this past year.

(Jane's delivery of the above material had been somewhat slow and hesitant, but clear. It gave me the feeling of being uneven, but I note that the typewritten copy reads as well as any of the other material. Her head was down much of the time, as though she might fall asleep. Her voice did not lose volume. She appeared to be restless now, shifting about on her chair. Some of the pauses between phrases were indeed quite long.)

Then we shall proceed.

There will be varieties of adjustment; this also is to be expected. In the long run this procedure will take less out of Ruburt, and we of course will not exceed our usual regularity. Since we are trying something new I do not know how far we shall proceed this evening, for I do not press for quick, but press for thorough and safe progress. And even now, woe to me if I make a wrong move, for Ruburt would most certainly rise up in arms.

There are however many advantages to this sort of procedure, when and if we become used to it. There are few disadvantages, none having to do with health or safety, incidentally. Not the way we shall handle it.

A short dissertation. There is never any ending to what has begun. In larger terms, there has been no beginning as you think of it.

(It was now 9:30. Jane's delivery was very halting.)

Frameworks change their form, yet the form that they had still remains. The inner energy of which we have spoken constantly renews itself, and recharges itself as it passes from one field of activity to another.

As it forms new fields of activity then, it increases its own ability for such renewal. The fields themselves are energy potentials. You must recall our discussions concerning fragments. Fragments of this type have all the potentialities of the parent, inner energy. You understand that: the parent, not apparent, energy?

("Yes.")

(It was 9:35. Thus it took Jane five minutes to deliver the above two paragraphs. For the material on fragments see the very early sessions; it is scattered throughout them.)

Therefore they constantly create energy. All energy is what you may call mental energy. It creates itself in multitudinous forms, which then re-create fields, replenish each other. No energy is lost. No energy is meaningless.

(Jane used several long pauses delivering the above paragraph. One of them was so long I thought she had fallen asleep. She sat motionless on her chair, her head resting upon one hand. Yet her diction was very clear.)

Every action affects every other action. Mental enclosures are energy units possessing all the characteristics of such units as I have previously given you. You know that all action is basically mental action, as fields replenish each other. As no action is meaningless, so the dream universe and the physical universe constantly replenish each other, and mental actions are performed in both universes, being camouflage acting symbols for inner action.

The actions in the various fields affect each other. These actions burn almost like twin fires in different worlds, but they illuminate vastly different landscapes. And while their nature is basically the same, it is always the differences that you notice.

We have proceeded well for a beginning. I suggest you break, not into pieces; and that Ruburt now snap back to himself.

(Break at 9:45. Jane's eyes immediately opened as her head came up. She looked sleepy, and reached for her glasses. She did not smoke or drink during delivery. She said her state of dissociation was deeper, that she was "way out." She heard her voice however, and my answers. She was surprised at the amount of time that had passed. She remembered the pauses, but had thought they were "nothing."

(Jane was not frightened at the new development, but still felt uneasy about relinquishing control, as she put it, during a session. For instance, she worried about not knowing the time, yet once the session began she thought nothing of it. She did feel she had given consent for the experiment. She did not think Seth would try "pushing through" any startling information tonight.

(Jane moved over to the couch before the session resumed, and remained there once she began dictating again. Again her eyes closed, again her hand went to her chin, and again she used frequent and sometimes long pauses. Her diction was good. Resume at 9:59.)

We will not attempt to push much material through this evening, since we are trying a new venture.

In all respects there must be complete honesty here, and conditions should be reached where there is no fear of ridicule on Ruburt's part, or fear of lack of successful data, or failure.

All like communications have similar roads to follow, and all such communications must evade censorships. Some distortion of material is bound to occur, and is no reflection upon Ruburt, or indeed myself, and certainly not on you Joseph, but is instead a natural result of the type of communication itself, which attempts to surmount and pass through different fields and many barriers. This of course everything being equal.

As long as our attempts are completely honest, aboveboard, there is no more disgrace in any distortion of message than there is in a like distortion in usual communication, such as the misreading of a letter.

This should be clearly understood, for our progress depends upon a feeling of trust, and fears of this nature will impede us. You may consider the whole above paragraph stated again, it is that important to us.

We will also initiate more question periods in the future, Joseph. I believe that you would enjoy them.

Ruburt's idea of writing down his daily predictions is an excellent one, and will help him develop his abilities. Within a short time Ruburt will give me more freedom, I believe. That is, he will, I hope, allow me to speak with more freedom.

This is enough for our initial serious attempt with this procedure. We will have Wednesday's session as usual, unless it conflicts with your circumstances because of the season. I will understand if this is the case.

My fondest wishes to you both. Ruburt may return now, and we will close our session. One note: I hope in the future to be able to add in dimension now and then to our sessions, opening up vistas to Ruburt to illuminate other avenues to complement any given discussion. We have done very well this evening. Indeed, my heartiest wishes to you both.

(End at 10:16. Jane was fully dissociated as before, and again looked sleepy when the session ended. This time she was not aware of anything except her voice. She was not aware of the darkness. Her attention was elsewhere.

(Jane said it would be easier to block any material that frightened her while she was pacing about. The new method, when she sat quietly, with the added ingredient of the long pauses, made blocking probably more difficult. The pauses interrupted the sense of the material to some degree. This might remove the impact from words or phrases that ordinarily would alert her to block them.

(Jane was quite intrigued because she had no conception of darkness or light while delivering material. She wasn't aware of using her voice. She heard the words after they were spoken, but could not retain them.

(While delivering the last paragraph of the session, Jane had the parallel perception or feeling that Seth meant she might receive visual data while dictating.)

(The following data are from Jane's psy-time notebook:

(December 28, Monday, 11:30 AM: I saw a pair of eyes close to me, looking straight at me. They were moist and very dark, wet but not soft. They were not human eyes, yet did not appear to be animal either.

(December 29, Tuesday, 11:30 AM: Achieved a terrific sense of well-being, of suspension and lightness. I had the sensation of rising.

(December 30, Wednesday, 11:30 AM: Voices were in conversation with me. I believe they were people I know. I could not retain what was said. I think Dick Roberts, editor at Dell, said something about going to California for a publishing firm. Yet now I am not sure.)

SESSION 117
DECEMBER 23, 1964 9 PM WEDNESDAY AS SCHEDULED

(This is the shortest session to date. Jane had been working in the kitchen all day in preparation for the holidays. I had been working overtime also and was very

tired. At 8 PM Jane began to clean up after her baking marathon in the event there was a session, although she wasn't sure there would be one. She had not felt Seth about. I wondered what part conditioning might play in the schedule we had become used to.

(Both of us lost track of the time. We were standing beside our Christmas tree when Jane took off her glasses and began to speak for Seth, in a voice somewhat stronger than usual. She walked to the couch and sat down, her eyes closed once again. She spoke rather slowly. The following is my reconstruction of the brief and somewhat enigmatic session.)

There is no necessity for taking notes.

There is something here that you can put to good use in your own daily lives. This event you are about to celebrate did not take place historically. Nevertheless you can use it, and we will go into this in sessions in the near future.

There will be no session. If I may, however, I would like to look in on you at various times over the holidays.

(The session was over in a minute or two. Jane said she was surprised at the abrupt way it began. She also said that as soon as she began to speak she felt cold. The sensation passed as soon as the session ended.)

SESSION 118
JANUARY 4, 1965 9 PM MONDAY AS SCHEDULED

(Because of the holidays we did not hold sessions for Monday, December 28, and Wednesday, December 30.

(The following data are from Jane's psychological time notebook: December 31, Thursday, 11:35: A rather amazing experience of "ecstasy," the strongest I've experienced so far. No voices or visions, however. Now an hour later traces of lightness and suspension still linger. Also a small nagging feeling of rising. January 4, Monday, 11:30 AM: No results in particular.

(As session time approached Jane became increasingly nervous. She felt this way because of our rather long rest, and the recent developments in the presentation of the sessions themselves. She had no idea of the subject matter for the session, nor did she know whether she would sit with her eyes closed or pace about as usual.

(As it developed she did both. She was sitting down as 9 PM arrived. She then took off her glasses and began to pace slowly about the room. Once again her eyes were dark. Her voice and rate of delivery were normal.)

Good evening.

("Good evening, Seth.")

I will indeed vary the procedure. We will benefit greatly through various experiments within our sessions however, and some of these should be quite important to our overall progress.

Ruburt may feel betwixt and between, as indeed at times he is, but only occasionally. We must have some experiments to progress. It seems that we should supplement our lectures, at least now and then. Also, if Ruburt is experimenting as he is with the trance state in psychological time experiments, it is a good idea that some of this experimentation be carried on by him under our excellent supervision; and after consideration I think that you will agree.

He has fought me a good deal of the time. However this is also to his benefit and to yours. We do not want any willy-nilly trance states, spontaneous or undisciplined. He knows what he is doing. You have been negligent this past week, and yet this also adds to your confidence, in that you know that it is up to you both ultimately, and not ultimately up to me, whether or not these sessions are held.

I presumed that you knew this.

We have left many loose ends since our last session. I have told you that it is possible to tune in on the dream universe. You know this is done during sleep. It can also be done in the so-called waking state.

There are quite a number of your psychological time experiments that we will have to discuss. One of the reasons why we have not gone into them as yet is that you have tuned into other realities, and the realities must be explained before your experiments can be discussed.

(I now became aware that Jane seemed to be pacing about the room with her eyes closed, or very nearly so. Certainly they were far from being wide open, as they usually were when she was on her feet. From my position they appeared to be closed, but from the confident manner in which she moved about the room I thought she could see a little at least.)

A few of them did involve a tuning into the dream universe. There are many stations, so to speak, to tune into, and at present you touch the dials rather indiscriminately. Planes of actuality of one sort or another everywhere exist. I mean that literally. The apparent emptiness of outer space is far from empty, but these are not necessarily worlds that you could visit with the most advanced imaginable spaceship.

Many of these planes of actuality can never be explored by any physical vehicle. They would appear as incomprehensibly vast as your single planet would appear to a single fly, who set out to examine it. Perception of its characteristics would be impossible. To you physical objects would seem so far separated in space that you would lose your way, and not perceive realities as they there existed at all.

You would not be able to perceive a sufficient amount of data to make any deductions. This is not to say that such planes or fields of actuality cannot in some manner be perceived, but they will escape physical perception or exploration. In dreams, when the self is somewhat free from camouflage, perhaps it is possible for the self then to travel spontaneously into such fields of actuality; but since they are as bizarre to the self as is the dream world itself, then there is no way, usually, for the sleeper to distinguish between the universe of dreams or other actualities.

These fields or planes are more various than you can imagine, and they are formed in the same manner, basically, as your own universe was formed, and many of those inhabitants tune in on your universe spontaneously and quite accidentally. But the inhabitants of most such planes are no more aware of your actual existence than you are of their existence.

In most cases there simply is no way for such fields of actuality to meet, although indeed they are formed by the same energy, but along lines which cannot meet.

I suggest your break.

(Break at 9:26. Jane's eyes opened wide, and once again she looked sleepy. Her delivery had not been slow, however. She said she was in a deeper trance state than when her eyes are fully open.

(Part of the time her eyes were fully closed as she paced about the room, Jane said, but she could not give me a percentage estimate. The rest of the time her eyes were "cracked open" just enough for her to see. Jane thought Seth intended that she begin the session sitting down; instead she got up, and we think it reasonable that as compensation Seth introduced the nearly-closed-eye experiment.

(After break Jane again resumed pacing. Again her eyes were nearly shut, but now occasionally they opened as usual. This was infrequent. Her voice was unchanged, her glasses once again off. Resume at 9:34.)

It will be impossible to go into even a fraction of such planes of actuality.

We will only concern ourselves with a few, those of which I am at least partially familiar. These planes of actuality, of course, all operate within the spacious present, and with a value climate. While portions of them may protrude into physical actuality, they will do so with varying proportion.

Many of them barely exist in a physical manner at all. Others to you would appear physically lopsided, with all of their matter concentrated, so to speak, in one place. The actuality of a plane, the validity of a plane, is not necessarily determined by its material makeup. On some planes this is so, but on a small number only.

Your mistake is in judging existence by its protrusion into matter as you are familiar with matter, and this attitude indeed will persist into any foreseeable future without basic change. This attitude is a defense mechanism, most understandable, since your plane or field of actuality is so involved in its relationship with material construction. There is a freedom, however, in independence from material construction that inhabitants are familiar with in other actualities.

I am myself, now, to a large extent so freed. Were it not however for the basic independence of the inner self from matter, human life as you know it would also be impossible.

We must also clear up some points on other topics. We will shortly be concerned more directly with discussions of individual dreams. It is necessary that a firm ground be prepared for such discussion. There are various doorways into the dream universe: chemical doorways, electronic doorways, and psychological doorways. All three must be opened at once, that is simultaneously, but any one door will automatically open the others.

They open infrequently in the waking state. When they are clicked open, usually but not always chemically through a momentary imbalance, the physical organism itself is connected to the dream universe, as well as to your physical universe; and to some degree the physical organism can be affected through this connection.

(Jane now sat down in a wicker chair opposite my writing table. She had not been smoking while delivering the material. Her eyes almost shut, she groped about on the table for her cigarettes, lit one and then leaned back with her eyes closed.)

It is not understood that this connection exists, but metabolism is to some degree influenced by the physical organism's dream connection. The physical organism is not only open to, but to some extent influenced by, many more areas of actuality than is supposed; and its survival is determined by a large variety of factors as yet hardly considered possible by your scientists or doctors.

This is not to say that a man has no control over the physical state of his own organism. It is to say that many more factors go into the construction and maintenance of the physical organism than you realize. Subconsciously, man manages to balance these influences, and there are physical mechanisms within the organism whose purpose it is to deal with such data.

The pores of the skin are such mechanisms.

There are many more. It is known now that the physical organism exists as many things. It even exists as radio waves, and to creatures who cannot perceive matter but can perceive radio waves, your physical body appears quite differently than it does to you. The whole physical organism contains checks and balances of which your scientists are still not aware, and I must also mention that for all its mandy-pamby, astrology has a strong basis, although it is only one small portion of the whole story, and not indeed the whole kettle of tales.

The physical organism itself then, even as you know it, exists and moves and reacts and influences, and is influenced by, many fields or planes of actuality; and its existence as you know it in your universe is determined by and dependent upon its existence within other fields, of which man is still intellectually ignorant.

I suggest your break.

(Break at 10:03. Once again Jane looked sleepy as her eyes opened. She was much more dissociated than when she paced about the room with her eyes open, she said, and also in a deeper state than when she was moving about with her eyes shut part of the time.

(Jane said she had the idea that Seth got her to sit down by letting her smoke. Just before she sat down she was beginning to feel "strained," as though she had to reach for what she was saying. As soon as she sat down the feeling of strain vanished. As soon as she did sit down, Jane began to take longer pauses between phrases at times, as she had done in the last session. But as before her diction remained clear, her voice normal.

(When she began dictation again Jane remained seated. Her eyes were closed, her glasses off, and she was smoking. Resume at 10:12.)

The physical organism also has capabilities and freedoms which it uses constantly, and of which the intellect is not yet aware.

The physical organism protrudes into many fields of actuality, and is to some extent perceived within these fields, and influences those fields as they influence the physical organism. It is because you conceive of the body as existing within one field only that you have not had more success in dealing with human illness.

There are automatic processes that are constantly carried out by the body, of which you are intellectually unaware. When a stoppage of one of these processes occur, there are ways of setting them into motion. These involve not surgery but a proper communication and adjustment, made through or by way of the subconscious to the inner self.

The inner self, which has been called the soul, has connections through the entire physical organism, and is not concentrated in any one portion. More adjustments are made by the physical organism than you know, and when I say that it exists in many fields, I mean that it actually not only appears within them, but is a part of them in an intimate manner, that the physical organism as it is materialized within your universe is actually a coming together and merging that has its existence, and is a blending of data from many planes, that would be considered foreign by the intellect.

The physical organism as you know constantly changes, and cannot be said to be the same from one of your moments to the next. To you it appears as a solid duration. On many of the fields within which it exists it is seen as constantly flickering, as say a fire.

The overall pattern of organization in a physical sense must be maintained however, and always under the auspices of the inner self, which is not imprisoned by its construction, although like any good guardian it spends most of its time at home, in maintaining the structure.

The molecular structure indeed is fairly rigid. The inner self is not so bound to such a formal alignment, and is thus free to travel in ways which the body, because of its formal molecular structure, finds impossible.

This has been a fruitful session, and I am pleased to find us back on schedule. You will discover that this evening's material on the physical organism in particular will be most helpful, particularly in future sessions. We will sometime or other deal with the maintenance of the organism, and then you will need this material. I hope it explains the <u>comparative</u> (underline comparative) rigidity of pattern which composes the body, which allows it to maintain apparent constancy; and one of the prices it must pay for this is a stabilization of a kind that the inner self is not bound by.

I will now end our session. My most fond wishes to you both, particularly since this is the beginning of your new year. May it be a fruitful one.

(End at 10:36. Once again Jane was well dissociated. And again she was not conscious of light or dark, or images. She was aware of her voice speaking however.)

SESSION 119
JANUARY 6, 1965 9 PM WEDNESDAY AS SCHEDULED

(The following data are from Jane's psychological time notebook: January 5, Tuesday: No results in particular. January 6, Wednesday, 11:30 AM: Achieved a light trance first, then felt as though my hands were crossed, but knew they weren't. Extreme sensation of lightness and rising, as if from some pressure beneath me. Left hand moved occasionally of its own accord.

(John Bradley, of Williamsport, PA, visited us yesterday. He has witnessed several sessions. He could not attend tonight's session but left with us a question concerning transubstantiation; John wanted Seth's comments on the literal results, if any, of this Catholic ceremony.

(Jane has been reading Jung for the last few days. This afternoon she told me

she thought Seth might talk about the self-conscious inner ego. As session time approached she had no idea of what her procedure would be—whether she would sit, stand, pace, open or close her eyes, etc. She was still worried also about the time element when her eyes were closed, and we agreed that I would ask for breaks if it seemed the monologues might carry past the customary half-hour limit.

(She was sitting opposite my table in a wicker chair as 9 PM arrived. She did not get up, or remove her glasses, but began to speak in a normal voice with her eyes closed and her head down somewhat. She was smoking.)

Good evening.

("Good evening, Seth.")

Ruburt should learn much of advantage from the book by Jung which he is reading. And I would like to mention here that I am not Jane's animus.

(The word was unfamiliar to me and I asked Jane to repeat it. She did so but I still did not understand it very clearly, and decided to wait until I could refer to Jung myself.

(It will be recalled that in the 83rd session, August 31, 1964, [in Volume 2], Seth commented on the work of Freud and Jung, and mentioned some of the distortions Jung's work in particular contains.)

You will understand, Joseph, when you read the book.

Jane's animus is indeed quite a different sort of chap from myself, much more omnipotent to Jane's subconscious. I will indeed speak concerning the inner ego, which is the organizing principle within the subconscious, but which looks into other worlds; toward worlds in which it has its origin, and does not have awareness of itself or possess self-consciousness within the physical universe. Its attention and focus is, rather, directed elsewhere, so that it appears to be dormant. But it is not.

It is the ego or directive consciousness behind all personified aspects of the subconscious; in dormant fashion however, and contrary to Jung's propositions, within the subconscious and in those personified aspects of it will be found remnant memory personalities of past reincarnated selves. They may be called shadows and yet they are not powerless. The inner ego, the directive organizer of the subconscious, also is the part of the self which is familiar with activities and methods of which the outer ego is ignorant. It is this organizer who directs not only the movements of the physical body from within, but directs from within those intimate survival mechanisms, without which the physical body could not exist, and upon which the existence of the outer ego is so dependent.

It is this inner director who maintains all of these functions, and who is responsible for the physical health. It is this director to whom you must communicate when health fails. There are ways of doing this which we will discuss at a later date. It is this inner director who chooses the dream symbols in such a way that they will be meaningful to all layers or areas of the subconscious, and who is responsible for the amount, rate and type of subconscious data which is given to the outer ego by means of the intuitions.

If the outer ego would be content to work on an equal basis with its inner counterpart, then many severe difficulties would be sidestepped.

(Jane now paused, waved a hand and frowned. She was still sitting down, and had indeed slid quite a ways down in the chair; with her feet up on the register, she was actually very nearly in a prone position as she spoke. Her eyes were closed.)

I forgot, you wanted the spelling. It is a-n-i-m-u-s.

The outer ego, being of later development, is jealous of its position and would have all knowledge at its fingertips. This is impossible. It cannot stand to have anything hidden, but the very mechanism of its own behavior is hidden from itself, and it knows only the feel of its own surfaces.

In many respects it is a reflector, the surface of the self looking outward. While this is necessary, the whole remainder of the self could not be left to an organizer or caretaker who did not focus his attentions within the depths but sat, as it were, on the front porch of the house, leaving the inner workings unattended. The outer ego does not want to meet the inner ego. The outer ego does not want to admit the existence of the inner ego. As the eye cannot see its own pupil without a mirror, so the outer ego could not even see itself, were it not that the inner ego hides in the depths of all reflections.

When the outer ego, from the surface of its consciousness, reflects the outer world, it sees reflections of the inner ego which are the images within its own eye; and as the self creates matter subconsciously within its own eye, and as the self creates matter subconsciously and not consciously, and as the self creates matter in line with inner and not outer expectations, so then does the ego, in viewing the material universe, come face to face with the face of its own inner ego; and the outer ego cannot escape from this inner self.

I now suggest your break.

(Break at 9:30. Jane's eyelids were heavy, and she had trouble keeping her eyes open for some few minutes. She had been well dissociated, she said, going into a deep trance after the first sentence or two. Her pauses were not overly long, and she knew what she was saying as she gave voice to it, but then forgot it.

(Jane's definition of Jung's animus is the male characteristics incorporated in the female subconsciously. Anima would be the female characteristics subconsciously incorporated in the male.

(Jane said that when she delivers material while sitting and with her eyes closed, she is aware of a feeling of resistance at going into the dissociated state. The

feeling is not strong, but she is aware of it. Once more now she resumed dictation while sitting down and with her eyes closed. At times she was again in the prone position, which she achieved by sliding down in the wicker chair, and elevating her feet upon the register. Resume at 9:44.)

Nor could I possibly live up to Jane's animus. I use the name Jane here rather than Ruburt because the animus belongs to Jane and to the present personality.

Talk about reflections, because Ruburt has an anima!

Scientists have glimpsed the complications of the human body. They have scarcely glimpsed the complicated realities of the mind. If it were understood that the areas of the subconscious are indeed populated by many and various subpersonalities, then they would not wonder that the human body is sometimes so besieged with ailments, or that the dominant personality so often appears in contradictory terms.

The subconscious is not a cellar piled high with explosives, rocking at the foundations of the ego. The subconscious contains a collection of diverse, varied and vital personalities who represent the losers when the time arrived to send one of them to the topmost level, or to the surface of the self.

The choice was made and is always made by the inner ego, who does this appointing according to his knowledge, or its knowledge, of the personality's qualities. Any of these subconscious personalities could have learned in some fashion to cope with the outside world as well as the present dominant ego, but for various reasons of inner development they could not be so trusted.

These subpersonalities are not unconscious to themselves. They are conscious of themselves, but they are not conscious of themselves in relation to other selves. They are conscious of needs and drives, and of their existence. They are different from the inner ego or director in that the inner ego is conscious not only of itself, but of the outer ego, and is aware of the existence of the outer world, although not too much concerned with it unless the whole self becomes jeopardized through the actions of the outer ego.

The inner ego knows when to apply safety valves, and is aware of the danger before the outer ego is alerted. The inner ego is concerned with maintaining the foundations and balance, which is very important, of the whole self, and it is open to messages from the overall entity. The inner ego receives messages through the inner senses, and is aware of realities which the outer ego cannot afford to recognize because of its specialization. In some important aspects the outer ego is supposed to represent to some degree the subdominant personalities who still dwell in the subconscious. When the outer ego is narrow, and poorly represents these subdominant personalities then they rise up in arms, and when conditions are favorable attempt to express themselves through a momentary weakness on the part of the dominant ego. But without even doing this they may momentarily take over or express themselves through a single function, such as speech or motion, while the outer ego is blissfully unaware.

I suggest your break.

(Break at 10:06. Jane's eyes opened slowly. She said she was so well dissociated that she could not remember what she said. She vaguely recalled hearing her voice. She was not bothered by any conception of time while speaking; yet she still wanted to be sure she "came out" on time.

(During break I mentioned John Bradley's question on transubstantiation. Jane's voice was quite strong, indeed loud, when she began dictating again. She remained seated with her eyes closed, and was smoking. Resume at 10:16.)

The consciousness had its origin in the subconscious, from which it sprang. The consciousness was not at one time the center of the subconscious. However, the inner ego was always the center of the subconscious.

As the self became more involved with objectivity, the subconscious, of itself, began the formation of the consciousness, which evolved as portions of it became specialized for the purpose of out-terialization.

(Out-terialization, above, is just as Jane pronounced it.)

The center of consciousness, that is the center of outward consciousness, the outer ego, is finally chosen by the inner ego after certain portions of the inner self show greater tendencies for objectification; these portions of course grouped around one of the subconscious subpersonalities which then wins out to become the outer ego, the manipulator for and the spokesman for the whole self.

This outego, among its purposes, has the duty of expressing not only itself but to a lesser extent those various hidden personalities which compose the subconscious. In larger terms and in more comprehensive terms, the whole self, the whole field of the complete subconscious and inner self, reaches back to the entity. There is no end to the past projection or existence of the subconscious of any given self; and though it is not understood in your field, there is no end to the forward thrust of the subconscious of any given self.

At death on your plane the ego merely changes the focus of its awareness. We have come through very well this evening, and I will here end our session. My fondest wishes to you both. We will take up the question of transubstantiation, as asked by our friend, at a not distant date.

("Good night, Seth."

(End at 10:29. Jane struggled to keep her eyes open. She was well dissociated, she said, and for some minutes after the session ended remembered only the last sentence

she had delivered. Her voice had been loud, her diction clear. She had been very restless in her chair, ranging from an upright sitting position to a practically prone one.

(Jane said she now believes her traditional pacing about has become a distraction largely; she thinks she no longer wishes to pace, except when she feels brief periods of resistance at the ego's surrender on this point. On the whole she feels there is much less resistance to delivering the material while less active physically. She receives the data clearer this way. She is also not so aware of outside distractions, such as traffic passing the house, people in the hall outside our door, etc.

(Jane said her voice sounded to her as though it issued from a point perhaps a foot in front of her mouth. This was a new feeling as far as she could recall, although she wasn't sure whether or not it began at last break.)

(The following data are from Jane's psy-time notebook:

(January 7, Thursday, 11:30 AM: Mentally I saw Mother's old house. Recalled writing a poem as a child that I had completely forgotten, and at the time it had seemed tremendous to me. I recalled only the first two lines: "My backyard is a garden, In beauty unsurpassed." I saw the old kitchen linoleum in color, and the outside cellar roof. I recalled an item on the roof I had been trying to paint lately. I couldn't see it clearly. My left hand moved by itself.

(January 8, Friday, 11:30 AM: Feeling of hands crossed again. Saw outside myself clear silhouette of full-leafed tall bush or type of tree, against a dim red background. The leaves were distinct and separate. Also mental conversation I've forgotten.

(January 11, Monday, 11:30 AM: Saw a pair of scissors. Later, while resting, I received a mental impression of Linda Butts and perhaps her mother Betts. I am not certain it was Linda, but whoever it was was either very angry or frightened. Linda and Betts could have been arguing [although this is unlikely; as far as I know Linda is away at school.] All of this was a mental impression, more of a jumbled <u>sense</u> of sound and emotional clutter, with but vague images. I did not see Linda clearly, yet assigned this data to her.

(Right after this I felt a most odd sensation, one I can describe only as a definite, strong cluttering motion, jumbled, inside my head; like angry or upset symbols not translated into <u>specific</u> information, with a sense of sound in it. It was as if I picked up someone else's physical and emotional jumbles.

(At the same time I felt the same sensation, although to a lesser degree, in my left kneecap, which instantly snapped or jerked my leg up. All this was direct and kinetic on my part.

(The time was approximately 6:30 PM.)

SESSION 120
JANUARY 11, 1965 9 PM MONDAY AS SCHEDULED

(By 8:55 PM Jane was uncomfortable and nervous because she didn't know what Seth was going to talk about. This feeling was heightened of course because she was also not sure whether she would sit with her eyes closed during the session, or pace about. She reminded me of Seth's suggested phrase to bring her out of the trance state every half-hour, should she show signs of remaining in it for longer periods.

(I had placed the Kennedy rocker opposite my writing table. Jane remained seated as the session began. She put her feet up on the register, and rocked back and forth lightly as she dictated. Her eyes were closed for the most part, although she was smoking as the session began. Her voice was a little stronger than usual; it might also be noted that for the most part the pauses she uses during delivery are not now as long.)

Good evening.

("Good evening, Seth.")

First of all, on a jovial note, may I remark upon the new furniture arrangement, adding that for your purposes the second room divider will prove most advantageous.

It appears that I have lectured you constantly, and I'm afraid of late in quite a dry, official manner. But in some session in the near future we will have a less formal and more friendly time. I am concerned with getting material to you, but I am also concerned that we do not lose the basic friendly nature of our communications.

As far as our experiment with this new procedure, it is coming along well. We are taking it gradually and gently, and upon any occasion when Ruburt feels momentarily panic-stricken, though I do not believe he will, by now he will merely come out of his state more or less automatically. I believe that this signal has now been set up as a precaution.

We will speak this evening concerning the importance of the existence of planes or fields of actuality which are as yet generally unrecognized within your own field. Due to mankind's present general insistence upon recognizing no other fields of actuality but his own, the advance of knowledge is curtailed. No efforts will be made to determine the existence or importance of actualities when such actualities are not believed to exist to begin with, particularly when such a discovery would shatter the very foundations of knowledge as it now exists.

It is precisely because of this failure, because of man's endeavor to explain data in terms of his own field only, that so much seems either unexplainable, mysterious, or beyond the realm of intellectual comprehension. By following such a course mankind severely limits the amount of data that reaches his own perception. He tries, therefore, to construct a model of the universe with only a handful of available clues.

The clues which he does not look for would lead toward not mere dry generalized facts, but facts that are at the basis of the universe as he knows it. Facts indeed that make such a universe possible, facts that would revolutionize science, and most of all the science of medicine, and the field of psychology. The study of so-called extrasensory perception is now considered an isolated bizarre domain, unrelated to other fields of knowledge. The reason for this is that the data that would connect such a study to all other fields of interest is not recognized. The study of the inner workings of the self is closely connected to the study of the universe as it exists in all its levels of reality.

The pieces to the puzzle are at mankind's fingertips, but he has put together an awkward, ill-fitting miniature model universe of a puzzle with which he is afraid to part. If the physical universe existed on a physical field only, indeed this would be the greatest miracle of all, for it would be impossible. The inner vitality of which we have so often spoken, and whose ways I have described, this inner vitality is the force which itself forms the physical universe, and without which no such manifestation would be possible. Yet this inner self, this inner vitality, is one of the main clues which man refuses to recognize, calling it an unreasonable assumption, but not willing to examine it for those characteristics which show it to be the most reasonable and logical of phenomena.

In other sessions I have explained precisely and in detailed fashion the steps by which this individualized vitality forms its own energy into molecules and atoms, which are the basis for further more advanced gestalts. For his refusal to pursue the examination of such forces, mankind suffers greatly the results of his own ignorance.

I suggest your break.

(Break at 9:25. Once again Jane's eyes opened sleepily. She had been fully dissociated, she said, much farther out than in earlier sessions before she began to sit down. Her cigarette had become a distraction. She listened to herself speak as though listening to a recorder.

(Again Jane began dictating while seated in the rocker. Now her voice was louder and her pace faster. Her eyes were closed. Resume at 9:34.)

Your own universe has its existence within many fields, and exists as an actuality, exerting force, within these fields.

Force of various kinds is also exerted by these fields upon your universe. Until it is thoroughly understood little real progress can be made. Mankind still deals with surfaces, depending mainly as he does upon the powers of the outer ego, whose purpose it is to deal only with surface reality.

This is not to say that such surface reality is not vital and important, or that some information about its own nature cannot be gleaned from its study; but only a small amount can be so obtained. The other fields of which I speak exert their influences upon the physical organism as it exists. These forces are dealt with and balanced by the subconscious, and not by the outer ego.

Excess of chemicals within the body are drained off by the subconscious through its ability to act as a channel between fields of actuality. The chemicals are sent as projections into other fields which need such chemicals. Certain energies from other planes or fields are also projected into this field, where they are used.

Transformation of energy from one field to another continually goes on. I cannot stress too strongly the fact that in practical actuality the body exists within many fields, and it cannot be explained or understood when it is considered a product of one field only. Nor can it be much aided in times of physical difficulties, for the basic causes of the problems is not known, and treatment at best is haphazard.

In <u>all</u> instances of ill health, the psychic inner forces are being misdirected. The aim of medicine should then be to aid the inner self to direct its own energy along other lines. Now. With the above, the psychic forces may be misdirected in several main ways, and with several resulting malfunctions. Energy may not be properly directed toward releasing from the physical field of the body excess chemicals into other fields. A buildup of such chemicals can be deadly, leading to among other things forms of insanity, schizophrenia, and other disorders which show themselves in mental or personality symptoms.

It is possible to treat such disorders from a chemical standpoint, as is sometimes being done, but the acquired artificial chemical balance will in most cases not be maintained, because the inner self, the deep subconscious, has not been signaled that an error is being made. Ideally of course such an error should not occur. There are also reasons why the deep subconscious has allowed such difficulties to come about, and in most cases the basic reason here is a lack of understanding and communication between the various portions of the self, so that seemingly the left hand does not know what the right hand is doing.

The first treatment should always include the setting up, once more, of such communication, and we will have more to say later on this subject.

Existence within any field is more complicated than you dream either possible or reasonable. It depends upon simultaneous actuality in so many fields, and delicate balances and communications, the balances in all cases being determined by the efficiency of the communications.

I mentioned earlier the connection between excess chemicals and the dream field. Now. Before we take a break, let me tell you that hormones within the physical body have not only a chemical but an electric, rather electromagnetic, basis and reality, and that these also are connectors with other fields of existence.

I now suggest your break.

(Break at 9:58. Jane was well dissociated, hardly being able to recall anything of what she had said. Again sitting down, and with her eyes closed, she resumed in the same rather loud and clear voice at 10:10.)

So-called extrasensory perception, and many connected endeavors, merely represent the recognition, by some, of those important pieces of data which are usually not recognized.

Successful experiments along these lines appear as disconnected happenings merely because the context in which they have their existence, and which makes their existence possible, is not known or recognized. Telepathy goes on constantly, my dear friends, in all fields of actuality. Telepathy goes on within the body between the cells. Telepathy exists because no systems are truly closed systems.

Clairvoyance exists and is possible because of its basis within the spacious present, and this is not known because man will not accept the available data. Clairvoyance exists because matter and energy are one and the same thing. There is clairvoyance within the organs of the physical body itself, because the organs of the body are not, quote, "just" matter, but energy which has composed itself into matter. Such inner data continually and automatically is accepted by every other portion of the human framework except by the outer ego. Even this outer ego, however, acts all unknowingly often on the basis of such information, which it will not admit it has received; and often such action saves it from dire circumstances.

As you know, at one time it was necessary for the ego to focus exclusively upon outer data, but the channels never closed between the inner self and the ego. The ways for communication between the two have been left open. If they had not been left open, man would have no knowledge at all, nor any hint, of his basic inner existence. There is no real dual state. The inner self will make itself known. For the species this present period is transitory, but the length of this period, if drawn out, could bring about results most unfortunate.

Two main possibilities come to mind. One, a continued lack of acceptance of the inner self could lead to worldwide catastrophe, as the ego runs wild. Two, the inner self, restrained and denied for too long a period, could explosively overwhelm the ego so that existence in the physical field was made most difficult, since the ego is equipped to handle such manipulation. Ego domination must indeed be halted, but it must be replaced with a balance between the outer and inner selves. Other matters briefly mentioned this evening will be more thoroughly discussed then also.

My best regards to you both, and to Ruburt bravo.

("Good night, Seth.")

(End at 10:29. Jane came out of her deep state slowly as usual. She remembered little of the material. She said Seth's bravo referred to the fact that she is acquiescing in the new developments during the sessions; namely, delivering the material while sitting down and with her eyes closed.)

SESSION 121
JANUARY 13, 1965 9 PM WEDNESDAY AS SCHEDULED

(Jane had no idea of the material for the session as time for it approached, but she was not nervous as she was last session. Once again she began dictating while sitting in the rocking chair opposite my table. Her eyes were closed and she was not smoking. Her glasses were off. Her voice was rather quiet, but clear, and she spoke at a comfortable rate without undue pauses.)

Good evening.

("Good evening, Seth.")

I wanted to add here that evidences for those other fields of actuality <u>can</u> be found even within the body itself; that is, within the physical body. But these evidences are not recognized for what they are, attempts being made to the contrary to fit these into the framework of conventional knowledge, where indeed they fit but poorly.

Also, such placement of them is misleading when other deductions are drawn. Such evidences of other actualities could serve as important clues, which if followed could then begin to unravel the secrets which are secrets merely because of man's refusal to pursue them.

These clues could lead to proper understanding, so that it would be known that the physical body does exist in many fields of actuality, and through the study of various portions of the body many glimmerings could be received concerning the various fields of actuality themselves.

To study the human body from only the physical standpoint, or to consider it as exclusively a physical phenomenon, is to severely limit your perception of it, and of reality as a whole. To study psychology exclusively in terms of the brain's effect upon the physical body is likewise hampering and limiting, for the brain is merely that portion of, that very small portion, of the mind which is apparent within matter. As such within your physical field the brain is subject to the laws of your field. The mind, having its existence within the scope of the physical field but independent of it, is a much more fruitful subject for study; and not of course study through means of physical instruments or of operations performed. In any case the mind cannot be found by such procedures.

The mind will be found to be closely allied with the spacious present. The mind's capabilities, if studied, would lead man into a realization of these other fields of actuality of which I have spoken. The mind deals with intangibles, but it does not deal with unrealities. Again, the validity of an actuality is not to be determined by its appearance within matter alone. The ingredients of matter are first of all intangible ingredients, and the study of the mind and a study of the processes by which the mind creates its dream images could lead to a basic understanding of the manner in which man subconsciously produces the physical images of his own material universe.

This study alone would involve an introduction into a knowledge of other fields of actuality. Biology has made many strides, but it must finally be concerned with that intangible which is behind all organisms, and it will be forced to the initiation of an entirely new field, along the lines of basic organic psychology. It will be forced to recognize the innate ability of <u>all</u> cells for what we may call telepathy, for there will be no other solution in answering many questions.

In the most simple of living structures telepathy is a necessity for communication, particularly before the inside energy is concentrated sufficiently to form any sort of more complicated pattern or nerve structure. Even when such nerve structures and physical complications are evolved telepathy operates, still a necessity as a communications system within the physical structure, and still handling data which cannot be carried through any physical medium, simply because it is untranslatable by its nature into physical materialization.

These points are all extremely important. Much will be said yet to clarify the term telepathy itself, since there are many types, which you should be able to see from what I have said. This in itself is a complicated subject, and yet when I am finished it will be shown that telepathy is an intimate, innate ability within <u>all cells</u>.

I suggest your break.

(Break at 9:27. Jane was well dissociated, unaware of outside stimuli. Her eyes opened slowly. She said she feels the material is more "concentrated" than it used to be—that is, that the same amount of information is contained within fewer words.

Certainly the sessions are not as long as they used to be. Jane also said she does not believe she will smoke anymore while dictating, since that too has become a distraction.

(Sitting with her eyes closed, Jane again began speaking in her quiet voice at 9:36.)

Now. On its simplest level, and this is hardly simple, but on its most basic level, what you call telepathy operates in the following manner.

Telepathy on this level is the intangible, nonmaterial communication of inner energy, or inside energy, to the physical materialization of itself within the physical field. This elementary telepathy is not the communication of thought as such, but is the communication of intent, desire and purpose. It is therefore the communication of inner energy to various still-forming aspects of itself, a blazing, so to speak, of invisible paths or bridges. And at the same time the laying down of these intangible paths serve as the inner framework over which or upon which future physical lines or structures will be laid.

No physical communication systems, such as nerves and so forth, are accomplished before these invisible inner energy telepathic structures are first set forth, for these impress within the unformed physical structures the habits and ways which the physical structures will then follow; and these inside telepathic lines continue to exist within the physical structures after they are completed, and for a while after the physical structures have been broken down.

I have until this point said very little about the so-called astral body. For one thing I dislike the term. For another, I did not want to discuss such points until I had first prepared you for not only their existence, but their purpose and logic.

(Many sessions ago Seth stated he did not like the term, astral body, but said nothing else about it. See the 40th session, [in Volume 1].)

You can perhaps now see where this so-called astral body has its origin and purpose. It is actually the intangible but actual framework formed by inner energy, about whose lines or, actually, reference points, the physical framework is constructed. Now. This sort of elementary telepathy has existed as a necessity since the first formation of inner energy into matter. Some of our past sessions, particularly those explaining the initial appearance of matter, will set you clear, and you will see that the explanations I gave you then would have to involve such elementary telepathic communication between cells.

As inner energy forms more complicated gestalts through the processes that I have earlier explained, then inner energy continues its communication with the physical matter that it creates about it. When inner energy desires to construct a more complicated gestalt, then it must telepathically communicate this intent and purpose through the matter which it collects about itself, forming a more complicated inner telepathic pattern first, that can then be filled in with physical matter. The manners in which telepathy operates are difficult to explain because of the divergence of definition held by the ego and by the inner self of any given individual. To the human being it must appear that telepathy is a mental or psychic communication occurring between two or more entirely separate selves. The ego, you see, has one definition for the self, and its own idea of the limitations of itself.

The ego considers itself <u>the</u> self, and considers anything outside of its self as being either <u>non</u>self or another such separate identity, and so the individual man is led to believe that telepathy is basically a communication between two or more basically alone, separate and aloof selves. Telepathy does not operate at the level of the ego, although its actions may protrude into the domain of the ego. Telepathy operates within the inner self, within various levels, different levels of the subconscious, where the ideas of separation and limitations of self are not nearly so limiting.

The type of telepathy which is most commonly thought of as telepathy is of course not the elemental type of which I spoke earlier, but a different variety. This particular, more advanced telepathy could not and did not occur <u>in its most complicated form</u> until the development within your plane of psychically developed personalities. This development involved separations and concentrations of energy into self-conscious identities. This development was an advancement, yet this advancement led also to a separation and objectifying of consciousness, into dual segments of subject and object.

I suggest your break.

(Break at 10:07. Jane was again well dissociated. She resumed in a louder voice, again while sitting down and with her eyes closed, at 10:14.)

I have explained in the past the potentialities and unlimited qualities of the self. You may refer to those discussions if you wish for background here.

(Among others see the 40th session, April 1,1964, for material on tissue capsules; and the 41st for material on the spacious present.)

You can see that the inner self is much more spacious and unlimited than the ego self, and that while divisions occur they may vary, and the boundaries of the inner self constantly change.

Inner telepathic communications exist whenever the inner self reaches out, wherever its sympathies or vitalities are attracted. In a manner we will later discuss, psychically it surrounds information, operating psychically almost in the same manner that a simple amoeba physically will surround food.

This may not be a very apt analogy, but the principles are sound behind the analogy. This is complicated to explain, and yet an explanation is sorely needed, for telepathy operates mainly when similarities and attractions are set up, when like attracts like; and not, as it would seem, when as it appears one alien or separate identity is connected with another.

What I am trying to get across here is that, because of the superficial studies done so far, it seems that telepathy operates with separateness because of the limitations set by the ego on the definition of self. It is the similarity, or sympathy, of those in telepathic communication that makes telepathy possible. The limited idea of the self held by the ego clouds and distorts the main issue, for the ego is not conscious of the underlying bonds of sympathy that serve to merge, momentarily, the identities involved.

This, dear friends, is quite enough for one session. I have given you some meat. Next time I will add the sauce. My best and fondest regards to you both.

("Good night, Seth.")

(End at 10:27. Jane was again well dissociated.)

SESSION 122
JANUARY 18, 1965 9 PM MONDAY AS SCHEDULED

(While trying psychological time on January 18, Monday, 11:30 AM, Jane achieved the following results: "Extreme feeling of weightlessness. I had no sense of physical pressure upon the bed, but one of suspension. In recent experiments I have been getting a strong sense of vibration and movement in the beginnings of the sessions."

(Jane did not feel well, but decided to attempt the session anyhow. Once again she spoke while sitting down, and again her eyes were closed. Her rate of dictation was about average, her voice normal. She did not smoke during the session.)

Good evening.

("Good evening, Seth.")

This procedure, in which Ruburt sits quietly, is indeed less flamboyant than our previous methods, but it has many advantages, and it is beneficial that we experiment along various lines.

Your interest in these sessions must indeed compete with ordinary daily endeavors, and there will be, as you realize, fluctuations in your interest and indeed energy. The regularity of our sessions is our best insurance that they will continue. Ruburt is of course free, when he feels indisposed, to call a session off, but I would prefer when possible that some sort of a session be held, if only a very brief one.

You may of course, Joseph, also call off a session for similar reasons of your own. You are not to feel bound to the sessions, but should have them because you want them. Anything else would defeat their purpose.

To continue along the lines of the various fields of actuality in which the human body exists, these fields or systems, being open, are also fields with particular identity, within which certain inner and particular laws operate. Forces entering these fields, by the very act of entry, become transformed into the sort of data that can be accepted by the given field. The field is open then, but data passing into it is in a different form from the form it had before entry. There are electrical fields of actuality which are fields in which the dominating data is electrical, in the same manner that the dominating force or data within your plane is material.

In this field, electrical force is the main method by which inner energy expresses itself. This is rather difficult to explain, and yet later it will not seem so. Personality gestalts within this field are built up electrically, with electric components, without physical matter. In this field possibilities and actualities are electrically computed. Your own personalities in some manners exist within this field.

This field projects itself, as should be obvious, into your own field of actuality, and as such the personality itself has its existence in both fields; and both systems, being open, are dependent one upon the other, and a failure to survive in one system threatens survival in the other. This particular electrical field is one of the most closely allied with the physical field; comparing the whole setup to your known physical universe, the electrical field would be one of the close planets of your own system.

Existence in this field has great importance, particularly as far as the physical brain mechanism is concerned, and there are far more connections here than your scientists have yet discovered. The nerve impulses leap and connect the two fields continually, and interrelate them in a most intimate manner. Only infrequently does the electric field protrude visibly in your field, yet in its own field it is indeed tangible, but not in terms of matter. This field is also concerned with what you call growth in your own field. Electric impulses within atoms and molecules are part of the structure of your physical universe, while matter is not perceived directly in the electric field itself.

Where matter would exist there, a concentration of energy forms what you could think of as a body form, body meaning mass, yet it would not be matter in your terms. Such manifestations in the electric field are much more powerful, in terms of intensity per mass unit, than anything you know. This is a very important point, which will come up with us again in the future.

Now again: regardless of current scientific thought, there are at least three different kinds of electric force which your scientists have not yet discovered, and one of these has much to do with the intensity of thoughts as they are formed in the intangible mind, and translated to the physical brain and then into action, as the case may be.

I suggest your break.

(Break at 9:28. Jane was well dissociated as usual. Her delivery had been brisk but it slowed up somewhat when she resumed, again sitting down and with her eyes closed, at 9:35.)

It is not simply that some weak electrical force exists within the physical body, but that a portion of the physical body has its actual existence within a strong force field; that the whole physical body has counterparts, so to speak, within this force field, and that so far man has discovered only the comparatively weak electrical charges of one particular kind in general, that most obviously protrudes into the physical universe.

The physical body, in other words, exists as an electrical body that is not material, that has a peculiar mass but no weight, whose characteristics are apparent in terms of not varying shapes, but varying intensities and concentrations of electric force. In some respects there are differences. The mind, which is not physically represented in the material body, does exist electrically. The brain, which exists physically, is a part of the mind in the electric structure. The organs exist electrically. The skin does not exist <u>within</u> this electric counterpart, although the physical skin does contain electric force.

Now. If you could see the body as it exists within the electric field, you would certainly not recognize it, for its shape would bear no resemblance to the physical shape as you know it. The electric counterpart to the physical body exists, then, as an identity formed by various electrical systems operating more or less as one. It is an electric reality in which most certainly even thoughts exist as actualities, ever-moving spheres of more or less independent electric systems.

Emotions are also, then, actualities within the overall electric system, existing not as representations of feeling, but as definite charged action. I want if possible to get the idea over that this system involves realities that are directly experienced and vivid, and also that in some ways emotions and thoughts are more directly perceived in that field than your physical field. They are more readily apparent, with more force behind them acting directly upon the electric environment, without any intermediary steps; that is, <u>they</u>, emotions and feelings and thoughts, exist immediately within the environment as electrical forces within that system. In your system they need to be translated and given reality by a method of interrelationships. Your field attains its actuality only as a result of the cooperating merger of many other independent systems.

The trouble has been that your scientists see or perceive electrical and chemical systems, for example, only in their relationship with the physical system. They do not realize that these systems exist in universe actualities of their own. And the electrical and even chemical systems play a much larger part within the physical system than matter plays within their systems. They could both exist without the world of physical matter, but the world of physical matter could not exist without them.

I suggest your break.

(Break at 10:01. Jane was dissociated as usual. She resumed in the same manner as before at 10:13.)

As within your field inner energy is translated into physical matter through means which I have earlier described, within the electrical system inner energy is translated into the characteristics peculiar to that system.

Because your system is dependent upon the electrical system in one way or another, counterparts exist within the electrical system for all such phenomena. However, the electrical system contains phenomena that does not appear within your system, although some projections from it may be perceived. These projections so far have never been understood, since they have not been studied objectively, but only in their relation to the physical field.

Matter has little effect within the electrical system, but the effects of the electrical system upon physical matter are great. Now. Thoughts, human thought, has an electric reality; a human thought exists as an independent electrical action, and as such it continues to exist within the electrical system long after it has <u>left</u> its point of origin. This is another important piece of information that will also be referred to later.

The thought, as an electrical reality, is not subject to the physical laws that bind the physical body. The durability of the thought as an electrical act is determined by its initial electric charge. This electric charge can propel the thought, as an electrical action, through the apparent dimensions of your physical time in such a manner that it can exist simultaneously within your past and your present. Because a thought, as electric action, may exist both within your past and your present, this is not to say that it becomes <u>two</u> electric actions, one existing in the past and one existing in the future. Rather the one electric action or thought is simultaneously projected, through a peculiarity of its axis, so that it appears within your field, not in two places at once, but in two times at once.

All thoughts, as mental or electric actions, do not necessarily so appear by any means. I hope to go into these matters more deeply at our next session. Nor have I forgotten that I spoke of an informal session; when your recorder is fixed we will have such a session, when you can be relieved for once from your note taking, Joseph. And I will even make room for questions.

My fondest wishes to you both.

("Good night, Seth."

(End at 10:32. Jane was dissociated as usual. She now said she felt better than she had before the session began.)

SESSION 123
JANUARY 20, 1965 9 PM WEDNESDAY AS SCHEDULED

(While trying psychological time on January 19 and January 20, Jane achieved excellent states of "ecstasy" both times.

(Jane had no idea of the material for the session before it began. She sat once again in the Kennedy rocker, across from my writing table, and dictated the material with her eyes closed. She did not smoke during the dictation. Her voice this evening was rather soft; she used some pauses but they were not very long ones for the most part.)

Good evening.

("Good evening, Seth.")

I am glad to see the progress that is being made on the book dealing with the Seth material.

I would like to speak on some of the topics that were discussed in our last session. If you recall, I said that thoughts and also emotions existed as electric actions, and once initiated are then in independent existence. That is, they are actualities apart and independent from their point of subjective origin.

They are brought into existence in a subjective manner, but they then are independent action, and as such may continue to exist in duration within the physical field, according to their original electric potential. In turn these thoughts or emotions, as electric actions, can affect other actions; and influence patterns can be set up, and are set up. The subjective habits of individuals are largely responsible for their own attractions to various types of such electric actions, and here indeed like attracts like.

Various emotional factors within each personality cause what we may call a characteristic emotional climate. Certain types of thoughts and emotions are entertained therein. Since these are electrical actions, they set up strong electrical fields of attraction within the personality, easy electric paths. Uncharacteristic thoughts or emotions must then meet with some resistance. Habit, then, has not only a psychological, but an electrical and psychological nature and implication.

It will be easier (i.e., there will be less resistance; put that in parentheses) for a given individual to accept certain ideas or emotions therefore, and more difficult for him to accept certain others. I have spoken about fields and systems. While no system is closed, each system has at its furthest reaches sufficient resistance to form sufficient-enough boundaries, so that its own identity is retained.

So does the personality, through negative charges, cause boundaries to be set about its own emotional system. It will accept most readily those thoughts and emotions, or electric actions, which attract it, which have a similarity to its own charged emotional climate; and it will have greater resistance to those which have the greatest dissimilarities. It is, therefore, most advantageous to study well those thoughts and emotions which are habitually accepted by any given personality.

The emotional climate, though intangible, is intimately known by each individual as it exists within himself, and it is the best indication of his physical condition, for thoughts and emotions as independent electrical actions have great influence directly upon the physical mechanism, acting indeed as electric storms which flash through the entire nervous system; or as great stabilizers as the case may be, and with of course many middle varieities of influence.

Thought and emotion then, is not only generally related to the physical mechanism, but as electrical actions, thoughts and emotions act directly upon the system. Again here you see, however, that it is the individual himself who initiates his own emotional climate, and then suffers or enjoys the results.

We must go much further into this particular subject. Nevertheless it must be clearly understood that thoughts and emotions are actualities in <u>themselves</u>, that directly work upon the physical mechanism. Any thought or emotion is bound to directly affect the physical body. Because thoughts and emotions, as electrical actualities, are independent from their subjective point of origin, a given thought or emotion, initiated by an individual, may be rejected by him and cast out. If the thought or emotion is similar to those usually <u>accepted</u>, then this will take time, for new electrical patterns must be set up. But an idea, thought or emotion so rejected still has independent actuality, and <u>may be</u> attracted to the emotional climate of another.

Many psychological intangibles, including dreams, have such an electric reality, and do exist as electric actions. They are to be reckoned with. The connections between the emotional climate and physical health have never been clearly understood, because emotions were not known to have such electrical reality. They were not known to <u>directly</u> affect the system. More is understood as far as the chemical relationships here.

I suggest your break.

(Break at 9:34. Jane was well dissociated. Her eyes opened slowly at break time. She said her voice as she dictated sounded to her as though "it was two feet above my head."

(In a somewhat louder voice, and displaying more animation, gesturing frequently even though her eyes remained closed, Jane resumed at 9:42.)

The point here is that you are, yourselves, familiar with such a small portion of reality.

You are familiar with such a limited portion of the actuality of your own thoughts. These thoughts are things, so to speak, as real as a chair; but you are acquainted only with their purely subjective reality. They have great force within the electric field, great attractions. If you could fully understand or comprehend directly the reality of a thought in its full actuality, you would be amazed at the power behind it.

Its manifestations are greatly concentrated, and its patterns attract mass, but in different terms in the electric field. There is, therefore, a similarity existing between an individual's dreams and thoughts and emotions and physical condition at any given time. The mind, as separate from the brain, the mind exists purely and simply in the electric system or field, and does not project itself directly into the physical field although its effects appear within it.

Each thought or emotion exists then as electric action within the mind. The action is transformed and translated, and is sent to the brain where its effects directly are felt, and the brain then initiates reactions. Thoughts and emotions then, being independent however, are not bounded by or held within the physical body. The physical barriers of skin, for example, the physical limitations of that structure, do not exist and are not recognized by thoughts or emotions. They recognize only electrical systems.

Every individual is pelted, so to speak, with numberless such electrical actions constantly. He accepts only those where mutual attraction exists, and is usually not aware of their possible origin outside of his own system. The fact that thoughts and emotions have an actuality outside of the subjective sense may appear appalling to some. Unless the fact is accepted, however, the human physical structure will never be understood.

Positive and negative thinking is more than a turn of phrase. Dimensions do indeed exist within this electrical field of which I have spoken, and it should be understood that I speak of an independent electrical field, and not of the weak, apparent electrical effects that can be observed within the brain or nervous system. The electrical reality of emotions and thoughts represents a thought dimension that has been completely neglected; and in it there are other dimensions; as within your field there is apparent space and time and height and thickness, so in the electrical system there is intensity and what I will call space reality, electrical mass and potentiality, which is different from intensity and polarity.

All electrical actions exist with those characteristics. They amount to an overall existence as valid as your own. In many ways it could be said that the physical system is an effect caused by this electrical field. There is still much to be covered here. There are units, working backward from your system, for convenience's sake, whereby your very physical weight is in electric form, an actuality beside the one that you know.

I suggest your break.

(Break at 10:06. Jane was fully dissociated, unaware of all outside influences. She resumed in the same manner, sitting down and with her eyes closed, at 10:12.)

Electricity is one of the attractions which make the existence of physical matter possible.

You can see now how a subjective experience can have an electrical reality, and through this reality directly affects the human physical structure. Dreams, also being electric actualities, depend upon an electric system of patterns to communicate their data to the various levels or areas of the inner self.

In the past I spoke of the innate capsule comprehension, which exists within all cells. These are also electrically coded. Whole comprehensions can thus exist within physical structure while taking up no physical space. Dreams are particularly interesting from this viewpoint, as the original dream experience is a direct electrical experience, decoded electrically, subjectively then translated for the various areas of the inner self. All seemingly purely subjective experiences which take up no physical space, but are emotionally or subjectively felt, all such experiences exist first of all electrically.

(Jane smiled broadly while delivering the above material. She spoke with much emphasis and rapped upon my table several times. Her eyes remained closed.)

The human system then translates the experience, but its original existence and actuality is electrical. This is why your dream locations take up no physical space, either within your skull or in your physical universe; and yet I have said that these dream locations did exist. Their existence is electrical, and they partake of the dimensions of the electrical system as I have given them to you.

Dreams are felt directly through electrical patterns, and then decoded. The original experience, then, again, is an electric one, and the effects are instantly felt by the human system, according to the original intensity of the charge. I have not spoken much concerning the dream universe, since first it was necessary that you understand the electrical actuality of emotions and thoughts.

I shall have more to say on this subject shortly.

You will also remember that I spoke long ago of the connections between emotions and physical weather. The electrical system is also of import here. Also our mental genes and mental enzymes, of which we will also speak more fully.

This has been an excellent session. I hope you are not all charged up. I will now let you out of my charge, and not charge you for the privilege of our session. My fondest regards to you both.

("Good night, Seth."

(End at 10:30. Jane was dissociated as usual. She ended the session with a smile.

(For some material on cellular comprehension, see the 29th session, among others. Mental genes are mentioned in the 26th session, among others, and mental enzymes are dealt with in the 13th, 16th, 19th, 20th sessions, among others. Dreams and related phenomenon have been discussed in many sessions. Emotions as connected with physical weather was rather extensively discussed in the 56th session.

(Note: The first mention of the translation of thought took place in the 8th session. See Volume 1, page 40.

(The first mention of mental enzymes took place in the 8th session. See Volume 1, page 41.

(Mental genes were first mentioned in the 9th session. See Volume 1, page 46.

(See sessions 86 and 87 for material on mental enclosures, and Session 87 also for material on capsule comprehension.

(See the 44th session for material on dream locations.)

SESSION 124
JANUARY 23, 1965 10:50 PM SATURDAY UNSCHEDULED

(This session was unplanned. Bill Macdonnel, who has witnessed several sessions and has been involved in some of the effects obtained during sessions, was visiting us. He did not feel well, and I was quite lethargic. Jane was restless however, so we began to try various small ESP experiments. We tried for physical effects without success. After an hour or so of this, Jane decided to call on Seth. I brought out my notebook.

(Jane sat down at about 10:30. One light was on in the living room but this bothered her, even though she sat with her back to it. I turned this light off then and turned one on in the kitchen; this cast an indirect light into the living room, enough for me to see to write.

(But this light also bothered Jane, to such an extent that within a few minutes she switched it off. This left the room lit spasmodically by the lights from passing

traffic. We waited in the dark room. Jane finally began to speak, rather rapidly, and in a voice a little heavier than usual. At the same time she rose and began to pace slowly about.

(I could not distinguish her features. I tried to take notes in this poor light, but gave up after half a dozen lines. What follows is a reasonably accurate reconstruction of Seth's material. The first paragraph, however, is a verbatim transcript.)

I only suggest that you watch Ruburt as he moves; and I must remind you that upon other occasions when results had been achieved, your minds had been focused along these directions for a long period of time, comparatively speaking, and whether you realized it or not your psychic energies had been so focused. Whether you are consciously aware of it or not, the subconscious focus at all times must be achieved first. Even when you did not realize that such a focus had been achieved it had been achieved.

More matters than you know enter into such achievements. All of your forces are relatively scattered this evening, Mark's in particular. Ruburt's insistence upon darkness was an attempt to increase your inner concentration. At times during regular sessions, I have introduced effects, but for various reasons you have either failed to observe them, or have not been able to.

(It will be remembered that Mark is Bill Macdonnel's entity name.

(Jane now sat down. Her chair was against a wall, and out of the direct line of reflected traffic lights, although I could see shadows pass across the white blur of her face. Again, I could not distinguish her features.)

I suggest you watch Ruburt's face. If any effects are to occur they will take place within three minutes.

(We sat quietly for perhaps one minute. I observed no change in or about Jane. Bill said nothing. Jane then spoke.)

If you see any effect, it will be the aura.

(For some little time longer we waited without observing any change relating to Jane. Our cat Willy moved about the dark apartment in a normal manner, apparently not sensing anything strange to him. Jane finally switched on a light, saying that Seth was gone.

(I had not seen an aura about her. Bill said that at first he thought he might have, but then discounted it upon second thought because the impression he had received had been so fleeting and faint; he could not be sure of anything.

(I had thought Seth would stay, to say something about why results had not been good, but Jane said the session was over. She was not nearly as dissociated as usual. She had felt "weird" at finding herself pacing again during delivery, when she had just become used to speaking while being seated. End at approximately 11:00.

(See the 68th session for the change in Jane's features, witnessed by Bill and me.

See the 102nd session for Bill's cognition of open eyes upon Jane's closed eyelids. It will be noted that the 102nd session was also unscheduled, and that it dealt with the subject of obtaining physical effects.)

SESSION 125
JANUARY 25, 1965 9 PM MONDAY AS SCHEDULED

(Once again throughout the session Jane delivered the material while sitting down, and with her eyes closed. Her voice remained rather quiet. Occasionally her delivery slowed down, but seemingly in compensation it would then speed up. She did not smoke during the session, and her glasses were off.)

Good evening.

("Good evening, Seth.")

I am pleased, as always, to begin another session, and we will cover a variety of rather allied subjects this evening.

These will include material that directly follows from our previous sessions; and also a few comments concerning experiments which you have been carrying on, more or less on your own.

We have been speaking of the electric reality and actuality of thoughts and emotions, and of dreams, and of all such experiences which appear to be purely psychological in origin, and take up no space in your physical universe.

I have also mentioned that the electrical field has its own variety of dimensions, with which you are not familiar. Now indeed this electrical field in which thoughts and emotions and dreams have an independent actuality, this field contains depths and dimensions of a sort most difficult to explain.

Depths are contained within this system that are not depths in terms of space, but rather definite depths and dimensions in terms of varying intensities. There is also here a duration that is closely connected with intensity, but not with continuity in terms of time, as it is usually understood in the physical field.

In the electrical field it is the intensity of any given actuality that determines this sort of duration, and the intensity can project such an actuality into many dimensions at once. The intensity of a given actuality within the electrical field, of itself, determines the <u>other</u> dimensions of the actuality. In the physical universe, height and thickness determine to a large degree the potentialities, physically speaking, of any organism. Within the electrical system, intensity is also responsible for the potentiality, duration and electrical mass, which is a mass of a different sort; a mass that takes up no space, and is not made of matter as you know it, but mass whose <u>thickness</u> is one of varying electrical intensities which form a definite shape, a separate field more or less, an electrical coded counterpart for physical matter.

It is difficult to explain this to you, since old concepts must be used in a new way. But in this electrical system a travel through time would merely involve a journey through intensities. This has many implications, as you should see when you read it.

(Jane, here, took quite a long pause, one of the few such that she used during the session.)

There is indeed an electrical journeying through these intensities. There is constant motion in this system, as in all others, and the constant motion within the electrical system makes motion possible within your own system; and "time" is indeed, here, an electrical impulse that grows by <u>intensity</u>, and not by moments.

To speak of backward and forward is meaningless. There are only various electric pulsations of varying intensities, from strong intensity to ever stronger, to weaker, to fading and again to stronger ever stronger. Since strong intensities are indeed natural results of weaker intensities, it would be meaningless to call one present and one past. Yet within your physical field, and with physical time, you ride the waves of these pulsations, so to speak.

When the pulsation is weak you call it past, when it is strongest you name it present, and the one that seems to <u>you</u> not yet as <u>strong</u> as present, you name future. For you make the divisions yourselves, and in such a manner have made the framework and all the possibilities, potentials and limitations inherent within a system set up with a divided time system.

I suggest your break.

(Break at 9:27. Jane was well dissociated as usual. She resumed in the same manner at 9:35.)

Nor, in the electrical system, is there distance in terms of space or time.

There is, again, depth which is a depth of intensity; and yet within this depth of intensity there exists distances in terms of action, which is a fairly new idea in these sessions.

You conceive of action in terms of time, since within the physical field a given action appears to actually take up time, almost in the same way that a chair seems to take up space. The chair of course does not take up space, but is part of what you call space. Nor does the action take up time. It is <u>part</u> of what you call time. Nevertheless, in the electrical system there is distance in terms of action. Each action is separate and not continuous with other action, in terms of continuity.

The distance occurs within the intensity of an action within the electrical field, as to say, you could fall <u>into</u> depths of intensity. The falling into would itself involve action. The action as it happened, then, falling through the intensity, would be falling into what I mean by distance. Dreams have this kind of distance. Again, as a simple analogy, in a dream you may travel down a road. This involves distance in <u>essence</u>, although within your physical universe the particular road does not exist, so that spatially no distance would exist.

I mean that the distance would not exist spatially, but the distance would exist. Action within the electrical system, then, would involve this same sort of distance without space; the road would then be an imaginary road of <u>intensity</u>.

Now, I would like to make some comments concerning your own experiments.

They can indeed be beneficial. As certain conditions were met, however, before our sessions began, so certain conditions must be met before your experiments in other directions bear fruit. Sometimes you meet some of them, sometimes you meet none of them. Yet a trial and error period is extremely necessary, and in your cases natural, and should not lead to discouragement.

As in many other instances I do not try to push you, for you must learn many things by yourselves, and your own subconscious will pace you. You will learn as you learn. You know that a conscious determination such as Ruburt occasionally shows will get you nowhere. A deadly seriousness <u>can</u>, but is not necessarily detrimental.

Some discipline is of course needed. But a sense of spontaneity is most important, and indeed a momentary lapse of critical attention. I bring this up now since there is a connection here, if you will excuse a pun, but there is a connection here with the electrical field. You realize now that psychological conditions have their existence within electrical reality, and so certain frames of mind will then be duplicated within the electrical field.

Many effects are built up in this manner. Any personalities, any entities, that do enter your physical plane must use some camouflage material <u>if</u> they are to be physically perceived. In such circumstances Ruburt would act as a sort of director, gathering together the subconscious energies of those with you, and making those energies <u>available</u> to any possible entity.

The energies would be transformed literally into electric patterns, which such an entity could then use. But many conditions are necessary for this transformation.

Friday, or Saturday, were poor evenings for various reasons, having to do with weather, emotional climate, and also having to do with Mark's physical and emotional state. Had you been proficient the night might have been successful.

We will have more to say in the future, regarding such experiments in general. Naturally it is possible to have very successful experiments along these lines. Again, conditions must be met. Subconsciously you will make your own progress. You will simply not have visiting apparitions Monday through Saturday, nor will you ever be certain ahead of time, regardless of proficiency, as to the success of such ventures. There is too much involved. You will learn by doing.

I suggest your break.

(Break at 10:05. Jane was deeply dissociated as usual. Mark is Bill Macdonnel's entity name. The unscheduled session with Bill present took place last Saturday, January 23.

(Jane began speaking again, in the same manner, at 10:12.)

There is one point of help I can give you.

Holding hands is most helpful. The feet, however, are also significant in placement. The best arrangement when possible physically would be to have each individual sit with his feet together; and if possible a circle being made also with the feet, or at least an arrangement where the feet touched.

Sitting in various separated portions of the room usually is a disadvantage. Under some circumstances, as our sessions, this makes no difference.

Your room dividers are even beneficial from this standpoint. Incense is good from two standpoints; of negative ions from smoke, and also because scent, smelling itself, has an electrical reality. Semidarkness merely aids in dissociation and concentration, and the lessening of camouflage data is helpful.

Various people will of course be of aid or a hindrance. Some alcohol in the system is, as I have told you, beneficial. For your purposes drinking to excess is not beneficial. Wednesdays, Saturdays and Sundays, for various reasons I will not go into now, may give you a slight edge. At many times other days, because of weather, will take up the advantage.

It is good for Ruburt to wear dark clothing, not for any dramatic effect, but again for practical reasons that we will discuss thoroughly at a later date. Red can be a good color to wear under certain conditions, or violets. Yellow should be avoided. These are merely aids.

The recorder worked because you wanted the recorder to work, and expected it to work. An excellent demonstration, my friends, on your parts, not mine.

If you are tired, I suggest a brief break, and I will speak very briefly before closing the session.

(Break at 10:26. Jane was dissociated as usual. Her eyes opened slowly; she now looked tired.

(During last Saturday's effort Jane, Bill and I sat in different parts of the room,

not holding hands of course. We had been using incense during the evening. This is a habit we have cultivated somewhat since Bill introduced us to incense at the 86th session. We have not used it on session nights however, since.

(Sunday night while we had company Jane and I got out the recorder on the spur of the moment; to our surprise we found that it worked perfectly. In fact, the quality of the tapes we made was superior to any made before the machine ceased working several months ago. Recently Jane and I had been talking about putting the recorder in shape again so we could record some more sessions. The last session we recorded was the 70th, on July 13,1964, with John Bradley as a witness.

(Again sitting down and with her eyes closed, Jane resumed at 10:33.)

All of this takes development. And, again, rather than force an intensification before the subconscious is ready for such experiences, I would much prefer that you carry on as you have been, at your own pace. There will be failures. This is to be expected, but you will learn from your mistakes, as well as from your successes.

This sort of growth allows also for the development of inner discipline, that will grow simultaneously with inner spontaneity; and a screening process of sorts develops that is indeed beneficial for your own protection. You two work very well together. Ruburt displayed good sense Sunday evening, in following your advice not to try to continue, but stopping where you did. And it is well for him to do so.

There will be an interaction good for you both. It was natural for him to want to continue, under the circumstances, but to continue would not have been wise. You will learn to feel your way.

My fondest regards to you both.

("Good night, Seth."

(End at 10:39. Jane was dissociated as usual.

(We tried an impromptu seance with our guests, Judy and Lee Wright, Sunday evening. We burned incense during the evening, and while holding the seance sat at a coffee table and held hands.

(As in the case with Dee and Joe Masters on the evening of November 24,1964–see the 110th session–some results were obtained that did not involve Seth in any way. This time Lee Wright seemed to respond to Jane's suggestions; these suggestions were not specifically directed at Lee, but were generalized statements designed to set a mood, etc. In both of these instances Jane appeared to act as an agent or catalyst. She does not yet know how she accomplishes this, but feels intuitively that it is so.

(It is of interest to note that Judy and Lee do not know about Seth, or the existence of the material. Twice during the seance Lee obtained effects or results which

seem to fit in with Seth's description of some of the inner senses and their use. Once he achieved a feeling of transportation psychically to another room; the other time he felt the room we were all gathered in had enlarged a great deal. Jane and I have both approximated these sensations during psychological time experiments also.

(Lee Wright also breathed very heavily during the seance, felt a great relaxation, and yet also felt he could end the experiment at any time. After the second effect he wanted Jane to continue. I felt that enough had been done for a start, and Jane acceded to my wishes.)

SESSION 126
JANUARY 27, 1965 9 PM WEDNESDAY AS SCHEDULED

(John Bradley, who has witnessed several sessions, was a visitor this afternoon but not a witness this evening.

(While trying psychological time on January 25 and January 27, Jane achieved her now customary state of lightness or "ecstasy" to a fair degree.

(Again Jane delivered the material for the session while sitting down, and with her eyes closed. She spoke at an average rate of speed, with a few long pauses. Her voice was normal for the most part, her glasses off.)

Good evening.

("Good evening, Seth.")

We will speak again concerning a variety of interrelated subjects.

First of all, let me make it plain that while I speak of separate fields and systems, you must remember that they are all <u>one</u>. Traces of each system will be found in each system, because no field or system is basically closed, although they may appear closed.

They are closed enough to retain identity and separateness of characteristic natures, but because they are all formed from inner vitality, they are actually interrelated; and when I describe fields or systems I describe many portions of one reality, many faces of one reality.

In such a manner a simplicity is given which is helpful in explanations, but it must be kept in mind that <u>all</u> these explanations are extremely simplified. Dreams have a definite effect within the physical system. They are in part sparked with the aid of the physical system, but they do not <u>happen</u> within the physical system. They are not directly experienced by the physical system, but only translations of the original dream experience is felt by the actual physical system.

The dream experience is felt directly by the inner self. Dreams have an electric actuality, as I have told you. In this electrical actuality they then exist independently of the dreamer, although he still applies the dream to himself. In the same manner do thoughts and emotions have the electric reality of which I have spoken. Therefore, within the electric system, dreams, thoughts and emotions exist as actualities, and in what you may call a tangible form, though not in the form of matter as you are familiar with it.

All of these systems are intimately connected and delicately balanced, and an alteration in one sets up an alteration in each of the others. There is no escaping this interrelationship. A man's thoughts, then, are far more reaching than he knows. They exist in more dimensions, they affect worlds of which he is unaware. They are as concrete, in effect, as any building. Thoughts then appear in many guises within many systems, and once created cannot be withdrawn, and once set into motion cannot be stopped. The same applies for dreams.

All of this material concerning fields and systems will be most valuable when read in connection with our fifth dimension material.

(For some material on the fifth dimension, see the 12th session in Volume 1.)

Now. The inner self and the subconscious are not present in the physical universe, insofar as they take up no space within it. They exist within the electrical system. They affect the physical system and operate closely allied with it. Nevertheless they will not be found within the physical system.

Thoughts are psychoelectric patterns, set up by the mind, and transformed to human codes by the brain.

The mind is always with you. The particular brain is the physical mechanism that translates the thoughts of the mind. It goes without saying then, that the brain belongs to the physical system, and here in clear terms you see the smooth cooperation that exists. Thoughts are initially psychoelectric patterns in pure form, productions of the inner self that must be translated in order to be used by the physical self.

Inspiration is often a more or less instantaneous translation, occurring for various reasons which I will give you later, without the benefit of the brain's intervention. It is this strangeness that is often noted. The individual seems not to know where the thought comes from, because he does not recognize the characteristic mark of his brain upon it. And indeed such a mark is lacking, for inspiration originates with the inner self.

I suggest your break.

(Break at 9:28. Jane was well dissociated as usual. While she was delivering the material our cat, Willy, jumped up on her lap and began to playfully pull and tug at her wool sweater. Jane did not appear to be bothered by this, but since Willy kept it up I finally dislodged him rather than take the chance of him interrupting

Jane. She said she was aware of him as she spoke, but that was all. This is the first time Willy has paid any attention to Jane for many sessions.

(Jane resumed dictation in the same manner at 9:36.)

In a most ingenious manner, then, all of these systems, while individual, are portions of one unified reality.

The outer senses cannot perceive the unity. The outer senses can only perceive the apparent diversity within the physical system alone, for the outer senses do not perceive directly any other system but the physical one.

The inner senses can be thought of as transformers, where various kinds of data is sent to proper channels within the personality, channels which bypass ordinary physical channels. They then can exist side by side. There are various reasons, which I have not yet given you, that allow for the traveling of the self through physical space and time. These reasons have to do with the electric actuality of the inner self, and with that counterpart of the physical body which exists within the electric field.

Personal identity, the basic "I", is a product of the subconscious, and as such it exists as an actuality within the electric field; because of this it is basically independent of the physical field, held to it mainly by the ego. The ego directs the identity toward physical orientation. This is an important point.

The ego does not exist within the electrical field. The ego is a product of the physical field, formed from physical birth on. The inner identity and individuality, as you know, has its origins long before this. The inner self adopts an ego in order to allow manipulation within the physical universe, and yet part of the ego is composed of portions from the inner self, while the bulk of the ego is allowed to develop through physical heredity and environment.

The breath of life, so to speak, is breathed into the ego by the inner self, but from that point on the ego is independent.

(Jane now took a very long pause, rocking quietly with her eyes closed.)

All of these influences have a part in the formation of the physical individual, and his existence is dependent upon a balance being maintained. In some instances, to use an analogy, serious short circuits do occur, intensities of power accumulate. The dream universe, for example, may intrude with unusual sharpness. The systems lose complementary balance, but on the whole the systems operate together most efficiently.

Even the electric reality of a dream is decoded, so that its effects are experienced not only by the brain, but in the furthest reaches of the most minute cells in the human body. Dream experiences long forgotten are forever contained as electrically coded within the cells of the physical body. If an effect is felt in any one portion of human experience, then you can be sure that such an effect is felt in all other possible ways, whether or not such an effect is immediately obvious. This is also an extremely important point to remember.

I suggest your break.

(Break at 9:58. Jane was well dissociated as usual. She resumed in the same manner at 10:06.)

Every effect of any kind, experienced by the human being, exists as a series of electrical signals and codes, that in themselves form a pattern that is an electrical pattern.

They exist within the cells, or I should more properly say that the cells form about them. These electric coded signals then form electric counterparts of complete experience, as it has been felt by any given individual. It is, the pattern is, then independent of the physical system, while residing within it. In other words, each individual from birth on forms his own counterpart from built up, individual, continuous electric signals. At physical death his personality then exists in its complete form, and of course escapes the sort of ending that it would suffer if it were an integral part of the physical system.

This electrical pattern is the personality, with all the experiences of its earthly time. It then can join or partake of the inner self. In other words, though the ego was adopted originally by the inner self, and was a product of physical heredity and environment, it does not die; but its existence is changed from physical reality into electrical reality. It is still individual. No individuality is lost, but it becomes a part of the inner self, and its experiences are added to the total experience of the many personalities that have composed the inner self.

In the composition and buildup of the personality, you can easily see that dreams, thoughts, emotions and psychological experiences are far more important than any mere physical data. To the personality a joy or a sorrow is far more actual than a table or a chair.

Tonight's material, taken with our last few sessions, should add new dimensions to much of the knowledge that you had previously. I am very pleased that Ruburt is keeping his dream notebook. Correlations will indeed be found, and the habit of subconscious focus in this manner will certainly bring results.

The material given here on dreams will add depth also to previous material on the subject, and should be studied in that manner. A note here: Ruburt has indeed discovered something at which I hinted, though in a different connection. In his daily predictions he has begun to notice that one phrase seems to stand for more than one event in some cases.

I spoke of this in connection with dreams, saying that they were cunningly constructed, so that any particular symbol would have a meaning for various levels of the subconscious. The appearance of this in Ruburt's predictions represents a first glimpse of real progress.

(See the 93rd session, among many others, on dreams.)

During our next session I will go into this much more thoroughly, for the matter is not only interesting but extremely informative, and we shall spend a good part of our next session dealing with it.

Perhaps I shall look in on you before then. In any case my best regards to you both, and I will close our session. I may indeed see you before then. Sometime, who knows, you may see me too; and <u>that</u> will give Ruburt something to brood over.

His confidence however is slowly growing, but definitely growing. And as it does so shall we progress.

("Good night, Seth."

(End at 10:32. Jane was dissociated as usual.

(Seth had something to say about the electric nature of ideas in the 86th session.

(See also the 8th session [in Volume 1] for the translation of thought.)

SESSION 127
FEBRUARY 2, 1965 9 PM TUESDAY (MAKEUP FOR MONDAY)

(On February 1 I began to make a list of daily predictions, as Jane has been doing for some time now.

(Due to the work involved in hanging my first one-man show of paintings, at Harris Hill Inn, last night's regularly scheduled session was not held.

(In addition Jane and I visited Jim and Marian Spaziani, our landlord and his wife, to make arrangements for them to attend the session for next Monday, February 8. The Spazianis will also bring a mutual friend.

(Jane and I anticipated no difficulty in holding the session tonight instead of last night. She had no idea of the material to be discussed. As usual she sat in the rocking chair, across from my table. She began speaking on time and in a quiet and clear voice, with few long pauses. Her glasses were off and her eyes remained closed while she delivered material throughout the session.)

Good evening.

("Good evening, Seth.")

There is no reason to blame yourselves if you occasionally miss a session. However, it is a good idea to make it up.

We were speaking, among other things, of intensities, and this is connected with both dream symbols and other such data. Dreams, having an electrical reality as I explained, must be decoded to have meaning to various levels of the subconscious and the personality. In Ruburt's predictions he has only begun. There will be other significant data that will be observed, as he learns to use his ability. And much of this significant material that he will observe from his predictions will also apply to dream symbols.

This has to do, again, with intensities, which are decoded in many and complicated fashions. The meaning, so to speak, must be separated and made meaningful to many psychological areas, some of which would not even seem to speak the same language.

(It might be worth noting here that many sessions ago Seth stated he was substituting the word "area" for "level," when a reference to the subconscious was made. The reason being that the subconscious is not divided into neat levels, but is made up of many interconnecting and complicated corridors, rooms, etc.

(I would also like to state here that Jane's predictions, made daily, have recently begun to prove out with what seems to be an amazing frequency. Their effectiveness runs in cycles, but her percentage of "hits" or partial hits has steadily increased.)

To be so decoded, there are also delicate manipulations in terms of fine distinctions. An intensity pattern is made up of electrical signals. Each slight variation in intensity is meaningful from this information, as to physical time; placement in space and the like must be comprehended, and this particular specific type of information is a relatively small part of the original dream experience, which is composed of electrical pattern, thick only in terms of intensity.

The various levels of the subconscious and the personality are attuned to the particular intensities of the dream experience which they can perceive and interpret, and which has meaning to them. The dream experience is much larger and, again, more concentrated than is supposed.

(Here, our cat Willy jumped up on Jane's lap as she sat while dictating. He had just eaten and was getting playful. Jane did not appear to be bothered, but to be sure I lay my notes aside and put Willy in another room. While I was moving about Jane sat quietly. I did not speak to her during the episode.)

It is also constant, but simultaneous, and not continuous in terms of one event following the other.

Various portions then of the entire self are attuned to their own intensities, picking up signals, interpreting only portions of the whole dream experience. I am using the term dream experience because it is a familiar word to you. However, the dream experience, you see, represents only a portion or particular range of intensities from a larger experience. In dreams you perceive but part.

I have told you that you create your dreams, in actuality, not in theory alone. You create an actuality, a dream universe, as real as the physical universe. It simply cannot be directly perceived within the physical universe. There is always interaction. You can perceive the dream experience, you can receive its particular intensities, because you have created the dream experience within the universe of those intensities. But the dream universe and the dream experience, like thoughts and emotions, are independent of you in existence. You influence the dream universe but you cannot stop a dream experience after you have created it, and you must create it within the small range of intensities available for its existence, for there are no other conditions or agreeable ranges of intensity within which the dream experience can exist.

You must, then, project or materialize the dream universe outside of the physical self in an electric reality, and then reinterpret it, because the original dream experience has an electric reality that cannot be perceived or used, even by its creators, until it is decoded.

I suggest your break.

(Break at 9:25. Jane was dissociated as usual. She resumed in the same manner at 9:32.)

The dream universe, the dream experience, is only a small portion of another experience.

The experience of emotions and thoughts and other psychological realities that do not take up space physically within your universe, all represent portions of, small portions of, what I will for now term initial experience. Psychological reality, emotional reality, and the reality of thought also become valid to human personality through their existence as various intensities. All psychic realities are in this classification also. All of these, with the dream experience, are received and recognized by various levels of the self, through their identifying intensities.

They are then decoded and the experience is translated or interpreted into meaningful data. In the original dream experience then, the electrical reality of the dream is broken down, so to speak, into its varying intensities, by the mind.

The mind then formulates meaningful psychological symbols, but still in terms of electric symbol, and only in the brain are the particular symbols then sent to the various levels of the human personality.

One symbol will be meaningful to many portions of the personality. The symbol will be the same. That is, any given symbol will be the same, but it will be so chosen by the mind that it will have definite meanings to various portions of the self, and the meanings may be quite different. In the breaking-down process the intensities are separated into the most minute values, each value an electrical impulse representing any one of many references. And all of these references are contained within a given impulse, electrical impulse, that will be decoded by the mind.

The mind breaks the impulse down into more specific terms, collects or attracts within separate fields those impulses within the same general range, and then forms from them a new electrical pattern, composed of impulses now more meaningful to the individual, because they have been somewhat deciphered and put together in a more recognizable form.

This form is the electric symbol. It is received by the brain and changed into a more or less pure psychological symbol. Or in case, in the case, of a dream, it is changed into a dream symbol. The dream as perceived by the mind then, is a pattern of electrical impulses, all more or less within a particular range of intensity.

The mind breaks down this pattern into still more refinements of intensities, each refinement making possible a refinement of meaning. The dream is then passed on to the brain, where the electric symbol becomes a psychological or dream symbol. <u>No intensity of impulse is actually ever the same as any other</u>.

It is for this reason that such a rich diversity in such symbols is possible, and it is for this reason that one symbol can have various meanings to different levels of the personality. The various meanings of any given symbol are expressed and recognized as the intensity ever so minutely changes. This, as I have explained, also has something to do with your idea of physical time.

Within the mind the dream has an electrical reality. Within the brain the dream has an electric and psychological reality; a much weaker electrical reality. That is, it still exists as an electrical reality, but it is not recognized as such by the brain or the psychological awareness of an individual. To the individual the dream has only a psychological reality.

I am going to give you a break, and then discuss what I meant by difficulties of interpretation concerning predictions and dreams.

(Break at 10:01. Jane was dissociated as usual. She resumed in the same quiet manner, sitting down and with her eyes closed, at 10:10.)

When I spoke of interpretation of data in predictions, or clairvoyance, I was not speaking in terms of psychological interpretation.

For such material to be made meaningful to the conscious personality, a training of abilities along the lines of interpretation is definitely required in most cases. Such material is a part of what we termed the initial experience, which is of electrical nature, received through the mind, broken down there as explained, and then received by the brain where it is changed or interpreted to psychological symbol form.

It has changed, in other words, as far as pattern is concerned. New patterns are formed, groupings of intensities that will be meaningful to various levels of the personality. To make such data meaningful to the conscious self requires other steps of subconscious interpretation that actually have to do with an electrical regrouping and realignment.

This cannot be done, obviously, at a conscious level. The subconscious can be trained to do so, but usually it is necessarily hampered in that it cannot use those ranges of intensity which make up meanings to the ego. Hence the appearance of what you may call distortions.

This data must be interpreted in such a way that the conscious mind then can give a prediction, say, but also in such a way that its reality exits simultaneously with consciousness, but never so replacing consciousness that the ego grows alarmed. This is often done by the use of symbols which are not immediately apparent to consciousness, and thus are allowed through. Then it is too late for the ego to close its gates against them. But the symbols chosen must be of a nature so that they <u>will</u> become meaningful to consciousness, to as large an extent as possible after emergence.

The experimentation with daily predictions will show you quite clearly, with practice, the nature of such distortions, as you see the difference between the predicted event and the event that occurs. Also for economy and for the reason given above, symbols may stand for more than one physical reality, and so may they in some of the earlier predictions given in this material.

We have spoken of expectations. These, you see, are electrical realities, which may explain their importance; for you not only sometimes predict so-called future events, but you create their actuality within the electrical field, and therefore insure their existence one way or another within the physical field.

I told you that in measuring your physical time, you actually measure intensities. Your creations in the electrical universe may be said to appear <u>as your future</u> in the physical universe. This point is extremely important, and will explain many other questions. My use of terms such as electrical universe, and so forth, is merely for the sake of simplicity. They are all one, but to explain them I must seem to dissect them and separate them, so that you may see their various identities. This has been a most fruitful session, in terms of significant material. I will not keep you now, but do intend that we hold our regular session tomorrow evening, as planned.

("Good night, Seth.")

(End at 10:30. Jane was dissociated as usual.)

SESSION 128
FEBRUARY 3, 1965 9 PM WEDNESDAY AS SCHEDULED

(Jane remained seated, and spoke with her eyes closed, for the entire session. At times her delivery was slow. Her voice was pitched somewhat lower but not louder; she did not wear her glasses and she did not smoke while delivering material.)

Good evening.

("Good evening, Seth.")

I see that we are holding two sessions in succession. Quite unusual.

Man has always attempted to examine those realities that he could perceive through the outer senses. Because of the apparent objectivity involved, this has been comparatively easy for him to do. The entire inner universe is far more varied, more complicated, than your physical universe, yet it could be conceived of as the same sort of universe with certain substitutions being made.

You could imagine it for example as having a shape, but the shape would not be formed by matter, but by pattern masses; and all the multitudinous portions of it, the shapes on it, would be composed in terms of mass intensity. To bring this even clearer, you could even imagine that the whole inner universe was an organism, of which your universe represented but one small portion. Yet in using the inner senses, you yourselves probe into this universe, and at least in analogy dissect it, the inner self acting as the imaginary knife.

In such imaginary dissection, at first only small sections of it are exposed. Change our knife image now into an imaginary rocket ship, so that our dissection involves many more dimensions. The rocket ship would be the inquiring inner self in motion. This inner self in motion is bound to set up ripples of counteraction. All this will be in terms of electric impulse.

Realities existing within this electrical universe are built up through counteractions with the human personality and others. All psychological realities and experiences which are not materialized within the physical universe have their actual reality and existence within the electrical universe.

Thoughts have shape in terms of intensity mass, though you cannot see their shape; your outer senses do not perceive it. You see within yourself the various shapes of dreams to a certain extent. You do not see the dream itself, for even here, after giving a dream reality, electrical existence, you must break it down into simpler terms so that you can perceive what you have indeed created.

But thoughts have shapes, as do dreams. I use the word shape for simplicity's sake, but the electrical universe is composed of dimensions which are perceived by the inner self, for the inner self also has existence within the electrical universe. If all of this sounds farfetched, then remember that the shapes that you perceive meaningful, many other species within your own field cannot perceive at all.

I suggest your break.

(Break at 9:24. Jane was dissociated as usual. She resumed in the same manner as previously at 9:31.)

It follows that the whole self has an actual reality and existence within many fields beside the physical field.

The brain, because of its purpose and its close connection to camouflage manipulation, does not have a primary existence within the electrical universe, although it has a secondary existence within it because of its connection to the purely electrical mind.

The physical body is formed about its electrical counterpart, yet they are both intertwined in completely different dimensions. All the knowledge gained by the present ego is retained in electrical form, as is all experience so retained. The camouflage material will be discarded as a physical gestalt, as far as the individual is concerned. The matter of the physical body will simply be used in other gestalts, in the manner that I have explained in earlier sessions.

The idea image of the physical body is of course retained by the individual. The idea shape may be used or not used, according to when and in which manners the personality wishes to extend itself. It is no longer necessary for locomotion, and its senses, electrically coded now, are no longer necessary, since they were adopted to meet the demands of a particular field in which the personality no longer has any prime interest.

In codified form these outer senses still exist, and with codified memory any sensuous or sensual data that has been experienced may be experienced again. And with some, though very few personalities, such experiences are indeed constantly played back, though of course not indefinitely.

(Seth had something to say about psychic remembrance of earthly phenomenon as long ago as the 9th session, December 18,1963. See Volume 1, page 46.)

I told you once that with your outer senses you could not directly experience a concept. Perhaps now you will see why this is so. <u>We</u> can travel through the varying intensities that make up a concept, and therefore experience it directly, as, say, you can move through a storm or a sunny day. It is not so much that you move through as that you directly experience. You are inside and not outside of the day or the storm.

(Among others, see the 37th and 38th sessions [in Volume 1] for material on concepts and some of the inner senses.)

To be inside a concept is to be inside an electrical field formed by varying intensities, each intensity meaningful, distinct, simultaneous and separate, yet all taken together forming a particular electrical field. I told you, I believe, that it is an error to think at all in terms of size when fields are mentioned. In a way I cannot yet explain to you, these fields of intensity, while having mass in terms of intensity, do not have size.

All depths here, and all dimensions here in the electrical system, are all in terms of intensity alone. And for a reason too difficult now to explain, intensity, while having a certain sort of mass that is not matter, of course, does not have anything like your idea of size.

(Giving this information, Jane also came through with a big smile.)

Its dimensions are in terms of values and value fulfillments. The apparent shapes, if you could see them within the electrical system, would seem to appear and disappear as pulses became stronger or weaker. Each and every thought and dream and experience that any human being has had exists as an individual, distinct electrical impulse of particular, unduplicated intensity. It exists not only isolated for example, or detached, but it exists as a part of the electrical pattern of that personality who originally created it. It is still a part of his electrical pattern, but it does also exist independently of him.

I suggest your break.

(Break at 9:59. Jane was again well dissociated. She resumed in the same manner at 10:06.)

Now. Basically and ultimately, all pathways and all journeys and all experience are electrical.

At a later date I will explain the true nature of this electrical reality, since your idea of electrical reality is extremely limited, and within your field it is perceived but dimly, as a mere shadow of itself.

I told you at one time that my form was somehow a man's form. I use the form rarely. The electric reality of it, coded in a particular range of intensities, is now in my possession, in what you may call capsule form, though this is not a good analogy. But an explanation will have to wait until you understand more clearly the nature of electrical reality itself.

Now, if you will follow me closely you will obtain a hint at least of the structure of the inner self. It is composed, that is, each inner self is composed, structurally of a particular range of electrical intensities with which various personalities have their identities insured, since their identity is composed of particular intensities within the range.

These personality intensities are themselves formed within ranges that would appear minute, but contain within them, truly, eons of experience. In our further discussions concerning the nature of electrical reality, we will also come closer to an understanding of those pyramid gestalts of which I have spoken.

(See the 81st session for some material on psychic pyramid gestalts.)

This electrical reality will be a basis for many future discussions, and you will see the basis behind my contention that dream locations indeed exist in actuality. It is important also to realize that psychic gestalts are built up electrically, and that many positive attractions exist between and within various electrical fields, so that there is constant motion and travel between them.

Various intensity identities may, therefore, appear within other fields while still retaining actuality in their own.

I am going to end our session. I wish you both a fond good evening.

("Good night, Seth."

(End at 10:23. Jane was well dissociated as usual.

(Jane felt that this was all Seth wanted to say on the above material this evening, hence his abrupt end to the session. She thought he had more material on the subject ready but did not want to start in on it now. She believes it has to do with the electrical makeup of the entity itself.)

SESSION 129
FEBRUARY 7, 1965 APPROX. 11:15-12:00 PM SUNDAY UNSCHEDULED

(Recently Jane and I have made friends with a younger couple from Texas, Judy and Lee Wright. They have lived in Elmira [NY] for a year, and are interested in psychic study.

(Prior to this evening Jane and I had not mentioned the Seth material to them, although the four of us have tried a few ESP experiments on weekends. See page 231 of the 125th session. Tonight's experiment began rather spontaneously and ended with Seth making an entrance, although I for one had not particularly planned it that way.

(In the beginning the four of us sat on the floor, grouped around our coffee table and holding hands as suggested by Seth in the 125th session, and as we had done before. Jane spoke for some little time in a repetitious voice, as a way of inducing a relaxed state within us, but no phenomena of any kind appeared. Dim lights were on. We had been using our recorder earlier but were not recording these monotonous inductions, and as will be seen this was a mistake on my part.

(We became cramped physically. Jane's voice also tired, so to relieve her I began to speak. Now Jane, Judy and Lee were prone upon the floor by the divan. Our idea was that our receptive state might make it possible for one of us to speak for another personality should one be present, or for another level of the self. I did not try to bring

Seth into the experiment. I had been speaking for perhaps ten minutes, however, when Jane abruptly began to speak for Seth from her prone position. She lay flat on her back but soon sat up.

(This of course startled our guests, but they listened without interruption. Jane's voice was quite loud and somewhat deeper than usual. Indeed, she displayed much more animation than she has for any of our regular sessions since she began to deliver the material from a sitting position. Her eyes remained closed now however, but she spoke much more rapidly and gestured often.

(The recorder was not on, and I was not taking notes. I thought the session might be short and decided to rely upon my memory for a reconstruction. I soon regretted this, for Jane talked rapidly, in high good humor, and at some length. She took a break eventually, and I then set up the recorder. What follows then is a brief summary of the first half of the session, based upon our memory, and a verbatim transcription of the second half.

(Seth began by stating that he had been with us throughout the evening. He said we had chosen a poor method of experimentation, if we did not want to contact him, since Jane has been conditioned to respond through him when we sought contact with discarnate entities. My idea had been that Jane might speak for another personality, such as in the Sarah Wellington or the Malba Bronson instances. See Volume 1, page 64 for the former, and 103 and 127 for the latter.

(Seth expressed much pleasure at being able to speak in a natural manner, without dealing with the usual philosophical and complicated subjects that make up most of the sessions. My own thought, as soon as he began to speak, was that I had made a mistake in method, since his appearance was a complete surprise to our guests. Seth reinforced this by saying that in the future I should be careful if I did not want it to happen again. Jane and I now like to prepare witnesses beforehand, since the material has become so lengthy and complicated that it is increasingly difficult to explain briefly.

(Seth repeated several times that he felt in fine form, and Jane's voice and manner so indicated. I asked some questions designed to keep the material on the level of reincarnational data, since our guests had done some reading on the subject. Seth said I had not known Lee Wright before, but that I had been "involved" with Judy in a past life. It was indeed in my Denmark existence, he said, "the life of which you are now so ashamed." In that life Judy had been a man, and a sailor. This reminded me that Seth had given similar data for our friend Bill Macdonnel; he too had been a sailor in a Denmark contemporary existence, but as I recall I did not ask Seth whether Judy and Bill had known each other in that life. As it happens, Bill had been a guest also earlier tonight, leaving just before the session.

(Judy's entity name was given as Rayuk, and Lee's as Wonlin. While speaking

Jane was now up on her knees, gesturing freely. Her eyes remained closed and she did not get up and pace about. Break came after 11:30. I had plenty of time to get the recorder set up. Jane resumed at 11:40 in the same rather strong voice, but at a somewhat slower rate.)

Our material has been excellent, but I have missed the emotional contact. Ruburt, because of the change in our practice, has been somewhat uneasy, and for this reason the more friendly atmosphere that he had enjoyed earlier had deserted us. The state which he has achieved this evening, with your help Joseph, allowed us to achieve that informality to some small degree.

If indeed I still sound like a lecturer, and somewhat of an old fuddy-duddy, it is because old rockhead Ruburt continues in his own ways, as is to be expected.

If it were [done] differently we would never have achieved the results that we have achieved.

We have everything in order now. He now, however, is a stiff old thing. I cannot make him move about as I would move now. We achieved this earlier but the conditions were different.

I would sit with you now as a friend at the party and converse, but it is a trifle difficult as you should understand. I am doing very well with him, however, and your two guests are doing very well themselves, considering the circumstances.

I realize also that your precious recorder is playing, and I would suggest that now and then it be put to such good use.

("That's why we wanted to get it fixed; and as you said, we did it ourselves."

(See the 125th session, page 231.)

You had help.

At one time these two were brother and sister. At this time, 1602, in England, the man committed an act which put him greatly in his sister's debt. He was from a good family. He was however cruelly-natured in many respects. It was a time when such cruelty was indeed accepted, and sensitivity was hardly a way of life.

(Here, Seth of course was referring to Lee and Judy.

("Can you give us the family name?")

Manheuton. Part of the family had been from France. I am not clear on all of this. He owed gambling debts. It was because of these gambling debts that he wronged his sister, and it was because of that wrong that they now once more have come together at a different relationship.

As you should know here, I do not speak in terms of payment, I do not speak in terms of suffering, of making up. I do not speak in terms of his being forced to make up. I speak in terms of his own choice. For his own development he chose to make up, because of a past lack of sensitivity, because of a certain exhilaration felt in those days in cruelty, and because in those days his emotions held no sway, but what he considered cold reason led him on. But this reasoning, divorced from emotions led him into his own betrayal.

This time we see the development of the personality. We see that balances have been made here, we see the emotions having stronger bearing upon the personality. We also see, as I mentioned in your own case Joseph, we see an attempt to overcompensate. As once he would not trust the emotions and does not trust his reason, this being an attempt to compensate. Indeed its purpose is a good one, but any compensation of this sort must be balanced by the personality itself in all cases.

There was difficulty with the left foot at one time. There was at one time difficulty with the forefinger of the left hand.

(Unfortunately, we are unable to distinguish here as to whether Jane pronounced the word forefinger, or the two words, fourth finger. Her diction was not quite clear enough on the tape for us to distinguish between the two. The question arises because after the session Lee Wright said that as a youngster he had injured the forefinger of his left hand. Indeed his finger bears even now a scar near the tip. Seth's use of the phrase "at one time," could refer, we suppose, to either a past life of Lee's, or an earlier period in his present one.

(Lee said he didn't recall any injury or trouble with his left foot in this life.

(Prior to the session, neither Jane or I had noticed any scar on Lee's finger.)

Death came at one time from a knife wound. The involvement between the two personalities of the man and the woman at this time is a good one, as far as commitments previously in other lives is concerned. We find here also a balance of strong points and weak points, and again, compensations.

("Can you give us the location of the town or village in England?")

I cannot now. It was a locality rather close to Wales. There was mining nearby. I believe that there was a family crest; I think two dragons, the image of Saint George, and a shield on the crest.

I will close now our brief session, giving you all my best regards, and I will see you tomorrow evening.

One point, Joseph. I believe that this evening has been a breakthrough for us.

("In what way?")

In the way that I have mentioned earlier, in that the emotional atmosphere, the psychological climate, is coming through once again, and we will be clearer.

There should be an extra dimension added to the material, and now and then the freedom for some informal discussion. With your recorder we may be able to arrange a more comfortable conversation, although as you realize as far as the material itself is concerned, it is rather weighty material and I must sort of hit you over the head with it. If I did not hit you over the head with it I'm afraid that you would not get it at all.

I do not say this to make you feel inferior, or Ruburt. It is simply that it is difficult to mix the material with a light atmosphere, although I do believe we can retain the emotional closeness which does seem to be beneficial. I now give you all my fond good wishes. My best regards to your two visitors, and we may indeed meet again.

("Good night, Seth."

(End at approximately midnight. Jane was quite well dissociated, she said; about the usual state she has been attaining recently.

(It will be noted that although Seth evidently wanted her to pace about, she did not do so. She was very active as far as gesturing was concerned, and her delivery was quite animated. But the closest she came to getting to her feet was when she rose to her knees while speaking.)

(The following recent notes are from Jane's psychological time notebook.

(February 1, Monday, 11:30 AM: I heard voices but forgot most of them. I remember the word "chlorine." I saw a pinup lamp on an adjacent wall, where we have no wall. I saw a road with white guardposts and possible red lanterns. I saw this road as though I was traveling on it, heading straight ahead. It was a gray day. The sensation of forward movement was most definite, up and down low hills. I saw houses on both sides of the road in the distance, like our nearby village of Chemung.

(February 8, Monday, 11:30 AM: Good state achieved. Once briefly I saw a bright white light, as though it was approaching me. Upon opening my eyes after the experiment I lay staring at the walls of the room. I then experienced a definite feeling of "separation." During psy-time, I had an odd physical-like sensation, as though I was ready to leave my body. But I believe I became alarmed and prevented this from happening.)

(And these additional notes:

(February 5, Friday, While getting supper in the kitchen this evening, I heard Lee Wright's voice, although I could not understand what he said. I heard his southern accent clearly. He was not visiting us.

(February 7, Sunday, 10:45 PM approx.: While trying our seance with Lee and Judy Wright, I had a quick impression that a man stood to one side of me. He wore I believe a dark suit of some kind. It was not Rob or Lee, and Judy sat opposite

me on the divan. When I turned quickly to look there was no one there. No one else saw it, upon my questioning.

(February 10, Wednesday: While resting briefly just before noon, I saw a woman in some kind of ski outfit, in the lower branches of a tree. Just as I wondered what she was doing there, she fell. I did not see her face. She was about average in size, perhaps a little larger than me.)

SESSION 130
FEBRUARY 8, 1965 9 PM MONDAY AS SCHEDULED

(Due to illness, the witnesses scheduled for this session did not appear.

(Jane felt quite lethargic and sleepy as the day wore on, but did not believe this state had anything to do with our active weekend. She worked well at her writing this morning, but grew increasingly drowsy as the day wore on. She has been reading the book The Self in Transformation, *by Herbert Fingarette, Basic Books, 1963, NY and London. She considers it excellent.*

(After supper Jane took a nap. After the nap she still felt drowsy. She mentioned this to me, but I had no real intimation that she was in anything but a very relaxed state. I suggested she have coffee, which she did. Jane also wanted to hold the session. She had no idea of the material to be covered.

(Once again she spoke sitting down and with her eyes closed during the whole delivery. She used some pauses; I will try a new method of indicating them where they occur in the text. Her voice was very quiet, yet clear. She did not wear her glasses.)

Good evening.

("Good evening, Seth.")

I would have thought that my friend Ruburt would have realized what he was about.

A combination of circumstances has momentarily disrupted his orientation. I am going to hold a fairly brief session, and then I will have some suggestions. In fact, I will give the suggestions now.

The book which Ruburt has been reading tended to turn him inward. (*Pause.*) He is becoming fairly proficient now in the use of the trance state, and in its controls. However, so slowly did he slip into a semitrance state that he did not realize what had happened. His energy today was turned inward more than it was turned outward.

The slight but perceivable feeling of lightness in his hands could have given him notice of this fact. The situation began as he completed his psychological time experiment this morning, and has continued. He was neither wholly oriented to the inner world nor to the outer, and therefore was not efficient in either.

The symptoms of such a semitrance state include the sleepiness and drugged feeling with which he was afflicted; though these were only mildly disagreeable, they should be taken as signs that orientation is inefficient. The lightness of the hands is another such symptom. That is, these symptoms, noticed when the individual is supposed to be going about his normal physically-oriented day, can then be taken as a sign that the personality does not have all of his energies properly directed for the case at hand.

I am going to suggest that our friend take a walk when we are finished here, a brisk one. The situation is in no way alarming. He has been used to the trance, and of course with what you call the normal waking state, and has not happened to become acquainted with this transition phase. He passes through it so quickly as a rule. As a transitional step, it is most necessary. Otherwise however it does not allow efficient behavior in any particular reality.

What we are looking for here, and indeed one of the purposes of our sessions, is efficient use of various portions of the self in the perceptions of their own realities, and of an overall perception of each of the various portions of the self by the whole self, which transcends the others even while it is composed of them.

This involves efficient, complete use of the outer senses in their perception of camouflage reality, and of joyful, effective behavior and manipulation within that field of camouflage in which you spend a certain level of your existence. When you operate within it you should indeed experience it completely, in as many phases as possible, and <u>be</u> it to a much greater degree than is usually achieved, the conscious mind using itself then in experience, and thus knowing itself. And then the switch to use of the inner senses. The great contrast then refreshes the whole self. (*Pause.*)

The inner senses therefore should also be used as fully as the outer senses. Experience within both realities lets the inner or whole self know more fully its own potentialities and its own selfness.

The state into which Ruburt fell as a rule allows no such focus in either reality, but a suspension. It is necessary only as a transition. I will again suggest that for the present psychological time experiments be carried on once a day. There is no reason to give further time to it, in the evening, at this time. This is aimed at Ruburt. We want contrast. (*Pause.*) This transitionary stage is rather difficult to perceive. He was beginning to wonder himself, and since it is his first real experience with it as an isolated state, it is understandable that he did not recognize it for what it is.

The outer senses are dulled, but the inner senses have not yet been turned on. The state is an unhappy one, where sharpness of perception is extremely limited. I am speaking at length about it because its lethargy could be harmful under certain circumstances. All the more so since the obvious, more noticeable symptoms of the trance state itself are absent; and therefore the state could pass unnoticed for some time.

I suggest your break.

(Break at 9:30. Jane was dissociated as usual. She reported she understood the gist of what she was saying, whereas usually she has little or no idea.

(She told me that after taking her nap after supper she began to get "suspicious," especially so when she became aware of her light hands. She was going to tell me about it, but then decided she didn't know what to say. But she felt "disconnected," and recalled her psychological time experience of the morning, in which she felt "separated." See page 248.

(Jane now felt better than before the session began. She resumed in the same quiet and clear voice at 9:33.)

A plunge into the world of the outer senses will be immediately restorative; although I know Ruburt has no inclination to take a brisk walk this evening, I suggest that he do so.

It has often been said that the subconscious has a generalized focus, but the subconscious and inner senses have as strong and vital and intensified a focus as the focus of the conscious mind. The phenomena perceived is merely of a different nature, and in this state of which I have spoken no real intensification is possible.

I do not believe that any future difficulty will occur. (*Long pause.*) What we would like is the ability to fully perceive both the inner world and the outer world, to alternate between them. But we should be <u>in one</u>, and know it, and know ourselves in it. Or we should be in the other and know ourselves in it; and finally, while we are in one reality, we should be able, even in it, to hold our knowledge of the other. In this way our whole selves achieve a freedom.

The semitrance state does not allow a clear awareness in either world. It is passed through very quickly as a rule, both on the way into a trance and on the way out of one. It is of course a part of both realities. This goes without saying. It is true that there is much this evening that could be added to our previous discussions, but Ruburt, particularly after last night's session, should rest. And I would also suggest that he forget his psychological time experiments until next Monday.

For this reason I will close the session. He should take a brisk walk, and turn his mind into some innocent diversion, play of a sort. My best wishes to you both.

("Good night, Seth."

(End at 9:48. Jane was dissociated as usual. She was surprised at the quick ending to the session; she had hoped Seth would discuss other material also. She now felt much better, but did not care about going for a walk. However we went for one together, and before the evening was through she was her old self.)

SESSION 131
FEBRUARY 10, 1965 9 PM WEDNESDAY AS SCHEDULED

(The following notes are from Jane's psy-time notebook:

(February 11, Thursday: While resting, I somehow got a message about Fred Anderson. He was invited to go to some affair. There was some kind of fee involved. He decided to go but not to pay the fee.

(February 12, Friday: While resting I heard or saw "Londondale," and heard or saw words, "Our ways are not your ways." Was Londondale a coat label? I also had a feeling of enlargement and projection, an inner projection. I felt filled and at the same time light, a resemblance to the way I felt when reading the poetry for the recorder, during the Father Trainor experiment yesterday. This feeling came upon me right after I had asked my subconscious to give me some idea of what had happened during the tape recording, when the voice I used seemed to belong more to Father Trainor than to me.

(Jane felt fine today. She'd had no aftereffects either yesterday or today from her inadvertent semitrance state of last Monday. See the last session. She spoke this evening while sitting down and with her eyes closed, and in a quiet and clear voice. Her pace was very slow and filled with pauses. If I indicated her pauses as in the last session, their frequency would mar the text.)

Good evening.

("Good evening, Seth.")

We have seen that dreams and thoughts and psychological experiences all have an electric reality.

We have seen that all experience is retained in electrically coded data within the cells, and that the material of the cells forms about this coded experience. We have seen that the ego begins, sparked into being, by the inner self, greatly influenced by heredity and physical environment; and that this ego as it continues to exist gradually builds up an electrical reality of its own, as its experiences form into coded data within the cells.

At any given point, the ego is as complete within electrical reality as it is psychologically complete within the physical universe. This includes of course the retention of its dreams, as well as the retention of purely physical data.

I mentioned that the electrical universe is composed of electricity that is far different from your idea of it. Electricity as you perceive it within your field, is merely an echo emanation, or a sort of shadow image of these infinite varieties of pulsations, which give reality and actuality to many phenomena with which you are familiar, but which do not appear as tangible objects within the physical system.

I can say little until much more background is given, but this electrical reality is vastly dense.

(Jane now took one of her frequent pauses. At break she told me that as she spoke the word dense, and during the pause, she had a rather strong mental image of a field of points of light. These points of light were many-layered, she said, as though she looked at a picture of a galaxy that was not flat. On a vast scale the myriad points of light compared to the density in the electric field, on a very tiny scale.

(Jane also said the above image almost escaped her, before she realized she was receiving information two ways at once.)

We run into difficulties, for I do not speak of denseness as you probably think of it. This is a denseness that does not take up space. This is a denseness caused by an infinity of electrical fields of varying ranges of intensity. Not only are no two of these electrical fields identical, but there are no identical impulses within them.

The gradations of intensities are so minute that it would be impossible to measure them, and yet each field contains in coded form the actual living reality of endless eons; contains therefore what you would call the past, present and future of unnumbered universes; contains the actual coded data of any and every consciousness that has been or will be, in any universe; those that have appeared to vanish, and those which seemingly do not yet exist.

In our past sessions I have explained time distortions, and you are familiar with the spacious present. So it should be no surprise to realize that basically the future is in existence now, and the past has never been swept away. In <u>your</u> physical field you merely look away, or turn your focus from one point to another.

(See the 41st session for material on the spacious present.)

The actuality of what I call the past has not gone out of existence, and the future exists in actuality in the past. These last notes were merely for your own edification, and I will continue.

This density is extremely important, for it is a density of intensities. And it is the infinite variety and gradations of intensity that makes all identities possible, and all gestalts, all identities in terms of personalities and fields and universes. It is this density, this infinite variety of intensity, which allows for both identity and of change.

I suggest your break.

(Break at 9:27. Jane was well dissociated. Her eyes opened slowly. I now became aware that my right hand felt "fat," or enlarged. When I mentioned this Jane then became aware that both of her hands also felt this way to some small degree. I had noticed the same sensation perhaps two hours or so before the session. I had tried to quickly cut a paper tape to use in measuring the circumferences of my fingers, but before I could do this the sensation disappeared.

(See Volume 2, page 5 in the 43rd session for a brief explanation of the hand phenomenon. Also the 43rd and 47th sessions.

(Jane resumed in the same quiet and slow manner at 9:39.)

The electricity that is perceivable within the physical plane or field is merely a projection of a vast electrical system that you cannot perceive because of the nature and construction of the physical system itself.

The electrical system possesses many dimensions of reality that cannot be perceived within the physical system. So far scientists have only been able to study electricity by observing the projections of it that are perceivable within their frames of reference. As their physical instruments become more sophisticated they will be able to glimpse more of this reality, but since they will not be able to explain it within their known system of references, many curious and distorted explanations of reported phenomena will be given.

(Jane now took a very long pause.)

Yet the inner self offers so many answers, for the inner self is a portion of each individual; and yet it operates outside of physical systems of reference. It is of itself free of all distorted effects peculiar to the physical system. The study of dreams—your scientists consider such work beneath them. Why has no one suspected that dream locations, for example, have not only a psychological reality, but a definite actuality?

A study of dreams, of dream locations, is most important. Dream locations do <u>not</u> take up any space physically, it is true, but they are composed of electrical mass density and intensity. Here is another point. Energy is expended in work in dreams. <u>Definite</u> work may be done in a dream, but the physical arms and legs are not tired.

(See the 44th session for material on the dream locations, the expanding mind, the value climate of psychological reality.)

This would seem contrary to your known laws, yet no one has looked into the reasons for this seeming contradiction. We shall spend some considerable time with it at a later session. Nothing is static. Everything moves and changes. Electrical identities move and change. Now. Within the electrical universe there is constant motion. There is negative and positive reaction, and infinite degrees or gradations between.

(Now Jane took another long pause.)

It is most difficult at this time to even hint at the myriad complexity and dimension of the electrical actuality as it exists, when you consider that each of your own thoughts is composed of a unique intensity of impulse, shared by nothing else, and that the same may be said for every dream that you will have in your lifetime; and that all your experience is gathered together in particular ranges of intensity, again completely unique, codified; and that the summation of all that you are exists in one minute range or band of intensities, then you will see how difficult it is. For all human beings are likewise so electrically composed, and everything else, with few exceptions within your physical field, whether or not it even exists as physical matter. Yet I tell you that this not only applies to your physical field but to all fields.

Your field is contained within its own unique range of intensities, a tiny band of electrical impulses a million times smaller than any one note picked at random from the entire mass of musical composition that has been written, or ever will be written.

Yet as you know, none of this is meant to give a sense of futility, for uniqueness brings its own responsibility.

(Jane now took her longest pause of the evening. She sat without moving for over a minute.)

This material, as I have mentioned, is difficult. I must put the words into Ruburt's mouth, and now and then we travel where words are not enough. Insight and intuition, in a flash, can traverse a thousand words.

I suggest your break.

(Break at 10:07. Jane was dissociated as usual. Her eyes opened slowly. She said she has no feeling of strain during the pauses. She thinks Seth is trying to make clear things that almost cannot be put into words, however; that while she sits waiting he assembles words for her to speak. Jane hears nothing within during pauses, all is quiet.

(She resumed in the same very slow and hesitant manner at 10:15.)

I am not going to go too deeply into this, because you are not ready. But because of the truly infinite range of intensities available, every individual has limitless intensities available within which he can move.

All motion is mental or psychological motion, and all mental and psychological motion has electric reality. The inner self moves by changing or moving through intensities from your physical field. Each new psychological experience opens up a new pulsation intensity, and therefore gives greater actuality within the electrical field.

To move through intensities within the electrical system gives the result, on the physical field, of moving through physical time.

Here is a clue for so-called astral travel. Again, the inner self has limitless intensities of pulsation available to it. When the inner self in its constant motion travels through an impulse range which it has once experienced, to the ego this will appear as a journey into the past.

When the inner self achieves an impulse or intensity that is new to it, to the ego it will seem a journey into the future.

In actuality of course both impulses exist simultaneously. The inner self knows this, but the ego does not. All of this material should add dimension to your understanding of capsule comprehension, and of the initial appearance of consciousness within the physical field, as I explained it earlier.

The material in these last sessions will be basic for further discussions. We are going much deeper into the meaning of reality, and the aspects of reality. Our present procedure is working out very well, and it is enabling me to discuss matters that were too complicated for our earlier method. Before we close I want you to understand that your experiments in psychological time add to your mobility and subconscious manipulation within the electrical universe. And all psychic experience must have reality here, that is, within the electrical system. There is no psychic experience which does not have such electric reality. Your psychological experiments give you familiar ground there to walk upon, to travel on; grounds of reference and even of safety.

This is why I speak often of more or less disciplined experiments, with slow gradations. For following our analogy, your psychic footpath is then composed of stones laid out in some order, and not too far from one another, that can lead you both away from the ego and back to it safely.

I will now close our session.

("Good night, Seth.")

(End at 10:37. Jane was dissociated as usual. She feels the recent sessions are better than we think they are.)

SESSION 132
FEBRUARY 15, 1965 9 PM MONDAY AS SCHEDULED

(This afternoon Jane and I met a friend of John Bradley's, Mrs. Lorraine

Shafer, Horseheads, NY. She borrowed a copy of the first 23 sessions.

(Jane spoke for the session while sitting down and with her eyes closed. Her voice was somewhat heavier throughout, her rate of delivery somewhat faster than usual.)

Good evening.

("Good evening, Seth.")

First of all, Ruburt may continue with his daily psychological time experiments. But these are to be carried on but once daily, and if he tries any other sort of experiment, such as he tried with the Father Trainor poetry session last week, then he is not to attempt his regular psychological time experiment for that day.

One half-hour a day is more than sufficient, considering these sessions. And also, I am at present against these fairly frequent sessions where, on the one hand, Ruburt pretends that he is merely resting; that is, he pretends to himself, but actually he is expanding his energies, and expending them just as quickly, for this amounts to more than one psychological time experiment daily.

You were quite correct, Joseph, in cautioning Ruburt against the poetry session the other evening. He knew this but was obstinate. It is not only a case of being obstinate, however. I have told you that it is extremely limiting to regard the ego as the complete self or personality, or to think that the ego makes up the entire identity.

The identity, indeed, is as much and more the inner self as it is the ego. This has been mentioned in the past, but Ruburt became so fearful of his own spontaneity in early life that he was more or less forced, out of fear, to deny the validity of his identity with the inner self. On some occasions, as the other evening, he spontaneously accepts this identification, particularly when alcohol acts as a depressant.

Then he dares to go forward, only then he must rush. The spontaneity is good, the lack of caution is not. The experience concerning the poetry was a legitimate one. All in all however, Ruburt did entirely too much last week.

We are dealing with delicate balances that must be maintained. With the schedule that I have suggested the inner energies are vividly and intensely focused, but for a short period of your time. This allows for an excellent utilization of the abilities already developed, and permits, again, excellent concentrated inner focus. Too many attempts at this time do not permit this brief but excellent intensification, and can lead to that peculiar semitrance state in which Ruburt found himself last week.

A complete change from intense focus outward to intense focus inward is most beneficial, but this does not mean that every few minutes found available be spent in psychological time experiments. Brisk walks should be a daily part of Ruburt's schedule in any case, and walking also refreshes the inner self.

I do not approve of a whole day being given over to the sort of experimentation carried on by Ruburt last week in the Father Trainor sessions. In one respect I do agree with Ruburt, in that any future experiments with friends would be of better advantage carried out using chairs at a table, and actually making as few suggestions as possible.

A few drinks, again, are even beneficial, but too many drinks do not belong.

I suggest your break.

(Break at 9:30. Jane was not as deeply dissociated as she has been recently. She knew the gist of what she had said. Looking back at the Father Trainor episode, she said she was somewhat frightened in retrospect, and would not conduct such a lengthy experiment again.

(A copy of Jane's account of the Father Trainor affair will be found at the end of this session. This took place on February 11, Thursday, and parts of it are recorded. A shorter repetition, also recorded, was given for Judy and Lee Wright on the evening of February 12, Friday. It was this occasion to which I objected.

(It will be noted that in the 12th session, January 2,1964, Seth, without being asked by us, stated that he "knows" Jane's old friend, Father Trainor. Father Trainor was an Irish Catholic priest who visited Jane and her ill mother regularly, for years, during Jane's grade and high school days. He has been dead for some time. Jane has a photograph of him.

(Jane resumed in the same manner at 9:39.)

We now have a good deal of spontaneity and freedom within our sessions. A good deal, simply because we are working within a framework of discipline.

I quite understand Ruburt's curiosity when Father Trainor's voice did indeed come through, although far from perfectly. And it did represent another phase of Ruburt's developing abilities. But these abilities must be trained. I do believe that Ruburt has learned an important lesson. As his abilities do develop, it is even more important that he take walks, and that some frequency in daily contact with others is maintained.

I do not mean daily social hours. Now and then experiments with guests are fine. However, his energies on weekends as a rule should be more outgoing, and I am sorry that it has been necessary to curtail your dancing activities. Going out is an excellent way of recharging energies, by contrast. Spontaneous short humorous plays, such as you sometimes do with your recorder, is an enjoyable relaxation.

I am not saying that you should not talk about our sessions or allied subjects with friends, only that one night or sometimes two, of social discourse should certainly contain some more outward enjoyments. It would do Ruburt no harm either to resume his painting. His time as a rule is very busily engaged, and usually with mental work. It is all the more important therefore that his leisure have some outward aspect to it, and when possible of an active nature.

His Saturday housecleaning, believe it or not, is excellent for him. The short story work is a very good balance actually, for both his poetry and the book of mine that he is working on. I had meant to mention this earlier. The people, the young people with whom you work, Joseph, are very good guests for you to have. Mark is good for you both, and in many instances his impulse to get you both out of the house has been a good one.

(Mark is the entity name for our friend, Bill Macdonnel.)

I am not saying that you should always spend your weekend evenings in one particular manner. Evenings at home with guests are very good, but again, such evenings should not constantly be taken up with experiments and discussions, though they have their place at such gatherings now and then.

I am not saying you should always go dancing, but this is an excellent relaxation for you both, and leaving the house or visiting at someone else's home is also good for you both. I would not take so much time this evening with this material if I did not feel that it was important enough to warrant it. Surely you and your friends could go dancing together when you can afford it. Surely, you can for example go with Mark to one of his jolly haunts. Even though no physical activity such as dancing is available the change is still good.

Surely you can have enjoyable evenings at home without experiments, though again at times these have their place. Our sessions themselves are always in a state of becoming. We hope to become more proficient. I do not want Ruburt to become overinvolved. I would prefer that he channels his new abilities <u>mainly</u>, though not exclusively, in our sessions.

As far as the sessions themselves are concerned in relation to Ruburt, your love and reinforcement are necessary; and on your part the atmosphere of confidence, which indeed you have always given him, this will allow him the greatest possible development of ability within the sessions, and of course will further the sessions themselves.

The fear of failure is insidious, and it is this which must be combated. All in all he does very well. I suggest your break.

(Break at 10:05. Jane's eyes opened slowly. She reported that she was much more dissociated than during her first delivery. She resumed in the same rather heavy voice at 10:16.)

These suggestions are in the way of setting up checks and balances that will maintain you at your best levels. Now and then it seems that such a session as this is necessary.

Now, on session days Ruburt should rest one half-hour. I mean rest or sleep. You should both keep up your exercises. You diet has been good. I am trying to look at your situation from all angles while I am about it, to see if any other adjustments should be made.

(Jane now took a rather long pause.)

I do not see any other adjustments needed at this time.

You have both done very well during the winter season. Your uneasy period, Joseph, or the period in which you have a tendency to become so, has passed. Our friend's, our dear Ruburt's, has not yet passed, which is why I am giving the suggestions now. His overall condition, however, is very good, indeed, and if my suggestions are followed I anticipate no difficulty for him. It is important he get sufficient rest, particularly now through early spring.

If possible, also vitamins from now till early spring. This for you both, incidentally. Ruburt's uneasy period usually begins in middle January. However this year he has avoided it largely. His energies quicken however from then until early spring, and I did not want him to get into the habit of channeling them inwardly to any overbalanced degree. I think this will now be avoided.

These energies now will, I believe, go into our sessions, and into his own work. And some arrangements for physical outlets will help also.

We will have so many dreams to discuss when I finally get to them. They will be handled in groups. Much of the background material has been given to you, so it should not be too long before we begin such a prolonged discussion.

I am very pleased with both of your experiments and with your progress, and particularly, Joseph, with your portrait work. You will do very well along this line.

One small note. Upon another occasion I would like to speak about Mark's recent seizure. He is very loyal, particularly to you, Joseph, and is indeed in his own way as trustworthy a friend as you have ever had; this having to do with past experiences also.

(While visiting us on a recent weekday evening, Bill Macdonnel ruptured a blood vessel in his nose. It bled to such an extent that after half an hour we called the emergency room at one of the local hospitals. Bill lost much blood and became quite ill. Just as the hospital instructed us to take him there, the bleeding stopped. Being afraid to move very much Bill spent the night with us. He was better in the morning, although the bleeding resumed briefly. It developed that Bill has been troubled by this ailment since childhood. Jane and I did not know about it, however, and this was his first such seizure in over a year.)

My very best wishes to you both. We shall have an excellent session

Wednesday, when I hope to finish up some of the material which we have been discussing, at least. Even I, through you, look forward to your springtime. If now and then you ever want an additional session, under most circumstances I will agree. I do not mean extra sessions for witnesses particularly, since these sessions are open to anyone who is sincerely interested. I simply mean that if you ever feel the desire for an additional session, I would comply.

Again, my best and most fond wishes to both of you. I do not mean to be hard with Ruburt, but I did wish to make necessary suggestions which I felt were needed now.

("Good night, Seth.")

(End at 10:37. Jane was well dissociated. Once in a while Jane and I have discussed extra sessions, but usually we do not have the time, particularly when other experiments like the one involving Father Trainor crop up. Occasionally we would like a session dealing with some specific problem, and may try this approach. Also one involving questions and answers.)

(Notes from Jane's version of the Father Trainor experiment of February 11, 1965.

(I am not sure exactly what happened, much less what caused it. I'm writing a prose sketch of Father Trainor. I thought that if I tried reading G. K. Chesterton's Lepanto, *and Gray's* Elegy in a Country Churchyard *the way Father Trainor used to, my memory would be refreshed. I wanted to describe his poetry readings for the sketch.*

(I stood up and began to read. The sudden volume and depth and timbre of my voice was instantly apparent, and startled me. I read all of the Lepanto *and part of the* Elegy *in this manner. My voice boomed—I sounded more like Father Trainor than like myself. The volume of my voice was really tremendous.*

(When I finished this I kept wondering about it. Why hadn't I thought to record it? What was the change in my voice? Had I imagined or elaborated on perhaps just a small change? I tried to do it over, on tape. The reading this time was not as striking as the first time, but still there was certainly something definitely going on.

(After lunch I decided to try again. At lunch I played the tape for Rob, then while posing for him I suggested to myself that I would go into a trance as soon as I began to read, and that Father Trainor would indeed use his voice to speak through me, if he was available. I then started all over again with the readings. Except, for what reason I do not know, I turned the recorder on but forgot to depress the "record" button.

(This performance was as good as the first one. I felt carried away by the voice, almost outside of myself, very light and disconnected from this voice. But I do recall

that the book itself, which I held as I paced, was heavy. I grew cold and tingled as I read. My hands perspired quite a bit, perhaps from holding the book. Rob came out of his studio to listen to me. When I discovered that I had recorded nothing this time I felt cheated, because to me this reading had been most unusual.

(I was so angry that I did the whole thing over again. Lepanto *is a four-page poem. This time the performance was about like the second one, already recorded. Perhaps if I feel subjectively right about doing it again, I may try it tonight. I don't know where the volume comes from, the deep manlike tones. Perhaps it is what actors call merely projection, breathing from the diaphragm. I wasn't conscious of breathing any differently than usual, but if this was a subconscious production that wouldn't make any difference. But where would the male aspect enter, unless it be a woman's attempt to mimic as best she could the voice of a man she had admired?*

(Rob suggested another possibility: that as a medium I am starting to learn to let others in contact with me speak out. Perhaps, because I knew Father Trainor, I let his voice come through as a starter.

(My comments added:

(Something did take place. The medium allowing others to speak through her is the best guess I can make at this time. It seems reasonable, if Jane's abilities are growing, as the material suggests.

(As a check I suggested later that Jane try reading a different poem, one not read by Father Trainor, to see if she could summon this powerful new voice at will. I wanted to see if something Jane had no emotional involvement with, via memory, could also be used to summon voice changes. Nothing happened. To begin with Jane could not consciously summon nearly the volume of voice, and within a few lines she was so hoarse she had to rest. She said Father Trainor always read the Lepanto *and the* Elegy *on his Sunday visits, and that she could not remember his reading anything else.*

(The volume and male inflection Jane achieved during her various readings was quite amazing. I noticed that toward the end of each verse of the Lepanto *she would reach a crescendo of volume and emotion that was indeed thrilling. For brief periods her voice would sound very alien. For other periods, during what seemed to be letdowns, I would know the voice was hers. But still it would be much stronger and lower in timbre than her natural voice.*

(This voice was not the Seth voice by any means. Even at its strongest Seth's voice is a dry and intellectual one. The Father Trainor voice was very emotional by contrast. I do not believe that the Father Trainor voice at its best exceeded Seth at his best, and vice versa.

(It might be added that during the whole day's experimentation Jane did not suffer from any voice fatigue, nor did she have any aftereffects the next day. She bore

up as well as when she was conducting three-hour Seth sessions, although today's experiment lasted something like five or six hours. I was afraid that she would overdo it however.)

SESSION 133
FEBRUARY 17, 1965 9 PM WEDNESDAY AS SCHEDULED

(The day after the last session Jane realized that she had burned herself on the back of her right leg, just above the heel. While it was not overly severe, the burn was deep enough to have formed a scar; yet she could not recall when she had been burned. She later realized she had done it during the last session.

(During sessions now, Jane sits in our rocker across from my writing table. She usually faces our big bay window. Beneath the window is a heater, covered by a metal window seat. At times this "seat" becomes too hot to touch. At times also, Jane sits with her feet propped up on this seat while dictating. Checking, she discovered that while in her usual position with her feet up, the burn coincided exactly with the edge of the seat. I had wondered at times about the seat becoming too hot, but had taken it for granted that Jane automatically lowered her feet when it became too warm. Evidently she had neglected to do so, at least once, yet had felt no pain. I would also remember had the session been interrupted by her. Both of us have speculated about whether she is less sensitive to pain while in her trance state.

(Jane's voice was quite dry tonight, and it remained so when she began dictating. The hoarseness gradually cleared up as the material unfolded, however. She spoke at a rather steady rate, with some pauses, and with her eyes closed.

(Note also the variation in the opening of the session.)

Now my dear friends...

Though we speak in definite terms of the inner self, the entity and the ego, neither the inner self, the entity or the ego are stationary and complete. We freeze them, so to speak, in order that we might hold them within our grasp, but we cannot, nor is there a time, as such, when they will be completed or finished.

They are forever in motion. They change constantly. As you cannot hold even the ego in the palm of your hand, so you cannot hold the inner self within the mind. They always escape in essence.

The entity should therefore not be thought of as completed. The electric universe, of which you know so little, is a reality, and yet it is also a symbol of another reality. For behind even this electrical universe there is a reality which cannot be explored in terms of speech; for all consciousness, while having an electric reality, has a reality beyond even this.

It is the vitality of the universe, and all universes, which causes the electrical reality, and the vitality of the universe, composing everything that is, cannot be touched. It is touch, but touch not as it is conceived of in your terms. This vitality is the most immediate and intimate aspect that composes the camouflage appearance within all fields. And yet it is by far more than the camouflage.

It has many realities, forming all universes and all fields. It is indeed within you, as you are within it. It is not formless, but takes many forms. It is above all never static and never completed.

(There came a knock upon the door. At times I had wondered how Jane would react to an interruption while in her new and deeper state. I now had at least one answer: Her body jumped in her chair, and her eyes popped open as though from shock. For a moment she appeared to be disoriented. Then she answered my query to the effect that she was all right.

(Bill Macdonnel, who has witnessed several sessions, was at the door. He remained for the balance of the session. Jane had thought Seth would continue the interruption as our first break, but shortly she announced he wanted to continue. When she resumed her voice was abruptly quite a bit deeper and stronger, and it remained so for the balance of the session. Resume at 9:17.)

It is indeed closer to you than your breath.

Many sessions ago I used the analogy of air within your physical field, comparing it with the vitality of the universe, in that you are not as a rule conscious of air. Yet it is part of everything within your field. And also, that most inaccessible, most inward and seemingly most mysterious portion of the inner universe, which you seek, is so a part of you that you are unaware of it even though in it you have your very existence.

When I speak of the electrical universe, indeed this represents but one more facet of reality. But all of these universes are indeed <u>one</u>. You remember our discussion concerning density of intensities. Here is the secret, if you could but see it: Even though the electrical universe might seem to you far divorced from what you know, nevertheless <u>you</u> dwell within it. Your own emotions have an <u>independent</u> existence within it. And your own possibilities within it are unlimited. But even this is also a camouflage.

I give my greetings here to Mark, who has lately entered, and you may now take your break.

(Break at 9:26. Jane reported that she was well dissociated to begin the session, and even more so after Bill's arrival. She resumed in the same deeper and louder manner at 9:35.)

The difficult point here that we must always return to, is that beneath all camouflage exists that which has no need of camouflage, but simply is.

Yet this initial experience is not completed and it is not finished. And while it does not need expression through camouflage, it exists in a fuller and more vivid nature than you can at present imagine.

So when I told you to look where there was nothing, then I spoke because this uncamouflaged experience can be most directly perceived where nothing is perceived with the outer senses. In one sense anything that you can see or feel or touch is not real, and yet in another sense it is the nature of all reality.

Neither, then, is the ego ever finished, nor the inner self, nor the entity. Each field of existence merges into every other, and yet each retains its own identity. The subconscious layers of the self dwell also in many realities, and here I speak of actual fields and not fantasies.

Personalities within, that are not dominant within the ego, are dominant within other fields of actuality, though they appear as mere shadowy influences within your own.

The gestalt patterns of which I have spoken is the basis here, and yet all members within such gestalts are themselves independent, possessing identity and separation even while they cooperate in a complicated pattern. It is arbitrary; that is, from your viewpoint you arbitrarily choose certain portions of reality and call them units, marking them off. But your divisions do not affect the nature of these gestalts, as my discussion speaks of separate universes without affecting the nature of any universe one whit.

The idea that I want to portray is a difficult one, for as you know everything that is, is conscious. And everything that is, is also self-conscious, in degree according to its abilities; and everything that is therefore contains identity and separation, even while it is part of a large and complicated gestalt.

No identities are blurred, but it makes no difference to the identities where you or mankind happens to draw a line, saying "Here we have A, and here we have B."

A small frog for example may be more likely seen not as a frog isolated, but as one part of the pond in which he lives; and the pond part of the forest in which it lies; and the forest part of the earth; and the earth itself part of the universe, which is part of another universe.

It makes no difference to the frog, to the nature of the frog, and it changes no smallest cell within him, if you choose to enclose what you call him, as an idea unit called frog, or whether you consider instead the complete picture. The identities still remain the same.

I suggest your break.

(Break at 9:55. Jane was again well dissociated. She resumed in her heavier

voice again at 10:05.)

Such explanations are needed only because we are speaking in terms of indirect experience.

All true knowledge is direct experience. It cannot be classified, it cannot be named, it cannot be set down in black and white. True knowledge is only experience, direct experience, and a matter of the inner senses.

Even my explanations to you involve a verbal dissection, which in itself distorts the very nature of the matter under examination. All our discussions concerning the electrical universe do not bring you closer to experience of it. You are in direct contact with it. But again, as you cannot hold your own breath, so you cannot hold that which is even more intimate, and which forms the very personality which attempts the examination.

Direct experience alone will bring you such knowledge, and yet it will not be held by the conscious mind or by the ego, although flashes of the experience may be momentarily projected within these realms. Such knowledge indeed is communicated to the various levels of the self through dreams, as you should know.

And again, dreams are themselves never completed, but continue on whether or not your perception of them continues. For dreams also are gestalts. When you look into the mirror you see the camouflage image. You do not see the ego, though you know that it exists. But the idea, ego, is in itself an arbitrary unit chosen for particular reasons. It is not a thing. You have drawn lines, imaginary lines, and made an arbitrary boundary. This does not mean that the ego does not exist.

It means that the word is nothing, and that it is merely a symbol for that which you can neither see nor feel nor touch. It is merely a symbol for that small particle of yourselves which you permit your consciousness to perceive. It is a symbol to express that portion of an unseeable self, that is brought most obviously into operation for purposes of manipulation of the physical image within a camouflage field.

The ego then, is only part of a much larger self, but because consciously you do not perceive the whole self you arbitrarily make a unit from a truly indivisible identity, and call this the "I." This designation, this classification, in no way affects the nature of that indivisible self. It merely affects your own conscious attitudes. You succeed in cutting off, in theory, one portion of the self from the whole self.

This duality then affects your own perception in a most diverse fashion. It sets man against himself. We will go into this matter more clearly at our next session, as it will lead us further into some new areas.

This has been a most fruitful session. My best regards to all of you. I would suggest that you keep watch on your Miss Callahan from Thursday on of next week.

("Good night, Seth."

(End at 10:25. Jane was fully dissociated, she said. Miss Callahan is an elderly retired teacher who lives in the front apartment of our second floor here. Oddly enough, she had her first stroke almost exactly a year ago—February 17,1964. Since her illness then, Seth has dealt with her to varying degrees on February 17, as well as in the 29th, 31st, 33rd, 44th, 46th, 54th, and 56th sessions, among others. Jane has also had clairvoyant dreams involving Miss Callahan.

(After leaving the hospital, Miss C returned home, to live with a housekeeper. Miss C, preferring to be alone, finally let the housekeeper go a few weeks ago. She has been quite weak since the onset of her illness, and lately has looked weaker since doing everything for herself. Jane visits her rather often just to keep an eye on her. Miss C's memory is very poor now, and evidently her energy is low also. She is extremely thin.

(See also the 63rd and 83rd sessions about Miss Callahan.)

SESSION 134
FEBRUARY 22, 1965 9 PM MONDAY AS SCHEDULED

(Jane was upset about her work this evening, so much so in fact that she would have missed the session had I not been too lazy to go dancing. It was a bitterly cold and windy night. While we were discussing our problems 9 PM arrived, so we held the session.

(Jane spoke at a fairly normal rate, in a voice that was for the most part quite strong and loud. She sat down, and her eyes were closed. She was also smoking during the first part of the session. She actually began speaking at 9:02.)

The weather is indeed stormy.

The inner discipline, the inner utilization of energy, the inner channeling and direction of energy on Ruburt's part in these sessions, would have been impossible but a few years ago.

This involves on his part not a conscious, but a subconscious change of habit. The <u>new</u> habit he has acquired very well. The psychic explosions that have been fairly regular with him in the past, have been minimized to some considerable degree since our sessions began. No one is endeavoring to tamper with his personality, however, and it is his natural reaction to turn aggression, when it arises, outward in some manner, while he is almost superstitiously careful that it not be directed at another individual.

This is with him a fairly healthy reaction, and less disruptive than he thinks. You have been distrustful to some degree concerning Ruburt's fidelity to the sessions, precisely because the sessions have become important to you. Ruburt at this time would not dispense with the sessions, although it is true that he sometimes consciously resents the discipline involved in their regularity.

Subconsciously however, the very regularity is reassuring to him, since a fairly permanent pattern exists despite the flux and flow of conscious inclination. I am not going to give over a full session to these matters. However some comments will be helpful.

Without Ruburt's now and then, really rather petty explosions, the stability of his working habits and the stability of emotional reactions would not be nearly as regular. The explosions are after all small ones, and of a harmless nature, that have a definite balancing tendency. Nor, my dear Joseph, are these explosions, though this is quite an exaggerated phrase, nor are these <u>his</u> alone; for he takes up also <u>your</u> hidden frustrations and angers, feels them deeply, though consciously he does not know this; and he then in these small explosions rather harmlessly dispels pent-up, small but potent emotional bombshells that belong to you both.

There is also, though this will vanish, a strong giving of self in these sessions on Ruburt's part, a giving of self that involves the momentary giving up of emotion. And when he is angry he does not want to give his anger up. What will vanish is any feeling on his part of being subconsciously drained, as he does feel <u>occasionally</u>, and only when he is perturbed at something else.

The material itself however shows that we are coming along very well, and able to get across delicate shadings of meanings that would not have been possible earlier. Our sessions have had a stabilizing effect upon you both, and will so continue.

I will let you have your break now, and then I will return to our other material.

(Break at 9:24. Jane was well dissociated. She said the time had gone so fast it appeared that only two or three minutes had elapsed. She resumed in the same rather strong manner at 9:34.)

Only one more additional note here concerning the above.

On a conscious level you, Joseph, are much more given to regularity, and therefore more concerned when Ruburt shows signs of irregularity. It is however with him, <u>as</u> with you, the peculiar mixture of discipline and regularity with spontaneity that makes the sessions possible; and this quality in Ruburt, even of rebellion, that allows the sessions to continue.

For without a rebellious nature <u>neither</u> of you would have permitted the sessions to begin. From this mixture *all* creativity comes. Our regularity of sessions is now a necessity. This does not mean however that at times *a* session cannot be missed, or that such a missed session should be considered a significant symptom. Overall our schedule will be maintained, but we do not want rigidity, merely the spontaneity that comes, and the freedom that is achieved within discipline.

This may not seem so to you, but because *subconsciously* and basically, though not consciously, Ruburt trusts both his own intuition and the validity of our sessions. He will not allow the rambunctious portion of his personality to upset our schedule, but because he trusts all this *subconsciously*, he will not be as disturbed as *you* are if a session is missed.

This is because you are more apt to place stress upon regularity as a matter of your temperament, though you trust your intuitions in the sessions, as he does.

We have truly done much in a year. We will do more. If you were in Ruburt's position, you would be more willingly regular than he; but my dear Joseph, *your* critical sense would block me much more than his, particularly in details. And in your position Ruburt would not do as well as you do.

You have set up more blocks than he has. He will be more vulnerable or receptive to your moods than *you* are to his. You fear moods more than he does, because of the constant emotional gyrations in which your mother is constantly involved. You fear *Ruburt's* moods also, for this reason, fearing that you might be swept away by them. For as a child you feared you would be swept away by the raw emotions of your parents, and you feel insecure at such demonstrations. As I have said, you two temperamentally balance each other well.

You know by now that emotions even change the physical cells, sweeping through them as wind through branches, and leaving imprints in many realities, leaving imprints within the reality of dreams, the physical reality, and in electrical reality, in terms of coded systems.

There should be an easy flow and acceptance of such emotions, wherein they come and go; but ego often holds them tightly, for its own purposes, in which case they become imprisoned, and become stronger than they were. The origin of emotions is something that we still have to discuss, for there are many origins.

Some emotions originate within the personality, but others are simply like winds that are then rationalized and *held*. Emotions are indeed motion, and not static, and will pass to be replaced by others, unless the ego holds them back.

Emotions also are electrically coded, and also have an independent electrical reality. On a physical level they are both chemical and electrical. The validity and strength of emotions cannot be overestimated, for they represent in only slightly tinged form the uncamouflaged vitality of the universe as it passes through the inner self. Emotions represent, therefore, this vitality before it has been constructed into camouflage.

It has been tinged psychologically in its entry through the subconscious, but that is all. Emotions are the most vital tools with which you have to work. It is for this reason that you must learn how to use them.

I suggest your break.

(Break at 10:00. Jane was well dissociated, and still amazed now at the rapid passage of time during her delivery. She resumed in the same strong manner at 10:13.)

Joseph is now facing the fact of his own aggressions, as he never really did to any strong extent in the past. Consciously recalling the dreams is excellent, since the subconscious data is at least to some extent consciously assimilated, and in the dreams aggressive tendencies are indeed released and worked out in an actual manner, as satisfying to the subconscious as if they were worked out within the physical field. And to some extent through muscular action, even in dreams such aggressions find physical outlet also, and save you quite a few aches and pains, by the way.

Again, you Joseph feared aggression in the past so strongly that you would not allow yourself to even recall such dreams a year ago. Ruburt has no such knowledge of aggressive dreams, a very few, and this is also significant. He fears violence. This is one of the main reasons for his own occasional explosive moods.

He is too meek in many ways, for he is not basically a meek temperament, and for this reason I always encourage him in physical activities. He is more than you afraid to face natural aggression, and both of you are fearful here.

I will not go into particular dreams now. The dream to which you refer was not a warning concerning either of you, however.

I have to some extent attempted to tie in personal material with more general information this evening. Ruburt's psychic state is much improved over his usual late winter state, and this seasonal susceptibility is also somewhat responsible for his occasional, really deep feelings of discouragement.

These feelings of discouragement, however, though much deeper in the past, should be dissipated as quickly as possible in all cases, and then the energy used in a new plunge into work. There are no tendencies now worth speaking of, but the discouragement could in certain circumstances turn into an unhealthy despondency, and his intuitional urge to counteract it by seeking out people is a sound one.

(Just as our wall clock indicated 10:30 PM, an unfortunate thing happened. Our cat Willy had several times jumped up on Jane's lap as she spoke. Since this disturbed Jane's trance state to some extent, I had been trying to keep him away from her.

(Willy now jumped up once more. Reaching for him to make him move, I grabbed his tail and at the same time nearly lost my balance. I pulled Willy backward. He came loose, but at the same time his claws came out in a reflex action. I heard them scrape across Jane's lap. Jane's eyes snapped open and she cried out. It was evident that the cat had scratched her through her dress. Jane clearly did not know what had happened exactly; she appeared to be dazed. I said nothing, not wanting to pull her out of her state any more abruptly. I was then surprised to see her sit quietly, finally close her eyes, and go back into her full state. If Willy's scratches hurt she gave no sign. Indeed, Jane smiled as she began speaking again. Resume at 10:31.)

You would have both been incapable of producing your present work even a year ago.

I will here add Joseph, that you did indeed paint an excellent likeness of me, as I was, and as my entity is. I am sure you know to what I refer.

And do not fall, either of you, into winter doldrums. For I am a jolly snowman, and I will not melt in the springtime. You are both progressing in your work. Creative work does not grow in even ways, but in seeming sudden bursts of activities, and in seeming wastefulness, which is not waste at all.

My best good wishes to you both.

("Good night, Seth."

(End at 10:35. Jane was well dissociated, as before. She did remember something scratching her, and it developed that Willy had drawn a few spots of blood.

(I have just finished an oil painting of two heads, male; one of the characters appealed greatly to Jane, and had since the beginning. I had not given it much thought, beyond wondering where I had gotten the idea for the painting to begin with. I had taken it somewhat for granted that the faces I painted were the result of some kind of telepathic information or subconscious memory. In the past Seth has stated that I often use these sources of information for my portraits. The head Jane likes is of a blond man, quite heavyset and evidently of a massive build. The features are rather regular, although the nose is somewhat prominent, the jaw square, the eyes blue. Jane does not care much for the other head in the painting, although as I worked on the picture I was as much intrigued by this head as by the other.

(I have been keeping a record of my dreams for several weeks now, emulating Jane's example. It is a fascinating experience, and already appears to have borne some small fruits as far as clairvoyance is concerned, and self-understanding. Lately the dreams have featured a lot of aggressive action on my part, and it had been my own

idea also that this aggressiveness released was a good thing.

(The particular dream Seth refers to on page 270 concerned one I had on the night of Sunday, February 21. In it a man received news of his wife's death via his inner senses, by which he sees her apparition appear before him as she dies many miles away. The apparition I saw in the dream was not of Jane, but still the dream was very vivid, and somewhat upsetting. I believe it has elements of clairvoyance, and that possibly I disguised the identity of the apparition I saw in the dream.)

SESSION 135
FEBRUARY 24, 1965 9 PM WEDNESDAY AS SCHEDULED

(John Bradley, of Williamsport, PA, was a witness to the session. This is the first session he has attended since that of the 95th, October 7,1964. However John has visited us often since then, and is reading the sessions regularly.

(Perhaps because of the presence of a witness, Jane was nervous before the session began. Once again she dictated while sitting down, and with her eyes closed. She spoke quite rapidly, in a voice somewhat louder and deeper than usual, and continued in this vein throughout the session. She was also more animated than usual, and used much emphasis and many gestures. Pauses were quite rare.

(It will be remembered that Philip is John's entity name, and that Bill Macdonnel's entity name is Mark.)

Good evening.

("Good evening, Seth.")

([John]: "Good evening, Seth.")

I will here welcome Philip to our session. Since he is acquainted with our later material, I will continue along the same lines.

Much of the information that you have been receiving lately <u>can</u> be partially verified by physicists and mathematicians. That is, verification is <u>possible</u>. This does not mean that it will necessarily come about.

Your letter, by the way, to the publisher, was an excellent move on your part. The book being prepared by Ruburt is coming along well. Some more work is needed on pages 52, 70 and 90. If he will reread these sections the necessary changes will occur to him. <u>I</u> will see to it.

(After the session, Jane said she had no idea offhand just what material is on those particular pages of the Seth manuscript. But she does not want to look at them until she is ready to go to work on them.)

It is most pleasant this evening, with our small group. I am still working with Ruburt in an attempt to make the sessions more congenial, although necessarily it takes a while for him to become accustomed to our new method of delivery.

The Mr. Gottlieb of whom you have been speaking will soon find himself in other difficulties, I am afraid. We will now return to our other discussions.

I have said that the electrical universe is, again, a materialization of a sort of inner vitality, of which everything is composed. This vitality has a reality independently of any and all such materializations, which brings us to a most interesting point.

It is most difficult for <u>you</u> to contemplate the existence of that which is independent of its own materialization. This vitality fills all other forms while it is itself, in <u>your</u> terms, formless. But our discussions concerning the electrical universe should have led you into intangibles.

It should be easier now for you to understand this vitality, since we have already spoken in terms of reality existing by means of intensities. You will recall that I spoke of distances in terms of action, and that these distances occurred not in a perceivable framework of the sort with which you are familiar, but that I spoke of distance that had its reality in terms of the varying intensities within any given electrical actuality.

(See many of the recent sessions, particularly from the 125th on.)

Therefore, traveling through such distance would involve travel through the electrical intensities that go into the existence of any given action as it electrically occurs. This idea of action within action, of distance and movement within action, is a fairly new one in our sessions.

No electrical reality is composed of simply <u>one</u> impulse. Although we must speak in these terms for simplicity's sake, every electrical impulse is of itself composed of a truly <u>endless</u> variety and range of intensities. In other words, each electrical impulse contains within it its own infinity of variations.

It is difficult here to do more than simply give you the statement. If you will, at your leisure, consider the makeup of your own dreams, you may partially and intuitively understand what I mean, for the distance in dreams is endless, though <u>you</u> may go but a little way; yet this distance as we have said, does not take up space. <u>This</u> comes close to evoking an understanding of distance as it occurs electrically, existing <u>within</u> an action.

I suggest your break.

I do not, and I have said this before, want any of you to break up into pieces, for I am not sure that I could put you back together again.

(Break at 9:20. Notice that break came quite early. Jane was well dissociated, she said, and her eyes opened slowly. She resumed in the same forceful manner at 9:30.)

The intensities merge one into the other. Even the words which I use to describe them are at best poor symbols, for when I speak of an action, it would seem as if I spoke of one indivisible concrete completed issue, and such is not the case.

No action basically is ever completed. This statement will later lead us into further realms. All possibilities are open to an action, an electrical action. And again, within it are an infinity of variations and depths of intensities, which give it a reality in many dimensions simultaneously. Where strong intensities are felt, then the actuality will be said to project within the field of reality which falls within the range of that particular intensity group.

Such electrical realities then, through the strength of their intensities and their particular range, are projected into some fields, but not projected into others. Any so-called travel through time involves then a traveling through such intensities. This is obviously impossible for the physical camouflaged self, but it is not impossible for the inner self, which as you know has its own electrical reality, which is again composed of particular impulses and intensities.

All depth, all dimension and all distance is therein contained within the electrical universe. There is here, as I have said, no such thing as size in your terms, or shape in your terms; but there is, again, distance, which is not absolute but varying, and which can be said to exist both backward and forward indefinitely within the infinite intensities. And all reality within any given field basically occurs within such intensities.

Once more, your own inner psychological experiences, and the inner life of every individual, can lead you to some understanding along these lines. Nor, as I said earlier, should this seem so strange. Mankind names and identifies even what he cannot see, and he divides and he separates. As I mentioned, when you look into a mirror you do not see your ego. You can never see it. You experience it directly, and so do you experience directly this sort of distance of which I speak.

But as you cannot find life by dissecting a frog, you cannot find this sort of distance by exploring space. When you dissect the frog you destroy that which you had been seeking. You are left with camouflage. Only by direct experience will anyone know of these matters.

Again, by looking where nothing seems to be, you will find much. And by exploring that which you cannot touch, you will discover that which is even closer to you than touch, for the outer sense of touch is one of the most close counterparts of direct experience that you have. And it contains dimensions and gradations and varieties that cannot be recorded by scientific instruments, and this comes near in its own way to the infinite varieties present within one electrical action.

I would also suggest Joseph, that will all due respects, that within your crowded schedule you find time now and then for your psychological time experiments. As many teachers say, practice makes perfect, and lately in this respect you do not exactly deserve a gold star.

Nor does Ruburt. He either goes overboard and overdoes, or does nothing in that respect, and I believe in other respects. The half-hour limit should always be maintained, however. You should be able to experience now, directly, the sort of distance to which I have referred.

I will now suggest your break.

(Break at 9:50. Jane was dissociated as usual, and again had trouble opening her eyes. They "felt like they were glued shut," she said. She thought her trance state was somewhat deeper than usual even when she is seated.

(She resumed in the same strong manner at 10:00.)

I find the conversation most amusing, and I myself will have a hand with any critics.

And if I do not seem spiritual enough for anyone who reads the material, then let it be said that I have never pretended to be the Holy Ghost. Such a remark is also based upon your definition of spirituality, which is at best limited in your contemporary society, and whose limited definition is indeed the result of the duality which has besieged mankind now for centuries.

(Seth talked about this duality as long ago as the 25th session, in Volume 1.)

What I have been telling you this evening, and my discussions in all our sessions, all my comments, have been concerned with basic and simple facts, not alien to mankind's nature, but more intimate to him than touch. The very fact that over one hundred and thirty sessions have been devoted to such ABC's is, in itself, adequate proof of how mankind has indeed divorced itself from the nature of its own spirit.

I am always amused and somewhat agitated at talk of so-called spirituality, when barriers have been effectively set up, cutting the nature of man into halves, and I will effectively deal with any such criticism. You will not have to open your mouths. Indeed, I would prefer, under such circumstances, that you would not speak out.

Most of our material will indeed be shown as valid. I do not speak in any of these matters as far as definite times and places are concerned, nor do I intend to. Ruburt is egotistical enough as it is, and you Joseph are so determined. We will continue on. The material will see wide circulation; and at a time when you are both able to handle such circumstances.

I show to you those facets of my personality with which you can attune yourselves most readily. I am indeed <u>here</u>, and <u>with</u> you more than you realize. For you see, your experience of <u>me</u> now exists in electrically coded data <u>within your own systems</u>. I am myself. I still exist, however, in electrically coded data within, or about, yourself; as I have explained that <u>all</u> individual experience is so electrically coded and retained.

<u>I</u> thought that you would understand this automatically, but apparently you did not. I am <u>pleased</u> with Philip's interest on our behalf. And I do indeed keep my eye out, so to speak, on <u>his</u> behalf.

There are many reasons why such a rapport was first established and then continued. And there will be in the future an event that will bind the three of you together.

I here mention once more that you keep some watch upon Miss Callahan, and would indeed suggest that Ruburt, for a period of three or four days, brings up the mail to Miss Callahan. This will prevent Miss Callahan from attempting the stairs, at least for this purpose, and it is during the afternoon periods that concern is felt here.

(It is Friday night as I type this, two days after the session. To date Miss Callahan appears to be all right. Jane saw her at 3 PM, mail time. Jane has been picking up Miss Callahan's mail as suggested, and also sometimes manages to look in on her at another time of day.

(Miss Callahan is not completely alone. She now has a woman who cooks her noon meal for her, and usually stays with her until about 1 PM.)

During our next session we will go more deeply into those pyramid gestalts of which we have spoken in the past, and perhaps consider from another viewpoint entirely the scope and nature that make up the idea of gods. Within certain frameworks these pyramid gestalts do have an electrical reality, but their existence goes beyond <u>not the range but the nature</u> of electrical reality. And <u>because</u> of the strength of their intensity, they are projected within <u>every other field of actuality that exists</u>.

I will now close our session. When the three of us are together upon some other occasion, then perhaps we shall see about your effects. Show me, show me, <u>show</u> me, Ruburt. And here you see this: Because Mark has seen what Mark has seen, our Ruburt is dubious. Why? <u>Because</u> Mark has seen what Mark has seen!

Mark's abilities, while untrained, are excellent. He is naive and childlike. For this reason his abilities allow him to see what has been put before him. I would say more along these lines. However Ruburt would not take it kindly, and I am after all in his debt to <u>some</u> degree. My heartiest wishes to all of you. <u>If</u> you prefer, I will consider prolonging the session. However, we shall end it as usual if you prefer.

("I guess we'd better.")

Then by all means do so. I will give you one little puzzle, Joseph: The number five, a Saturday evening. And that is all I will say.

("Good night, Seth."

(End at 10:29. Jane was again well dissociated. John Bradley said the material was much harder to follow, when given verbally, than it was the last time he witnessed a session. It was much more complex. John also said he tried to communicate with Jane mentally while she was speaking, concerning his company, Searle Drug. But since Jane did not mention the subject John considered his efforts a failure, for whatever reason.

(Jane finished the session in good humor, particularly the comments on physical effects, Mark, and the like. And I am curious about my little puzzle.)

SESSION 136
MARCH 1, 1965 9 PM MONDAY AS SCHEDULED

(Jane dictated while sitting down, and with her eyes closed. Her voice was quiet and clear. She spoke at a fairly rapid rate, and smoked part of the time.)

Good evening.

("Good evening, Seth.")

Before we begin with other material. I would suggest that Ruburt set aside one day a week for the marketing of his own manuscripts.

During the rest of the week, he should if possible forget about the marketing aspect. This is a suggestion, and that is all.

The components of the electrical universe are drawn from all energy, in a manner that could be described as a cosmic juggling act. For this energy is never still, and it goes without saying that no electrical impulse is <u>stable</u> from one instant of reality to the next. That is, it is <u>never</u> the same or identical impulse. It is not <u>identical</u>. It is not therefore of the same intensity, though it may contain the same approximate electrical mass.

Change alone allows for the possibility of identity within any universe, for without change there can be no value fulfillment, no experience, and no identity. Portions of the electrical universe are projected into many fields. Therefore electricity to some degree is recognized as a reality within many fields.

Practically, your own identities exist electronically, as I have explained, in codified form. At some later occasion, we shall go into <u>seeming</u> duplications, for such duplications are only apparent, of a nature that could be compared to a reflective result. In such cases almost, though not entirely without exception, such a duplicate is projected by an original electronically. We are not quite ready yet for this material. I wanted however to mention the possibility of such occurrences, since such projections have and do happen with some frequency.

If you will consider the projection of a thought, that is intangible, so that it affects another individual, and hence both directly and indirectly affects the action of physical matter, then you may consider the possibility of other such projections. We have here a rather delicate point. I have said that there are no duplicates. Yet you may say, are not some thoughts duplicates? The variations may indeed be slight, but the variations are always present. A thought transmitted knowingly or unknowingly by "A" is not precisely the same thought when it reaches receiver "B".

The thought originally held by A is still retained by A, yet a seemingly identical thought reaches B. A has lost nothing. That is, in sending the thought, in trying to duplicate the thought, he himself still retains it, so what is passed on to receiver B? This is rather important, since an explanation will do much to account for the frequent difference that occurs in telepathic communications.

Whether or not A, the sender, knowingly transmits this apparent duplicate, at the point of its transmission the sender forms an electrical impulse pattern that is supposed to duplicate the original thought. But no such identical duplication is possible, as far as I know, within reality of any kind.

A side note: Identical twins, for example, are hardly identical.

As soon as the attempt is made to duplicate the original thought, then we find that the attempt itself strains and pulls; the impulses change minutely or to a greater degree. The point that I want to make here is that any attempt at such duplication actually forces, because of the nature of the attempt, the impulses to line up in a different pattern. When B receives the thought, it is already a new thought, bearing great resemblance to the original, but it is not the identical thought.

In this case action forces change, and by the very nature of action no such duplications can occur. It may be said, for practical reasons, that A and B have identical thoughts. But the thoughts are not identical.

I suggest your break.

(Break at 9:25. Jane was dissociated as usual. She resumed at a much slower rate, still in the same quiet voice, at 9:32.)

An identity is by definition and nature, one.

An identity can appear, be perceived in more than one place, but in such a case there is but one identity being viewed from many perspectives.

We will be going into some matters that may appear complicated in the telling, but this is only the effect, again, of the necessity to use words in single strung-out fashion, one before the other. Regardless of any seeming contradictions that might appear before this particular subject matter is covered, identities by nature cannot be duplicated.

I cannot explain everything at once, and so obviously many questions would remain unanswered until we can get to them. For the original thought, as an identity, to actually be transmitted to a sender, you would have to face the inevitable result: If the identical thought were actually transmitted from A to B, then A would have it no longer. Since A obviously may still have the original thought, then B has not the identical thought; not an exact duplicate, but instead a similar but still unidentical thought.

Prime identities cannot be duplicated. Duplication, exact duplication, is always merely an effect of insufficient knowledge. In some cases two thoughts may indeed appear identical, but whether or not examination can show it, such exact duplication is impossible. Now. When receiver B receives this transmitted thought, he may react and interpret that part of the thought that is similar to the original.

He may, on the other hand, react to and interpret portions of the thought that are not similar. He may then react and interpret the similarity or the difference. His reaction here depends on several circumstances, including the intensity of the electrical pulsations that compose the thought, and his own inner facility in reacting to particular ranges of intensities. Habitually individuals establish various overall frequencies that they are able to handle, for various reasons that I believe I explained to you somewhat earlier.

An individual will therefore feel more at home operating within certain frequencies, and he will feel less at home with others. The original thought is used as a pattern, therefore, for the creation of a new electrical reality, which may or may not be directed at any given receiver. It is obvious that the attempt to duplicate is present; and were it not for this attempt to duplicate, then there would be little similarity between any separate identities.

Because of the nature of this material, I will suggest another break.

(Break at 9:54. Jane was well dissociated. She said she thought it was a good session, because "my head feels as though there's absolutely nothing else in it but the session." She thought Seth was trying to use her abilities as best he could, in order to present the material without mix-up.

(Jane resumed in a little faster manner at 10:02.)

Identical realities, therefore, do not exist, and any such appearances should be a tip-off that an error has been made.

Now. The nature of the thought that is received by our sender B is determined by many factors. We shall merely consider a few of these. These include, to begin with, the original intensity of the thought as A possesses it, A's ability to duplicate the thought as far as possible, the relative stability of the electrical thought unit as it is formed by A, the familiarity or unfamiliarity of the range of frequencies that compose the new thought to any intended receiver.

The receiver will understand and interpret in general the intensity range that he is in the habit of using himself. Some, or a portion of, the transmitted thought may fall within his range, and some may not. He may pick up the portions of the thought which are similar to the main thought, in which case some scientific proof of sorts can be achieved.

It may happen however that the dissimilarity is what falls within his particular accustomed range, in which case proof would be inadequate. Such thoughts will be received by those individuals in whom a variety of circumstances happen to occur simultaneously.

Now. I have told you that emotions also possess an electrical reality. Thoughts formed and sent out within the impulse range of emotion often succeed because of the peculiar nature of emotional electrical impulses themselves. They have a particularly strong electrical mass. They also usually fall within powerful intensities. For reasons that we will not discuss, this evening, thoughts formed under a strong emotional impetus will carry greater vividness, have a greater tendency toward duplication, and are apt to be interpreted with some success.

Also, all individuals have had familiarity with emotions, as they exist within electrical intensities, and are accustomed to reacting to them. The whole process is instantaneous. However, the thought which is now an approximation of the original thought, and actually an identity of its own—

(There now came a knock on the door. It was 10:23. Once again, as in the 133rd and 134th sessions, Jane was shocked out of her trance state. She was disoriented, groping for her bearings. I signaled her to sit quietly, rather than to further the shock by getting up to answer the door. We waited until the knocking stopped. As before, Jane then drifted back into the trance state, and resumed at 10:25.)

The thought is changed once more by the receiver.

He does not interpret the thought. He interprets its meaning, and forms a new thought identity.

With our new system of communication, interruptions are shocking to Ruburt. I suggest that we end this evening's session.

("Good night, Seth.")

(End at 10:28. Jane was dissociated as usual. We did not like to see the session end so abruptly. Since interruptions have evidently become something of a hazard because of Jane's deeper trance state, we have decided to move the sessions into our

bedroom. We have room for a desk and chair there; but better yet, the room is isolated from our entrance by three doors. They add up to a soundproof barrier.

(Jane said that an interruption while she is in this new deeper state is like being doused with ice water. It is really shocking, and she does not want to go through it if it can be avoided.)

SESSION 137
MARCH 3, 1965 9 PM WEDNESDAY AS SCHEDULED

(This session was held in our bedroom. The doors were closed. The quiet was quite unusual. We were also free from the fear of interruptions. Evidently the new setting was also a little strange to Jane, for she did not begin speaking until 9:02.

(She sat down as usual, kept her eyes closed, and used a rather quiet voice. Her pace was average at the beginning, but became progressively slower as the session wore on.)

Good evening.

("Good evening, Seth.")

The new arrangement should work out well, now, although it would not have in the past.

Our last session was an extremely fruitful one, and much of that material will be important in our future discussions.

We will further consider this evening the nature of identities. In our earlier discussions concerning the nature of matter, we made it plain that each individual created any given material object, through use of the inner senses, and following certain rules which were mentioned.

Since any materialization is in effect a mediation between what we may call an ideal which is, by nature, of itself not materialized, and a practical working perceivable symbol of the ideal, each materialization must be composed of some camouflage elements. Within the physical field these perceivable symbols are composed of matter, which is a conglomeration of atoms and molecules. Each individual, creating, say, his version of any given chair, uses entirely different atoms and molecules in his subconscious construction of it.

He sees or perceives only his own construction. A rereading of sessions dealing with the nature of matter will help you here. The chair created then by any given individual, and perceived by him, is an identity in that it exists at any given time, without any exact duplication. Basically, for any duplication to appear, the exact atoms and molecules would have to be used, and this is obviously impossible.

The chair is an identity, and yet at no given moment is it the same chair, for already the atoms and molecules that compose it have changed, and been replaced by others. This process is explained thoroughly also in the mentioned previous sessions.

(Among others, see the 60th-65th sessions.)

There are obviously many kinds of identities. Now in our last session I told you that our imaginary sender "A" does not transmit a given thought. He does not even send an exact duplicate. Action, the very action of transmission, alters the nature, the electrical reality of the thought itself. This is an extremely important point.

Nor does the receiver receive the thought in the same condition. The thought, the original thought, is retained by A. A, however, forms a thought as nearly identical as his possibilities allow it to be. This he transmits to B. But B can't receive the thought in its present condition, for the act of receiving a thought also changes it. He forms a thought as nearly identical as possible, and interprets it.

Action can never be considered apart from that which is seemingly acted upon, for action becomes a part of structure. Action begins from within, and is a result of inner vitality inherent within all realities. Some action is always present. Action itself is not a thing alone. It is not an identity. Action is a dimension of existence.

I suggest your break.

(Break at 9:26. Jane was dissociated as usual. She resumed in the same quiet manner, but at an even slower rate, at 9:31.)

Action is a dimension arising out of existence.

It cannot be considered separately. It may appear in many guises, due to the nature of the particular reality of which it is part, and it involves much more than motion. Action may be considered also simply as the spontaneous nature of the inner vitality toward various expressive materializations.

There is no separate outside identity or force, such as "force;" the two words here are being used with different meanings. There is no separate force that causes action. All of these points are extremely important, and if I speak slowly it is to insure words as nearly correct as possible. Action is perceivable in some cases, and not in others.

Action is more like growth than force. It is a by-product of any reality, and a part of all reality. You should be able to see many implications here when you read this material over. Again, action involves more than movement, as you think of movement, for value fulfillment is action. A dream involves action. Not only the action within the dream, but the action of dreaming itself.

You may here get a glimmering of the connection between certain types of action and distance, as I have mentioned it briefly. There is always action within action, and any reality or any experience is instantaneous action. Motion is the type of action with which you are most familiar, but motion attains its importance within the physical field only because of your particular outer senses. For much action is entirely unperceived by you, particularly on a conscious level.

The continued existence of your physical body is determined by action, although consciously you are not aware of this most of the time. Action may not seem to be going any place. Action, by its nature, while part of every reality, necessarily changes that reality and forms from it a new reality. This should be obvious.

There will be much more in this material when you read it, than you may at first realize. Action approximates as nearly as possible that portion of inner vitality or energy which cannot be completely materialized within any camouflage, within any plane. Action itself cannot be directly (underlined) perceived for this reason. But is effects upon camouflage can often be perceived.

This material is leading up to some future discussions, and the nature of action will be most important. Action is as valid whether the act is conscious and voluntary, or whether it occurs within a dream or within a thought. It is as much a reality either way. Again, it is not an outside force. It arises from within the inner vitality of which all camouflage is composed. To some degree it is a result of inner vitality's attempt to completely express itself in materializations, and its inability to do so.

I suggest your break.

(Break at 9:56. Jane was dissociated as usual. She resumed in a very slow manner at 10:04.)

As yet your scientists and physicists have a very limited concept of action. Their laws concerning action and force will only apply within the physical field.

Action is basically electrical, but within your field only the most obvious forms of electrical action have been perceived. In this one respect your technology has let you down, but the electrical manifestations of which I speak could not even be searched for, or anticipated within your physical field, until the reality of man's psychic nature began to make itself known. And it is only now beginning to become apparent.

Discovery of these other electrical realities will explain much that previously could not be explained. All realities with which you will be concerned, and with which mankind is intimately concerned, are built up electrically. A dream is as valid an electrical reality as a lightning bolt, the difference being that the lightning bolt projects itself into your awareness through the outer senses.

We shall have to consider, later, color as it appears in dreams, but this is not the time for such a discussion. Identities exist within dreams also, and here the same nature of identities applies, as those given earlier. The laws of action also apply here in the dream reality.

(Jane now took a very long pause. She had paused many times while speaking since last break.)

Action is not affected by time as you know it. Action also takes place within the spacious present. You may, however, only perceive parts of action in your time breakdown. Ideally, psychological time experiences will allow you to perceive action more clearly and directly. The ego attempts to control action by standing apart from it. Any such division is arbitrary, and in no way affects the nature of action itself. All that changes is your perception of it.

By slowing down his perception of action, man imagines that he lengthens time. This of course is not the case. He merely succeeds in perceiving action as bits and pieces, and fights its flow. On the one hand action is indeed simultaneous, yet in it all action is contained, for it occurs within the unlimited spacious present. In dreams action is given more freedom, and allowed to flow in a less hampered fashion.

The result is an effect of <u>more</u> rather than less time, and in many cases the deepening of perspectives. Action does not occur along any given line or direction exclusively, though you may perceive its motion in only one direction. It is a portion of other dimensions. Here again consideration of dreams in terms of action should make this point fairly clear.

In dreams also, where no space as you know it exists, you have complete freedom of space. When the ego gives up its hold upon what it considers control of action, then as in dreams almost any action is possible. And when the ego gives up its claim of space in a dream, all space is available.

We may end the session. Or if you prefer you may take a break and I will continue.

("All right then, I guess we'll take a short break."

(Break at 10:26. Because Jane did not appear tired, I took the opportunity of adding a little material to tonight's very slow session. Jane was dissociated as usual, and said she was not aware of speaking so slowly. She spoke at a much faster rate, when she resumed at 10:34.)

Action <u>always</u> involves change.

Again, it may not involve motion in <u>terms</u> with which you usually refer. There are many kinds of motion, for example, that you do not perceive as motion within the physical field.

Action tampers with identity, yet were it not for action identity would be impossible. It may, here, sound like a contradiction; but to remain an identity, an identity must completely renew itself, and each renewal is indeed a termination. Yet without the termination no new action on the part of the identity would be possible. And without action no identity can be aware of its own existence.

Remember here, however, that by action we do not necessarily mean motion as you perceive it. Action is the breath of inner vitality, of which all materializations of any kind are composed. It represents, again, the relationship between unexpressed inner vitality and materialized vitality.

There is always an imbalance here that may of itself be termed action. It cannot be perceived as any one thing, for it is a relationship and a dimension. It can be perceived most directly, and with less distortion, in the dream state. For here it is allowed the freedom of itself. Here you have also the inner vitality that has not been materialized within the realm of material camouflage. You have the tendency of this inner vitality to materialize, and its inability to completely do so. In the dream state the tendency for this vitality to materialize meets with little resistance. Action within actions result, without physical space. Distances appear and are experienced as such. Action is much less limited. Rather, action itself is not less limited, but you can experience action with less limitations, for the ego which erects such limitations lets down its guard.

I would suggest that this session and the last session be read over most carefully. For again, they will be used as a basis for further material. My best and heartiest wishes, and a very pleasant good evening.

("Good night, Seth."

(End at 10:50. Jane was dissociated as usual.)

SESSION 138
MARCH 8, 1965 9 PM MONDAY AS SCHEDULED

(On September 26, 1964, Jane and I sent sessions 39-91 to the publisher, Frederick Fell, NY, NY. On February 16, 1965 we asked for the return of the material. On March 5, 1965, F. Fell wrote that the sessions were being carefully read.

(See pages 102, 107, 114, 125 and 136 for some predictions of sales concerning Jane's writings. Page 102 is a psy-time experiment of Jane's; the rest are statements made during sessions. They range from October 30, 1964 to November 11, 1964. The sessions are 102, 103, 104 and 106. The letter of February 16 to F. Fell was referred to by Seth in the 135th session.

(Jane has been studying psy-time regularly, and reports that almost as a matter of routine now she attains what she calls an "excellent state", involving a feeling of much lightness and separation from her physical self. She believes she is on the verge of being able to travel from her physical body, and is getting used to the idea very gradually. She often feels herself to be partially "out" of her body, but as yet always exercises control to avoid going too far, too fast.

(Once again we held the session in our back bedroom, and found it very peaceful and quiet behind closed doors. Jane had no idea of the material for the session. She spoke while sitting down and with her eyes closed. Her voice was quiet and clear throughout the session. Her rate of delivery was again quite slow; some of her pauses were long. She began speaking at 9:01.)

Good evening.

("Good evening, Seth.")

We will continue this evening in our discussion of identities and action.

Unfoldings continually occur, and all identities, with a few exceptions, contain within them also other identities, not duplicates. Our discussion in the past concerning gestalts should make this point clear. The frameworks and boundaries, the extents and limitations of identities, are not physical.

(For the material on psychic gestalts, see the 59th, 62nd, 81st, 96th and 128th sessions, among many others.)

Identities may be termed action which is conscious of itself. For the purposes of our discussion, the terms action and identity must be separated. However basically no such separation exists, for an identity is also a dimension of existence, action within action, an unfolding of action upon itself; and through this interweaving of action with itself, through this reaction, an identity is formed.

The reality of such an identity then exists <u>within</u> the action. The energy of the action, the workings of action within and upon itself, forms identity. There are other causes here that we will consider later. Yet although identity is formed from action, action and identity cannot be separated. You will remember our previous definition of action, for this will make this evening's discussion easier to understand.

(See the 137th session.)

Identity then, <u>is</u> action's effect upon itself. Without identities action would be meaningless, for there would be nothing upon which action could act. Action must, therefore, of its very nature, of itself and from its own workings, create identities. Again, action and identity cannot be separated. This applies from the most simple to the most complex.

Once more, action is not a force outside that acts upon matter. Action is, instead, the inside vitality of the inner universe. It is the dilemma between inner vitality's desire and impetus to completely materialize itself, and its inability to completely do so. This was also discussed briefly in sessions dealing with the first appearance of matter within the physical field.

(See the 60th session, among others, along with the aforementioned material on psychic gestalts, etc. See also the 137th session.)

Action is therefore a part of all structure. Here again is an apparent dilemma, an exquisite imbalance whose result is consciousness and existence. For consciousness and existence do not exist because of delicate balances, so much as they are made possible by lacks of balances, so richly creative there would be no reality as it is understood to be, if balance were ever maintained.

I spoke of this second dilemma. The first dilemma is that which exists when inner vitality struggles to completely materialize, though it cannot completely materialize. The reasons for its inability to completely materialize have been given in a previous session, and I will discuss the matter again at a later date.

(See the 133rd session among others.)

This first dilemma results in action, and from action's own working upon itself we have seen that identity was formed, and that these two are inseparable. We will discuss the second dilemma after your break. I suggest your break now.

(Break at 9:27. Jane was well dissociated. She said she believes she is farther "out" when the sessions are very slow, as tonight. The pauses could last for an hour as far as she is concerned or knows.

(Jane said some subjective feelings are difficult to put into words. While talking about action and identity, she had an inner perception of a whole concept, of some kind of inside visual sense of action without seeing any object. She said this description is as direct as she can make it. While experiencing such a thing, Jane said she is not conscious of being apart from the experience. Rather, she seems to be part of it.

(This appreciation of concepts is, according to Seth, the using of some of the inner senses, and he has mentioned this many times. He has called the 4th inner sense the conceptual sense, and began to develop upon this about a year ago, March 23, 1964, in the 37th session.

(Jane resumed dictation in the same slow and quiet manner at 9:37.)

I will shortly comment upon Ruburt's inside experience which you have just noted, as it is directly connected with the material now under discussion, and indeed is an example of the matter of which I have been speaking.

First we will speak of our second dilemma.

(Jane now took a very long pause.)

Action, having of itself, and because of its nature, formed identity, now also because of its nature would seem to destroy identity, since action must involve change. And any change would seem to threaten identity.

It is however a mistaken notion that identity is dependent upon stability. Identity, because of its characteristics, will continually seek stability, while stability is impossible. And this is our second dilemma.

It is this dilemma, precisely between identity's constant attempts to maintain stability, and action's inherent drive for change, that results in the imbalance, the exquisite creative by-product that is consciousness of self. We have a series of creative strains. Identity must seek stability while action must seek change, yet identity could not exist without change, without action, for it is the result of action, and not apart from it but a part of it.

Identities are never constant, as you yourselves are not the same consciously or unconsciously from one moment to another. Every action is a termination, as we discussed earlier. And yet without the termination, identity would cease to exist, for consciousness without action would cease to be conscious.

Consciousness therefore is not a thing in itself. It is a dimension of action. It is an almost miraculous state, made possible by what I choose to call a series of creative dilemmas.

I will add a word here, only to remind you once more to read those sessions regarding inner vitality and the initial appearance of physical matter, for that discussion will help you with this one.

(Jane took a very long pause.)

It should be fairly easy to understand now how the second dilemma evolved from the first. I have said that the second dilemma resulted in, and constantly results in, consciousness of self. Now. Consciousness of self is not the same thing as consciousness of ego self. Consciousness of self is still consciousness directly connected with action.

Ego consciousness is the result of our third dilemma.

I suggest your break.

(Break at 10:02. Jane reported she was as well dissociated as she has ever been. She used to be afraid that when she was "way out" she would be empty, but she has discovered the state is not like that at all.

(Groping for words, Jane explained that she feels as though she is "wresting" material [not implying a struggle however] from Seth or some other source with a deep part of her consciousness that is below her ego consciousness. She feels that just recently she has in some manner begun to experience concepts in a more involved, different dimension of consciousness. It is a state of perception she hadn't attained before, perhaps until as recently as the last session and this one.

(Indeed, Jane said, although she now thinks she was aware of this grasping of concepts in the last session, she did not mention it because her conscious awareness of it was so fleeting. Even now, she cannot say how long during the session itself she is involved in this manner. It is a very rich experience. Jane also believes the quiet back room we now use for the sessions is very helpful.

(She resumed in the same quiet and slow manner at 10:13.)

The ego is a state resulting from the third creative dilemma, which happens when consciousness of self attempts to separate itself from action.

Since this is obviously impossible, since no consciousness or identity can exist without action, because they are inseparable, we have our third dilemma.

A note of further explanation here. The difference between consciousness of self as a result of our second dilemma, and ego consciousness as a result of our third dilemma, should be made very clear.

Consciousness of self involves a consciousness of self within, amid, and as a part of action. Ego consciousness, on the other hand, involves a state in which consciousness of self attempts to divorce itself from action, an attempt on the part of consciousness to perceive action as an object. Here we see that ego consciousness, in this attempt, strives to perceive action not only as separate, but to perceive it in such a fashion that it appears to ego that action is not only separate from itself, that is separate from the ego, but that action is initiated by the ego, and a result rather than a cause of ego's own existence.

These three dilemmas represent three areas of reality within which inner reality, or inner vitality, can experience itself. And here we have also the reason, or one of the reasons why, inner vitality can never achieve complete materialization. The very action involved in vitality's attempt to materialize itself adds to the inner dimension of inner vitality.

Action basically can never complete itself. Inner vitality, materializing in any form whatsoever, at once multiplies the possibilities of further materialization. At the same time, because inner vitality is self-generating, only a minute fraction of inner vitality is needed to seed a whole universe.

Inner vitality attempts therefore to materialize itself completely, and yet because of its very nature, with each materialization it increases itself, making the attempt impossible. This is the basic dilemma, from which all types of reality spring. This of course leads us to the necessity for further discussion concerning the nature of inner vitality itself.

You may take a break, and I will continue, or you may end the session as you prefer.

("We'll take the break then."

(Break at 10:31. Jane was dissociated. She feels she has attained a visceral

knowledge of concepts, meaning that she feels them within. She also realized she was aware of what she dictated to me during the session, although not the word-for-word order of the material. She called this a psychological experience. She obtained the information one way, and passed it on to me another way.

(Jane also now realized that she had at her command the full contents of the 60th session, although again not in word-for-word order. This is the first time she has been aware of this experience. She did not feel tired, nor did she look it to me.

(She resumed in the same quiet voice, though at a somewhat faster pace, at 10:42.)

In line with the statement that action necessarily changes that which it acts upon (in parentheses: which is basically itself), then it follows that the action involved in these sessions changes the nature of the sessions.

I have spoken often of consciousness also as being merely the direction of focus. Action implies infinite possibilities of focus. Action never happens along a straight line, although at times you may perceive it in such a fashion.

(Seth-Jane had some material on consciousness and the direction of focus in the 94th session, among others.)

Action exists within action. There are dimensions of action from which all diversity arises. All individuality that seems to be swept away because one action seems to terminate another, such individuality is indeed the result of the dimensions of action.

I will discuss this more thoroughly. However, at present Ruburt is experiencing many more dimensions of action. He is experiencing action gestalts.

(Jane now took another very long pause.)

To some degree he becomes action. Like every other consciousness he is <u>always</u> action, but this evening he experienced to some degree action directly, without the usual attempt of the self to separate from action.

I mentioned in our last session that this material would be the basis for many future sessions, and so I will certainly make no attempt to cover the material this evening.

It is true, then, that another dimension has been added to our sessions, and I hope to instruct Ruburt along these lines of more direct perception as our sessions continue. I have told you that such developments could be expected. These are natural unfoldings, and such developments will occur according to their own nature, and in their own time. I expect that this latest one may involve of itself still another.

My fondest regards to you both. Our next session will continue along these lines. Good evening.

("Good night, Seth."

(End at 10:58. Jane was again well dissociated.

(She felt Seth could have continued, but did not push her. Jane feels now that these recent developments mean she has given some kind of consent to go along with the sessions into a deeper trance state, to step back farther from her ego. A step at a time, very cautiously.

(Jane thinks that tonight her ego didn't experience anything, although some part of her did. She thinks her ego gave at least tacit consent. And yet her ego assimilated the experience. She feels that this evening's session was good because of her experience with past sessions. She felt light at times during the session. At times she was not conscious of being in her body; yet neither was she conscious of being anyplace else.

(Jane said an interaction takes place between us that makes the sessions possible. It happens within her, she is the one doing the experiencing, yet I am also necessary. She has a feeling of effortlessness on her part, and is not at all afraid.)

SESSION 139
MARCH 10, 1965 9 PM WEDNESDAY AS SCHEDULED

(The session was held in our back room. Jane spoke while sitting down and with her eyes closed, in a low clear voice and with quite a few pauses. She had no idea of the material for the session before she began speaking. She began at 9:01.)

Good evening.

("Good evening, Seth.")

I am most pleased with our sessions of late.

Though both of you give much in time, energy and dedication and effort to our sessions, you will receive much more than you give. I tell you this now but you will know it without my telling you so, before too much of your time passes.

Action itself cannot be directly perceived. It cannot be seen nor touched. Its nature can never be examined from an objective viewpoint. The objective viewpoint will, at best, give but hints and signs. Action, to be examined in such a manner, would have to be stopped. You cannot tamper with action, not with the basic nature of action, because any such tampering causes it to change.

Action can be experienced directly, however, but only when no effort is made to tamper with it. It must be plunged into. Once more, action is not a function of structure. Action is inseparable from structure. Structure is action. Identities are action, as I have explained. Your idea of action as it occurs within dreams comes closer to the real nature of action than does your idea of muscular force. For in dreams the ego makes little attempt to impede action. Though in dreams you see or feel your arm move, your legs run, still the arm and the legs of the physical body may not move.

You cannot touch the action. You cannot touch the action, now, of your own arm as you write. You see the results of the action. You can feel effects of the action, but you cannot directly perceive the action itself. Since identity is dependent upon action, then it should be seen that it is impossible for an identity to attain stability, since total stability would destroy it.

We come here also to one of the other causes of the dreaming state, beside those of which we have spoken in the past. The mind, of itself and separated from the ego, must still be action, and therefore never still. Since action of any kind, being composed of inner vitality, must seek materialization, the dreams become the constructions of that dream universe of which, again, we have spoken. But action can never complete itself. The dream once begun continues, and the dream universe itself forms anew other constructions.

(Jane now took a very long pause.)

Here is an analogy. Imagine then the inner vitality being some cosmic sphere, but a sphere of more dimensions than you can imagine. Its motion could be called action, but this is deceptive because action is the basic nature of the sphere itself. Action is its composition. Action is that from which it is, therefore it moves, it acts outward. But all outwardness turns ultimately inward, and then again outward in all directions. And each inward action forms a new dimension that must, again, be thrust outward toward utilization.

Yet each outward thrust turns again inward; and of itself, because of the nature of action, is the creation of new action.

I suggest your break.

(Break at 9:28. Jane was well dissociated. On a reduced scale, she said, she was again aware of the concept of action without object, dealt with at some length in the notes to the last session.

(Jane now added the information that the concept of action reminded her of the "red chair episode." See the 104th session, page 126. Jane as Seth was talking about a sale of her work, which has not even yet taken place: "A woman might have something to do with one sale, through influence. An office with a modern red leather chair, small room, stories high, not at all elegant..." This session took place on November 4, 1964. After the session Jane was able to give a more detailed description of the red leather chair. For this see page 126.

(Jane resumed in the same quiet and slow manner at 9:36.)

Now. To continue with our analogy, this cosmic sphere which we have imagined would be a model for every action.

Because of its own nature it must act, yet no action can ever complete itself. The sphere would act in as many ways as were open to it, and every action changes that which is acted upon. Therefore each action would create a new reality. In such a manner are all fields activated.

If you will remember the three creative dilemmas discussed in our past session, you will see that we have here the reason for our self-perpetuating universe, the reason for termination within it, and the inherent necessity for change. If one thought were held forever, no other thoughts would follow, no action would follow, and no identity. In your own intimate psychological experience, in the intimate psychological experience of every individual within your race, you will find recognition of the thought.

Thought cannot be seen or touched. Thought is action. A thought within your field must vanish, be terminated, disappear, before it can be replaced by another. The identical thought will not return. A very similar thought may return, but the two thoughts will not be identical, although you may perceive them as identical. This is an error of perception.

No two actions are ever identical. We must mention here also a little regarding pulsations and the appearance or semblance of continuity. Every action involves a pulsation; you will recall we spoke of the pulsation of atoms and molecules.

(For some material on pulsation see the 60-65th sessions, among others.)

Now. I have just told you that one thought must terminate before another thought can appear. Although this might sound as if I am speaking in terms of continuity, I am not. The action of our imaginary sphere upon and within itself is simultaneous, and in all directions. All actions occur basically within the spacious present, but all action cannot be aware of itself except as it attempts further action, i.e., materializations.

While so materialized, action is aware of itself in two basic ways: through its innate comprehension of itself, and through a secondary, more limited but more focused perception of a self belonging to such a materialization. The innate comprehension of course involves us with the inner self. The secondary self belonging to the materialization gives us, within your field, the ego.

Action does not involve time as you know it. Action does not involve space as you know it. The semblance of continuity is merely the result of a choosing of some actions from an infinite number of simultaneous actions.

I suggest your break.

(Break at 10:03. Jane was well dissociated. She said she no longer fears running past regular break time every half-hour, as she once did, especially when she began to deliver the material sitting down.

(While speaking tonight, Jane said she has within a definite "feeling of a pulsation"; it might be likened to the perpetual opening and closing of a fist, she said,

with each opening and each closing creating a new reality, and thus moving itself perpetually on.

(Jane resumed at a somewhat faster pace at 10:11.)

I have several things I want to say.

First I want to make certain that action is understood, insofar as we have discussed it. Action is the inner vitality of all reality. It seeks to utilize itself in as many ways as possible. Its action, its attempts at outward materialization, however, must result in the creation of new inner vitality, for this is the stuff of which it is composed. And this new inner vitality will then seek materialization, and so the cycle is never completed.

The word materialization is used because it is applicable within your field. Nevertheless, as you know such materializations hardly all result in the construction of matter.

One word to you, Joseph. I do most honestly and sympathetically understand your own problems. The sessions and any work resulting from them will never detract from your painting, although upon occasion it may appear that you suffer timewise. The sessions have greatly increased your ability to use your inner visions and intuitions, and to free them so that they can be directed into your paintings.

(This, I can attest, is most certainly true.)

A note now concerning thought, as it is a form of action with which all men are familiar. Here you can see that your ego accepts thoughts as a part of its identity. Thought's actions are accepted by the ego, yet the ego seems to stand apart from them; and because of ego's nature it fears to plunge into the action of a thought. For it, the ego, has but recently pried itself from action, and so perceives action now as if action were a province of the ego, and not the other way around.

But ego's seeming independence from action is basically meaningless, since ego is also action, and can never be otherwise. Any such separation of action from itself only adds to the totality of action, in that it increases action's ability to perceive itself from as many viewpoints as possible. Perspectives represent action's action upon itself. Any one dimension must result in another dimension, for the action within any given dimension can never complete itself, but will continue.

(Jane now took a very long pause.)

I do not want to push Ruburt in any way. And to prevent the possibility of his attempting to take another step, now, I will close our session. My fondest regards to you both.

("Good night, Seth."

(End at 10:32. Jane was again well dissociated. She said she was quite aware of Seth's affection for us both at the end of the session.

(Jane said that at the end of the session she felt a definite, although not very strong, sensation of pulsation within her head. It was as though her head moved physically in a pecking motion, she said, demonstrating for me. Of course I had observed no such movement as I watched her while she dictated.

(Jane said she found herself then considering just sitting quietly in her chair, after the pulsation had manifested itself. It was as though the idea "came" to her, rather than anything she deliberately dreamed up herself. It was at this point, she believes, that Seth decided to end the session.)

SESSION 140
MARCH 15, 1965 9 PM MONDAY AS SCHEDULED

(On November 4, 1964, Jane unwittingly achieved a trance state, during psychological time, that lasted for several hours. See the 103rd session. On February 8, 1965, through a combination of reading certain material and another psy-time experiment, she again put herself into a dissociated state. Seth called this one a semi-trance. See the 130th session.

(Today Jane again achieved a prolonged state that was begun during a psy-time experiment. She usually tries her experiments from 11:30 to 12:00 noon; today when I arrived home at 12:15, she mentioned that her hands felt light. This is a sign Seth said to be alert for, in the 130th session. As we ate lunch Jane finally admitted that somehow she had failed to snap out of the desired state at the regular end of her psy-time period.

(The state appeared to be progressing slowly, as in the above two instances. Jane had a tendency to stay put, as she described it; that is, if she was sitting down she did not want to move, etc. She tried working. Although she could type she found herself making mistakes. I then suggested we go shopping and run our other errands earlier in the day than usual, thinking the physical activity would help.

(While we were out the state reached its peak, so to speak. Jane functioned all right, but felt as though she could "fly," as though her feet would not come back to earth. She had to concentrate on each task in order to see it through, be it shopping, walking, etc. She had no trouble speaking, and when we met a friend she talked quite animatedly.

(The state had lifted after supper. Both of us wanted to hold the session in order to learn what had happened. Jane felt she had unwittingly given herself improper suggestions during the experiment. She had also achieved a good state yes-

terday, Sunday; indeed, this was the first weekend during which she had tried psy-time, and she speculated that she had overdone it by experimenting for ten days in a row. I felt she had alerted her ego somehow, and that it was balking at going through the usual psy-time routine. This experience, Jane said, wasn't very enjoyable, whereas the one of February 8 had been great fun. Today she had felt "half dissolved."

(Jane did not feel overly tired as session time approached. She had no idea of the material beforehand. Once again we held the session in our small back room, and Jane spoke sitting down and with her eyes closed. Her manner was somewhat more animated than it has been lately, and her voice was deeper. She spoke at a normal rate.)

Good evening.

("Good evening, Seth.")

There is no real need to fret or worry concerning Ruburt's experiences of today. However, I am afraid that we must temporarily clip his wings, for indeed he would go too fast, too soon.

These things vary with personality; with Ruburt, while the ego cannot directly or immediately participate in such, shall we say excursions, it nevertheless must be kept up to date, and give consent. The concentration of energy on Ruburt's part is increasing. His capability for such <u>focus</u> is increasing.

(This reminded me that Jane recently remarked that when she tries psychological time now, it is the usual thing for her to achieve what she calls an "excellent" state.)

When such focus of energy quickens, it will often then propel itself onward, having built up momentum. This is what occurred today. The ego, in anger, would not allow the suggestions made to be carried out. The energy that would have been used in what you may call, for now, astral projection, was dammed up. The difficulty lay not necessarily in the particular suggestions given. The trouble was that the energy that <u>would</u> have been used to carry out the suggestions was dammed up by the ego.

The ego simply feared the sudden increase of concentrated energy, and fought on general principles. For a week Ruburt should try <u>no</u> outside experiments of <u>any</u> kind. After this period we shall see. But there will not be a return to his past routine for quite a while.

Other substitutes may prove adequate and effective, while offering more opportunity for checks and balances. The experience was exhausting for him, and such experiences are to be avoided.

Psychological experiments as whole present him with an excellent means of using his energies. However at times we must, as now, cut him down. There is a possibility that he will be tired tomorrow, although I hope not. Such a pulling of one part against the other is psychically fatiguing.

I did indeed contemplate putting off our session for this reason. I suggest now that you take your first break, as we will take it somewhat easy for tonight.

(Break at 9:18. Jane was not as well dissociated as usual, she said; running water somewhere in the house annoyed her while she was speaking. She said she did not feel tired and didn't want a short session. She resumed at a faster rate at 9:25.)

Tonight's session will indeed be a brief one.

Caution is always intelligent action in such matters. Ruburt has been in enough of a trance as it is. However, even the action of speaking for me this session is beneficial, as far as he is concerned. That is why I held the session to begin with.

I did indeed attempt to tell him to use caution, immediately after his last psychological time experiment. It is, of course, necessary that you learn through direct experience; and my warning you against various uncomfortable effects would not mean nearly as much if you did not, Ruburt, experience a few of them.

Were it not for my supervision, you could easily have experienced more of these. Our next session will cover much material, and I presume that Ruburt will be in much better condition to hold it.

(Jane now smiled. Her delivery had been rather quick and animated throughout the session, giving the impression that Seth was more than a little amused by the day's events.)

Perhaps we can lengthen it. However, I do not feel that Ruburt should remain in a trance state today, any longer than he already has. If our caution slows down the material, there is no need to worry about time. We have plenty of it.

Patience, my pigeons. And if Ruburt continues feeding his pigeons as he does, then they will all be as big as barns.

My most sincere wishes to you both. I feel your emotions also, at times. My fondness for you both grows. Remember, also, that Ruburt's abilities are extremely promising, which is why we must be careful when and how he uses them.

As for you, Joseph, you were extremely helpful to him, because of your presence and your understanding. I will bring our short session to its close.

("Good night, Seth."

(End at 9:26. Jane was not as well dissociated as she has been in recent sessions. Toward the end of the session she received a feeling, a concept, from Seth to the effect that she shouldn't feel bad at the short session. Seth, she said, thought it "cute," and "silly," that we should be so concerned, when we have all the time we need to get all

the information we want.)

SESSION 141
MARCH 17, 1965 9 PM WEDNESDAY AS SCHEDULED

(Yesterday, Tuesday, Jane suffered no apparent psychic fatigue from her prolonged trance state of last Monday. See the last session. She has of course tried no psychological time experiments since then.

(Jane and I had an interesting little adventure this evening. Jane walked to our neighborhood store while I set to work typing. Since she did not return as soon as usual, I became a little concerned. More time passed, and my concern increased. I continued typing. Then I found myself picking up my pen. On a scrap piece of paper I wrote down: "Jane is at the Piper's. 6:45 PM." The thought had come to me clearly.

(Jane returned at 7:05 PM, and confirmed my thought. She had indeed, on impulse, visited Bob and Mary Piper, friends of ours whom we had not seen for many months. She had not consciously been thinking of visiting them when she left me. She recalled mentioning my name often in conversation with Mary Piper, particularly to the effect that I might be concerned because she, Jane, did not return promptly. It will be recalled that the Pipers witnessed the 73rd session [See Volume 2].

(Once again the session was held in our back room, and Jane spoke sitting down and with her eyes closed. She does not wear her glasses at all during sessions now. Her voice was rather quiet, her delivery contained pauses as usual.)

Good evening.

("Good evening, Seth.")

The experience this evening concerned telepathic communication between the two of you.

We will continue our discussion concerning action and identities. I have said that identity is a part of action, and basically inseparable from action. Identity attempts to form meaningful patterns and relationships from action. Consciousness is action that perceives itself. The ego is action's attempt to stand off from itself.

Action may show itself as motion, but it is much more than motion in the terms which you usually use, and motion is but one small dimension within action's realm. All types of consciousness represent a different focus of energy's perception within itself. There is no past or future to action. All action is simultaneous. Identities, some identities and some forms of consciousness, particularly the ego, perceive a past or a present, but this is merely the result of the manner in which such identities and consciousnesses view available data.

A consciousness is characterized by the particular ways in which it views or perceives available action. It is characterized by the type of action which it is more likely to perceive. It is characterized by the pattern of perception itself.

Since action is not apart from structure, but is indeed the formulator of structure, then it is obvious that generally the type, nature, extent and scope of characteristic perception patterns of a consciousness will determine its physical structure, and not the other way around.

There is no one particular pattern followed by consciousness in its perception of itself as action. Mankind is more familiar with certain patterns and relatively unfamiliar with others. Any action changes itself. Nothing is constant. This rule is not forced upon action from some outside agency, but is simply a part of its own nature.

Action, you may say, is carried away by itself. Reality possibilities are endless. You are familiar with very small portions of reality. Your perception characteristics at this time dictate and limit the aspects of action that you can perceive. You can, however, focus very clearly on other aspects. And particular types of consciousnesses and identities are merely the result of action's formation into perception patterns with which it can focus upon certain aspects of itself.

It may be thought that such perception patterns or identities may be limited, but this is hardly the case. For without them, whole portions of reality would never be perceived. There is much here that will take us a long while to explain, for the line can theoretically be drawn anywhere in the formation of identities and consciousness. And herein lies your freedom.

I suggest your break.

(Break at 9:25. Jane was well dissociated, as usual. She did not remember the content of the material.

(She was aware, she said, of a pulsation within while dictating. It was definite but not very strong. Jane likened it to the vibration one might feel through the floor of a house, say from traffic passing close by. At break, now, she checked to see if this was the effect she had sensed, but it did not seem to be, although traffic does pass our house rather heavily at times.

(Jane also likened this feeling, which she called feeling a "certain way," to the rhythmical, not-too-strenuous opening and closing of a hand. Note also that she used this hand analogy to describe a pulsation in the 139th session. *See page 295.*

(Jane resumed in a voice a bit stronger at 9:31.)

The dimensions of consciousness are not arbitrary. They are not clearly drawn. They are open, they are action.

They are a dimension, as I mentioned. Consciousness is not one thing, therefore consciousness is not of itself limiting. Boundaries may be set up in terms of a self. A self is a gestalt of action perception patterns, which are formed together through attraction.

This, when it occurs, and this particular formation into a self may or may not occur, but when it occurs it is a result of our second previously mentioned dilemma. The self as you know it is in actuality a self plus an ego.

(For material on the three creative dilemmas of inner vitality, see the 138th session.)

The ego, if you recall, is self's attempt to set itself apart from action, and to see or perceive action as an object. The ego attempts to attain stability and dominance, and resents change. It seeks to limit certain perceptions, to block out many perceptions of which the self is knowledgeable. In this way limitations become fairly rigid.

An ego could be compared to a small dam in this respect. However, action constantly forms perceptual patterns in which it can view itself. Again, these patterns are formed one within the other, and they could be said to form that imaginary structure which we called the fifth dimension, so many sessions ago.

(See the 12th session, of January 2, 1964 [in Volume 1].)

A particular consciousness is a gestalt of these conceptual patterns; but there is nothing to prevent a consciousness from increasing itself by experiencing other conceptual patterns or patterns of perception. This assimilation would increase, not decrease, any given consciousness. We use, or you use, words merely as a convenience. We therefore say that a consciousness is a gestalt of patterns of perception, by which action knows itself. But the patterns of perceptions may grow, and the consciousness reach out. The consciousness has changed. It is no longer the same consciousness, since it has extended itself. Yet it is the same consciousness, on the other hand, because it is that which has extended itself. So words can confuse us.

A consciousness can be said to be a gestalt of patterns of perception then; and while the definition stands, it can only apply to any given consciousness for the breath of an instant, since the patterns of perception, being action, have already changed; and the particular consciousness of which we spoke, and which we tried to limit and pin down, is gone.

Yet as you can see, what it was when we spoke of it is still present in what it will by now have become. The ego, through its own nature and characteristics, attempts to limit such change, but it succeeds only in limiting itself by limiting its perceptions. It still must change, as is obvious. But it changes along certain lines, moving within certain patterns of perception which are characteristic of it.

It cannot maintain stability, for all its efforts, and it cannot in any way limit the self. <u>It</u>, the ego, merely does not perceive because it will not perceive those other perception patterns, and that larger scope with which the <u>whole</u> self is constantly involved.

I suggest your break.

(Break at 9:55. Jane said she was even more dissociated than during her first delivery. Seth, she said, felt very pleased with himself when he referred to the fifth dimension material; as if to say, "See, this material is why I couldn't explain any more of the fifth dimension to you, way back in the 12th session."

(Jane resumed in the same manner at 10:02.)

This material on action, and identities, and consciousness, will add much to your understanding of dreams, of the whole self, and of other facets of reality of which I will speak shortly.

The self, then, is not static by any means. It has no arbitrary boundaries. The term itself is used only for convenience; and indeed the concept of the self is a concept of the ego, which considers <u>it</u>self the self.

The self then, being action which has formed itself into gestalts of pattern perceptions, by which it knows itself, this self changes constantly. And <u>within</u> the range of effective perception, starting at any particular point, there are patterns within patterns. For convenience's sake we will have to limit our discussion to some degree, taking the self as a particular gestalt within, or composed of, a particular range of perception patterns; though in actuality the range may be smaller or larger at any given time.

The self then, unknown to the ego, perceives itself in a vast variety of experiences, and in, indeed, a vast number of realities. Each of these so-called realities, for one blends into the other, could be termed, or viewed as, a separate field. Each is therefore composed of the characteristic perception patterns that happen to lie within it, and these so-called minor fields could then be termed <u>other</u> selves, or minor selves, from the standpoint of the self that we are considering.

From the standpoint of these seemingly minor selves, however, the viewpoint would be entirely different. If we take for example a particular range of various perception patterns, for convenience's sake, and label them one self, then the various patterns within would appear to be minor selves forming the whole.

If however we changed our arbitrary boundary points, then the minor selves at either end would now seem to be portions of <u>other</u> selves. For practical purposes it may be said that a self is composed of a gestalt of perception patterns, within which a fairly constant efficiency is maintained. This is the best definition I can give you at this time.

As this effective field of perception patterns changes, so do the apparent boundaries of the practical self. It is imperative that we move away from the concept of a self as an indivisible, rigid and limited reality. Indeed, I hesitate almost to continue, since I do not want to confuse you.

The fact is, that any given self, as we have described the self, may have more than one ego, though these egos will not be aware of each other, even though operating simultaneously. You have information on the inner ego. There is also a dream ego, in that there is within that reality field a directive part of the self that is concerned with the construction of purpose and meaning.

You may take a break now, and if you prefer I will then continue briefly.

("Okay."

(Break at 10:25. Jane was again well dissociated. For material on the inner ego, the self-conscious self behind the self-conscious self, see the 28th session.

(Jane resumed in the same manner at 10:29.)

You can here indeed see where I am leading you.

The deeply and strongly dimensioned sphere I used as an analogy for an action, if you recall, for any portion of action; you can now indeed further imagine one entity being composed of such an action, with egos like many faces looking outward in all directions, and each perceiving vastly different fields of reality; looking inward and outward, backward and forward as it were, through and beyond. And yet each action, or entity, is a part of another, and is both within and without another. And none of it is meaningless, and yet in a basic manner all of it has the meaning that you give it.

And what meaning you give it is there, and part of it, since you who project the meaning are yourselves part of it. The inner self is, therefore, that inner portion of action which forms the egos, and the selves, through the dilemmas of which I have spoken.

Part of the self knows, and knows that it knows. Part of the self knows, and does not know it knows. The creative dilemmas of which I have spoken are the basis for all realities, and the heart of all meaning.

I will now close a most excellent session.

("Good night, Seth."

(End at 10:37. Jane was well dissociated as usual.

(She reported that at the end of the session she received a strong emotional feeling from Seth. It was directed toward us and was to this effect: "Through action, see how I'm a part of you both now, and how foolish it is of you to worry about identities, when all identities are so bound together."

(Jane quoted this to me immediately after the session ended, and I include it here without change. My point is to show that she did not have time to consciously tinker with the thought, to recompose it in a literary sense, etc.)

SESSION 142
MARCH 22, 1965 9 PM MONDAY AS SCHEDULED

(Neither Jane or I felt well, but we also didn't want to dispense with the session unless we had to, or Seth decided to.

(Jane began at 9:02. She spoke while sitting down and with her eyes closed, as usual, and in a quiet voice. Her delivery was broken by pauses, also as usual.)

Good evening.

("Good evening, Seth.")

If you will forgive me, you do not seem in the mood for much action this evening.

There are some points that should be mentioned concerning the definition of the self, or a self, as I gave it to you during our last session.

The definition of course stands. I merely would like to be sure that the correct interpretation is given to the definition. The self, or a self, is not any particular thing, as I told you. It is true that there are no boundaries to enclose it within safe confines, where it can be said, "Here is the self."

It is also true however that this lack of boundary allows for possibilities of development and expansion that would be impossible with a limited self. The self is not nebulous. Action changes itself, as we have described. Any self, therefore, is never the same self, but action contains within itself its own comprehension.

Because there is no time, as you think of time, we will not say that action retains a memory of all its previous actions or selves, for this would be misleading. Action is aware of itself in all of its spontaneous and simultaneous workings. The self that you are, in a basic sense, is the self that you were in past instances within this existence, the self or series of selves that you were in previous existences within the physical field, and also the myriad selves that you are now, in various perception experiences unknown to the ego.

Your self is all this, as well as the selves that you would call future selves. I wanted to make it clear that the self at any moment, while being no one thing, being indeed a series of simultaneous happenings, so to speak, is however far from meaningless, containing within it full inner comprehension of its various portions.

Once again I make the point, a seeming paradox: The self constantly changes. The self at any given moment is not the self that it was, yet it is that which it was, since it is that which changed.

It acts upon itself, being action. The inner self also changes, but it is also that which changes itself. We come now close to a definition finally for the entity, which cannot really be defined, because in your terms it escapes definition.

However, the entity can be partially defined as the sum of all the selves within a given range of action, the simultaneous totality which on the one hand then cannot yet exist, since action can never complete itself, yet representing that impetus forever frustrated on the part of action for complete materialization.

The blueprint is action's intent. The selves are action in progress toward this blueprint.

I suggest your break.

(Break at 9:27. Jane was well dissociated. She said she started "feeling things" again toward the end, when Seth began to talk about the entity. It was something concerning what it was like to be an entity, yet so vague it couldn't be put into words, really.

(Jane resumed in a slightly stronger voice, and a faster rate, at 9:35.)

There are selves within selves. Each self is interwound with all others, and yet each self, being composed of action, has within it the powers of action toward change, development, expansion, and the drive toward fulfillment.

Herein also lies the freedom of each self: not being limited. We have spoken in the past of capsule comprehension. It is indeed a characteristic of action, indivisible from action, equally interwoven within it.

Therefore each portion of action is aware of its simultaneous experience within all levels. Again, action carries itself along. Each self is therefore aware of its previous gestalt affiliations. Now. Identities may or may not have egos. An atom is an identity—

(Jane had been delivering the above paragraph with many pauses. I now began to sneeze, without warning. Jane sat quietly, waiting for me to stop. Her eyes remained closed, and she rocked back and forth gently. My sneezing certainly constituted an interruption of sorts, yet Jane's reaction to this was placid, her trance state unbroken. Had someone pounded on the door abruptly and broken Jane's state she would have been painfully aware of it.

(Many sessions have dealt with capsule comprehension, some of them being the 24th, 27th, 29th, 62nd-64th; the 87th and 131st particularly, as well as later ones.)

Do you want a break?

("No, I'm all right now.")

It is a self materialized in physical form. It is conscious of itself as belonging to action. The fact that it may be part of a larger gestalt self in no way belittles its own identity. It is conscious of the gestalts of which it is part.

It is materialized action, a self, part of other selves, as you are part of other selves. The intensity here is different. You, any human being, represent a capability, an attraction, an electrical field of great intensity that is capable of efficiently acting as a unit within the physical field.

You may also be part of a self operating within other fields, and operating also within another system of units. The inner self operates as a relay station, as a reference point for the various seemingly disconnected selves. It is only through contact with the inner self that knowledge of the whole self can be found.

The inner self could be called, then, the nucleus, the original point of action from which all the other emanations that form the whole self began. There is here you see no limitation upon the direction in which action may move, nor any limit to the dimensions which action may create.

The inner self would be then any given outthrust of original action outward, as explained earlier. This outthrust would, because of its nature, instantly send further outthrusts in as many directions as possible for it. And because it is action, and because no action can complete itself, and no action can completely materialize, then each outthrust or materialization would result in an inthrust; not into the original action from which it came, but into itself.

This gives us the creation of new inner selves, and all this is of electrical composition, and you should recall the information given you concerning the manner in which electrical fields are formed.

(See the 122nd-127th sessions.)

Again, this is no reason to feel that the individual is nothing, simply because he is one of so many. Action develops according to value fulfillment, and value fulfillment has little to do with size or numbers; and action turns to consciousness. Action working on itself becomes consciousness, and in speaking of consciousness I do not necessarily mean what you mean by the word.

Your concept of consciousness is fearful and limiting, and depends for its existence upon ignorance and barriers, barriers that divide parts of the self from others, from other parts of the self, and from other selves, and from experiences of the selves.

Value fulfillment opens the many eyes of the self to its various portions. It enables the self to expand, to join in a gestalt with other selves. It is only your ego which leads you to believe that such an expansion would result in a lessening of consciousness on the one hand, or an invasion of other selves on the other.

My dear friends, there is so much here to be said. There are freedoms available that mankind never uses, or very seldom uses.

I suggest your break.

(Break at 10:09. Jane was dissociated as usual. She did not remember the material, and delivered it with many pauses intermingled, some of them quite long. Both of us felt much better than when the session began.

(I might add here that my arbitrary designation of an average pause on Jane's

part might run to perhaps ten seconds. A long or very long pause thus would run twenty or thirty seconds. These are not rare. As said before, while in the state Jane is not aware of the pauses; as far as she is concerned they might as well not exist; or conversely, they could be an hour long.

(Jane resumed at a faster pace and in a louder voice at 10:22.)

And yet in another sense all selves are one self, in that all selves are action.

But action must attempt to materialize itself and fulfill itself completely. It cannot do so, and the result is the formation of many selves, that are a part of action, and formed from action; and therefore each self must continue in the creation of other selves.

Selves are not destroyed. They change into other selves, and yet are still themselves, for each new self is also the previous self which changed through acting upon itself. There will be no huge contraction of action back into itself, in those terms. There may very well be a conscious realization of each self, that it is a part of the original actionself.

Lest we forget, action is another word for inner vitality. Selves are formed also by effective ranges of comprehension, which may be expanded. They cannot be contracted, for action cannot wipe out comprehension of itself. The electrically coded data of which we have spoken cannot be removed, for an action cannot withdraw a previous action.

You understand that when I speak I am not saying that continuity, in terms of past and present, exists. I am using these terms merely for your convenience. An action can never negate itself. There may be counteraction, but no action can be wiped out.

The ego is indeed a necessity within the physical field at this point of man's development. The ego is in a state of becoming, however. The ego is not what it was centuries ago, and it will not be the same centuries from now. It, the ego, will not admit the change, but its refusal to admit change in no way stops change.

Efficient manipulation within the physical field will soon require that other portions of the self be utilized and recognized. In a manner of speaking, the ego can be compared to the nationalistic state of nations, necessary indeed for man's development, but already growing passé, and perhaps even mitigating against the survival of the species, where once it aided that survival.

The worldwide view of man as a species, worldwide brotherhood, in no way hampers or endangers the individual man, and in no way endangers nations, but will represent one of the main hopes of mankind, without which no nations will endure.

In like manner, when the ego concept is discarded as a concept, as the concept of nationalism will be discarded, so the individual self will not lose but gain. The individual self will expand, as the individual man will be capable of expanding when the old idea of nationalism is finally overthrown, and he can be benefited through learning of, and cooperation with, other men as brothers upon your planet.

But as it is not wise to dispense with the idea of nationalism without gradual growths of understanding and preparation, and while the idea of nationalism cannot suddenly be dispensed with, so also the ego cannot be, and will not be, overthrown overnight; and even when it is finally left behind, it will still be used as a handy reference point; and through all this the self will not lose but gain, for all expansion outward, and expansion inward is a gain, and all boundaries, whether inward or outward, are hampering and limiting. Basically, the self is not limited. The self does not need imaginary fences to protect its privacy, or its safety or its solitude. Only the ego is afraid of challenge, and therefore speaks of such limiting safety.

If the self were the ego then indeed such precepts would be necessary, but the ego is a small part of the self. Necessary indeed, still, but less necessary than it once was.

I suggest your break. Or if you prefer we will end our session.

("All right then, we'll end the session."

(End at 10:45. Jane was well dissociated. This last delivery was much more rapid. Jane said she felt carried away, as she had been in the Father Trainor episode. See pages 261-63. This took place on February 11, 1965. During this experiment, while reading some poetry aloud that the now-dead Father Trainor had often read to her when she was in high school, Jane's voice had taken on an enormous male volume and strength. To me it had sounded alien. Jane said it was Father Trainor's voice, at times, or a close approximation. I can only say it was not the Seth voice; I had never known Father Trainor.

(Jane said that tonight her voice felt as though it was being projected out of her as she dictated, that she was swept along by energy other than her own, "like a sail filled with wind." The voice was all around her, she said, yet she had no sense of invasion. She was very pleased at recognizing the feeling of the Father Trainor episode. She felt supported, like flying, yet not disembodied.

(Jane also said she wasn't sure the session was over. I had asked for its end in order to spare her fatigue, as a matter of routine. She barely had time to give me the above information, when she sat down again, resumed her trance state, and began dictating. 10:48.)

We will close here this evening's session, since I believe you need your rest. However, I will have something to say Wednesday concerning Ruburt's experience this evening. He is indeed doing very well.

My fondest regards to you both.

("Good night, Seth."

(End at 10:49. Jane again was well dissociated, and her voice was, briefly, loud and strong. She has manifested few voice changes since she began to speak while seated, and with her eyes closed.

(Jane said that as soon as she resumed her seat she felt carried away. She entered the state more rapidly than she would like. Also, the end came so quickly that she found herself groping briefly, in an effort to "put herself together again." The experience made her uneasy.

(Jane said she believes Seth is using these experiences, within the experience of the session itself, as a compensation for the psychological time experiments he has requested her to abandon for a while. It will be remembered that in the 140th session Seth stated that at times Jane would advance "too fast, too soon", with her own experiments. She speculated that these recent experiments within experiences were Seth's ideas re a more controlled approach.)

SESSION 143
APRIL 5, 1965 9 PM MONDAY AS SCHEDULED

(Because of illness on my part this is our first session since March 22; thus we missed the regularly scheduled sessions of March 24, March 29 and March 31. This is the longest gap in the flow of the material since the sessions began on December 2, 1963. Both of us were eager to resume. Jane remarked last night that the enforced layoff was making her rather nervous. It was, she said, the same kind of nervousness she used to experience before each session, during the early months.

(Jane has not been experimenting with psychological time since Seth suggested she stop at the time of her prolonged trance state of March 15.

(Lying in bed in a drowsy state last night, Jane received the following items, she believes from Seth. She woke me to tell me about them:

(About my illness: "Some things you have to work out for yourself."

(Also about my illness: Seth doesn't like to give warnings of future events, particularly when they may be only strong possibilities, yet avoidable. In these cases the suggestion itself could, under some conditions, bring the events about.

(About the subconscious: According to Freud the subconscious is often held to blame for present ego difficulties. This is not so in many cases—the real trouble being that the present ego did not assimilate the subconscious experience. Seth has discussed Freud and Jung to some extent, in the 83rd and 119th sessions, among others.

(Once again the session was held in our secluded back room. Jane spoke while sitting down, and with her eyes closed. She does not wear her glasses at all during sessions now. Her voice was quiet, her initial pace rather slow. Her delivery speeded up as the session progressed, and her voice became somewhat louder.)

Good evening.

("Good evening, Seth.")

I did indeed communicate briefly with Ruburt last evening. He reported my words correctly.

In regard to your illness, no healing of any sort can ever take place without inner understanding and psychic comprehension. My interests are those of an educator. Any healing brought about from the outside may be advantageous in the short run, and I would be only too willing to help in a situation involving illness, particularly of a serious variety, even though the advantages of my help would be surface ones.

I realize that such surface help at times could be most desirable. Basically however in your case the illness was not serious, and the advantage that you would derive from my help in a healing capacity would have been outweighed entirely by several disadvantages that are almost always present, in the case of healing that does not originate from inner comprehension.

(Seth has discussed this inner comprehension and physical illness in the 98th, 99th and 120th sessions, among others.)

I would have been removing the problem from you, and in this instance depriving you of the opportunity of solving it, and therefore of adding to your own energies and abilities. As it was, your illness was shorter by several times than it would have been had it occurred last year, and certainly much shorter than it would have been were it not for the understanding that you have derived from these sessions.

I certainly do not mean to sound less than compassionate. My bedside manner may leave much to be desired, and my potions and pills are not those that come in a doctor's black bag.

However, I can indeed do more, in that my pills are pills of knowledge, which are indeed, my friends, somewhat difficult to digest. But you do not mind.

("No.")

(Jane delivered the above paragraph with a broad smile.)

The basic source of your difficulty was not new. It did not even, except superficially, represent a dangerous lapse or relapse on your part, into those truly dangerous and quite disastrous negative battles of thoughts, which eventually in any individual can and often do lead the integrated self into annihilation.

The illness did represent, however, a needed warning, materialized into physical reality as illness. A warning that after all there had been a recent tendency on your part, though slight, to slide into negative thinking. The illness was meant to bring you up short, to make you think.

It was no coincidence, however, that you plunged into reading the New York papers during your stay in bed. Not that it is intended that you should close your eyes to world events, but that in your particular case there are times when, to you, such concentration upon world evils becomes extremely unwholesome.

Your reactions at such times are not good for yourself, and your reactions are not good at such times for the conditions which bring them about. Such reactions actually worsen the conditions that you would change. I am not suggesting that you adopt a bland, idiotic, male Pollyanna smile, nor that you shout love, prosperity and health from the rooftops while the world below is steeped in poverty and ignorance.

However it is your duty, and the duty of every individual insofar as it is within his power, to maintain his own psychic health and vitality; according to the strength of this vitality he will protect himself and others. Negative expectations, far from protecting either the individual or those with whom he comes in contact, will actually, to a greater or lesser degree, turn as destructive as any epidemic.

I suggest your break. How do you like my pill?

("Very good.")

(Break at 9:26. Jane was dissociated as usual; that is, she had achieved a good state. She smiled as she ended the monologue.

(I spent eight or nine days in bed, the victim of what is generally called a virus. At no time however did I blame a virus, feeling that the real cause was psychic, thus permitting the virus to come to the fore. I was somewhat embarrassed at having "goofed" psychically. As time passed, and while I pored over several daily New York City newspapers plus Elmira's daily paper, I came to realize to a small extent that poor expectations on my part had much to do with my falling ill.

(I finally reached the point where I told Jane, the day before this session was due, that I had decided to stop reading the New York papers so thoroughly. I found it a sad experience to read about the race situation, Viet Nam, the conditions of life and crime in New York City, etc., although of course I realized that much of this news meant something was being done about some urgent problems.

(For some other examples of the psychic power of negative expectations, see the 9th, 15th and 17th sessions, involving Jane and me at York Beach, Maine. Also see the 17th and 66th sessions for material on the death of our dog, Mischa.

(Jane had begun the session rather slowly and softly. As it progressed her pace speeded up and her voice acquired more volume. She resumed in this manner at 9:34.)

Such newspapers as you read do a definite service, that should not be overlooked or thoughtlessly condemned.

They definitely open the eyes of many who would otherwise pay no attention. Particularly in the race question they have performed a great psychic service, for they have aroused deep, creative, constructive emotions on the part of people who otherwise would not have been involved. And these constructive energies have helped change the situation for the better.

Such dire conditions cannot be pretended out of human existence, nor should they be. But in your case, you *are* aware of man's inhumanity to man. It is well that you are, but you must not allow this knowledge to weigh like a mountain upon your being, so that *you* are pinned under and your energies sucked away. This is the danger for which you must be alerted.

I am aware that you would prefer that I continue with my discussion upon action. But indeed we have here quite a practical application, and I intend to go into other earlier symptoms that should have, and did not, give you warning.

Ruburt sensed one in particular, and did indeed react in a manner that you found annoying. Ruburt's feelings and lack of action as far as the publishing house was concerned left much to be desired, and in time his lack of action would have caused an unpleasant reaction on his own part. However he correctly, if subconsciously, interpreted your attitude toward the publishing house as being basically dangerous to you. And so it was.

Note: The attitude was partially justified, but the portion that was not justified was a symptom of a new appearance of negative thought on your part. And *because* such negativism is a psychic problem to *you*, it was potentially dangerous.

Your attitude was, in some manner, more realistic than Ruburt's, and yet his attitude was the healthier. Both of you went too far in opposite directions, as is characteristic of your own natures: you are *sometimes* inclined, and underline sometimes, to be overly pessimistic; and Ruburt is sometimes inclined to be not overly optimistic but overly docile, as far as his connections with the outside world are concerned.

His nature is independent, but the independence is blunted when he is not sure of what he is dealing with. You felt his reaction to your attitude strongly, and you should have questioned yourself at that point. Ruburt was able to counteract the temporary but overall negative storm by his own creative energies, and focus strongly to protect you both.

He would not have been able to do this a year ago. You have learned something from this illness, and you will be stronger for it, but you would not have learned it if it had not run its course, and if you had not faced the reason behind it.

You of all people should realize that when valid concern for world problems turns into an obsession with world injustices that wipes out all, or threatens to wipe out all personal enjoyment, then trouble is on the way. For enjoyment is a weapon. The man who is capable of joy is capable, to a large extent, of changing his world. Joy is not a weak spineless idiot either. Its backbone is stronger than bitterness.

Joy is the muscle of action, and without it there would be no action. If I speak strongly to you at times, it is because this tendency, while <u>much less</u> now than formerly, must be kept very well in control, Joseph.

Basically this concern for human welfare is indeed virtuous, but overindulged in it becomes loaded with possibilities that could be most unfortunate. You knew I was going to light into you this evening, as Ruburt would say. What I want, here, is the balance. Neither plunge yourself into the ignorance, doubts and injustices, so that you can see nothing else, nor close your eyes to them. <u>But there must be a place within you where these do not exist</u>, or the freedom of the inner self will be hampered, as far as its connection with the ego is concerned. Your deep consideration for human problems has indeed helped lead you to these sessions.

I suggest your break.

(Break at 10:01. Jane was dissociated as usual. The pace of the dialogue had been quite fast, and Jane's voice had acquired some volume. She resumed at the same fast rate, although in a quieter voice, at 10:12.)

There is one matter that I should clear up.

There was a possibility at one time, for a particular period of time, when for various reasons your Miss Callahan was in <u>danger</u> of falling down the front flight of stairs. For several reasons the possibility was strongest when she went for the mail.

Her anxiety is high upon such occasions. I suggested that Ruburt bring up the mail for her, to cover that period of possibility. He did so. The fall did not occur. But the strong possibility for it did exist.

I know that you wanted me to explain. I am extremely cautious as far as giving warnings, since suggestion could play a part in bringing about the event which looms, merely as an unfortunate possibility, but not definitely as an actuality.

(Just before tonight's session I told Jane I hoped Seth would clear this matter

up. See the 133rd and the 135th sessions. The 133rd session also contains a list of previous sessions in which Seth has dealt with Miss Callahan to varying degrees. Miss Callahan, a retired schoolteacher, was also acquainted with Frank Watts. It was Jane's initial contact with the Frank Watts personality, through the Ouija board, that led to these sessions. F. Watts has been dead perhaps twenty years, and is one of the personalities making up the Seth entity.

(Also see the first page of this session for material on the power of suggestion. For other material on suggestion and related subjects like illness, see the 68th, 98th, 99th & 120th sessions.)

There is much to be said along these lines, but you still need preparation, in terms of information, before you can benefit as much as you should. We come here for example into many questions. The future, in your terms, is not foreordained, and is at no moment fixed.

It is true that what will occur, in your terms, has already occurred in other terms, and that it is possible to perceive beyond your now into your so-called future. But here I am very careful of tampering, for tampering with "your" present tampers with "your" future. I suggest that in the last sentence you place the word your in quotes.

(See the 134th-137th sessions for some material on time travel.)

When we have discussed further the nature of action, then we can delve further into these questions, for they involve thrusts of action, and are intimately connected with energy's action upon itself.

I am going to suggest also that Ruburt continue with the procedure as far as psychological time is concerned, that is, that he lets it go until I tell him otherwise. The experience, the subjective experience, of the last session, on Ruburt's part, was meant as a practical demonstration of the limitless self. I am very pleased that we did so well with it, and various other such controlled experiments can be expected in the future.

(See page 308.)

The conditions of our sessions allow us, on the one hand, more freedom, and on the other hand more control. Also they add to the value of the sessions themselves. We will have much more to say concerning the limitless self, in connection with action.

The material, our material, will indeed be published. A firm but not too impatient attitude is the most beneficial on your parts.

At any time that you may wish it, you can indeed make up sessions. However, I will not suggest it. It is up to you.

(This information came through, I presume, because earlier I had been joking with Jane about making up the sessions we had missed. I doubt if it is possible; our

daily routine is busy enough now.

(Jane now gave a broad smile.)

You have taken your medicine very well this evening.

A note I wanted to add: It was indeed no coincidence either that your house was so filled with guests when you became ill. Your Sonja was drawn by your own inner vehemence. It was very well that she did not spend more time with you.

Ruburt, without realizing it, entered into psychic swordplay with her, for her own chronic and critical inner bitterness sought out your own. On some other occasion I will discuss this particular character with you, for there is much to be learned here.

The others did not come for the same reason, although your illness was the cause of their visits. John, your Philip, was definitely called as a reinforcement, and he responded. The other two visitors were neutral psychically. I will say more of this at a later date, when it will be pertinent to another discussion.

My heartiest regards for your health. You may here take a break; or, considering your convalescence, I will end the session.

("We'll take a short break, then."

(Break at 10:36. Jane was well dissociated. Since we had missed three sessions, I thought we could continue a little longer.

(Our host of visitors during my illness was another subject we'd hoped Seth would discuss this evening. From March 24 to April 2, Jane and I received a total of 21 visits from 16 different individuals. Of these 16, 7 had witnessed sessions. Some of the visits lasted for hours and left Jane very tired.

(Since the visitors began to appear on the first day I was in bed and within a matter of hours, Jane and I soon thought it more than coincidence. We had 4 visitors the first day, 3 the second day, 5 the third day, 4 the fourth day, etc. Moreover two of our first four visitors, Sonja Carlson and Louis D'Andreano, were from out of town.

(Sonja bought a painting from me on November 18, 1964, and is mentioned by Seth in the 108th session of that date. Louis witnessed the 89th session, held in Rochester, NY, and was also discussed by Seth in the 90th session. Another visitor that first day was Jim Beckett, who witnessed the 47th and 49th sessions. Thus Jim and Louis were the two neutral visitors referred to by Seth.

(Philip of course is the entity name for John Bradley, who has witnessed several sessions. While visiting us on the second day of my illness, John said that events transpiring within the drug firm he represents, Searle, appear to bear out predictions made by Seth some time ago. Seth had mentioned a time limit of several years for some of these predictions to work themselves out, and counseled patience on John's

part. See the 37th session, of March 23, 1964, and the 70th session, of July 13, 1964, among others.

(My younger brother, William Richard, also from Rochester, NY, was a visitor on March 28. He is custodian of the second carbon of these sessions, and witnessed the 89th session. Another visitor was Bill Macdonnel, entity name Mark, and several times a witness. On file I have a complete record of the 21 visits Jane and I received.

(Jane now resumed at an average rate of speed at 10:43.)

They were called by your illness for various reasons.

The two neutral parties came earnestly, however, with a subconscious desire to help. They were drawn by your predicament, and psychically aware enough to be sensitive to it. However, they were not able to rally any noticeable psychic force of their own.

Had the conditions been different, or the situation worse, they would have so rallied. Philip added his constructive energy to Ruburt's, in Ruburt's attempt to counter your inner vehemence, and you helped yourself to the admittedly small degree of which you were capable at the time.

Sonja, all unwittingly, came to prey upon the situation. She herself is in desperate need of help. Ruburt sensed this, and if his own abilities had not been so strong, Ruburt would have ended up in a most unfortunate situation; for he attempted, for a time, to counter the wholesale destructive tendencies open in your house.

He did have some support from you, for you see you were far from powerless this time. The other assorted company during the week was most beneficial indeed. From this standpoint you were indeed not alone, and it was not a time for you to be alone, although you may have wished for privacy.

I could indeed continue now along other lines. However I think it best that you retire for the evening. I did not neglect you, either, while you were ill, but the circumstances did not warrant a direct action on my part. I was here. I kept an inquiring, sometimes severe, sometimes amused, sometimes concerned, but always watchful eye upon the household.

And now my best regards to you both. I am glad that we resume our sessions once again. Ruburt had a vacation of sorts, but I will see that there is action enough for him now.

("Good night, Seth."

(End at 10:58. Jane was well dissociated. She said she retained an awareness of the gist of the material given during her first monologue, but that in successive monologues she lost all idea of what she had said.

(It might be noted that now her eyes open quite easily at break time and at the

end of the session. When she first began to speak while seated, and with her eyes closed, she had difficulty opening her eyes.

(Jane had told me that during my illness she hadn't felt Seth around. There were times during my illness when I had an actual feeling of disbelief at the steady parade of visitors. I did not see them all. I soon became aware that I felt better after talking to the ones I did see, and once I realized this I rather deliberately tried to capitalize upon this apparent exchange of energy. Sonja Carlson visited us twice; almost at once I understood the negative character of her thoughts, and decided not to let it bother me. I was concerned about Jane bearing the brunt of this, however.)

SESSION 144
APRIL 7, 1965 9 PM WEDNESDAY AS SCHEDULED

(Mrs. Lorraine Shafer witnessed tonight's session. She was introduced to the Seth material by John Bradley, who has witnessed several sessions and read much of the material himself. Lorraine took her own shorthand notes of the material. She has also offered to do some typing for Jane and me.

(Since Jane began to achieve a deeper trance state, and to speak while sitting down and with her eyes closed, she has become much more sensitive to interruptions. For this reason we have been holding recent sessions in a protected back room. This room is too small to hold three people comfortably however, so for the session we moved back out to the living room. Most of the sessions have been held there. We chanced interruptions but none developed.

(Jane was a little nervous before 9 PM. Once again she spoke while sitting down and with her eyes closed, and in a voice somewhat stronger and faster than usual.)

Good evening.

("Good evening, Seth.")

May I wish you all a pleasant evening, and I hereby acknowledge the presence of our guest.

There will be more later to follow, concerning the predicament in which <u>you</u> found yourself, Joseph. However, we will save it for another time.

The information which Ruburt learned this morning is correct in essence, and you will see that the data I gave you many sessions back is coming to pass.

(See Volume 2, page 158 of the 63rd session, of June 17, 1964. I doubt if this data would be entered on the record had not Seth mentioned it without prompting. It concerns the husband of a friend of Jane's, and an involvement with narcotics. The couple no longer live in Elmira. Several Elmirans keep well informed concerning

them, and one Elmiran happens to work in the same out-of-state town in which they live.

(This morning Jane learned through this individual that the husband in question has been involved with narcotics, to the extent that it was treated in the newspapers at the new location. Jane and I have not seen these published reports.

(A companion prediction to this one, made by Seth at the same time and concerning the outbreak of a narcotics investigation in the Elmira area, within three months, developed as predicted.)

I have told you that action cannot deny itself. An action cannot be recalled, that is, called back out of existence. Once an action has begun, it will attempt completion. An action may be recalled in terms of <u>memory</u>, but it cannot be taken back, or denied or undone.

Your idea of consequences is derived from this fact. Nevertheless your idea of consequences takes into consideration only one small element of any given action. You perceive, in other words, only that part of an action which is projected into your own physical field, and this element you call the natural consequence of the original act.

You perceive however but one flicker, one small dimension of any given action as a rule. As in the case of your own illness, Joseph, you perceived the physical effect of the mental action, which was but a small portion of the event.

The entity name of our visitor is Marleno.

(Seth/Jane obligingly spelled out the name at my request.)

We find in the present personality knots, whereby action is not allowed freedom, particularly in terms of expansion. There is strong concentrated energy turned inward, but it is not turned inward far enough to be effective.

It is turned inward mainly in terms of the ego. There is awareness here of the inner self, but the main energy is knotted in tensions and exhaustions. At the same time the personality does not refresh its energies. If the energies of the personality were turned further inward, or on the other hand turned further <u>outward</u> toward the outside world, there would be an improvement in terms of additional, recharged energy.

The knot, or the main concentration of focus, in ego concern, prevents true refreshment, either through the inner self or from the outer world. The knot of energies is indeed caused by fear, and it <u>can</u> be dissolved. The knotted energies amount to a frozen immobility, where nothing is lost, but neither is anything gained.

The situation here can be eased, and it is within the ability of the present personality to do so. There is an inner generosity and a psychic, if you will forgive the word, sensitivity, that will be of great benefit to the personality. There is also, and I believe always has been, the desire on the part of the personality to untie or dissolve this knot of immobilized energy.

At one time the personality was involved with very early paper manufacturing, in I believe Belgium. The personality was then a male. The personality has always been involved with communication in one form or another in various lives.

Until this life the communications involved have been in outward manifestation. This time there is on the part of the personality an awareness of inner realities, of which the personality was not before concerned with. There is also a bewilderment, since in the past communication was easy. Now there is awareness of that which is not easy to communicate.

There is now an earnest desire to travel inward, but in the past the personality was involved with outward communication. The personality will always have communication as a main aspect. Nevertheless this life begins a new phase, where the communication involved will be, indeed, of a different variety. The knot of energy, among other things, quite a few other things, is caused by the temporary inability to change the focus of interests from outward to inward methods of communication.

I am not suggesting here that this individual turn all focus away from the outer world, far from it. I am saying that a release is necessary, and then a balance will be maintained.

In the past lives, again, desire for communication was strong. It is strong now. However, it is as if the personality stands before another door, where the abilities for communication can turn the knob, but he will not turn the knob. The personality stands in an anteroom, with all his knotted energies, in indecision, and will not open the door leading inward, and will not turn in the other direction, in the direction from which he has come, to the door that leads outward. It is the indecision here that is important.

Were the personality content between the two doors, there would for the present be little problems. I am not saying that the individual is ready to plunge headlong into a world of energetic psychic endeavor at this time, either. I am merely saying that the personality only now is discovering the inner reality of which so many are ignorant.

I suggest your break.

(Break at 9:34. Jane was dissociated as usual. Lorraine told us that her first name was Meredith, and that her mother in naming her Meredith Lorraine intended to call her Mary Lou, but never did so. There is a similarity here to the entity name, Marleno.

(Lorraine thought the last sentence of the monologue was significant to her. She

confirmed that she has been interested in communication and related work. One of her past jobs involved writing copy for a radio station.

(Jane resumed in a slower manner and a somewhat deeper voice at 9:45.)

There was a village in the southern part of France. 1230. The personality was a primitive mason. A crib turns over, a child is killed. 1645. Belgium. The personality died in infancy. Later the personality returns to Belgium after a lapse of fifteen years. Also a drummer boy in a civil war. There has been trouble with a hand, also an ear. At times a throat difficulty.

(After the session Lorraine told us she has had no throat, ear or hand difficulty.)

In general in the present, the personality should relate firmly with outer reality, and also come to grips with the whole self. There should be moderation, but a moderation that allows for spontaneity and a disciplined program of inner evaluations. The personality has been twice a man, once a woman, and once a female child who did not reach adulthood.

The name Kronski was a family name at one time.

(Again, Seth spelled out the name. Lorraine said it had no meaning for her.)

Now. Action is something like a mirror which reflects itself. In one action, basically, we can see all actions, and through one action we can reach the reality of all actions.

The apparent dimensions within action is caused by the separation of which we spoke, when action attempts to step aside from itself. Dreams are as much action as the movement of a muscle, and the movement of a muscle is indeed as sleeplike as any dream.

We are all within action. We are of it. To be outside of it is impossible. Choice however is limitless within it. In whichever direction we focus our abilities and energies, we seem to see new action, but it is merely our focus which has changed; and in changing, has formed new action.

For the benefit of our visitor, let me say that action is the vitality of the universe from which all realties spring. This will make our discussion simpler. Again, no action may be withdrawn. Nothing is motionless. Therefore, when our visitor hesitates between his two doors, he is not motionless, but uses as much energy in indecision as should be expended in purposeful direction.

Action cannot be dammed up, for it becomes explosive. There are many balances to be maintained. The dream world of which we have spoken so often is also action, and as such it affects all other action. It is not apart from your so-called physical universe, for the dream universe, through its connection with the inner self, also helps to construct physical matter—and this is no trifling matter.

It matters more than you know, and I will tell you what the matter is. How do you like that play on words, Joseph?

(Jane gestured and smiled broadly, turning her head toward me even though her eyes remained closed.

("It's beautiful.")

I suspect some hint of sarcasm.

("Oh no."

(Seth has dealt with dreams in many sessions. See the 44th, the 92nd-101st and the 122nd-131st sessions, among others.)

But after the lecture that you took from me at our last session I do not blame you, as long as it is not carried too far.

Now. As you know, among other things dreams reflect inner expectation. For our visitor's edification, dreams are created by each individual, and given actual molecular structure and reality, within a different field than the one with which you are usually familiar.

Dreams cannot be taken, however, as accurate descriptions of inner expectation, since too many other elements are involved.

Nevertheless, the actual individual dream world created by each individual will bear a close resemblance to the physical environment which is also created by the individual. And here we come to a subject that I mentioned briefly the other evening, and even now we will but touch upon it.

There is much involved. The individual, any individual, may construct many possibilities in the dream world. Having problems in the physical world, he may attempt to solve them through working them out on a dream basis, trying various solutions.

These possibilities then become actualities within the dream field. They exist as surely as they would if he acted in the same manner within the physical field. They are not myths, they are not imaginary, they do not vanish. They exist as reality within another field of actuality.

Consciously our individual may not know what he has done. Consciously he may not even know the problems which beset him, but which he has worked out on a subconscious level. But he will have chosen his solution, <u>and in the physical world an event will shortly occur</u> which will be close to a duplicate to <u>one</u> of those dreams which he has created.

When he dreamed the dream, and chose this possibility as the solution to his problems, he had already subconsciously chosen which event he would construct within the physical field.

This is a rather tricky point, but an important one. The other possible solutions, however, still exist as reality within the dream field, and as such they continue unfolding. Your past material on dreams will help you on this.

I suggest your break.

(Break at 10:22. Jane was well dissociated as usual. She spoke at a rather rapid rate comparatively, yet took some long pauses.

(The first part of the following material was delivered with many pauses, some of them long. When Jane sat down again and entered the trance state, she remained quite motionless, with her eyes closed, for over a minute before she began at 10:29.)

There was no personal connection between the three of you in past lives.

There was however a telepathic connection. The present personality of our visitor was aware of the sessions before Philip mentioned them. I expect that the association will continue. The number fifteen is an important one to our visitor.

(Jane now took a very long pause. It will be remembered that Philip is the entity name for John Bradley, who first mentioned the sessions to Lorraine. Lorraine told us later that she was not consciously aware of the existence of the sessions before John told her about them. She also said the number fifteen had no particular significance for her as far as she was aware. Seth mentions a period of fifteen years, however, in connection with past lives for her. See page 319.)

Once the personality was blind, physically, and evolved a communication by means of the texture of a particular type of cloth, the hemp. He could, for he was then a male, he could by educating his fingers, distinguish the most slightest variation of roughness and texture.

He was near to being a beggar, living in poverty. Reaching out to passersby and touching their garments, he could accurately tell their social and economic standing through the touch of the cloth. He sang for money or whatever was given him.

He was blinded in his teens, an accident, boys playing with stones. The fingers were very sensitive, and since then he has always developed the ability to use his hands to advantage in nimble ways. He was then brawny, strident. This is the personality's first experience with being a mother.

The daughter of the present personality, however, was once a sister. There were difficulties between the sisters. Now this relationship is one that irons out old difficulties. The youngest son was once the personality's father. Is it any wonder that the conscious mind does not retain in one life memory of its other existences?

Memory is there, within the inner self. Lessons learned in the past are drawn upon. You would indeed be laden with relatives if you were aware of such past relationships.

I am rather pleased with the evening's session. Indeed, I feel in rather good spirits, if you will again forgive the phrase. We will at our next session truly get down again to business, as far as our discussions on action are concerned.

There is still much to be said here. Nor was I flattered at Ruburt's surprise upon his discovery that what I told you in the past, concerning your friends, was coming to pass. He should have expected it. He is if anything more bullheaded than even I gave him credit for, and I gave him credit for a good deal of bull-headedness.

(See page 317.)

He is somewhat better than he was. He does not block me as much as he did, and our material has been coming through very well. However he could, it seems to me, show somewhat more confidence in my ability. He certainly shows enough confidence in his own, though not in his psychic ability. Ah, here he hedges. But I will run him around that particular hedge.

You may now do as you like. You may close the session, or you may take a short break and continue for a few social pleasantries.

("Well, I think we'd better close."

(As usual, I didn't want Jane to become fatigued. Seth had been building up to a state of high good humor, however, and I regretted passing it by. Truth was, though, that I was getting very tired also.)

I will then meet with you at our regular time. May I add that when I am feeling pleasant you should at least take advantage of it; for your own pleasure, of course, and not mine. I bid you a most fond good evening. However, I have been so concerned of late with our lessons that I have barely taken time to do more than say hello and good-bye, and I do indeed now and then feel like indulging in some more relaxed social discourse. And one of these evenings we shall have a social time.

All joking aside, I will indeed say good evening.

("Good night, Seth."

(End at 11:05. Jane was well dissociated. As the session ended she sat still, with her eyes still closed. It became apparent that she was having trouble opening them. She finally made it. "He didn't want to go," she said.

(Since her eyes appeared to want to close again, I then told her to go ahead with more dictation if she cared to. Resume at 11:08.)

I was hoping, Joseph, that we could have some give and take. However I have been unfair, and I will admit it. I realize that you have been ill, and I should not tease you. It is one of my failings. So I will now leave, though with some misgivings.

("Why?")

I leave out of due consideration for your convenience, to show that I can be magnanimous. My best and heartiest and final good evening to you all.

("Good night, Seth."

(End at 11:11. Jane was fully dissociated, she said, "really out." But as the session ended her eyes opened promptly.)

SESSION 145
APRIL 12, 1965 9 PM MONDAY AS SCHEDULED

(One afternoon during my illness, as I lay drowsily in bed, I had two distinct impressions. First, while my eyes were closed I felt that the "area of darkness" they encompassed to the left and the right was abruptly and definitely wider. This sensation was brief, yet lasted long enough for me to be sure of it.

(So was the second impression, which came immediately after. This time I suddenly "saw" a shorter left leg superimposed over my own flesh-and-blood leg of normal length. This new leg reached only to my knee but was complete with a foot and a knee as it stemmed from my hip. It could have been the leg of a dwarf.

(I thought the two impressions could be examples of inner expansion and contraction. I reminded Jane of them again just before the session tonight, in the hope that Seth might be ready to discuss them.

(Once again Jane spoke while sitting down and with her eyes closed. Her pace was slow, her voice rather low and husky. She was rather sleepy from a nap, and began at 9:01.)

Good evening.

("Good evening, Seth.")

It is good to be by ourselves again.

I am going to speak about your past condition, and I am also going to speak about action. Although the reason, or reasons, for your particular illness involves personal causes, indeed in one way or another all illnesses have a root within ego's attempt to stand apart from the action of which it is composed, so that at times it fights against itself.

(See the following sessions: 139, 141, 142.)

Part of what I am about to say may sound callous, but you should see that such is not the case. From the viewpoint of the concerned and conscientious ego-self, truly there appears to be great and disastrous evils that overflow like poison the cup of human existence.

When he sips of it, as you have sipped of it, and as all conscientious human beings sip of it, then indeed the taste is bitter. It is not too farfetched however to add that all, or many, medicines have unfortunately a foul taste, and that the child who sips such a medicine finds it difficult to believe that such a distasteful brew can do him good.

Basically, all action is. Basically there is no evil action. All is unfolding. With the limited perceptions that the ego has itself adopted, the whole is not visible, and it sees what it will see. Within your field, within your moral field, you must indeed strike out against that which appears evil to you.

This is a responsibility laid upon you by the code of limitations which the ego itself has adopted as a part of its own nature. You may find it most difficult to follow me here without any strong affirmation. However, as you do not blame, as you do not morally blame the wind for the tumultuous hurricane, and as you do not punish the wind, so you must somehow manage to understand that a wrongdoer, in your eyes, is no more or less to blame than this. It would be foolhardy to ignore the results of such activity. Nevertheless, I tell you now that there is much you do not see or know.

You see perhaps havoc within the physical field, and this is indeed to be faced and dealt with, and set straight, as aid is given to the victims of a hurricane. But you are familiar only with the results of action as they appear within the physical field, as long as you insist upon viewing your physical universe with the eyes of the ego-self; for the ego-self attempts to cut itself off from that action of which it is a part, and in so attempting it loses contact with this larger reality.

This loss of contact applies only to the ego. It does not apply to those other portions of the self, and it is through the inner self, through inner consciousness, that to some degree the nature of action can make itself known. And when it is made known it will be seen then—

(Jane now took a very long pause, one lasting at least a minute. During these periods she will sit quietly in her chair, her eyes closed, her hands usually unmoving in her lap. When she resumes she merely carries on with the thought at hand as though there had been no interruption.)

—that which you call evil represents a falling short of value fulfillment in a particular, or in any particular, case. There are always, as I believe you realize, those who court injustice and persecution. There are always those who persecute. There are those who murder, and there are those who seek to be slain.

They seek each other out for many complicated reasons. This whole subject is difficult but I will not simplify matters, as I could. I would prefer to discuss it most thoroughly. Nothing here must ever be taken as a justification for evil, in humanity's terms. For many practical reasons at this point, and please underline at this point, it is necessary that man fight against what he considers evil, for he strengthens himself immeasurably by so doing.

It is also true however, in a completely different framework, that evil is of his own creation, at least evil as he thinks of it. And if a crime is to be assigned in humanity's terms, often the victim is as guilty as the murderer, in basic terms, in terms of guilt that no court can weigh.

I suggest your break.

(Break at 9:34. Jane was dissociated as usual for a first monologue, meaning that she retained some idea of what she had been saying. While speaking aloud, she had the parallel thought that Seth felt this material wouldn't make him very popular in some quarters, among people who might desire to use this material for their own purposes.

(Jane now felt fully awake. She resumed in a light and faster voice at 9:45.)

We all have our roles. As we exist within various fields we focus upon these roles to the exclusion of much else.

That part of us as you know which deals with these roles is the ego, which lives intimately the role which was assigned to it by the whole self, of which it is a part.

The health and psychic condition of an individual is not primarily determined by the ego, however. It is only when the ego is allowed too much power that the individual is deprived of much of the inner vitality of the whole self. For the ego is acquainted with only its role. It can find refreshment only within the limitations of the reality which it was formed to meet; and when it looks about with the best of intentions and sees disasters and terrors, it does not know that these others also play their roles, and that the roles are temporary.

It becomes bitter and mortally frightened, with no place to turn, and it sickens the body, and shrivels, and concentrates more and more upon the morbid aspects of its environment, until it cannot even appreciate the splendid accomplishment of itself, and the joys that are peculiarly <u>part</u> of the ego.

This, temporarily, is something like what happened to you, Joseph. The inner self is aware of other realities. It is aware of the ego. Remember here the difference between consciousness of self and the ego, for the difference is important. The ego is but part of the self, part of the conscious self, but focused in one direction.

The inner self, feeling itself part of action, is aware of facets of reality of which the ego is ignorant. It knows that roles can be reversed. There is so much here to be explained, and so many questions that must be answered. For I tell you, at the risk of being misunderstood grossly, that there is only one reality, and value fulfillment, <u>which you may, if you like</u>, equate with goodness.

There is no such thing as evil, except for the phantoms which man has made. He sees hate in his own heart, what he calls hate, which is but fear, so he projects it into another man's face and says the man hates him; and he may slay the man. But the hate never existed, that is, what mankind thinks of as hate never existed.

Hate is unreasoning fear. Fear is caused by lack of understanding, by a lack of value fulfillment. Hate is that which is not love. Love is fulfilled, or fulfilling, value fulfillment. It is action that knows itself, and that glorifies in its parts, that is separated to know itself, and in knowing itself is no longer separated.

Hate is that which fears to join, and hence is separate, and that is all.

If all men could learn to love, in terms of which I have spoken, then there would be no need for any kind of punishment within your field, and the word would vanish from your vocabulary. The subconscious is not the cause or the carrier of hatreds.

The difficulty here is of an ego's refusal to assimilate subconscious experience.

The ego may assimilate only a part of a given experience. Sometimes it will not assimilate or accept an experience at all. Remember here again that there is a difference between the ego and consciousness of self. It is not necessary that the ego assimilate all experiences that are open to consciousness of self. Ego must have at hand, however, those experiences that are significant for manipulation within the physical environment.

Any gap of assimilation here can be most unfortunate, and sometimes disastrous. Consciousness of self, if you recall, is self-consciousness that still retains self as a part of action, self that perceives its existence within action. Ego, originally a part of this consciousness of self, splits off as previously explained, and attempts to dissociate itself from action, indeed to view action as a result of itself; that is, to view action as a result and not a cause.

Due to the difficulty of the material that I am trying to explain as concisely as possible, I suggest a brief break.

(Break at 10:15. Jane was more deeply dissociated. She had spoken steadily for half an hour, but upon coming out of her trance state felt that but a few minutes had passed.

(Jane resumed in the same rather light voice and faster manner at 10:26.)

There are many freedoms, Joseph, that you will learn to allow yourself.

You must not allow yourself to become constricted, for in constriction there is no expansion and little creativity. The daily walk that you plan is not only an excellent idea, but had you carried this through in the past, there is a good possibility that you would not have become ill. For there is that in the physical nature of your field that is automatically refreshing and renewing.

By way only of a suggestion, I would take advantage of the outdoors in the coming season as much as possible, for both of you.

Within the framework of your disciplined nature, you must allow now for more spontaneity. You will find it most rewarding in many ways. And the rewards will be reflected in your work. At the risk of a cliché, I must add here the ancient truth that only fear can hold you back, in <u>any</u> direction.

There is much that you can expect if you can free yourself from fear. You should allow yourself to travel. This is a physical form of expansion that should not be overlooked. Fear speaks for security. Fear causes to expect. The physical symptoms of old age are the physical manifestations of fear in the tissues. There is no reason why you, or any man, should not be strong and vital until death. You and Ruburt have learned much, and will learn more.

The inner self that knows its existence within action, has a firm foothold within reality. The ego can perform its function, fulfill its responsibilities within the physical field, and be free to know adequate joys and pleasures. But such an inner self must be renewed within action.

Your seasons, and the physical nature of your universe, is that part of action which is instantly renewing, and which automatically lets even ego feel its relation to that reality of which it is a part.

Your personal potentials, Joseph, are excellent. A knowledge of past lives would be most helpful to any personality, not only of lessons learned and of triumphs achieved; but also of problems passed and solved. We will have much more to say concerning what you may call moral problems, but such discussions will always be tied in with reality as it exists.

I wish you both a most pleasant evening. Nor have I forgotten your request, Joseph, that I speak concerning your two experiences when you were ill. However, a discussion of them will fit in much more conveniently with our next session.

My best regards again. My energy is often with you.

("Good night, Seth.")

(End at 10:42. Jane was well dissociated. She said she had a strong feeling of affection from Seth at the end of the session, as sometimes happens. Neither of us had said anything else when she resumed at 10:44, in a deeper voice.)

One small note, Joseph. Because I have given you so much advice, I did want you to know that I realize that you have already taken significant strides, as you will, I know, continue.

Ruburt will get his from me in due time. He is being directly helped in many ways through the mere fact of holding these sessions, for in speaking through him, he also to some extent partakes of my energy. The relationship between us, in fact, is one that we shall discuss most thoroughly in the very near future, for now you will be able to understand what you could not perhaps have understood earlier, concerning our communications in terms of actions involving actions.

I will indeed now close. And again, maintaining your discipline, nevertheless allow yourself freedom, for within you will find spontaneity, added dimensions and even new discipline.

("Good night, Seth.")

(End at 10:50. Jane was dissociated as usual.)

SESSION 146
APRIL 14, 1965 9 PM WEDNESDAY AS SCHEDULED

(Recently, just after retiring for the night, Jane had the feeling that momentarily she had left her body. Her actual sensation was one of returning to it. She could not say where she had been, if any place else. The sensation was extremely brief, she said, and hard to describe. Indeed, she had forgotten about it until just before tonight's session.

(Jane now misses trying psychological time quite a bit. It will be remembered that Seth suggested she give up this practice on March 15, 1965, with the comment that she had been trying to do too much, too fast. Jane believes the above experience stems from her psy-time experiments, for during some of them she had achieved a similar effect.

(Jane had no idea of the material for the session. Once again she spoke as usual, with her eyes closed. She began in rather a slow manner, but as the session progressed her delivery speeded up somewhat. Her voice was higher than usual.)

Good evening.

("Good evening, Seth.")

You realize that in order to speak of action it is necessary that it be discussed as though some aspects were isolated from others. But this is not the case.

In order that you understand it is necessary, as I have told you, for me to break down concepts. In this way much of the unity of certain phenomena may escape you. We have spoken at various times about specific portions of action's manifestations. We have discussed to some degree, for example, the nature of matter, the electrical universe, the dream universe, and such other topics as the layers of the subconscious and the nature of the whole self.

There is always the danger in such discussions that effects which are studied separately will appear to be separate in essence. But what we have been discussing in all these topics is, indeed, the nature of action. The personality as you know it is action. As such the personality however is not physically materialized. You cannot hold it in your hand. You can only observe it in motion, for it is never still, and to probe into it yourself is to change it.

In very important aspects it always escapes you, though you are partially what it is. Men speak of having their own personalities, as if the personality were a thing that they had in their possession, a thing fairly permanent, a concrete, always-to-be-counted-on possession.

But the personality is always in a state of becoming, and forever changes. The personality is an excellent example of action in one aspect. It is important here also to realize that while the personality is always in motion, the motion involved here is not one of mobility in space as you know it. It is most definitely motion in terms of value fulfillment.

There are here also thrusts in all directions, with certain identifying pulsations that underlie all, and that have their origins within the inner self. As the vitality of the universe forms, of itself, the boundaries of the various fields of activity, and as vitality itself takes on the coloration of the various fields and forms the camouflage patterns within them, so also vitality, in the form of emotions that the camouflage patterns of the personality, even while this vitality forms both emotions and personality for every individual, every consciousness, may be thought of as a separate field of activity; and all the data relating to fields of activity may be seen to apply to any consciousness as well.

(As I was transcribing the above involved sentence from Jane's dictation I was somewhat aware that it contained incomplete phrases. I thought it best to continue, rather than to backtrack in an effort to straighten it out. As usual my mind was on getting the next word on paper, rather than to critically appraise each one. Jane now took a long pause before resuming.)

We find once again a basic reality, that of the personality, which is accepted and recognized within the physical field, even while it does not appear there as a definite physical unit. It can indeed be examined but the examination itself, being action, changes it. For the personality, true to the roles of action, will seize upon the new action and form of it new realities and unities with itself.

The personality and the ego are not the same.

I suggest your break.

(Break at 9:22. Jane was dissociated as usual for a first delivery. She remembered the last bit of the material. She resumed in a deeper voice and in a slower manner at 9:29.)

The personality has strong connections with the inner self.

The personality is that consciousness of self of which I have spoken, which is aware of itself within, and a part of, action. The ego attempts to stand apart from action, and to stand apart from the personality, and to mold the personality into a more or less permanent and stable, dependent portion of the ego itself.

(Again, see the following sessions among others: 139, 141, 142.)

The ego would if it could, stop personality's motion and development for the security of stability. The ego would drive the personality into preconceived channels. This consciousness-of-self—I suggest hyphens between consciousness-of-self—this consciousness-of-self is seen in man as personality, as the human personality. It appears, however, in all types of consciousness to one degree or another.

Therefore, consciousness-of-self can appear with or without the existence of an ego. Consciousness-of-self is an attribute then of all physical species, regardless of their classification. Personality, human personality, is simply the name given to this class of self, as applied and seen within human beings. Personality changes and acts upon all other action. Personality, then, can be seen to operate as a field of action in identity; but identity that is conscious of its relation to action as a whole.

The peculiar and individualistic aspects of personality are the result of those camouflaging abilities of which we have spoken earlier. Those portions of the personality which escape ego's attempts to dominate are held suspect in ego's eyes. Ego considers them as invalid and dangerous to its own supremacy. When ego is forced to admit that personality changes, it will do its best to avoid this knowledge. The more rigid an ego is, the more danger there is that the individual will have difficulties in all kinds of adjustments.

Because of its nature ego does not want to adjust. It wants adjustments to be made to it. Because ego is another manifestation of action, it is of course impossible for its aims to be realized. For all its attempts at stability and control, ego itself constantly changes. Ego most of all resents and fights against time as you know it, yet ego is to a large extent responsible for your conception of time. Basically, ego fears both the past and the present. It fears the past because it has already lost control of the past. It fears the future because it is not yet in control of it. It seeks continuity of identity, yet it is forced to realize that the "I" of today is hardly the "I" of thirty years ago.

It is the ego which fears death so strongly. And yet the stability which ego so urgently seeks would, indeed, result in a death, since no further action would be allowed.

(Jane now took one of her very long pauses. For well over a minute she sat quite still, her eyes closed.)

Ego also fears spontaneity, for it cannot control action; being a part of action, most of its efforts of necessity are thwarted. Yet it is precisely this struggle between ego's struggles for stability, and the personality's attempt to expand spontaneously, that is at the basis of much of mankind's achievements, and that is certainly the basis for much of his art.

In his art we have the nostalgia of the ego for past time, and for lost control of a self that has already vanished, and changed into something new. It is ego who plans for the future, trying to anticipate the environment in which it must operate. Its anticipations, of course, then form that environment.

The ego therefore is a very necessary force within your field. It is also, regardless of current psychological beliefs, the basis for aggression, in general. All aggression is not detrimental, for example.

I suggest your break.

(Break at 9:59. Jane was well dissociated. She remembered none of the material. Her last delivery was broken by some very long pauses. She resumed in the same manner at 10:08.)

Because the personality is that part of the individual which is conscious of itself as a part of action, and therefore aware of its relation with action, the personality is that part of the individual which survives physical death.

The personality is not the whole self. It is a portion of the whole self, which is activated during a particular existence. The ego, as I have explained, does not vanish. However, it must always be remembered here that the ego is not the self-conscious self in its entirety by any means. It is simply a portion, a field of focus whereby the self attempts to objectify itself within the world of matter.

It simply ceases to so objectify itself, but it retains, or the self retains, memory of that objectification.

The personality necessarily continues to change after physical death. After physical death the personality simply ceases to project itself, as a rule, within the physical field, and no longer focuses within it.

The personality is much more extensive and expansive than you realize. Remember here our discussions upon the subject of the limitations of the self.

(See the following sessions: 141, 142, among others.)

Theoretically, the self is unlimited, if you will recall. The ego within your field is limited because of the nature of its rigidity. The ego operates as a partitioning agent. It directs and uses the abilities of the personality for manipulation in the physical universe. It can mobilize a smaller or larger amount of these energies according to its own strength. It has a small focus but a powerful one.

I mentioned earlier that the personality is an excellent example of action as it is sometimes projected into the physical field, while not appearing within it in tangible form. For here we see many of action's characteristics: the mobility that does not necessarily involve space, the thrusts outward, and the corresponding thrusts inward. We see action acting upon itself and constant change.

A thorough study of the personality will be an excellent exercise, and will lead you close to the nature of action itself. The experiences about which you asked, for example, involved actions of the personality and not, of course, of the ego. Expansion and contraction occur constantly as characteristic of action, as I have explained.

The ego is scarcely conscious of these. Your experiences occurred when the ego, because of your illness, was momentarily exhausted, its control lessened. The personality was then momentarily aware of realities that the ego would ordinarily attempt to block. These were pulsations, in actuality of corresponding strength, but interpreted differently by you.

(See page 323, of the 145th session, for a description of my experiences. Also see the 86th session.)

I will have more to say concerning this after I have developed certain subject matter that is important. If I did not make it clear, let me repeat that the personality is a <u>portion</u> of the inner self. There are interchanges here, so that certain parts of the personality will seem to vanish. In such cases, for various reasons, the inner self simply sees no reason for their continued focus in the physical field.

There is a very delicate balance always maintained, and later on we will have a whole section of our material that will deal with the personality in relation to other phenomena. We are speaking of it this evening mainly in terms of its reality as a part of action. As we speak of such subjects in their relation to various phenomena, again it must be kept in mind that such realities are being considered often from one aspect only, but that their reality extends into many other dimensions.

Many of these dimensions cannot be discussed at this time. But you will see, indeed, that the nature of action, or the nature of any reality, is greatly colored by the viewpoint or dimension from which it is examined. It is my purpose here to examine for you reality from as many different aspects as possible, lifting you from the limitations of your own dimensions, and allowing you the advantage of others.

I suggest your break.

(Break at 10:36. Jane was well dissociated. Although she had used pauses in her delivery the pace had been fairly fast, and my writing hand was tired. She resumed in the same fast and quiet manner at 10:45.)

It must, once again, be realized that there is no particular point where ego begins or ends.

There is no particular and definite line between the ego and the personality and the inner self. They must merely be discussed in such terms. There is, believe it or not, no particular and specific and definite boundary between what is self and not self. If we isolate such portions of reality for the sake of discussion, such isolation is artificial, and in no way affects the nature of reality itself.

Such a remark may appear so simple that it is not worth saying, but it is extremely important that it be understood. In like manner, there is indeed no particular boundary or line of demarcation between the dream universe and the physical universe. Any seeming barrier is artificial, for all these realities merge one into the other, and an action in one affects the other.

The self is extended, so to speak, existing within many dimensions. It extends as vitally and actually in the dream universe as it does in your own physical universe. It is as much a part of the electrical universe as it is a part of the world of psychological motivation. The intertwinings are infinite in all directions.

The ego fears death, yet in the space of your own physical lifetime portions of the self have undergone like transformations endless times, of which the ego is unaware.

We will continue with this discussion at our next session. You may, as you prefer, end this session now, or you may take a short break and continue it.

("Well, I guess we'll say good night then.")

In that case my best wishes to you both. It has been a most fruitful session. We may have a surprise session some evening, when we will deal with less weighty matters.

("Good night, Seth."

(End at 10:55. Jane was well dissociated as usual, and my writing hand was very tired.)

SESSION 147
APRIL 19, 1965 9 PM MONDAY AS SCHEDULED

(Last Thursday, April 15, as we were driving about Elmira on errands, Jane mentioned to me that she missed trying psychological time. She wondered when, if ever, Seth would allow her to resume. See the 140th session. Jane then received the information, she believes from Seth, to the effect that she might soon be allowed to resume psy-time, but only for fifteen-minute periods, and during the evening when I would be home with her.

(Today Jane received word from F. Fell, Inc., that they would like to schedule her book, Hidden Powers Within You; How to Make ESP Work, *for publication in the spring of 1966. Jane has the book partially written. One of the experiments*

she listed in the book for the reader to try led, of course, to the development of the Seth material in her own case. Thus the material will be an integral part of the ESP book.

(In the 92nd session, of September 28, 1964, Seth predicted the sale of this specific book by name. *See page 40.* *In the 104th session he gave details we think may refer to the offices of F. Fell in NYC, involving a red chair, certain individuals, etc. This material can be shortly checked out. A woman was mentioned as influencing a sale; Jane's editor, Mara Thomases, is a woman. She was not editor when the manuscript was submitted to F. Fell.*

(Seth has predicted sale of the ESP book, and of the material itself many times. The latest was in the 143rd session. See the notes preceding the 138th session for a partial list of such predictions. I will endeavor to compile a complete list of specific statements, by session number, and attach it to a succeeding session.

(Once again Jane spoke while sitting down and with her eyes closed. The session was held in our small back room. She used her now familiar combination of rather rapid delivery, broken by pauses. Her voice was quiet and clear. She began at 8:58.)

Good evening.

("Good evening, Seth.")

There are, as you know, actions within actions, thrusts forward and backward, in and out and in all directions. And so in Ruburt's manuscript there existed a vitality that of itself would bring about other actions, as indeed I foresaw.

(Jane now smiled.)

We have here an excellent focus of energy, an excellent use of action, that of itself propels itself onward; I might say, somewhat sarcastically: Oh, ye of little faith. Nevertheless, that which is obvious to me is not obvious, often, to you, and it is not too difficult for me to see why at times you appear to be lacking in faith when such predictions are made.

I am going to deal with some personal material here this evening, pertaining to Ruburt. I have left him alone in this respect for too long. I heartily suggest that he seriously begin to tackle the smoking problem, for his health in many small but significant ways will benefit.

Also, several basic causes for this habit no longer exist in fact. I will indeed help him to <u>some</u> degree, but I will not do <u>all</u> the work for him.

(Here, Jane shook her head most definitely.)

Smoking represents among other things, to him, a blanket of insulation, not only between himself and exterior reality, but a blanket between himself and interior reality. He is fully capable now of operating without such insulation, and it will be most beneficial for him to dispense with it.

I expect a serious attempt to meet this problem head-on, for he can triumph in this respect. I never do insist, but this is my recommendation. You will both find the coming season to be a most beneficial one, in terms of your work, and indeed of your health.

Ruburt is more stable a personality than he knows, and thus he can now handle himself without dependence upon artificial supports such as his smoking. He will find that work on his book will go very well, smoothly. And as I believe as I have told you, our material will indeed be published.

Action does not always move in what you would consider a straight line. Because you view action in narrow terms, usually seeing it in physical terms only, you are inclined to think of it, or any effort, as a straight line from one point to another. This is hardly the case.

Any action that affects the physical individual also has its reality within many other fields, and its effects and its nature are felt within them. A manuscript, or indeed any art form, contains action and sets up its own climate, either of psychological acceptance or rejection. This climate is more than the result of the materials or subject matter or nature of which the work is composed. It goes without saying that such a work actually contains a portion of focused psychic energy, which is action, and which has its effects.

The energy charge in this particular manuscript is not only very vivid, but well focused. It has already had a vivid effect on more people than you know.

I here suggest your first break.

(Break at 9:21. Jane was dissociated as usual; that is, she retained a very general idea of what she had been speaking about. Seth has dealt with her smoking habit rather lightly at various times. He was more specific in the 31st and 32nd sessions, tying it in with her past lives. See Volume 1.

(Jane resumed at a fair pace and in a quiet voice at 9:28.)

Ruburt may indeed resume psychological time experiments, however, and he did understand me correctly. His experiments for now should be limited to a fifteen-minute daily period, and they should be held in the evening or afternoon.

Joseph should be in the house. Then we shall see what develops.

I expect everything to go well. This evening's session will be a short one. Ruburt is quite exhausted, though he may not realize it, and he will be quite recovered by morning. The emotional activity, the contrasts of today, exhausted him, not one thing alone.

This again concerns the nature of action, and I will in our next session begin to discuss the emotions as they are related to, and part of, action. Ruburt's momentary exhaustion this evening is a simple, natural result here of ordinary counterthrusts of emotional action and reaction.

It is most important, again, to realize that action does not move in a straight line. Action may have mass. It may not have mass in other instances. Action will never have one effect only. This is a rather important point. Whenever an action seems to have but one effect, then there is a lack in perceptive abilities.

Action within your field may appear to be affected by your time, but only that part of action which is physically materialized will be so affected. Action may appear to be at rest, but is never at rest, or stationary, or permanent. Action may appear to have a beginning and an ending but this is, again, an error of perception.

(Seth had quite a bit to say about the "source of the source" in the 95th session.)

Action which is materialized within your plane appears within your field, and disappears from your field. This in no way affects the basic nature of action itself. That is, it does not change the basic laws of action. Action will change both within your physical field and outside your physical field. You are only aware of a small part of action, that portion which is materialized within your system.

You say that an action has begun when it enters your system. You say that an action is completed when it passes beyond your system. But the action, in those terms, began long before; and the action, in those terms, is never completed. Yet even the action as it occurs within your system is constantly changing in the ways which we have described, and this changing in itself implies infinities of beginnings and endings within action itself, with no ending, a real or permanent ending, and no beginning, a real beginning out of nothing. For each beginning carries within it action which has come before.

Again here, when I speak in terms of before and after, I speak only for your convenience, for there is no before or after, only all action within the spacious present, occurring out of itself, spontaneously, into all directions, and forming of itself all the infinite fields and systems of actuality.

I am here going to suggest another brief break, and then we will continue.

(Break at 9:46. Jane was fully dissociated. Seth introduced the spacious present in the 41st session. Jane resumed in the same manner at 9:58.)

You will both find the coming seasons fulfilling.

As the springtime progresses this will be an excellent time for Ruburt to cease his smoking, as his abilities renew themselves. Earlier in the year was a poor time.

(Jane has made several unsuccessful attempts to stop smoking in recent months.)

I believe that now you can trust this prediction: By summer he will have broken the habit for good, and it will no longer be a worry. The various unfortunate effects that seem to be caused by smoking are not caused by the cigarettes so much, as by those psychic habits which cause a personality to seek security within such habitual patterns that become compulsive.

When the inner patterns are broken the effects cease, but the inner patterns are associated by the personality with those outer habits. Indeed, the need for the habits creates the exterior habit. This is almost a mechanistic response that is confining, and indeed detrimental to expansion.

Some personalities need a habit security, and will switch from one habit to another. Ruburt is strong enough now so that this will not be the case. He should keep a close watch upon his smoking now, and immediately after his birthday he should break the habit completely. And I believe he will.

We will have a full session Wednesday. My best regards to you both. You will have most pleasant dreams this evening. And again, all of your energies are in ascendancy.

("Goodnight, Seth."

(End at 10:07. Jane was well dissociated.

(Seth's comment above on switching habits is of interest to me personally. It reminds me that although I quit smoking in 1959, I tried for the better part of two years, first, to cut down. I then found quitting altogether relatively easy. However, I immediately switched to chewing on toothpicks, and kept this up for well over a year. This habit then gradually fell away, practically without conscious effort.)

SESSION 148
APRIL 21, 1965 9 PM WEDNESDAY AS SCHEDULED

(Jane has not yet resumed her study of psychological time, even though Seth said it was all right for her to begin again on a daily fifteen-minute basis. See the last session.

(Jane did not feel at all well before this evening's session, and I was not at my best either. I suggested to Jane that she pass up the session but she wanted to have one if possible. We were both curious to see what Seth would say about basic causes, and as it developed we had some fairly good insights. We seem to have had good results recently, in applying the material to our daily lives. This application has been after the event in many instances, of course, and we hope to continue to improve in using it in a practical way to forestall various problems.

(The session was short. Jane spoke in a quiet voice, sitting down and with her

eyes closed; and, strangely enough, in a rather rapid manner.

Good evening.

("Good evening, Seth.")

I see that we are all in high spirits.

You realize that when one of you is indisposed, you may of course cancel a session.

There is, indeed, nothing seriously wrong with our cigarette smoker, Ruburt. Tension however has caused a disturbance. Tension arising, oddly enough, from the realization that his book will indeed be published. This tension will vanish. He needs to relax.

I was going to speak this evening rather in depth concerning action within action, as there is much to be said here that will show you how actual dimensions of action are formed. However, this will be a brief session. We have much time available to us, and need not worry over an occasional missed or short session, as long as our overall pattern is maintained.

(Jane now smiled.)

Ruburt may, if he wishes, delete the following from the record.

There is a definite connection between his desire to stop smoking, and the fact that he has found silver threads among the black. His ego image, or in this case Jane's ego image, is that of, among other things, a black-haired young woman, and that of a woman writer who smokes.

Disturbing the image in two ways at once is indeed difficult and I would suggest, as I believe you suggested Joseph, that the smoking problem be tackled. Let us not try to change our image overnight in too many ways at once. These matters also helped add to Ruburt's tension. It grabbed him rather viciously today.

I would suggest that Jane do what I presume is womanly, and to a woman logical under the circumstances. Purchase her preparation by all means, for here we have a clever attempt at trickery. To take focus away from the smoking problem, our Ruburt suddenly decides to go "a la naturel" as far as hair is concerned.

(Jane shook her head in mock concern, her eyes closed.)

This horror, these few white hairs, then very naturally become the reason to increase smoking, for he now has an excellent reason to feel sorry for himself.

I am going to save my planned discussion until our next session, and end this evening's session. It would be advisable if Ruburt enjoyed either light reading this evening, or perhaps your television. But no more heavy reading this evening.

(Before the session Jane had been reading a book on abnormal psychology. I noticed this and suggested she not read it, having in mind my recent experience with illness and my poring over the daily New York City newspapers. See the 143rd session.)

Perhaps you might rub his back before retiring. He should feel well in the morning. I would like here to mention once more my suggestions concerning outings. The two of you should, when financially feasible, go out for an evening of enjoyment once a week. The important point here being that you are outside of your apartment, and also that you are with other people. This suggestion is beneficial for you both.

I will make up for this briefer session, no doubt. My heartiest wishes to you both.

("Good night, Seth."

(End at 9:19. Jane was dissociated as usual for a first delivery. She was aware of the gist of the material. She wasn't happy with the short session, since once she has begun a session she has yet to mind continuing it.

(Jane also thought she knew something of what Seth had planned to discuss this evening, relative to action within action. It concerned the actions taking place within the action of dreaming, reincarnation, etc.)

THE SETH AUDIO COLLECTION

RARE RECORDINGS OF SETH SPEAKING through Jane Roberts are now available on audiocassette and CD. These Seth sessions were recorded by Jane's student, Rick Stack, during Jane's classes in Elmira, New York, in the 1970's. The majority of these selections have never been published in any form. Volume I, described below, is a collection of some of the best of Seth's comments gleaned from over 120 Seth Sessions. Additional selections from The Seth Audio Collection are also available. For information ask for our free catalogue.

Volume I of The Seth Audio Collection consists of six (1-hour) cassettes plus a 34-page booklet of Seth transcripts.Topics covered in Volume I include:

- Creating your own reality – How to free yourself from limiting beliefs and create the life you want.
- Dreams and out-of-body experiences.
- Reincarnation and Simultaneous Time.
- Connecting with your inner self.
- Spontaneity–Letting yourself go with the flow of your being.
- Creating abundance in every area of your life.
- Parallel (probable) universes and exploring other dimensions of reality.
- Spiritual healing, how to handle emotions, overcoming depression and much more.

FOR A FREE CATALOGUE of Seth related products including a detailed description of The Seth Audio Collection, please send your request to the address below.

ORDER INFORMATION:
If you would like to order a copy of The Seth Audio Collection Volume I, please send your name and address, with a check or money order payable to New Awareness Network, Inc. for $60 (Tapes), or $70 (CD's) plus shipping charges. United States residents in NY must add sales tax.

Shipping charges: U.S.-$6.00, Canada-$7, Europe-$17, Australia & Asia-$19
Rates are UPS for U.S. & Airmail for International—Allow 2 weeks for delivery
Alternate Shipping-Surface-$9.00 to anywhere in the world—Allow 5-8 weeks

Mail to: **NEW AWARENESS NETWORK INC.**
P.O. BOX 192, Manhasset, New York 11030
(516) 869-9108 between 9:00-5:00 p.m. Monday-Friday EST
Visit us on the Internet—www.sethcenter.com

Books by Jane Roberts from Amber-Allen Publishing

Seth Speaks: The Eternal Validity of the Soul. This essential guide to conscious living clearly and powerfully articulates the furthest reaches of human potential, and the concept that each of us creates our own reality.

The Nature of Personal Reality: Specific, Practical Techniques for Solving Everyday Problems and Enriching the Life You Know.. In this perennial bestseller, Seth challenges our assumptions about the nature of reality and stresses the individual's capacity for conscious action.

The Individual and the Nature of Mass Events. Seth explores the connection between personal beliefs and world events, how our realities merge and combine "to form mass reactions such as the overthrow of governments, the birth of a new religion, wars, epidemics, earthquakes, and new periods of art, architecture, and technology."

The Magical Approach: Seth Speaks About the Art of Creative Living. Seth reveals the true, magical nature of our deepest levels of being, and explains how to live our lives spontaneously, creatively, and according to our own natural rhythms.

The Oversoul Seven Trilogy (The Education of Oversoul Seven, The Further Education of Oversoul Seven, Oversoul Seven and the Museum of Time). Inspired by Jane's own experiences with the Seth Material, the adventures of Oversoul Seven are an intriguing fantasy, a mind-altering exploration of our inner being, and a vibrant celebration of life.

The Nature of the Psyche. Seth reveals a startling new concept of self, answering questions about the inner reality that exists apart from time, the origins and powers of dreams, human sexuality, and how we choose our physical death.

The "Unknown" Reality, Volumes One and Two. Seth reveals the multidimensional nature of the human soul, the dazzling labyrinths of unseen probabilities involved in any decision, and how probable realities combine to create the waking life we know.

Dreams, "Evolution," and Value Fulfillment, Volumes One and Two. Seth discusses the material world as an ongoing self-creation—the product of a conscious, self-aware and thoroughly animate universe, where virtually every possibility not only exists, but is constantly encouraged to achieve its highest potential.

The Way Toward Health. Woven through the poignant story of Jane Roberts' final days are Seth's teachings about self-healing and the mind's effect upon physical health.

Available in bookstores everywhere.

Printed in the United States
90368LV00002B/196-282/A